GOBI

2/18

W9-BVO-728

LOEB CLASSICAL LIBRARY

FOUNDED BY JAMES LOEB 1911

EDITED BY

JEFFREY HENDERSON

LIVY

X

LCL 301

LIVY

HISTORY OF ROME

BOOKS 35–37

EDITED AND TRANSLATED BY

J. C. YARDLEY

HARVARD UNIVERSITY PRESS
CAMBRIDGE, MASSACHUSETTS
LONDON, ENGLAND
2018

Library of Congress Control Number 2016957655
CIP data available from the Library of Congress

ISBN 978-0-674-99715-8

*Composed in ZephGreek and ZephText by
Technologies 'N Typography, Merrimac, Massachusetts.
Printed on acid-free paper and bound by
Maple Press, York, Pennsylvania*

CONTENTS

HISTORY OF ROME

LIBER XXXV

1. Principio anni quo haec gesta sunt Sex. Digitius praetor
in Hispania citeriore cum civitatibus iis quae post profectionem M. Catonis permultae rebellaverant crebra magis
2 quam digna dictu proelia fecit, et adeo pleraque adversa
ut vix dimidium militum quam quod acceperat successori
3 tradiderit. nec dubium est quin omnis Hispania sublatura
animos fuerit, ni alter praetor P. Cornelius Cn. f. Scipio
4 trans Hiberum multa secunda proelia fecisset, quo terrore
non minus quinquaginta oppida ad eum defecerunt.
5   Praetor haec gesserat Scipio: idem pro praetore Lusi-
tanos, pervastata ulteriore provincia cum ingenti praeda
domum redeuntes, in ipso itinere adgressus ab hora tertia
diei ad octavam incerto eventu pugnavit, numero militum
6 impar, superior aliis; nam et acie frequenti armatis adversus longum et impeditum turba pecorum agmen, et recenti milite adversus fessos longo itinere concurrerat.
7 tertia namque vigilia exierant hostes; huic nocturno itineri
tres diurnae horae accesserant, nec ulla quiete data la-

---

¹ Sex. Digitius (2); cf. 34.42.4, 43.7 for his election and provincial sortition.   ² P. Cornelius Scipio (350): for his appointment to Farther Spain, cf. 34.43.7.   ³ A bellicose Iberian
people in what is now Portugal (*Barr.* 24 D4; TIR K-29, 70). This
is the first mention of Roman conflict with them, and they were
not totally subdued until the time of Augustus.

BOOK XXXV

1. At the start of the year in which these things occurred, Sextus Digitius, praetor in hither Spain,[1] fought with the communities that had rebelled in large numbers after the departure of Marcus Cato. The battles were more numerous than noteworthy and most went so badly that Digitius passed on to his successor barely half the men he had himself been given. There is no doubt that all Spain would have been roused to rebellion had not the other praetor Publius Cornelius Scipio (son of Gnaeus Scipio)[2] fought many successful battles beyond the Ebro, intimidating no fewer than fifty towns into defecting to him.

Such had been Scipio's achievements as praetor. As propraetor, he also made an attack on the Lusitanians[3] when they were actually on the road homeward carrying enormous spoils after ravaging the farther province. He fought them from the third to the eighth hour of the day in an inconclusive engagement, being no match for them numerically but having an advantage in other respects. For he had joined battle with his men in a close-formed line and faced a column drawn out and encumbered by a herd of animals; and his were also fresh troops facing men fatigued by a long march. For the enemy had set out at the third watch; and in addition to this night journey there had also been three hours of daytime travel, and the battle had

8 borem viae proelium exceperat. itaque principio pugnae vigoris aliquid in corporibus animisque fuit, et turbaverant primo Romanos; deinde aequata paulisper pugna est. in hoc discrimine ludos Iovi, si fudisset cecidissetque hostes,

9 praetor[1] vovit. tandem gradum acrius intulere Romani cessitque Lusitanus, deinde prorsus terga dedit; et cum institissent fugientibus victores, ad duodecim milia ho-

10 stium sunt caesa, capti quingenti quadraginta, omnes ferme equites, et signa militaria capta centum triginta quattuor; de exercitu Romano septuaginta et tres amissi.

11 pugnatum haud procul Ilipa urbe est: eo victorem opulentum praeda exercitum P. Cornelius reduxit. ea omnis ante

12 urbem exposita est, potestasque dominis suas res cognoscendi facta est; cetera vendenda quaestori data; quod inde refectum est, militi divisum.

2. Nondum ab Roma profectus erat C. Flaminius prae-

2 tor cum haec in Hispania gerebantur. itaque adversae quam secundae res per ipsum amicosque eius magis ser-

3 monibus celebrabantur; et temptaverat, quoniam bellum ingens in provincia exarsisset, et exiguas reliquias exercitus ab Sex. Digitio atque eas ipsas plenas pavoris ac fugae

4 accepturus esset, ut sibi unam ex urbanis legionibus decernerent, ad quam cum militem ab se ipso scriptum ex

---

[1] praetor *Bχ*: propraetor *Mog*.

---

[4] Cf. 36.36.1–2 for the vow's fulfillment (in 191).

[5] Ilipa is probably Ilipa Magna (*Barr.* 26 E4; TIR J-30, 201), today Alcala del Rio in the municipality of Seville. The Lusitanians had evidently looted it before Scipio attacked them.

[6] C. Flaminius (3): quaestor in 209, curule aedile 196, praetor

followed the exertion of the march with no respite. Thus, the Lusitanians began the fight with a measure of energy and determination, and had initially thrown the Romans into disorder, but then it gradually became an evenly matched struggle. At this critical juncture the praetor made a vow of games to Jupiter should he drive back and cut down the enemy.[4] Eventually the Romans pushed ahead with greater ferocity, while the Lusitanians gave ground and then really took flight. As the victors pressed their advantage against those in flight, some 12,000 of the enemy were cut down, 540 taken prisoner—almost all cavalrymen—and 134 military standards captured. Losses from the Roman army totaled 73. The battle was fought not far from the city of Ilipa, and it was to this town that Publius Cornelius brought back his conquering army rich with spoils. These were all set out in front of the town and owners were given the opportunity to identify what was theirs.[5] The remainder was given to the quaestor to be sold, and the proceeds from them were divided among the soldiers.

2. The praetor Gaius Flaminius[6] had not yet left Rome when this was taking place in Spain; thus conversations between him and his friends[7] centered more on the failures than the successes there. Since a serious war had flared up in the province, and since he was to take over from Sextus Digitius the little that remained of his army (which itself was full of fear and dejection), Flaminius had tried to have the senate assign him one of the urban legions. To this he would add the soldiers he had enrolled

this year (193), and later consul (187). Assigned Hither Spain: 34.55.6.   [7] That is, his political supporters.

senatus consulto adiecisset, eligeret ex omni numero sex
milia et ducentos pedites, equites trecentos: ea se legi-
5 one—nam in Sex. Digiti exercitu haud multum spei esse—
rem gesturum.
6   Seniores negare ad rumores a privatis temere in gratiam magistratuum confictos senatus consulta facienda
esse: nisi quod aut praetores ex provinciis scriberent aut
7 legati renuntiarent, nihil ratum haberi debere; si tumultus
in Hispania esset, placere tumultuarios milites extra Italiam scribi a praetore. mens ea senatus fuit ut in Hispania
8 tumultuarii milites legerentur. Valerius Antias et in Siciliam navigasse dilectus causa C. Flaminium scribit, et ex
Sicilia Hispaniam petentem tempestate in Africam delatum, vagos milites de exercitu P. Africani sacramento
9 rogasse; his duarum provinciarum dilectibus tertium in
Hispania adiecisse.
   3. Nec in Italia segnius Ligurum bellum crescebat.
Pisas iam quadraginta milibus hominum, adfluente cotidie
multitudine ad famam belli spemque praedae, circumse-
2 debant. Minucius consul Arretium die quam edixerat ad
conveniendum militibus venit. inde quadrato agmine ad
Pisas duxit, et cum hostes non plus mille passuum ab oppido trans fluvium movissent castra, consul urbem haud

---

8 Antias, a Roman historian of the first century BC, was one
of Livy's sources, but not held in much regard by him. Cf. Introduction to vol. IX (LCL 295, xxvii–xxviii and *OCD* s.v.).

9 Minucius' province was Liguria (34.56.3–4). Arretium
(Arezzo) was an ally of Rome and had been a base for Roman
operations since the third century.

10 The Auser (now Serchio). Now it flows into the sea north
of Pisa, but then into the Arnus (Arno) close by (*Barr.* 41 C1.)

following the senate's decree and then select from the entire body a force of 6,200 infantry and 300 cavalry. This, he said, was the legion with which he would go into action since little confidence could be placed in Sextus Digitius' army.

The senior members replied that decrees of the senate should not be passed in response to rumors idly concocted by private citizens to suit the purposes of magistrates, and they said that nothing should be regarded as confirmed without written statements from praetors in the provinces or reports from their legates. If a state of emergency existed in Spain then it was their decision that emergency troops should be enrolled by the praetor outside Italy. What the senate really meant was that emergency troops should be recruited in Spain. Valerius Antias[8] records that Gaius Flaminius sailed to Sicily to raise troops, and that as he headed from Sicily to Spain he was blown off course in a storm to Africa, where he swore in some stragglers from the army of Publius Africanus. To these levies made in the two provinces, says Antias, Flaminius added a third in Spain.

3. In Italy the war with the Ligurians was escalating no less quickly. Pisae was now under siege by 40,000 men, their numbers increasing every day as word of the war spread and hopes of plunder rose. The consul Minucius reached Arretium[9] on the day on which he had ordered his men to muster. From there he led them to Pisae in "square" formation, and since the enemy had moved camp to a point across the river[10] no more than a mile from the town, the consul entered a city that unquestionably owed

3 dubie servatam adventu suo est ingressus. postero die
et ipse trans fluvium quingentos ferme passus ab hoste
posuit castra. inde levibus proeliis a populationibus agrum
4 sociorum tutabatur: in aciem exire non audebat novo milite et ex multis generibus hominum coniecto, necdum
5 noto satis inter se ut fidere alii aliis possent. Ligures multitudine freti et in aciem exibant, parati de summa rerum
decernere, et abundantes militum numero passim multas
6 manus per extrema finium ad praedandum mittebant, et
cum coacta vis magna pecorum praedaeque esset, paratum erat praesidium per quos[2] in castella eorum vicosque
ageretur.

4. Cum bellum Ligustinum ad Pisas constitisset, consul
alter, L. Cornelius Merula, per extremos Ligurum fines
exercitum in agrum Boiorum induxit, ubi longe alia belli
2 ratio quam cum Liguribus erat. consul in aciem exibat,
hostes pugnam detractabant; praedatumque ubi nemo
obviam exiret discurrebant Romani, Boii diripi sua im-
3 pune quam tuendo ea conserere certamen malebant. postquam omnia ferro ignique satis evastata erant, consul agro
hostium excessit, et ad Mutinam[11] agmine incauto, ut inter
4 pacatos, ducebat. Boii ut egressum e finibus[3] suis hostem
sensere, sequebantur silenti agmine, locum insidiis quaerentes. nocte praetergressi castra Romana saltum qua

---

[2] quos *B*χ: quod *Vat. Lat. 1852*[2]
[3] e finibus suis *Mg*: finibus suis χ: suis finibus *B*

---

[11] Modern Modena.

its salvation to his arrival. The next day Minucius also crossed the river and encamped about half a mile from the enemy. From this position, with some minor skirmishes, he protected the farmlands of the allies from plundering expeditions; but he would not risk a pitched battle—his men were raw recruits brought together from many tribes and not well enough acquainted to be able to rely on each other. The Ligurians, confident in their numbers, would offer pitched battle, ready for a decisive confrontation, and since they had so many men they also kept sending out numerous raiding parties in all directions along the borders of their territory. When large quantities of animals and other plunder could be rounded up, armed guards were at the ready to take them to their strongholds and villages.

4. When the Ligurian war had stalled around Pisae, the other consul, Lucius Cornelius Merula, took his army along the borders of the Ligurians into the lands of the Boii, and here the strategy employed in the conflict was far different from that used with the Ligurians. It was now the consul offering battle, and the enemy refusing engagement. And when no one came out to face them, the Romans would fan out to plunder, and the Boii preferred to see their lands pillaged without resistance than join battle to protect them. After wholesale devastation had been inflicted by fire and the sword, the consul left enemy territory and led his men toward Mutina,[11] the column proceeding without caution, as if passing through pacified territory. When they realized that the enemy had left their lands, the Boii began to follow them, marching stealthily and looking for a place for an ambush. During the night they passed by the Roman camp and occupied a ravine

5 transeundum erat Romanis insederunt. id cum parum
   occulte fecissent, consul, qui multa nocte solitus erat movere castra, ne nox terrorem in tumultuario proelio augeret, lucem exspectavit, et cum luce moveret, tamen tur-
6 mam equitum exploratum misit. postquam relatum est
   quantae copiae et in quo loco essent, totius agminis sarcinas in medium coici iussit, et triarios vallum circumicere;
7 cetero exercitu instructo ad hostem accessit. idem et Galli
   fecerunt, postquam apertas esse insidias et recto ac iusto
   proelio, ubi vera vinceret virtus, dimicandum viderunt.

   5. Hora secunda ferme concursum est. sinistra sociorum ala et extraordinarii prima in acie pugnabant; praeer-
   ant duo consulares legati, M. Marcellus et Ti. Sempronius
2 prioris anni consul. novus consul nunc ad prima signa erat,
   nunc legiones continebat in subsidiis, ne certaminis studio
3 prius procurrerent quam datum signum esset. equites
   earum extra aciem in locum patentem Q. et P. Minucios
   tribunos militum educere iussit, unde cum signum dedis-
4 set impetum ex aperto facerent. haec agenti nuntius venit
   a Ti. Sempronio Longo non sustinere extraordinarios im-
5 petum Gallorum: et caesos permultos esse, et qui super-
   sint partim labore partim metu remisisse ardorem pugnae;

---

12 Literally, "third men." They were the third line of the Roman battle formation in the Middle Republic. On the Roman
battle formation, see Introduction to vol. IX (LCL 295), lviii–lxv.

13 These were a body of elite allied troops.

14 For ex-consuls to be serving as military legates was unusual.
M. Claudius Marcellus (222) was consul in 196, Ti. Sempronius
Longus (67) in 194.

through which the Romans had to proceed. Since they employed insufficient stealth in doing so, the consul, whose practice it had been to strike camp in the dead of night, now waited for dawn so that darkness would not heighten the panic in a disorderly engagement; and although he was moving camp at daybreak he nevertheless sent a cavalry squadron ahead to reconnoiter. When a report came back on the size of the enemy force and its position, Merula gave orders for the baggage of the entire column to be brought together in one spot and for the triarii[12] to build a defense work around it. He then advanced on the enemy with the rest of his army drawn up for battle. The Gauls did the same when they saw that their ambush had been exposed and that they had to fight a regular, open battle where true courage would prevail.

5. The clash came at about the second hour. The allied left wing and the irregular contingent[13] were fighting in the front line under the command of two consular legates, Marcus Marcellus and Tiberius Sempronius, the latter of whom had been consul the previous year.[14] The new consul would at one moment be at the front standards, and at the next be holding back the legions in reserve to prevent them from charging, through eagerness for the fight, before the signal was given. He ordered the military tribunes Quintus and Publius Minucius to lead the cavalry of these legions outside the line to an open area and to attack with them from the unrestricted ground when he gave the signal. While the consul was making these arrangements, word reached him from Tiberius Sempronius Longus that the irregulars could not hold out against the charge of the Gauls; large numbers had been cut down, he said, and in addition the survivors had lost their ardor for the fight

11

legionem alteram ex duabus, si videretur, submitteret,
6   priusquam ignominia acciperetur. secunda missa est legio
et extraordinarii recepti. tum redintegrata est pugna, cum
et recens miles et frequens ordinibus legio successisset; et
sinistra ala ex proelio subducta est, dextra in primam
aciem subiit.

7   Sol ingenti ardore torrebat minime patientia aestus
Gallorum corpora; densis tamen ordinibus nunc alii in
alios nunc in scuta incumbentes sustinebant impetus Ro-
8   manorum. quod ubi animadvertit consul, ad perturbandos
ordines eorum C. Livium Salinatorem, qui praeerat alariis
equitibus, quam concitatissimos equos immittere iubet, et
9   legionarios equites in subsidiis esse. haec procella eques-
tris primo confudit et turbavit deinde dissipavit aciem
10 Gallorum, non tamen ut terga darent. obstabant duces,
hastilibus caedentes terga trepidantium et redire in ordines cogentes; sed interequitantes alarii non patiebantur.
11 consul obtestabatur milites ut paulum adniterentur: victoriam in manibus esse; dum turbatos et trepidantes viderent, instarent; si restitui ordines sivissent, integro rursus eos proelio et dubio dimicaturos. inferre vexillarios
12 iussit signa. omnes conisi tandem averterunt hostem. postquam terga dabant et in fugam passim effundebantur, tum
ad persequendos eos legionarii equites immissi.

---

15 Livy frequently adverts to the Gauls' lack of stamina and
intolerance of heat and thirst: cf., e.g., 10.28.3–4, 22.2.4.

16 C. Livius Salinator (29): curule aedile 204, praetor 202.
After the Gallic campaign he was praetor again in 191 and
reached the consulship in 188.

through either exhaustion or fear. He suggested that the consul send help in the form of one of the two legions, if he saw fit, before they were dealt an ignominious defeat. The second legion was sent in and the irregulars withdrawn. With fresh troops and a legion with a full complement of companies joining in, life was now restored to the battle. The left wing was also withdrawn from the engagement, and the right replaced it in the front line.

The sun was beating down with a fierce intensity on the Gauls, whose bodies are incapable of coping with heat,[15] but with their ranks closely ordered and the men leaning now on one another, now on their shields, they continued to parry the Roman assaults. When the consul saw this, he instructed Gaius Livius Salinator,[16] commander of the allied cavalry, to send in his horsemen at full gallop to break their ranks, and ordered the legionary cavalry to provide support. This violent cavalry charge at first unsettled and disrupted the battle line of the Gauls, and then broke it up completely, but without making the enemy turn to flight. This the Gallic officers kept trying to prevent, striking the backs of their panicking men with their spear shafts and forcing them back into line, but the allied cavalry rode among them and would not let them reform. The consul earnestly appealed to his men to put on a little more pressure; victory was in their hands, he said. They should press the attack as long as they saw the enemy in disorder and panic; allowing their ranks to be reformed would mean once more fighting the battle from the start and its outcome would be uncertain. With that he ordered the standard-bearers to advance. All then made a concerted effort and finally drove back the enemy. After the Gauls turned and scattered in flight in all directions the legionary cavalry were sent out to pursue them.

13   Quattuordecim milia Boiorum eo die sunt caesa; vivi
capti mille nonaginta duo, equites septingenti viginti
unus, tres duces eorum, signa militaria ducenta duodecim,
14 carpenta sexaginta tria. nec Romanis incruenta victoria
fuit: supra quinque milia militum, ipsorum aut sociorum,
amissa, centuriones tres et viginti, praefecti socium quattuor, et M. Genucius et Q. et M. Marcii tribuni militum
secundae legionis.

    6. Eodem fere tempore duorum consulum litterae
adlatae sunt, L. Corneli de proelio ad Mutinam cum Boiis
2 facto et Q. Minuci a Pisis: comitia suae sortis esse, ceterum
adeo suspensa omnia in Liguribus se habere ut abscedi
inde sine pernicie sociorum et damno rei publicae non
3 posset. si ita videretur patribus, mitterent ad collegam ut
is, qui profligatum bellum haberet, ad comitia Romam
4 rediret; si id facere gravaretur, quod non suae sortis id
negotium esset, se quidem facturum quodcumque senatus
censuisset; sed etiam atque etiam viderent ne magis e re
publica esset interregnum iniri quam ab se in eo statu
relinqui provinciam.

5   Senatus C. Scribonio negotium dedit ut duos legatos
ex ordine senatorio mitteret ad L. Cornelium consulem,
qui litteras collegae ad senatum missas deferrent ad eum,
6 et nuntiarent senatum, ni is ad magistratus subrogandos

---

17 This process, thought (probably rightly) to derive from the
regal period, involved the selection of surrogates if both consuls
either died or left office with no successors in place. The senate
selected one of its number as an *interrex,* whose main duty was
to supervise the election of one or both consuls. The *interrex* held
office for five days only, during which he he had to hold the election or appoint another *interrex* to replace himself.

Fourteen thousand Boii were killed that day, and 1,092 taken alive, along with 721 horsemen and 3 of their officers. Two hundred and twelve military standards were captured and 63 wagons. But it was no bloodless victory for the Romans either. More than 5,000 soldiers, Romans and allies, were lost, plus 23 centurions and 4 allied officers, as well as Marcus Genucius and Quintus and Marcus Marcius, military tribunes of the second legion.

6. Dispatches were brought from the two consuls at roughly the same time, one from Lucius Cornelius about the battle fought with the Boii at Mutina, and another from Quintus Minucius at Pisae. Minucius stated that it had fallen to him to preside over the elections, but the whole situation in Liguria was so precarious that he could not leave without it bringing destruction on the allies and damage to the state. If they concurred, the senators should send the message to his colleague that he should return to Rome for the elections since he had almost finished off his campaign. If Cornelius objected on the grounds that he had not been allotted the responsibility, then he, Minucius, would comply with any decision the senate reached. But, he continued, he entreated them to think long and hard about whether resorting to an *interregnum*[17] might not be more in the interests of the state than having the province left in such a condition.

The senate entrusted to Gaius Scribonius the task of sending two legates of senatorial rank to the consul Lucius Cornelius to pass on to him the letter sent to the senate by his colleague. They were to tell him that if he did not come to Rome for the selection of the new magistrates,

Romam veniret, potius quam Q. Minucium a bello integro
7 avocaret interregnum iniri passurum. missi legati renun-
tiarunt L. Cornelium ad magistratus subrogandos Romam
venturum.

8   De litteris L. Corneli, quas scripserat secundum proelium cum Boiis factum, disceptatio in senatu fuit, quia
9 privatim plerisque senatoribus legatus M. Claudius scripserat fortunae populi Romani et militum virtuti gratiam
habendam quod res bene gesta esset: consulis opera et
militum aliquantum amissum et hostium exercitum, cuius
10 delendi oblata fortuna fuerit, elapsum. milites eo plures
perisse quod tardius ex subsidiis qui laborantibus opem
ferrent successissent; hostes e manibus emissos quod
equitibus legionariis et tardius datum signum esset et persequi fugientes non licuisset.

7. De ea re nihil temere decerni placuit; ad frequen-
2 tiores consultatio dilata est. instabat enim cura alia, quod
civitas faenore laborabat, et quod, cum multis faenebribus
legibus constricta avaritia esset, via fraudis inita erat ut in
socios, qui non tenerentur iis legibus, nomina transcri-
3 berent; ita libero faenore obruebantur debitores. cuius
coercendi cum ratio quaereretur, diem finiri placuit Feralia quae proxime fuissent, ut qui post eam diem socii

---

18 As the Claudii and the Cornelii were bitter political oppo-
nents, the criticism voiced here by Claudius may have more to do
with family rivalry than Cornelius' military ability.

19 These laws had restricted the level of interest that could be
legally charged, but Livy may be exaggerating the problem as
most citizens had probably been too poor even to gain a loan.

20 A festival of the dead held on February 21; but there is a
problem as to whether this is the Feralia of 194/3 or 193/2. Cf.
Briscoe 2.23–24.

they would permit an *interregnum* rather than call Quintus Minucius away from an unfinished war. The legates on this mission brought back word that Lucius Cornelius would come to Rome for the selection of the new magistrates,

Controversy arose in the senate over the dispatch from Lucius Cornelius that he had written after the battle with the Boii because Cornelius' legate, Marcus Claudius, had written personal letters to several senators saying that thanks for the success in Cornelius' campaign should go to the good fortune of the Roman people and the courage of their soldiers. As for the consul, he had been responsible both for heavy Roman losses and for the escape of the enemy army that he had been given the opportunity to destroy. Losses had mounted because the men kept in reserve were too slow in coming to relieve those under pressure; and the enemy had slipped through the consul's fingers because the legionary cavalry had been given the signal too late and not been allowed to pursue the fugitives.[18]

7. It was agreed that no hasty decision should be taken on the matter and discussion was postponed until more would be present. For there was now another pressing concern: the citizen body was overwhelmed by interest payments and, although profiteering had been checked by numerous laws relating to interest on loans, a loophole had been used to circumvent them by transferring debts to allies not covered by the statutes, so that debtors were being crushed by unrestricted interest charges.[19] A way to end this was now sought, and it was decided that the day of the Feralia,[20] which had just passed, should be set as a

civibus Romanis credidissent pecunias profiterentur, et ex
ea die pecuniae creditae quibus debitor vellet legibus
4 ius creditori diceretur. inde[4] postquam professionibus
detecta est magnitudo aeris alieni per hanc fraudem con-
tracti, M. Sempronius tribunus plebis ex auctoritate pa-
5 trum plebem rogavit, plebesque scivit ut cum sociis ac
nomine Latino creditae pecuniae ius idem quod cum civibus Romanis esset.
6   Haec in Italia domi militiaeque acta. in Hispania ne-
7 quaquam tantum belli fuit quantum auxerat fama. C. Flaminius in citeriore Hispania oppidum Illuciam[5] in Oreta-
nis cepit, deinde in hibernacula milites deduxit; et per
hiemem proelia aliquot nulla memoria digna adversus
latronum magis quam hostium excursiones, vario tamen
8 eventu nec sine militum iactura sunt facta. maiores gestae
res a M. Fulvio. is apud Toletum oppidum cum Vaccaeis
Vettonibusque et Celtiberis signis conlatis dimicavit, exercitum earum gentium fudit fugavitque, regem Hilernum
vivum cepit.

4 inde *B*χ: deinde *Mg*
5 Illuciam: *Holk. 356*: Inluciam *B*χ: Iluciam: *ed. Rom.*

21 Here "allies and those with Latin rights" (*socii et nomen
Latinum*), but there are variations throughout Livy. This puts
together two groups with different sorts of treaties with Rome.
The Latins had closer ties, including marriage and commercial
rights, and the allies' treaties were generally less favorable. Both
were to provide troops when Rome was at war, and in military
contexts Livy does not distinguish between them.
22 The Oretani inhabited part of the eastern Sierra Morena
(Marianus Mons), and Illucia is possibly Ilugo, one of their towns
(cf. TIR J-30, 289 s.v. San Andrés, Venta de; *Barr.* 27 B3).

limit; allies who had made loans to Roman citizens after that date would have to declare them and from that day the creditor would be legally bound, with regard to money on loan, to abide by the rules of whichever judicial system the debtor selected. After this, thanks to the declarations made, the size of the debt accumulated by this fraudulent practice was uncovered and with the authorization of the senate a plebeian tribune, Marcus Sempronius, made a proposal to the plebs, which the plebs ratified, that allies and those with Latin rights[21] should be subject to the same laws dealing with loans as Roman citizens.

Such were events in Italy, political and military. In Spain the war was by no means as serious as the exaggerated reports had suggested. Gaius Flaminius took the town of Illucia in the territory of the Oretani[22] in Hither Spain and then led his men to winter quarters. Throughout the winter a number of engagements, none of them noteworthy, were fought in response to attacks made by marauders rather than by enemy forces, though the results were uneven and they were not without loss of men. More was achieved by Marcus Fulvius.[23] He fought a pitched battle with the Vaccaei, Vettones and Celtiberians near the town of Toletum,[24] and there defeated and put to flight the army of these tribes, and took their king, Hilernus, alive.

[23] M. Fulvius Nobilior (91): cf. 34.55.6 for his Spanish appointment. He was a friend of the poet Ennius, who later accompanied him on his controversial Ambracian campaign.

[24] Now Toledo: *Barr.* 27 A2, TIR J-30, 316–17. For the Vaccaei: *Barr.* 24 G3, TIR K-30, 230; Vettones: *Barr.* 26 D2, TIR K-30, 240; Celtiberians: *Barr.* 25 B–C 4, TIR K-30, 91–93.

8. Cum haec in Hispania gerebantur, comitiorum iam appetebat dies. itaque L. Cornelius consul, relicto ad exer-
2 citum M. Claudio legato, Romam venit. is in senatu cum de rebus ab se gestis disseruisset quoque statu provincia
3 esset, questus est cum patribus conscriptis quod tanto bello una secunda pugna tam feliciter perfecto non esset habitus dis immortalibus honos; postulavit deinde suppli-
4 cationem simul triumphumque decernerent. prius tamen quam relatio fieret, Q. Metellus, qui consul dictatorque fuerat, litteras eodem tempore dixit et consulis L. Corneli ad senatum et M. Marcelli ad magnam partem senatorum
5 adlatas esse inter se pugnantes, eoque dilatam esse con-sultationem ut praesentibus auctoribus earum litterarum disceptaretur; itaque exspectasse sese ut consul, qui sciret ab legato suo adversus se scriptum aliquid, cum ipsi ve-niendum esset, deduceret eum secum Romam, cum etiam
6 verius esset Ti. Sempronio imperium habenti tradi exerci-tum quam legato: nunc videri esse amotum[6] de industria
7 qui, si[7] ea quae scripsisset praesens diceret, arguere[8] co-ram, et si quid vani adferret, argui posset, donec ad liqui-
8 dum veritas explorata esset; itaque nihil eorum quae pos-

[6] videri esse amotum *Fr. 2*: videre . . . mon . . . *F*: videre se admonitum *Bχ*: videre sese amotum *ed. Rom.*: videri amotum *Novák*   [7] si *M.Müller*: *om. Bχ*
[8] diceret arguere *Bχ*: diceret et arguere *M. Müller*

[25] The supplication (*supplicatio*) was a period of collective prayer decreed by the senate in times of crisis or calamity, or for thanksgiving, especially for a victory.
[26] Q. Caecilius Metellus (81): consul in 206, he had held the elections for 204 as dictator in 205 (29.10.2–3).

8. As these events were taking place in Spain, the day
of the elections was approaching. The consul Lucius Cornelius therefore left his legate Marcus Claudius in charge
of the army and came to Rome. Discussing before the
senate his own achievements and the situation in his province, he lodged a complaint with the senators that after
such a great a war had been so successfully terminated by
a single victory, the honors due to the immortal gods had
not been paid. He then requested that the senators decree
a time of supplication[25] as well as a triumph. However,
before the question was formally put, Quintus Metellus,
who had been consul and dictator,[26] said that conflicting
letters had arrived simultaneously, one to the senate from
the consul Lucius Cornelius, and another from Marcus
Marcellus addressed to a large number of the senators.
For this reason discussion of the matter had been deferred
so the debate could take place in the presence of the au-
thors of those letters. The consul was aware that negative
comments had been made about him in his legate's cor-
respondence, said Metellus, and he had therefore expected him to bring the man to Rome with him, since he
had to come himself. And besides, it would have been
more proper for the army to be confided to Tiberius Sempronius, who held *imperium*, than to a legate. As it was, it
looked as if a man had been kept away who, if he articu-
lated on the spot the statements he had put in writing,
could make his charges publicly, and be charged himself
if any of his claims proved false, until the truth of the matter had been brought to light after close examination. It
was therefore his view that none of the consul's requests

9 tularet consul decernendum in praesentia censere. cum
pergeret nihilo segnius referre ut supplicationes decerne-
rentur triumphantique sibi urbem invehi liceret, M. et C.
Titinii tribuni plebis se intercessuros si de ea re fieret senatus consultum dixerunt.

9. Censores erant priore anno creati Sex. Aelius Paetus
2 et C. Cornelius Cethegus. Cornelius lustrum condidit.
censa sunt civium capita ducenta⁹ quadraginta tria milia
septingenta quattuor.

Aquae ingentes eo anno fuerunt et Tiberis loca plana
3 urbis inundavit; circa portam Flumentanam etiam con-
lapsa quaedam ruinis sunt. et porta Caelimontana fulmine
4 icta est, murusque circa multis locis de caelo tactus; et
Ariciae et Lanuvii et in Aventino lapidibus pluit; et a Capua nuntiatum est examen vesparum ingens in forum
advolasse et in Martis aede consedisse: eas conlectas cum
5 cura et igni crematas esse. horum prodigiorum causa decemviri libros adire iussi, et novendiale sacrum factum, et
6 supplicatio indicta est atque urbs lustrata. iisdem diebus

---

⁹ ducenta *Pighius*: centum Bχ

---

²⁷ Literally, "closed the lustrum," which refers to a special
ceremony of purification (*lustratio*) of the Roman people. It involved a procession and ended with a *suovetaurilia* (the sacrifice
of a pig, a sheep, and a bull), marking the conclusion of the censors' five-year term. Cf. Oakley 4.458–60.

²⁸ A river gate in the Servian walls between the Porta Carmentalis and the Porta Trigemina (Richardson 303, with fig. 58.15
[p. 263]). ²⁹ Also a gate in the Servian walls, on the Caelian
Hill (Richardson 300–301, also with fig. 58.9 [p. 263]).

³⁰ Probably meteorite showers. ³¹ The priestly college
of decemvirs advised the senate and individuals on religious mat-

should be officially granted for the moment. When Cornelius continued with no less persistence to push his proposal for the authorization of supplications, and for permission to enter the city in triumph, the plebeian tribunes Marcus and Gaius Titinius declared that they would use their veto should any senatorial decree be passed on the matter.

9. Sextus Aelius Paetus and Gaius Cornelius Cethegus had been elected censors the previous year. It was Cornelius who performed the census purification.[27] The census of the citizens totaled 243,704.

There were torrential rains that year and the Tiber flooded the level areas of the city. Some buildings even collapsed in ruins around the Porta Flumentana.[28] The Porta Caelimontana[29] was also struck by lightening, and so too, at several points, was the city wall in the vicinity. Stones fell in showers at both Aricia and Lanuvium, and also on the Aventine;[30] and news came from Capua of a huge swarm of wasps that had flown into the Forum and settled in the temple of Mars (these, it was reported, had been carefully collected and incinerated). Because of these prodigies the decemvirs were instructed to consult the Books.[31] A nine-day sacrifice was performed, a supplication ordained and the city purified.[32] In this same period Marcus Porcius Cato dedicated a shrine to Victoria

ters. One important duty was guarding the Sibylline Books and consulting them when ordered by the senate (usually after prodigies or disasters).

[32] The nine-day sacrifice was usual for celestial prodigies. On the purification ceremony, in which sacrificial animals were paraded around the city, cf. *OCD* s.v. *lustration*.

aediculam Victoriae Virginis prope aedem Victoriae M. Porcius Cato dedicavit biennio post quam vovit.

7 Eodem anno coloniam Latinam in castrum Frentinum triumviri deduxerunt A. Manlius Vulso L. Apustius Fullo Q. Aelius Tubero, cuius lege deducebatur. tria milia peditum iere, trecenti equites, numerus exiguus pro copia agri.

8 dari potuere tricena iugera in pedites, sexagena in equites: Apustio auctore tertia pars agri dempta est, quo postea, si vellent, novos colonos adscribere possent; vicena iugera pedites, quadragena equites acceperunt.

10. In exitu iam annus erat, et ambitio magis quam

2 unquam alias exarserat consularibus comitiis. multi et potentes petebant patricii plebeiique: P. Cornelius Cn. filius Scipio, qui ex Hispania provincia nuper decesserat magnis rebus gestis, et L. Quinctius Flamininus, qui classi

3 in Graecia praefuerat, et Cn. Manlius Vulso, hi patricii; plebeii autem C. Laelius, Cn. Domitius, C. Livius Salina-

4 tor, M'. Acilius. sed omnium oculi in Quinctium Corneliumque coniecti; nam et in unum locum petebant ambo patricii, et rei militaris gloria recens utrumque commen-

5 dabat. ceterum ante omnia certamen accendebant fratres candidatorum, duo clarissimi aetatis suae imperatores.

---

33 The temple of Victoria on the Palatine (Richardson 420) was dedicated in 294, though traditionally it was assigned to Evander. For the shrine of Victoria Virgo, cf. Richardson 421.

34 That is, Tubero had proposed the settlement, which was at Thurii (cf. 34.53.2). Castrum Frentinum is otherwise unknown.

35 A *iugerum* was about two-thirds of an acre.

36 C. Laelius (1), a *novus homo* and close friend of Scipio Africanus, under whom he had served in Spain and Africa: quaestor (202), plebeian aedile (197), and praetor (196).

37 The Sextian-Licinian legislation of 367 stipulated that only

Virgo near the temple of Victoria,[33] two years after he had promised it in a vow.

That same year the triumvirs Aulus Manlius Vulso, Lucius Apustius Fullo and Quintus Aelius Tubero established a Latin colony at Castrum Frentinum (it was by Tubero's law that it was established).[34] Three thousand infantrymen and 300 cavalrymen went there, a small number in view of the amount of land available. Infantrymen could have been awarded 30 *iugera*[35] per head, and cavalrymen 60. On the proposal of Apustius, however, a third of the land was set aside with which they could later enlist new colonists if they so wished. Infantrymen were then given 20 *iugera,* cavalrymen 40.

10. The year was now at an end, and campaigning for the consular elections had become more intense than it had ever been before. Many powerful men, both patrician and plebeian, were candidates: Publius Cornelius Scipio (son of Gnaeus Scipio), who had recently returned from his province of Spain with great achievements to his credit; Lucius Quinctius Flamininus, who had been admiral of the fleet in Greece; and Gnaeus Manlius Vulso were the patricians. The plebeian candidates were Gaius Laelius,[36] Gnaeus Domitius, Gaius Livius Salinator and Manius Acilius. But the eyes of all were focused on Quinctius and Cornelius; for both were patricians seeking the same seat,[37] and recent military achievements made them both attractive choices. But more than anything it was the brothers of the candidates,[38] the two most famous com-

---

one of the consuls could be patrician, though both could be plebeian (which happened for the first time in 172).

[38] Titus Quinctius Flamininus was Lucius' brother, and Scipio Africanus was Scipio Nasica's cousin (*fratres* can include cousins).

maior gloria Scipionis et quo maior eo propior invidiam,
6 Quincti recentior ut qui eo anno triumphasset. accedebat
quod alter decimum iam prope annum adsiduus in oculis
hominum fuerat, quae res minus verendos magnos homines ipsa satietate facit: consul iterum post devictum
7 Hannibalem censorque fuerat; in Quinctio nova et recen-
tia omnia ad gratiam erant; nihil nec petierat a populo post
8 triumphum nec adeptus erat. pro fratre germano non
patrueli se petere aiebat, pro legato et participe adminis-
9 trandi belli: se terra fratrem mari rem gessisse. his obtinuit
ut praeferretur candidato quem Africanus frater ducebat,
quem Cornelia gens Cornelio consule comitia habente,
quem tantum praeiudicium senatus, virum e civitate optimum iudicatum qui matrem Idaeam Pessinunte venientem in urbem acciperet.

10   L. Quinctius et Cn. Domitius Ahenobarbus consules
facti: adeo ne in plebeio quidem consule, cum pro C. Lae-
11 lio niteretur, Africanus valuit. postero die praetores creati
L. Scribonius Libo, M. Fulvius Centumalus, A. Atilius
Serranus, M. Baebius Tamphilus, L. Valerius Tappo, Q.
Salonius Sarra. aedilitas insignis eo anno fuit M. Aemili

---

39 Actually the previous year, 194; cf. 34.52.3–4.

40 Scipio was consul in 205 and again in 194, censor in 199.

41 In 205 the Sibylline Books, consulted after some strange
meteorological phenomena, recommended that the sacred stone
representing Cybele, the Great Mother (*Magna Mater*), be
brought from Pessinus in Phrygia to Rome. Scipio Nasica was
selected as the "best man" to receive the stone when it arrived in
Italy (cf. 29.14.6–14).

manders of their time, who added excitement to the race. Scipio had the greater distinction (which also left him more exposed to envy) but Quinctius' distinction was more current, since he had celebrated his triumph that year.[39] There was also the further consideration that the former man had now been constantly in the public eye for almost ten years—something that decreases respect felt for great men simply from overexposure—and had served as consul for the second time after the defeat of Hannibal, and as censor, too.[40] As for Quinctius, his entire record being fresh and recent could win him support; he had asked for nothing of the people since his triumph and had been accorded nothing. He kept emphasizing that he was canvassing for a real brother, not a cousin, and for his erstwhile legate and partner in the conduct of the war—he himself had campaigned on land, his brother at sea. With these arguments he secured victory for his brother over a candidate who had the support of Africanus (his cousin), and of the Cornelian family (with a Cornelius presiding over the election as consul), and also had the advantage of such a great vote of confidence from the senate, which had judged him the best man in the community to welcome the Idaean mother when she came to the city from Pessinus.[41]

Lucius Quinctius and Gnaeus Domitius Ahenobarbus were elected consuls: so little influence did Africanus have even in the selection of a plebeian consul (for he was supporting Gaius Laelius' candidacy). The next day the following praetors were elected: Lucius Scribonius Libo, Marcus Fulvius Centumalus, Aulus Atilius Serranus, Marcus Baebius Tamphilus, Lucius Valerius Tappo and Quintus Salonius Sarra. Marcus Aemilius Lepidus' and Lucius

12 Lepidi et L. Aemili Paulli: multos pecuarios damnarunt;
ex ea pecunia clipea inaurata in fastigio Iovis aedis posuerunt, porticum unam extra portam Trigeminam, emporio
ad Tiberim adiecto, alteram ab porta Fontinali ad Martis
aram qua in Campum iter esset perduxerunt.

11. Diu nihil in Liguribus dignum memoria gestum
erat: extremo eius anni bis in magnum periculum res ad-
ducta est; nam et castra consulis oppugnata aegre sunt
2 defensa, et non ita multo post per saltum angustum cum
duceretur agmen Romanum, ipsas fauces exercitus Ligu-
3 rum insedit. qua cum exitus non pateret, converso agmine
redire institit consul. et ab tergo fauces saltus occupatae a
parte hostium erant, Caudinaeque cladis memoria non
animis modo sed prope oculis obversabatur.
4 Numidas octingentos ferme equites inter auxilia habebat. eorum praefectus consuli pollicetur se parte utra vellet cum suis erupturum, tantum uti diceret utra pars fre-
5 quentior vicis esset: in eos se impetum facturum, et nihil
prius quam flammam tectis iniecturum, ut is pavor cogeret

---

42 M. Aemilius Lepidus (68), later praetor (191) and twice
consul (187 and 175); M. Aemilius Paullus (114), later also praetor (191) and twice consul (182 and 168).

43 Money raised from fines by the aediles was often used for
public projects; cf. 31.50.2, 34.45.5, etc., and Oakley 4.259–61.

44 Often mentioned in literature, it was in the Servian walls
between the Aventine and the Pons Sublicius (Richardson 310),
but its precise location is unknown.

45 The *Ara Martis* was in the Villa Publica (Richardson 245,
430–31), and the Porta Fontinalis in the Servian walls (Richardson 303).

46 Q. Minucius Thermus; cf. 3–4.1, above

Aemilius Paullus'[42] aedileship of that year was worthy of note. They prosecuted many cattle breeders; from the money raised they set up some gilded shields on the pediment of the temple of Jupiter,[43] and also constructed one portico outside the Porta Trigemina[44] (adding a market along the Tiber at the end of it) and a second that extended from the Porta Fontinalis to the altar of Mars,[45] on the way down to the Campus Martius.

11. There had long been no activity worthy of note among the Ligurians but at the end of that year two situations arose that were fraught with danger. An attack was made on the camp of the consul[46] and only with difficulty beaten off; and also, not much later, a Roman army was being taken through a narrow defile when Ligurian troops blocked the exit. Since there was no way through, the consul turned the column around and proceeded to march back. To the rear, too, the mouth of the pass had been seized by a number of the enemy, and the Caudine Forks disaster,[47] which they now recalled, was not only present in their thoughts but almost danced before their eyes.

The consul had about 800 Numidian cavalry among his auxiliary troops. Their commander assured him that he would break through with his men at whichever end the consul wished—he had only to tell him which end had the more villages. The Numidian would attack these, and before anything else would set light to their buildings so that the panic generated would force the Ligurians to quit the

[47] The infamous episode in 321 at a still unidentified location between Capua and Beneventum when, trapped in a pass, a Roman army was captured and sent under the yoke (Book 9.2–6).

LIVY

Ligures excedere saltu quem obsiderent et discurrere ad
6 opem ferendam suis. conlaudatum eum consul spe praemiorum onerat.
Numidae equos conscendunt et obequitare stationibus
7 hostium, neminem lacessentes, coeperunt. nihil primo
adspectu contemptius: equi hominesque paululi et gra-
ciles, discinctus et inermis eques, praeterquam quod ia-
8 cula secum portat, equi sine frenis, deformis ipse cursus
rigida cervice et extento capite currentium. hunc con-
temptum de industria augentes labi ex equis et per ludi-
9 brium spectaculo esse. itaque qui primo intenti paratique
si lacesserentur in stationibus fuerant, iam inermes seden-
10 tesque pars maxima spectabant. Numidae adequitare,
dein refugere, sed propius saltum paulatim evehi, velut
quos impotentes regendi equi invitos efferrent. postremo
subditis calcaribus per medias stationes hostium erupere,
11 et in agrum latiorem evecti omnia propinqua viae tecta
incendunt. proximo deinde vico inferunt ignem, ferro
12 flammaque omnia pervastant. fumus primo conspectus,
deinde clamor trepidantium in vicis auditus, postremo
seniores puerique refugientes tumultum in castris fece-
13 runt. itaque sine consilio sine imperio pro se quisque currere ad sua tutanda; momentoque temporis castra relicta
erant, et obsidione liberatus consul quo intenderat pervenit.

30

pass they were blockading and run off to help their respective peoples. The consul applauded the man and showered him with promises of reward.

The Numidians mounted their horses and started to ride toward the enemy outposts, but without attacking anyone. At first there could not have been a sorrier sight. Horses and men were puny and scrawny; the riders wore only a tunic and had no weapons apart from the javelins they carried; the horses had no bridles, and their very gallop was unsightly, running along as they did with necks stiff and heads outstretched. The Numidians, purposely enhancing the enemy's derision, would fall from their mounts and make themselves look ridiculous. The result was that the men in the outposts, at first attentive and prepared for any attack, were now for mostly sitting around unarmed watching the show. The Numidians would ride forward and then fall back, but little by little they were approaching the mouth of the pass, looking like men carried off unwillingly by mounts that they could not control. Finally they put in the spurs, broke through the midst of the enemy outposts and, riding out into more open country, set all the buildings bordering the road on fire. Next they put the torch to the nearest village and destroyed everything with fire and the sword. First smoke was sighted, then shouts were heard from panic-stricken people in the villages, and finally old men and children running in flight caused uproar in the camp. So it was that, with no plan and following no order, they all hurried off willy-nilly to protect their own property. In a moment the camp was left deserted and, delivered from the blockade, the consul reached the destination for which he had been bound.

12. Sed neque Boii neque Hispani, cum quibus eo anno bellatum erat, tam inimice infesti[10] erant Romanis quam
2 Aetolorum gens. ii post deportatos ex Graecia exercitus primo in spe fuerant et Antiochum in vacuam Europae possessionem venturum, nec Philippum aut Nabim qui-
3 eturos. ubi nihil usquam moveri viderunt, agitandum aliquid miscendumque rati ne cunctando senescerent consi-
4 lia, concilium Naupactum indixerunt. ibi Thoas praetor eorum conquestus iniurias Romanorum statumque Aetoliae, quod omnium Graeciae gentium civitatiumque inhonoratissimi post eam victoriam essent cuius causa ipsi
5 fuissent, legatos censuit circa reges mittendos, qui non solum temptarent animos eorum, sed suis quemque sti-
6 mulis moverent ad Romanum bellum. Damocritus ad Nabim, Nicander ad Philippum, Dicaearchus frater prae-
7 toris ad Antiochum est missus. tyranno Lacedaemonio Damocritus ademptis maritimis civitatibus eneruatam tyrannidem dicere: inde militem inde naves navalesque socios habuisse; inclusum suis prope muris Achaeos videre
8 dominantes in Peloponneso; nunquam habiturum recipe-

[10] inimici et infesti *Briscoe*: inimice infesti *B*χ: inimice infestique *Lips*.

---

[48] Livy now returns to Greece and the East, and his source is again Polybius. (For corresponding passages in Livy and Polybius, see Introduction to vol. IX, lxxviii–lxxxii.) It seems odd, given the previous chapter, that the threat of the Ligurians is not added here to the Boii and Spaniards.

[49] Probably the Panaetolic meeting in the spring of 193: cf. 31.29.1 and note.

[50] Thoas was their *strategos* but, as often, Livy uses *praetor*,

12. But neither the Boii nor the Spaniards, with whom there had been war that year, proved as fiercely hostile to the Romans as did the people of Aetolia.[48] After the armies were shipped from Greece, these had at first entertained the hope that Antiochus would come to take possession of a now-vacated Europe and also that neither Philip nor Nabis would remain inactive. When they saw no movement anywhere, they thought they should agitate and stir things up so their schemes would not atrophy through procrastination, and they called a meeting at Naupactus.[49] There their praetor,[50] Thoas, complained about the injuries the Romans had inflicted on them and about the position of Aetolia—of all the peoples and city-states of Greece, he said, the Aetolians had been shown the least respect following the victory for which they had been directly responsible. He moved that envoys be sent around the kings, not merely to sound out their feelings but actually to incite them to war on Rome with incentives appropriate to each. Damocritus was sent to Nabis, Nicander to Philip, and Dicaearchus, brother of the praetor, to Antiochus.[51] Damocritus told the Spartan tyrant that his power had been weakened because he had been divested of his maritime states, which had been the source of his soldiers, ships and seamen; he was practically confined within his own walls, he said, watching the Achaeans act as masters in the Peloponnese. If he let slip the opportu-

which he considers an equivalent Roman term. Thoas is for Livy the main architect of the war with Antiochus.

[51] All three envoys were important Aetolians. Damocritus and Dicaearchus were former *strategoi,* and Nicander would hold that position three years later.

randi sua occasionem si eam quae tum esset praeter-
misisset. nullum[11] exercitum Romanum in Graecia esse,
nec[12]Gytheum aut maritimos alios Laconas dignam causam existimaturos Romanos cur legiones rursus in Grae-
9   ciam transmittant. haec ad incitandum animum tyranni
dicebantur, ut cum Antiochus in Graeciam traiecisset,
conscientia violatae per sociorum iniurias Romanae amicitiae coniungeret se cum Antiocho.

10   Et Philippum Nicander haud dissimili oratione incitabat; erat etiam maior orationis materia, quo ex altiore fastigio rex quam tyrannus detractus erat, quoque plures
11 ademptae res. ad hoc vetusta regum Macedoniae fama
peragratusque orbis terrarum victoriis eius gentis refere-
batur: et tutum vel incepto vel eventu se consilium ad-
12 ferre; nam neque ut ante se moveat Philippus quam Antio-
13 chus cum exercitu transierit in Graeciam suadere, et qui
sine Antiocho adversus Romanos Aetolosque tam diu sus-
tinuerit bellum, ei adiuncto Antiocho, sociis Aetolis qui
tum graviores hostes quam Romani fuerint, quibus tan-
14 dem viribus resistere Romanos posse? adiciebat de duce
Hannibale, nato adversus Romanos hoste, qui plures et
duces et milites eorum occidisset quam quot superessent.
15   Haec Philippo Nicander: alia Dicaearchus Antiocho; et

[11] nullum *Fr. 2*: et nullum *B*χ
[12] nec *Gron.*: nec propter *B*χ

34

nity now on offer of recovering what was his, he would never have another one. There was no Roman army operating in Greece and the Romans would not consider Gytheum or other coastal towns of Laconia a good reason for sending their legions into Greece again. These statements were designed to provoke the tyrant so that, when Antiochus crossed to Greece, Nabis' guilty conscience over having violated his friendship with the Romans by maltreating their allies would lead the tyrant to join him.

Philip, too, was being egged on by Nicander with arguments not dissimilar; and there was even more scope for persuasive argument inasmuch as the king had been brought down from a higher position than the tyrant, and the losses he had suffered were greater. Furthermore, there were references made to the time-honored renown of the kings of Macedonia and the victorious campaigns of that people throughout the world. The advice he brought would also be risk free both at the start and when carried through, said Nicander. For, he explained, he was not urging Philip to make a move before Antiochus crossed to Greece with his army; and in addition Philip had, over a very long period, sustained a war against the Romans without Antiochus' help. So when Antiochus now joined him, and he had as his allies the Aetolians—who had been a more formidable enemy than the Romans at that time— what strength could the Romans possibly have to resist him? Nicander would also add remarks about Hannibal's leadership; a born enemy of the Romans, he had killed more of their officers and men than now survived, he said.

Such were Nicander's comments to Philip, but those of Dicaearchus to Antiochus were of a different tenor. The

omnium primum praedam de Philippo Romanorum esse
dicere, victoriam Aetolorum, et aditum in Graeciam Romanis nullos alios quam Aetolos dedisse, et ad vincendum
16 vires eosdem praebuisse; deinde quantas peditum equitumque copias praebituri Antiocho ad bellum essent, quae
17 loca terrestribus copiis, quos portus maritimis. tum de
Philippo et Nabide libero mendacio abutebatur: paratum
utrumque ad rebellandum esse, et primam quamque occasionem recuperandi ea quae bello amisissent arrepturos.
18 ita per totum simul orbem terrarum Aetoli Romanis con-
citabant bellum.

13. Et reges tamen aut non moti aut tardius moti sunt.
Nabis extemplo circa omnes maritimos vicos dimisit ad
seditiones in iis miscendas, et alios principum donis ad
suam causam perduxit, alios pertinaciter in societate Ro-
2 mana manentes occidit. Achaeis omnium maritimorum
Laconum tuendorum a T. Quinctio cura mandata erat.
3 itaque extemplo et ad tyrannum legatos miserunt qui admonerent foederis Romani, denuntiarentque ne pacem
quam tantopere petisset turbaret, et auxilia ad Gytheum,
quod iam oppugnabatur ab tyranno, et Romam qui ea
nuntiarent legatos miserunt.
4 Antiochus rex, ea hieme Raphiae in Phoenice Ptolomaeo regi Aegypti filia in matrimonium data, cum Antio-
chiam se recepisset, per Ciliciam Tauro monte superato

---

52 The daughter became Cleopatra I after her marriage to the
king (Ptolemy V Epiphanes), and their son Ptolemy VI took the
title "Philometor." The wedding location, Raphia, near modern
Rafah in the southern Gaza strip of Israel (*Barr.* 70 E3), was

very first thing he said was that the booty taken from Philip had gone to the Romans but that the victory belonged to the Aetolians since it had been they, and no one else, who had given the Romans access to Greece and also furnished them with the strength to win the victory. He next enumerated the infantry and cavalry that the Aetolians would offer Antiochus for the war and the bases for his land forces and ports for his navies. He then resorted to a barefaced lie about Philip and Nabis, claiming that both were ready to restart hostilities and would seize the first possible opportunity to recover what they had lost in war. Thus were the Aetolians simultaneously fomenting war against the Romans throughout the world.

13. The kings, however, either did not react or else reacted too late. Nabis immediately sent men around all the coastal villages to instigate rebellion in them: and he won a number of important men over to his cause by bribery and by putting to death others when they obstinately stood by the Roman alliance. The Achaeans had been assigned by Titus Quinctius the responsibility of protecting all the coastal towns of Sparta; and so they immediately sent envoys to the tyrant to remind him of his treaty with Rome and warn him against upsetting the peace he had so eagerly sought. They also dispatched relief forces to Gytheum, which was by now under attack from the tyrant, and sent envoys to Rome to report on the situation.

That winter King Antiochus gave his daughter in marriage to Ptolemy, king of Egypt, at Raphia[52] in Phoenicia. He then retired to Antioch and, crossing the Taurus range

probably significant: it was where Ptolemy IV Philopator had defeated Antiochus III in battle in 217.

5   extremo iam hiemis Ephesum pervenit. inde principio
veris Antiocho filio misso in Syriam ad custodiam ultima-
rum partium regni, ne quid absente se ab tergo moveretur,
ipse cum omnibus terrestribus copiis ad Pisidas, qui circa
6   Sidam incolunt, oppugnandos est profectus. eo tempore
legati Romani P. Sulpicius et P. Villius, qui ad Antiochum,
sicut ante dictum est, missi erant, iussi prius Eumenem
adire Elaeam venere; inde Pergamum—ibi regia Eumenis
fuit—escenderunt.

7   Cupidus belli adversus Antiochum Eumenes erat, gravem, si pax esset, accolam tanto potentiorem regem credens, eundem, si motum bellum esset, non magis parem
8   Romanis fore quam Philippus fuisset, et aut funditus sub-
latum iri, aut si pax victo daretur, multa illi detracta sibi
accessura, ut facile deinde se ab eo sine ullo Romano aux-
9   ilio tueri posset: etiam si quid adversi casurum foret, satius
esse Romanis sociis quamcumque fortunam subire quam
solum aut imperium pati Antiochi aut abnuentem vi atque
10 armis cogi. ob haec, quantum auctoritate quantum consilio valebat, incitabat Romanos ad bellum.

    14. Sulpicius aeger Pergami substitit; Villius cum Pisi-
2   diae bello occupatum esse regem audisset, Ephesum profectus, dum paucos ibi moratur dies, dedit operam ut cum
3   Hannibale, qui tum ibi forte erat, saepe congrederetur, ut

---

53 Side is actually in Pamphylia (*Barr.* 65 F4) not Pisidia.

54 Cf. 34.59.8, where P. Aelius Paetus is mentioned as third
commissioner, but he does not reappear in Book 35.

55 The harbor of Pergamum (*Barr.* 56 E4).

56 That is, Eumenes.   57 For Hannibal's flight from Carthage, cf. Books 33.47–49, 34.60.

at the end of winter, came through Cilicia to Ephesus. From here, at the start of spring, he sent his son Antiochus into Syria to oversee the most remote areas of his kingdom so there should be no unrest at his rear while he was away, and then set off in person at the head all his land forces to launch a campaign against the Pisidians, who live in the area of Side.[53] Publius Sulpicius and Publius Villius (the Roman commissioners who had been sent to Antiochus, as mentioned above)[54] had been instructed to see Eumenes first, and they came to Elaea[55] at this time. From there they went up to Pergamum, site of Eumenes' palace.

Eumenes was eager to go to war with Antiochus. He believed that, if there were peace, a king with so much more power than himself would make a worrisome neighbor but that, if war broke out, the same king would prove no more a match for the Romans than Philip had been. Antiochus would either be totally destroyed or, if he were given peace terms after his defeat, much of what would be taken from him would go to him,[56] making defending himself against him easy thereafter without any assistance from Rome. Even if something went wrong, he reasoned, it was better to face whatever fortune had in store with the Romans as allies than to resign himself to Antiochus' domination in isolation or be obliged to do so by armed force if he refused. For these reasons Eumenes was using all his influence and every argument he could muster to goad the Romans into war.

14. Sulpicius, who had fallen ill, stayed on at Pergamum, but Villius headed for Ephesus when he heard that the king was involved in a war in Pisidia. While spending a few days in the city, he made a point of having frequent meetings with Hannibal,[57] who happened to be

animum eius temptaret, et si qua posset, metum demeret
4 periculi quicquam ei ab Romanis esse. iis conloquiis aliud
quidem actum nihil est, secutum tamen sua sponte est,
velut consilio petitum esset, ut vilior ob ea regi Hannibal
et suspectior ad omnia fieret.

5 Claudius, secutus Graecos Acilianos libros, P. Africanum in ea fuisse legatione tradit eumque Ephesi conlocu-
tum cum Hannibale, et sermonem unum etiam refert:
6 quaerenti Africano quem fuisse maximum imperatorem
Hannibal crederet, respondisse Alexandrum Macedonum
regem, quod parva manu innumerabiles exercitus fudis-
7 set, quodque[13] ultimas oras, quas uisere supra spem hu-
8 manam esset, peragrasset. quaerenti deinde quem secun-
9 dum poneret, Pyrrhum dixisse: castra metari primum
docuisse, ad hoc neminem elegantius loca cepisse, praesidia disposuisse; artem etiam conciliandi sibi homines eam
habuisse ut Italicae gentes regis externi quam populi Romani, tam diu principis in ea terra, imperium esse mallent.
10 exsequenti quem tertium duceret, haud dubie semet ipsum dixisse. tum risum obortum Scipioni et subiecisse
11 "quidnam tu diceres, si me vicisses?" "tum vero me" inquit
"et ante Alexandrum et ante Pyrrhum et ante alios omnes
imperatores esse."

[13] quodque β: quod $B\chi Mg$: et quod *Drak.*

58 Claudius is Claudius Quadrigarius (cf. Introduction to vol.
IX, xxvii–xxviii; and *OCD* s.v.), and Acilius probably the senator
referred to in *Per.* 53 as having written a "history of Rome in
Greek." While the episode also appears in Appian (*Syr.* 10) it is
probably fictional and did not occur in Polybius (cf. Briscoe
2.165–66).

there at the time, in order to sound out his attitudes and, if at all possible, allay his fear that he faced some threat from the Romans. Nothing was achieved in these discussions, but an incidental result—which might have appeared intentional—was that Hannibal began to lose credit with the king because of them and to become generally regarded with suspicion.

Claudius, following the Greek account by Acilius, records that Publius Africanus was on that delegation and conversed with Hannibal at Ephesus,[58] and he gives an account of one of these conversations. Africanus asked who Hannibal thought had been the greatest general, and Hannibal replied that it was King Alexander of Macedon because, with a small force, he had defeated countless armies, and because he had penetrated to the ends of the earth, visiting which lay beyond the hope of human beings. When Scipio then asked whom Hannibal would put second, he said that it was Pyrrhus: it was Pyrrhus who first taught the technique of laying out a camp and, in addition, no one had selected his terrain and deployed his troops with more finesse. He also had a way of gaining men's support so that the peoples of Italy preferred to be ruled by a foreign king than by the Roman people, despite their long hegemony in the land. Scipio went on to ask whom he considered third, and Hannibal replied that it was clearly himself. Scipio then burst into laughter and retorted: "What would your answer be if you had defeated me?" "In that case," Hannibal replied, "it would be that I am ahead of both Alexander and Pyrrhus, and all other generals."

12   Et perplexum Punico astu responsum et improvisum
adsentationis genus Scipionem movisse, quod e grege se
imperatorum velut inaestimabilem secrevisset.

15. Villius ab Epheso Apameam processit. eo et Antiochus, audito legatorum Romanorum adventu, occurrit.
2 Apameae congressis disceptatio eadem ferme fuit quae
Romae inter Quinctium et legatos regis fuerat. mors nuntiata Antiochi filii regis, quem missum paulo ante dixeram
3 in Syriam, diremit conloquia. magnus luctus in regia fuit,
magnumque eius iuvenis desiderium; id enim iam speci-
men sui dederat, uti si vita longior contigisset, magni ius-
4 tique regis in eo indolem fuisse appareret. quo carior ac-
ceptiorque omnibus erat, eo mors eius suspectior fuit:[14]
gravem successorem eum instare senectuti suae patrem
credentem per spadones quosdam, talium ministeriis faci-
5 norum acceptos regibus, veneno sustulisse. eam quoque
causam clandestino facinori adiciebant quod Seleuco filio
Lysimachiam dedisset, Antiocho quam similem daret sedem, ut procul ab se honore eum quoque ablegaret, non
6 habuisset. magni tamen luctus species per aliquot dies
regiam tenuit, legatusque Romanus, ne alieno tempore
incommodus obversaretur, Pergamum concessit; rex
Ephesum, omisso quod incohaverat bello, redit.

[14] suspectior fuit χ: suspectior B

59 The Carthaginians were regarded as cunning and deceitful
(cf. Walbank 1.412 for *Punica fides*). However, see Introduction
to vol. IX (LCL 295), xlv–xlvi, for Livy's change of attitude to
Hannibal from Book 21 to 39.   60 Famous Phrygian city (*Barr.*
65 D1), founded by Antiochus I and named after his mother,
Apame. The peace treaty between Antiochus and Rome would be
concluded there in 188 (cf. 38.38).   61 Reported at 34.57.4–59.8.

The cryptic answer with its Punic ingenuity[59] as well as its unexpected mode of flattery had a profound effect on Scipio, according to Claudius—Hannibal had set him apart from run-of-the-mill commanders as being one of incalculable worth.

15. Villius went ahead to Apamea[60] from Ephesus, and Antiochus also came there on hearing of the arrival of the Roman commissioners. The discussion at their meeting in Apamea was much the same as the one that had taken place at Rome between Quinctius and the king's ambassadors.[61] News of the death of the king's son Antiochus (who, as I noted a little eaerlier, had been sent into Syria) broke off the proceedings. There was intense grief in the palace and the young man was sorely missed. Such were the traits that he had already revealed that it was clear that he had the makings of a great and righteous king had he been granted a longer life. The extent to which he was loved and esteemed by all made his death all the more suspicious; people thought that the father had employed certain eunuchs—individuals who endear themselves to monarchs by performing such criminal services—to do away with him by poison, because he believed that having such a successor on his heels would be a threat to him in his old age. They also adduced as a motive for the covert act that the king had given Lysimachia to his son Seleucus but had not had a similar capital to give to Antiochus as a means of also keeping him at a distance by conferring that honor on him. Even so, a display of deep mourning overspread the court for several days and, not to be in the way at this difficult time, the Roman delegate repaired to Pergamum. The king abandoned the war he had started and returned to Ephesus.

7   Ibi per luctum regia clausa cum Minnione quodam, qui
princeps amicorum eius erat, secreta consilia agitavit.
8   Minnio, ignarus omnium externorum, viresque aestimans
regis ex rebus in Syria aut Asia gestis, non causa modo
superiorem esse Antiochum, quod nihil aequi postularent
9   Romani, sed bello quoque superaturum credebat. fugienti
regi disceptationem cum legatis, seu iam experto eam
minus prosperam seu maerore recenti confuso, professus
Minnio se quae pro causa essent dicturum, persuasit ut a
Pergamo accerserentur legati.

16. Iam convaluerat Sulpicius; itaque ambo Ephesum
venerunt. rex a Minnione excusatus et absente eo agi res
2   coepta est. ibi praeparata oratione Minnio "specioso titulo" inquit "uti vos, Romani, Graecarum civitatium libe-
randarum video; sed facta vestra[15] orationi non conveni-
unt, et aliud Antiocho iuris statuistis,[16] alio ipsi utimini.
3   qui enim magis Zmyrnaei Lampsacenique Graeci sunt
quam Neapolitani et Regini et Tarentini, a quibus stipen-
4   dium a quibus naves ex foedere exigitis? cur Syracusas
atque in alias Siciliae Graecas urbes praetorem quotannis
cum imperio et virgis et securibus mittitis? nihil aliud pro-
fecto dicatis quam armis superatis vos iis has leges im-
5   posuisse. eandem de Zmyrna Lampsaco civitatibusque
quae Ioniae aut Aeolidis sunt causam ab Antiocho acci-
6   pite. bello superatas a maioribus, et stipendiarias ac vec-

---

[15] vestra χ: vestrae B   [16] statuistis Bχ: statuitis *J. Gron.*

---

[62] Literally, "friends" (Lat. *amici,* Gk. φιλοι); they were high-
ranking officials in the entourage of the Hellenistic kings, serving
as military officers and also as court advisors. Minnio later reap-
pears as one of Antiochus' generals (37.41.1).

44

There, with the court closed for mourning, he engaged in secret discussions with a certain Minnio, who was the foremost of his courtiers.[62] Minnio had no knowledge whatsoever of foreign affairs and he assessed the king's strength on his successes in Syria or Asia. He thought Antiochus had the superior cause because the Roman demands were totally unjustified, but he also believed that he would prevail in combat. When the king avoided discussion with the commissioners—either because he had already found it unproductive or because he was still upset from his recent bereavement—Minnio assured him he would produce arguments to support his case and convinced him to have the commissioners invited there from Pergamum.

16. By now Sulpicius had recovered and so both commissioners came to Ephesus. Minnio apologized for the king's absence, and the meeting began without him. Minnio there opened the session with a prepared speech: "Romans: I see that you are using the specious pretext of liberating the Greek states; but your actions do not square with your claims and while you have established one set of rules for Antiochus you yourselves are following another. For how, I ask, are the people of Smyrna and Lampsacus more Greek than those of Naples, Rhegium and Tarentum, from whom you exact tribute and ships under the terms of a treaty? Why do you send a praetor every year to Syracuse and other Greek cities in Sicily with *imperium* and the rods and axes? The only possible reason you could give is that you have imposed these terms on them after military victory. You must accept from Antiochus the argument that the same condition obtains in the case of Smyrna, Lampsacus and the cities that lie in Ionia or Aeolia. These were defeated in war by his ancestors and made

45

tigales factas, in antiquum ius repetit. itaque ad haec ei responderi velim, si ex aequo disceptatur et non belli causa quaeritur."

7 Ad ea Sulpicius "fecit verecunde" inquit "Antiochus, qui, si alia pro causa eius non erant quae dicerentur,

8 quemlibet ista quam se dicere maluit. quid enim simile habet civitatium earum quas comparasti causa? ab Reginis et Neapolitanis et Tarentinis, ex quo in nostram venerunt potestatem, uno et perpetuo tenore iuris, semper usurpato nunquam intermisso, quae ex foedere debent exigi-

9 mus. potesne tandem dicere ut ii populi non per se non

10 per alium quemquam foedus mutaverunt, sic Asiae civitates, ut semel venere in maiorum Antiochi potestatem, in perpetua possessione regni vestri mansisse, et non alias earum in Philippi alias in Ptolomaei fuisse potestate, alias per multos annos nullo ambigente libertatem usurpasse?

11 nam si quod aliquando seruierunt, temporum iniquitate pressi, ius post tot saecula adserendi eos in servitutem

12 faciet, quid abest quin actum nobis nihil sit quod a Philippo liberavimus Graeciam, et repetant posteri eius Corinthum Chalcidem Demetriadem et Thessalorum totam

13 gentem? sed quid ego causam civitatium ago quam ipsis agentibus et nos et regem ipsum cognoscere aequius est?"

---

63 The three cities that Philip V called his "Fetters of Greece," since by holding them he could dominate Greece (cf. 32.37.4, Polyb. 18.11.5, Strabo 9.4.15).

into tribute- and tax-paying states, and now Antiochus is reclaiming his erstwhile rights to them. And so I would like a response from you on these points, if this is a discussion based on equity and not merely a search for an excuse for war."

Sulpicius replied as follows: "Antiochus has behaved with propriety. No other arguments being available to support his case, he has chosen to have anyone other than himself make these points. For what similarity is there between the cases of the states that you have compared? We demand of the people of Rhegium, Naples and Tarentum what they owe us under the terms of our treaty with them and we have done so ever since they came into our power, exercising our rights uninterruptedly and continuously without a break. These peoples have never, through their own actions or anyone else's, effected any change in their treaty, but can you say that the communities of Asia have likewise remained continuously the property of your realm once they came under the control of Antiochus' ancestors? Can you say that some have not been under Philip and others under Ptolemy, and that yet others have not affirmed their independence, with none disputing it, for many years? Will the fact that people were once in servitude, disadvantaged by the iniquity of a particular period of history, give others the right to enslave them after so many generations have passed? Is that not tantamount to saying that we accomplished nothing in liberating Greece from Philip—and that his descendants may reclaim Corinth, Chalcis, Demetrias[63] and the entire Thessalian people? But why am I pleading the cause of these city-states when it is fairer for us and the king himself to hear it from their own presentations?"

47

17. Vocari deinde civitatium legationes iussit, praeparatas iam ante et instructas ab Eumene, qui quantumcumque virium Antiocho decessisset, suo id accessurum regno

2 ducebat. admissi plures, dum suas quisque nunc querellas nunc postulationes inserit et aequa iniquis miscent, ex disceptatione altercationem fecerunt. itaque nec remissa ulla re nec impetrata, aeque ac venerant omnium incerti legati Romam redierunt.

3 Rex dimissis iis consilium de bello Romano habuit. ibi alius alio ferocius, quia quo quisque asperius adversus

4 Romanos locutus esset, eo spes gratiae maior erat, superbiam[17] postulatorum increpare, tamquam Nabidi victo sic Antiocho, maximo Asiae regum, imponentium leges:

5 quamquam Nabidi tamen dominationem in patria sua[18]

6 remissam, Antiocho si Zmyrna et Lampsacus imperata

7 faciant indignum videri; alii parvas et vix dictu dignas belli causas tanto regi eas civitates esse, sed initium semper a paruis iniusta imperandi fieri, nisi crederent Persas, cum aquam terramque ab Lacedaemoniis petierint, gleba ter-

8 rae et haustu aquae eguisse. per similem temptationem a Romanis de duabus civitatibus agi, et[19] alias civitates, simul duas iugum exuisse vidissent, ad liberatorem popu-

9 lum defecturas. si non libertas servitute potior sit, tamen omni praesenti statu spem cuique novandi res suas blandiorem esse.

[17] superbiam *Crév.*: alius superbiam $B\chi$: erat. alius *distinxit Walsh*   [18] sua *scripsi (app. Briscoe, comm. 2.297)*: sua et patriam Lacedaemonem $B\chi$: sua et patria Lacedaemone *Madvig*   [19] et $B\chi$: sed *Crév.*

[64] The conventional symbols of submission demanded by the Persians.

17. Sulpicius then issued orders for embassies from the city-states to be summoned. These had been given prior coaching and instruction by Eumenes, who assumed that whatever strength was lost to Antiochus would accrue to his own realm. Several were given an audience, and as each added its own protests and demands and combined valid with invalid ones they turned the discussion into a squabble. And so, with no concessions made or gained, the commissioners returned to Rome unsure of anything, no further forward than when they had arrived.

After sending off the commissioners, the king held a council to discuss the war with Rome. There the speakers tried to outdo each other in denouncing the arrogance of the Roman demands because the more abusive their criticism the more they would ingratiate themselves with the king. Those demands, they said, were imposing conditions on Antiochus, the greatest king in Asia, as if he were a defeated Nabis. Yet even Nabis had been left with sovereignty in his own country, while it was regarded as intolerable for Smyrna and Lampsacus to be doing Antiochus' bidding! Others argued that these states were of slight importance and hardly worth mentioning as reasons for so great a king to go to war, but that unscrupulous demands always began with insignificant ones—unless they believed that, when they asked the Spartans for water and earth,[64] the Persians truly needed a lump of turf and a drink of water! The Romans were now resorting to similar tactics with the two states in question, they said; and other states would defect to the liberating nation once they saw that the two had thrown off the yoke. Even if independence were not of itself preferable to servitude, everyone still finds the prospect of a change of circumstances more attractive, no matter what their present situation.

18. Alexander Acarnan in consilio erat: Philippi quondam amicus, nuper relicto eo secutus opulentiorem regiam Antiochi, et tamquam peritus Graeciae nec ignarus Romanorum, in eum gradum amicitiae regis ut consiliis quoque arcanis interesset acceptus erat. is, tamquam non utrum bellandum esset necne consuleretur, sed ubi et qua ratione bellum gereretur, victoriam se haud dubiam proponere animo adfirmabat, si in Europam transisset rex et in aliqua Graeciae parte sedem bello cepisset: iam primum Aetolos, qui umbilicum Graeciae incolerent, in armis eum inventurum, antesignanos ad asperrima quaeque belli paratos; in duobus velut cornibus Graeciae Nabim a Peloponneso concitaturum omnia, repetentem Argivorum urbem, repetentem maritimas civitates quibus eum depulsum Romani Lacedaemonis muris inclusissent, a Macedonia Philippum, ubi primum bellicum cani audisset, arma capturum; nosse se spiritus eius, nosse animum; scire ferarum modo quae claustris aut vinculis teneantur ingentes iam diu iras eum in pectore volvere. meminisse etiam se quotiens in bello precari omnes deos solitus sit ut Antiochum sibi darent adiutorem; cuius voti si compos nunc fiat, nullam moram rebellandi facturum. tantum non cunctandum nec cessandum esse; in eo enim victoriam verti si et loca opportuna et socii praeoccuparentur. Hannibalem quoque sine mora mittendum in Africam esse ad distringendos Romanos.

---

65 That is "adviser." He would later fight the Romans and receive a mortal wound in battle (36.11.6, 20.5–6).

66 Literally, "navel" (*umbilicus*), a reference to the "navel stone" (ὀμφαλός) in the temple of Apollo at Delphi, signifying that it was the center of the earth.

18. The Acarnanian Alexander was at the meeting. He had formerly been a friend[65] of Philip's, but had recently abandoned him to latch on to the wealthier court of Antiochus. Knowing Greece well and being not unacquainted with the Romans, Alexander had established such a close relationship with the king as to be party to all his secret plans. For him the question was not whether or not to go to war but rather where and how it should be conducted; and he would declare that he foresaw certain victory if the king crossed to Europe and established the theater of war in some part of Greece. Antiochus would first of all find that the Aetolians, who lived in the heart[66] of Greece, were up in arms—these were his frontline troops, ready to face the greatest hardships of the war. On the two flanks of Greece, as it were, there would be Nabis, who would wreak sheer havoc on the Peloponnese in trying to recover the city of Argos and trying to recover the maritime states from which the Romans had driven him before shutting him up within the walls of Sparta; and in Macedonia, Philip would immediately take up arms on hearing the clarion call to war. He was well acquainted with Philip's dynamism and temperament, said Alexander. He knew that he had long been churning over fierce resentment in his heart, like wild animals that are caged or chained; and he also remembered how often during the war Philip would pray to all the gods to give him Antiochus as his associate. If he now had that prayer answered he would not put off rebelling for a moment. Only Antiochus must not hesitate or hold back: victory depended on forestalling their enemy in both seizing strategic positions and securing allies. In addition, Hannibal should be immediately sent to Africa to distract the Roman troops.

51

19. Hannibal non adhibitus est in consilium, propter
conloquia cum Villio suspectus regi et in nullo postea
2 honore habitus. primo eam contumeliam tacitus tulit; deinde melius esse ratus et percunctari causam repentinae
alienationis et purgare se, tempore apto quaesita simplici-
3 ter iracundiae causa auditaque, "pater Hamilcar" inquit,
"Antioche, paruum admodum me, cum sacrificaret, alta-
ribus admotum iureiurando adegit nunquam amicum fore
4 populi Romani. sub hoc sacramento sex et triginta annos
militavi, hoc me in pace patria mea expulit, hoc patria
extorrem in tuam regiam adduxit: hoc duce, si tu spem
meam destitueris, ubicumque vires ubi arma esse sciam
veniam, toto orbe terrarum quaerens aliquos Romanis ho-
5 stes. itaque si quibus tuorum meis criminibus apud te
crescere libet, aliam materiam crescendi ex me quaerant.
6 odi odioque sum Romanis. id me verum dicere pater Hamilcar et di testes sunt. proinde cum de bello Romano
cogitabis, inter primos amicos Hannibalem habeto: si qua
res te ad pacem compellet, in id consilium alium cum quo
7 deliberes quaerito." non movit modo talis oratio regem
sed etiam reconciliavit Hannibali. ex consilio ita discessum est ut bellum gereretur.

20. Romae destinabant quidem sermonibus hostem
Antiochum, sed nihildum ad id bellum praeter animos
2 parabant. consulibus ambobus Italia provincia decreta est,

---

67 Cf. 14.1–4, above.   68 The famous story of Hannibal's
oath is also given earlier in Livy (21.1.4). In Polybius (3.11.5–7)
and Cornelius Nepos (*Hann.* 2.3) it occurs in the same context as
here (Hannibal's speech to Antiochus).   69 That is, from 237
to Zama in 202 (cf. 30.37.9).   70 The consuls elected at 10.10
above (L. Quinctius Flamininus and Cn. Domitius Ahenobarbus),
indicating that we are now in a new year, 192.

19. Hannibal was not invited to the meeting; he had aroused the king's suspicions because of his conversations with Villius,[67] and was thereafter accorded no honor by the king. At first, he suffered the rebuff in silence but then thought it better both to ask why the king had suddenly turned from him and try to clear himself. At an appropriate moment, he bluntly asked the king the reason for his displeasure and when given it he said: "When I was just a little boy, Antiochus, and my father Hamilcar was performing a sacrifice, he brought me to the altar, and bound me under oath never to be a friend of the Roman people.[68] I have campaigned observing this oath for thirty-six years.[69] It was this that drove me from my country in time of peace and this that brought me, an exile from my country, to your court. Led by this oath, if you frustrate my hopes, I shall go wherever I know power and military strength exist, searching the world over for enemies of Rome. So if any of your friends want to advance in your esteem by making allegations against me, let them find other ways of advancing at my expense. I hate the Romans and am hated by them. My father Hamilcar and the gods are witnesses to the truth of what I say. So when you reflect on war with Rome, regard Hannibal as one of your foremost friends; but if something disposes you toward peace, look for someone else with whom to discuss *that* course." These words not only impressed the king but even reconciled him with Hannibal. The council broke up with a decision for war.

20. In Rome people certainly had Antiochus marked out as an enemy in their conversations but so far they were preparing nothing except their spirit for this oncoming conflict. Both consuls[70] were assigned Italy as their prov-

ita ut inter se compararent sortirenturue uter comitiis eius
3 anni praeesset: ad utrum ea non pertineret cura, ut paratus esset si quo eum extra Italiam opus esset ducere le-
4 giones. huic consuli permissum ut duas legiones scriberet
novas, et socium nominis Latini viginti milia et equites
5 octingentos. alteri consuli duae legiones decretae quas L.
Cornelius consul superioris anni habuisset, et socium ac
Latini nominis ex eodem exercitu quindecim milia et
6 equites quingenti. Q. Minucio cum exercitu quem in Liguribus habebat prorogatum imperium; additum in supplementum ut quattuor milia peditum Romanorum scribe-
rentur, centum quinquaginta equites, et sociis eodem
quinque milia peditum imperarentur, ducenti quinquaginta equites.

7   Cn. Domitio extra Italiam quo senatus censuisset pro-
8 vincia evenit, L. Quinctio Gallia et comitia habenda. praetores deinde provincias sortiti, M. Fulvius Centumalus
urbanam, L. Scribonius Libo peregrinam, L. Valerius
Tappo Siciliam, Q. Salonius Sarra Sardiniam, M. Baebius
9 Tamphilus Hispaniam citeriorem, A. Atilius Serranus ulteriorem.

Sed his duobus primum senatus consulto, deinde ple-
10 bei etiam scito permutatae provinciae sunt: Atilio classis
11 et Macedonia, Baebio Bruttii decreti. Flaminio Fulvioque
in Hispaniis prorogatum imperium. Atilio in Bruttios duae

---

71 Cf. 7.5 note, above.

72 The exact phrase recurs below at 41.3 and 6 (cf. also
27.22.3, 42.28.6, etc.). It is used when the senate wishes to leave
a province unspecified to meet a possible emergency.

ince on the understanding that they would arrange by mutual agreement, or by lot, which should preside over the year's elections. The one to whom that responsibility did not fall was to be ready to take the legions wherever they were needed outside Italy. This consul was given permission to enroll two new legions, along with 20,000 infantry and 800 cavalry from the allies and those with Latin rights.[71] The other consul was assigned the two legions that the previous year's consul, Lucius Cornelius, had commanded, plus, from the same army, 15,000 infantry and 500 cavalry of the allies and those with Latin rights. Quintus Minucius, commanding an army in Liguria, had his *imperium* prorogued, and his forces were to be supplemented by the recruitment of 4,000 Roman infantrymen and 150 cavalrymen and by 5,000 infantry and 250 cavalry that were to be requisitioned for him from the allies.

The responsibility of leaving Italy for wherever the senate decided[72] fell to Gnaeus Domitius, and Gaul and administration of elections fell to Lucius Quinctius. The praetorian sortition of provinces then proceeded as follows: Marcus Fulvius Centumalus drew the city jurisdiction and Lucius Scribonius Libo the foreigners' jurisdiction. Sicily fell to Lucius Valerius Tappo and Sardinia to Quintus Salonius Sarra, while Hither Spain fell to Marcus Baebius Tamphilus and Farther Spain to Aulus Atilius Serranus.

However, the provinces of the last two praetors were changed, first by senatorial decree and then also by a resolution of the plebs: Atilius was assigned the fleet and Macedonia and Baebius Bruttium. Flaminius and Fulvius had their *imperium* prorogued in the Spanish provinces. For operations against the Bruttii Atilius was allocated the

55

legiones decretae quae priore anno urbanae fuissent, et ut sociis eodem milia peditum quindecim imperarentur et

12 quingenti equites. Baebius Tamphilus triginta naves quinqueremes facere iussus, et ex navalibus veteres deducere si quae utiles essent, et scribere navales socios; et consulibus imperatum ut ei duo milia socium ac Latini nomi-

13 nis et mille Romanos darent pedites. hi duo praetores et duo exercitus, terrestris navalisque, adversus Nabim aperte iam oppugnantem socios populi Romani dicebantur

14 parari; ceterum legati ad Antiochum missi exspectabantur, et priusquam ii redissent vetuerat Cn. Domitium consulem senatus discedere ab urbe.

21. Praetoribus Fulvio et Scribonio, quibus ut ius dicerent Romae provincia erat, negotium datum ut praeter eam classem cui Baebius praefuturus erat centum quinqueremes pararent.

2 Priusquam consul praetoresque in provincias proficis-

3 cerentur, supplicatio fuit prodigiorum causa. capram sex haedos uno fetu edidisse ex Piceno nuntiatum est, et Ar-

4 reti puerum natum unimanum, Amiterni terra pluvisse, Formiis portam murumque de caelo tacta, et quod maxime terrebat, consulis Cn. Domiti bovem locutum "Roma,

5 cave tibi." ceterorum prodigiorum causa supplicatum est:

---

73 Cf. 13.1, above.   74 *supplicatio:* cf. 8.4 note, above.

75 A Sabine town, birthplace of Sallust. Its remains lie some six miles northwest of L'Aquila (*Barr.* 42 E4).

76 Modern Formia, on the coast of Latium.

77 Levene (86) notes that this prodigy of the consul's talking ox stands out in the list, probably because it precedes a new war in which Hannibal, the Roman bogeyman, is to be involved.

two legions stationed in the city the previous year plus 15,000 infantry and 500 cavalry that were to be requisitioned from the allies. Baebius Tamphilus was ordered to construct 30 quinqueremes, to bring from the dockyards whatever old vessels were still serviceable, and to enlist crews. The consuls were also instructed to furnish him with 2,000 infantry from the allies and holders of Latin rights and 1,000 Roman infantry. It was claimed that these two praetors with their two armies (a land force and a navy) were being held in readiness for operations against Nabis, who was now openly attacking allies of the Roman people;[73] but in fact it was a matter of awaiting the return of the ambassadors who had been sent to Antiochus, and the senate had forbidden Gnaeus Domitius to leave the city until they returned.

21. The praetors, Fulvius and Scribonius, whose province was the administration of justice in Rome, were assigned the task of making ready 100 quinqueremes, in addition to the fleet that Baebius was to command.

Before the consul and the praetors could leave for their provinces, a supplication[74] was held because of a number of portents. There was a report from Picenum of a goat having given birth to six kids in one delivery, another of a baby boy born with only one hand at Arretium, and one of a shower of earth at Amiternum.[75] At Formiae[76] a city gate and wall were said to have been struck by lightening, and—most frightening of all—an ox that belonged to the consul Gnaeus Domitius was reported to have spoken the words "Rome, be on your guard."[77] A supplication was held in the case of the other portents, but the soothsayers

57

bovem cum cura servari alique haruspices iusserunt. Tiberis, infestiore quam priore[20] impetu inlatus urbi, duos pontes aedificia multa, maxime circa Flumentanam por-
6 tam, evertit. saxum ingens, sive imbribus seu motu terrae leniore quam ut alioque sentiretur labefactatum, in vicum Iugarium ex Capitolio procidit et multos oppressit. in agris passim inundatis pecua ablata, villarum strages facta est.

7 Priusquam L. Quinctius consul in provinciam perveniret, Q. Minucius in agro Pisano cum Liguribus signis conlatis pugnavit: novem milia hostium occidit, ceteros
8 fusos fugatosque in castra compulit. ea usque in noctem
9 magno certamine oppugnata defensaque sunt. nocte clam profecti Ligures, prima luce vacua castra Romanus invasit; praedae minus inventum est, quod subinde spolia agro-
10 rum capta domos mittebant. Minucius nihil deinde laxamenti hostibus dedit: ex agro Pisano in Ligures profectus
11 castella vicosque eorum igni ferroque pervastavit. ibi praeda Etrusca, quae missa a populatoribus fuerat, repletus est miles Romanus.

22. Sub idem tempus legati ab regibus Romam rever-
2 terunt. qui cum nihil quod satis maturam causam belli haberet nisi adversus Lacedaemonium tyrannum attulissent, quem et Achaei legati nuntiabant contra foedus maritimam oram Laconum oppugnare, Atilius praetor
3 cum classe missus in Graeciam est ad tuendos socios. con-

---

[20] priore *Bχ*: priore anno *T. Faber*: prius *Gron.*

---

[78] Cf. 9.2 above and note.

[79] Street running above the Forum Romanum and linking the foot of the Quirinal and the porta Carmentalis (Richardson 424 and fig. 19 [p. 69]).

ordered that the ox be attentively looked after and fed. The Tiber made a more violent attack on the city than on the occasion of the previous flood and destroyed two bridges and numerous buildings, particularly in the area of the Porta Flumentana.[78] A huge rock, which had been loosened by rainwater or else by an earthquake too slight to be otherwise perceptible, fell from the Capitol into the *Vicus Iugarius*[79] and crushed many people. Cattle were swept away in various parts of the flooded countryside and farmhouses were destroyed.

Before the consul Lucius Quinctius reached his province, Quintus Minucius fought a pitched battle with the Ligurians in Pisan territory. He killed 9,000 of the enemy and drove the rest in scattered flight back to their camp. The camp was attacked and defended in a furious battle until nightfall. During the night the Ligurians slipped furtively away and at dawn the Romans broke into an empty camp. The amount of booty found was disappointing because the Ligurians had been intermittently sending home the spoils they had taken from the fields. Minucius then gave the enemy no respite. He advanced against the Ligurians from Pisan territory and razed their strongholds and villages with fire and the sword. Here the Roman soldiers had their fill of Etruscan spoils, which had been sent there by the Ligurian raiding parties.

22. At about this same time the commissioners returned to Rome from the kings. They brought no information to justify opening hostilities in the near future, except against the Spartan tyrant, whom the Achaean delegation also reported as attacking the Spartan coastline in contravention of the treaty. The praetor Atilius was then sent to Greece with a fleet to protect the allies. As there was no

59

sules, quando nihil ab Antiocho instaret, proficisci ambo
in provincias placuit. Domitius ab Arimino, qua proximum
4 fuit, Quinctius per Ligures in Boios venit. duo consulum
agmina diversa late agrum hostium pervastarunt. primo
equites eorum pauci cum praefectis, deinde universus
senatus, postremo in quibus aut fortuna aliqua aut dignitas
erat, ad mille quingenti ad consules transfugerunt.

5 Et in utraque Hispania eo anno res prospere gestae;
nam et C. Flaminius oppidum Licabrum munitum opulen-
tumque vineis expugnavit, et nobilem regulum Corribi-
6 lonem vivum cepit, et M. Fulvius proconsul cum duobus
exercitibus hostium duo secunda proelia fecit, oppida duo
Hispanorum, Vesceliam Helonemque, et castella multa
7 expugnavit; alia voluntate ad eum defecerunt. tum in Ore-
tanos progressus et ibi duobus potitus oppidis, Noliba et
Cusibi, ad Tagum amnem ire pergit. Toletum ibi parva
urbs erat, sed loco munito. eam cum oppugnaret, Vetto-
8 num magnus exercitus Toletanis subsidio venit. cum iis
signis conlatis prospere pugnavit, et fusis Vettonibus operibus Toletum cepit.

---

80 Livy again uses a Roman term for a foreign political entity,
in this case perhaps a council of military officers who assisted the
chieftain (cf. Adam ad loc.)

81 Probably Igabrum (mod. Cabra, southeast of Cordoba):
TIR J-30, 198; *Barr.* 27 A4. The province of C. Flaminius (3) is
Hither Spain (34.55.6), and if Licabrum is Igabrum, he is operat-
ing outside it.

82 Marcus Fulvius Nobilior (91); his *imperium* was prorogued
in Farther Spain.

83 Vescelia: TIR J-30, 337. Perhaps to be identified with Vesci
(337–38). Helo (187): unidentified but perhaps Ilipula Halos.

immediate threat from Antiochus, it was decided that both consuls should leave for their provinces and they came into the land of the Boii, Domitius taking the most direct route from Ariminum, and Quinctius traversing Liguria. Coming from different directions, the armies of the two consuls laid waste the enemy's farmlands over a wide area. At first a few enemy cavalrymen with their officers went over to the consuls, then the entire senate,[80] and finally all people of any means or status, some 1,500 in all.

There were also successes that year in both Spanish provinces. Gaius Flaminius reduced the fortified and wealthy town of Licabrum[81] by means of siege sheds, and took alive the noble chieftain Corribilo. The proconsul Marcus Fulvius[82] also fought two successful engagements with two enemy armies, and took by storm two Spanish towns, Vescelia and Helo,[83] plus a large number of fortresses. Other towns went over to him voluntarily. Fulvius then advanced against the Oretani,[84] and after capturing two towns in their territory, Noliba and Cusibi,[85] proceeded toward the River Tagus.[86] In this area lay Toletum, a small city, but one with natural defenses. While Fulvius was assaulting it, a large force of Vettones came to support the Toletani.[87] Fulvius successfully engaged the Vettones in pitched battle, and after routing them took Toletum by siege.

[84] Pre-Roman Iberian or Celtic people north of the Sierra Morena (Marianus Mons) in Andalucia: TIR J-30, 256; *Barr.* 27 B3.

[85] Both unlocated: TIR J-30, 249 (Noliba); 167 (Cusubi [sic]).

[86] Modern Tajo.

[87] Toletum (Toledo) and the Vettones: 7.8 and note, above.

23. Ceterum eo tempore minus ea bella quae gerebantur curae patribus erant quam exspectatio nondum coepti
2 cum Antiocho belli. nam etsi per legatos identidem omnia
explorabantur, tamen rumores temere sine ullis auctori-
3 bus orti multa falsa veris miscebant; inter quae adlatum
erat cum in Aetoliam venisset Antiochus, extemplo clas-
4 sem eum in Siciliam missurum. itaque senatus, etsi prae-
5 torem Atilium cum classe miserat in Graeciam, tamen,
quia non copiis modo sed etiam auctoritate opus erat ad
tenendos sociorum animos, T. Quinctium et Cn. Octavium
et Cn. Servilium et P. Villium legatos in Graeciam misit;
et ut M. Baebius ex Bruttiis ad Tarentum et Brundisium
promoveret legiones decrevit, inde, si res posceret, in
6 Macedoniam traiceret; et ut M. Fulvius praetor classem
navium viginti mitteret ad tuendam Siciliae oram; et ut
cum imperio esset qui classem eam duceret—duxit L.
7 Oppius Salinator, qui priore anno aedilis plebi fuerat; et
8 ut idem praetor L. Valerio collegae scriberet periculum
esse ne classis regis Antiochi ex Aetolia in Siciliam traiceret, itaque placere senatui ad eum exercitum quem haberet tumultuariorum militum ad duodecim milia et
quadringentos equites scriberet, quibus oram maritimam
9 provinciae qua vergeret in Graeciam tueri posset. eum
dilectum praetor non ex Sicilia ipsa tantum sed ex circum-
iacentibus insulis habuit, oppidaque omnia maritima quae

---

88 He was to be a *legatus cum imperio*.

89 L. Valerius Tappo (350), one of the plebeian tribunes who
had advocated the repeal of the Oppian law in 195 (34.1.2–3).

90 These would probably be Malta and the Lipari Islands.

23. In fact, the wars in progress at this time caused the senators less concern than the prospect of the war with Antiochus, which had not yet begun. Although the entire situation was under repeated investigation by the commissioners, there were random and unsubstantiated rumors that were a mixture of truth and much falsehood nevertheless. Among them was the claim that Antiochus would send a fleet to Sicily immediately on reaching Aetolia. And so, although the senate had already sent the praetor Atilius to Greece with a fleet, it also sent a delegation to Greece, consisting of Titus Quinctius, Gnaeus Octavius, Gnaeus Servilius and Publius Villius, because an authoritative presence and not merely armed forces was needed there to retain the loyalty of the allies. It further decreed that Marcus Baebius should advance his legions from Bruttium to Tarentum and Brundisium and cross from there to Macedonia if the situation so required. The praetor Marcus Fulvius was also ordered by the decree to send a fleet of 20 ships to protect the coastline of Sicily, and the man who commanded the fleet was to have *imperium*[88] (and the commander proved to be Lucius Oppius Salinator, who had been plebeian aedile the year before). Furthermore, that same praetor was to write to his colleague, Lucius Valerius,[89] to alert him to the danger of King Antiochus' fleet crossing from Aetolia to Sicily and to inform him of the senate's decision, in view of this, that he should raise an emergency force of about 12,000 infantry and 400 cavalry to supplement the army that he already had. With such a force, Valerius would be able to protect the coast of the province that faced Greece. These troops the praetor raised not only from Sicily itself but also from the adjacent islands,[90] and he reinforced with garrisons all the

10 in Graeciam versa erant praesidiis firmavit. addidit ali-
menta rumoribus adventus Attali, Eumenis fratris, qui
nuntiavit Antiochum regem Hellespontum cum exercitu
transisse, et Aetolos ita se parare ut sub adventum eius in
11 armis essent. et Eumeni absenti et praesenti Attalo gratiae
actae, et aedes liberae locus lautia decreta, et munera data
equi duo, bina equestria arma, et vasa argentea centum
pondo et aurea viginti pondo.

24. Cum alii atque alii nuntii bellum instare adferrent,
ad rem pertinere visum est consules primo quoque tem-
2 pore creari. itaque senatus consultum factum est ut M.
Fulvius praetor litteras extemplo ad consulem mitteret,
quibus certior fieret senatui placere provincia exercituque
3 tradito legatis Romam reverti eum, et ex itinere praemit-
tere edictum quo comitia consulibus creandis ediceret.
paruit iis litteris consul et praemisso edicto Romam venit.
4 Eo quoque anno magna ambitio fuit, quod patricii tres
in unum locum petierunt, P. Cornelius Cn. f. Scipio, qui
priore anno repulsam tulerat, et L. Cornelius Scipio et Cn.
5 Manlius Vulso. P. Scipioni, ut dilatum viro tali non nega-
tum honorem appareret, consulatus datus est; additur ei
6 de plebe collega M'.[21] Acilius Glabrio. postero die praetores creati L. Aemilius Paullus, M. Aemilius Lepidus, M.
Iunius Brutus, A. Cornelius Mammula, C. Livius et L.

---

21 M'. *Grut.*: M. $B\chi$

---

91 P. Scipio Nasica (350). On his career, see Briscoe 1.162, and
for his electoral defeat the previous year, chapter 10, above.
92 M'. Acilius Glabrio (35): plebeian tribune 201, plebeian
aedile 197, praetor 196.

coastal towns on the side facing Greece. Rumors were also fueled by the arrival of Eumenes' brother, Attalus, who reported that King Antiochus had crossed the Hellespont with his army, and that the Aetolians were preparing themselves so efficiently that they would be under arms by the time he arrived. Both men were thanked, Eumenes in his absence and Attalus in person. Attalus was also awarded, by decree, state accommodation and entertainment, and given as a present two horses, two sets of horseman's armor, silver vases weighing a hundred pounds and gold vases weighing twenty.

24. When message after message arrived that war was imminent, it seemed advisable for the election of the consuls to take place at the earliest opportunity. A senatorial decree was therefore passed authorizing the praetor Marcus Fulvius to immediately send the consul a letter informing him that it was the senate's decision that he hand his province and army over to his legates and return to Rome, sending ahead an edict en route announcing the consular elections. The consul obeyed the letter's instructions and came to Rome after sending ahead the edict.

There was intense competition that year, too, as there were three patrician candidates competing for one position: Publius Cornelius Scipio, son of Gnaeus, who had suffered defeat the previous year,[91] Lucius Cornelius Scipio, and Gnaeus Manlius Vulso. The consulship was awarded to Publius Scipio, so that it appeared that a man of his distinction had merely had the honor deferred, not refused. As his colleague from the plebs Scipio was given Manius Acilius Glabrio.[92] The next day the praetors elected were: Lucius Aemilius Paullus, Marcus Aemilius Lepidus, Marcus Iunius Brutus, Aulus Cornelius Mam-

Oppius, utrique eorum Salinator cognomen erat; Oppius
7 is erat qui classem viginti navium in Siciliam duxerat. interim dum novi magistratus sortirentur provincias, M.
Baebius a Brundisio cum omnibus copiis transire in Epi-
8 rum est iussus et circa Apolloniam copias continere, et M.
Fulvio praetori urbano negotium datum est ut quinqueremes novas quinquaginta faceret.

25. Et populus quidem Romanus ita se ad omnes cona-
2 tus Antiochi praeparabat: Nabis iam non differebat bellum
sed summa vi Gytheum oppugnabat, et infestus Achaeis,
quod miserant obsessis praesidium, agros eorum vastabat.
3 Achaei non antea ausi capessere bellum quam ab Roma
4 revertissent legati, ut quid senatui placeret scirent, post
reditum legatorum et Sicyonem concilium edixerunt, et
legatos ad T. Quinctium miserunt qui consilium ab eo
5 peterent. in concilio omnium ad bellum extemplo capes-
sendum inclinatae sententiae erant; litterae T. Quincti
cunctationem iniecerunt, quibus auctor erat praetorem
6 classemque Romanam exspectandi. cum principum alii in
sententia permanerent, alii utendum eius quem ipsi con-
suluissent consilio censerent, multitudo Philopoemenis
7 sententiam exspectabat. praetor is tum erat, et omnes eo
tempore et prudentia et auctoritate anteibat.

---

93 Cf. 29.37.4, where Livy implausibly attributes the *cognomen* to Livius' father raising the price of salt as censor in 204. C.
Livius Salinator (29) would win renown as fleet commander in the
war against Antiochus (36.42–45, 37 *passim*) and go on to the
consulship in 188.
94 This famous *strategos* of the Achaean League was the greatest Greek statesman of his time, much admired by his compatriot
Polybius (both of them hailing from Megalopolis).
95 That is, as usual in a Greek context, *strategos*.

mula, Gaius Livius and Lucius Oppius, the last two bearing the *cognomen* Salinator[93] (it was this Oppius who had
commanded the fleet of 20 ships that went to Sicily). In
the interval before the new magistrates were to draw lots
for their provinces, Marcus Baebius was instructed to
cross from Brundisium to Epirus with all his troops and
keep them in the vicinity of Apollonia; and the urban praetor, Marcus Fulvius, was given the task of constructing 50
new quinqueremes.

25. The Roman people were certainly preparing themselves for every possible move by Antiochus and by now
Nabis was no longer postponing hostilities but was devot-
ing all his might to the siege of Gytheum and laying waste
the fields of the Achaeans, with whom he was furious for
having sent assistance to the beleaguered inhabitants. The
Achaeans for their part did not dare commit themselves
to war until their envoys returned from Rome as they
wished to know the will of the senate. After the envoys'
return they called a council meeting at Sicyon and also
sent a deputation to Titus Quinctius to ask his advice. At
the council meeting the opinions of all inclined toward
support for an immediate opening of hostilities, but a letter from Titus Quinctius recommending that they await
the Roman praetor and the fleet gave them pause. Since
some of the prominent citizens remained firm in their
opinion and others thought that they should follow the
guidance of the man whose advice they had sought, the
majority waited for Philopoemen[94] to express his opinion.
He was their praetor[95] at the time, and the leading man of
his day in intellect and authority.

Is praefatus bene comparatum apud Aetolos esse ne
praetor, cum de bello consuluisset, ipse sententiam dice-
8 ret, statuere quam primum ipsos quid vellent iussit: praetorem decreta eorum cum fide et cura exsecuturum, adni-
surumque ut quantum in consilio humano positum esset,
9 nec pacis eos paeniteret nec belli. plus ea oratio momenti
ad incitandos ad bellum habuit quam si aperte suadendo
10 cupiditatem res gerendi ostendisset. itaque ingenti consensu bellum decretum est, tempus et ratio administrandi
11 eius libera praetori permissa. Philopoemen, praeterquam
quod ita Quinctio placeret, et ipse existimabat classem
Romanam exspectandam, quae a mari Gytheum tueri pos-
12 set; sed metuens ne dilationem res non pateretur, et non
Gytheum solum sed praesidium quoque missum ad
tuendam urbem amitteretur, naves Achaeorum deduxit.

26. Comparaverat et tyrannus modicam classem ad
prohibenda si qua obsessis mari submitterentur praesidia,
tres tectas naves et lembos pristesque, tradita vetere classe
2 ex foedere Romanis. harum novarum navium agilitatem ut
experiretur, simul ut omnia satis apta ad certamen essent,
provectos in altum cotidie remigem militemque simula-
cris navalis pugnae exercebat, in eo ratus verti spem obsi-
3 dionis si praesidia maritima interclusisset. praetor Achaeorum sicut terrestrium certaminum arte quemuis clarorum

---

96 Cf. 34.35.5.

Philopoemen began his address by observing that it was a fine practice established among the Achaeans that a praetor, after putting a motion for war before them, should not express his own opinion and he bade them decide as soon as possible what they wanted done. Their praetor, he said, would faithfully and scrupulously carry out their orders and, as far as human wisdom could, make every effort to see that they did not regret their decision, whether it be for war or peace. That speech did more to spur them to go to war than if he had revealed a wish to lead it by openly advocating the campaign. The result therefore was a decision for war, with a huge majority, and the praetor was given a free hand with regard to the timing and strategy of operations. Apart from the fact that it was also what Quinctius wanted Philopoemen was himself of the view that they should await the Roman fleet, which could protect Gytheum by sea. Fearing, however, that the situation would not brook delay and that not only Gytheum but also the garrison sent to defend the city might be lost, he launched the Achaean navy.

26. To prevent any assistance being sent by sea to the beleaguered populace, the tyrant had also put together a small fleet comprising three decked ships and some pinnaces and cutters (his old fleet having been surrendered to the Romans under the terms of the treaty[96]). Wishing to test the maneuverability of these new vessels, and also to have everything well prepared for the forthcoming struggle, he had his crews and marines put to sea each day and gave them training in mock naval battles, since he thought his prospects for the siege depended on his intercepting any relief arriving by sea. The praetor of the Achaeans, while he was a match for any of the famous

imperatorum vel usu vel ingenio aequabat, ita rudis in
4 re navali erat, Arcas, mediterraneus homo, externorum
etiam omnium, nisi quod in Creta praefectus auxiliorum
militaverat, ignarus.
5   Navis erat[22] quadriremis vetus, capta annis ante octoginta,[23] cum Crateri uxorem Nicaeam ab Naupacto Corin-
6 thum ueheret. huius fama motus—fuerat[24] enim nobile in
classe regia quondam navigium—deduci ab Aegio putrem
7 iam admodum et vetustate dilabentem iussit. hac tum
praetoria nave praecedente classem, cum in ea Patrensis
Piso[25] praefectus classis ueheretur, occurrerunt a Gytheo
8 Laconum naves; et primo statim incursu ad novam et fir-
mam navem vetus, quae per se ipsa omnibus compagibus
aquam acciperet, divolsa est, captique omnes qui in nave
9 erant. cetera classis, praetoria nave amissa, quantum
quaeque remis valuit fugerunt. ipse Philopoemen in levi
speculatoria nave fugit, nec ante fugae finem quam Patras
10 ventum est fecit. nihil ea res animum militaris viri et multos experti casus imminuit: quin contra, si in re navali,
cuius esset ignarus, offendisset, eo plus in ea quorum usu
calleret spei nactus, breve id tyranno gaudium se effectu-
rum adfirmabat.

[22] ignarus. navis erat *Mg*: *om.* B*χ*
[23] octoginta B*χMg*: sexaginta *Briscoe dubitanter (vid. appa-rat. et comm. 2.183)*
[24] fuerat *Mg*: venit *χ*: *spat.* B
[25] Piso B*χ*: Tiso *Gel.*

---

[97] The figure is more likely to be sixty (Briscoe 2.183).

generals in experience and skill in the tactics of fighting on land, was also unfamiliar with naval warfare. He was an Arcadian, a man from inland who, apart from service as commander of auxiliary troops in Crete, had no knowledge of foreign lands.

There was an antiquated quadrireme that had been captured eighty years[97] earlier while transporting Nicaea, wife of Craterus,[98] from Naupactus to Corinth. Impressed with the reputation of this vessel (for it had once been a famous ship in a royal fleet) Philopoemen ordered it brought from Aegium although it was now quite rotten and decomposing with age. Then with the quadrireme as its flagship leading the fleet and with Piso of Patrae, the fleet's admiral, aboard, the flotilla was met by the Spartan ships coming from Gytheum. At the first collision with a new and sturdy vessel, the old ship, which was already taking in water at every joint, was immediately shattered and all aboard were taken prisoner. The flagship lost, all the other ships fled as quickly as their oars could take them. Philopoemen himself made good his escape in a light reconnaissance vessel and did not arrest his flight until he reached Patrae. The incident in no way crushed the spirit of a man who was a true soldier with a breadth of experience. Quite the reverse, in fact. Failure in the unfamiliar sphere of naval operations only gave him greater hope of success in one in which he had competence, and he repeatedly declared that he would make sure that the tyrant's jubilation was short lived.

[98] He was a half brother of Antigonas Gonatas and son of Alexander's famous general Craterus. We know nothing of the marriage to Nicaea or her identity.

27. Nabis cum prospera re elatus,[26] tum spem etiam
2 haud dubiam nactus nihil iam a mari periculi fore, et
terrestes aditus claudere opportune positis praesidiis voluit. tertia parte copiarum ab obsidione Gythei abducta ad
3 Pleias posuit castra;[27] imminet is locus et Leucis et Acriis,
qua videbantur hostes exercitum admoturi. cum ibi stativa
essent et pauci tabernacula haberent, multitudo alia casas
ex harundine textas fronde, quae umbram modo praeberent,[28] texissent, priusquam in conspectum hostis veni-
4 ret, Philopoemen necopinantem eum improviso genere
5 belli adgredi statuit. navigia parva in stationem occultam
agri Argivi contraxit; in ea expeditos milites, caetratos plerosque, cum fundis et iaculis et alio levi genere armaturae
6 imposuit. inde litora legens cum ad propinquum castris
hostium promunturium venisset, egressus callibus notis
nocte Pleias pervenit, et sopitis vigilibus ut in nullo propinquo metu, ignem casis ab omni parte castrorum iniecit.
7 multi prius incendio absumpti sunt quam hostium adventum sentirent, et qui senserant nullam opem ferre potu-
8 erunt. ferro flammaque omnia absumpta; perpauci ex tam
ancipiti peste ad Gytheum in maiora castra perfugerunt.
9 ita perculsis hostibus Philopoemen protinus ad depopu-

[26] cum prospera re elatus *Ald.*: quum prospere latus *Mg*: cum
prospera elatus re *Fr. 2: om.* Bχ
[27] castra *hic ed. Rom.*: *post* abducta *Briscoe*: *om.* Bχ
[28] praeberent Bχ: praeberet *Fr. 1*

---

[99] Pleiae, Leucae, Acriae: *Barr.* 58 D4. The town, rather than
the plain, of Leukai is probably meant.   [100] Latin *caetrati*; literally, "men carrying the *caetra.*" The *caetra* is a short Spanish

27. Elated with his success, and also confidently expecting there would be no further threat from the sea, Nabis decided also to shut off overland access by means of strategically placed guard posts. He withdrew a third of his troops from the blockade of Gytheum and pitched camp at Pleiae. This is a spot that commands both Leucae and Acriae,[99] where it seemed likely his enemies would bring up their forces. Nabis' base camp was here, but few of the men had tents and most had fashioned huts of intertwined reeds that they had covered with leafy branches merely to provide shade. Before he came within view of his enemy, Philopoemen decided to take him by surprise with a novel kind of military maneuver. He gathered some small boats together into a secluded anchorage in Argive territory and set light-armed soldiers aboard, peltasts[100] for the most part, carrying slings, javelins and other light weaponry. Then, hugging the coastline, he came to a promontory close to the enemy camp, disembarked and, marching inland along paths that he knew, reached Pleiae at night. The Spartan sentinels were asleep, assuming they had nothing to fear in the vicinity, and Philopoemen had firebrands tossed onto the huts on every side of the camp. Many were consumed by the flames before they were aware of the enemy's arrival, and those who were aware could bring no help. Everything was destroyed by fire and the sword; very few escaped the debacle to reach the larger camp at Gytheum. The enemy thus overwhelmed, Philopoemen immediately marched straight on to raid the

shield, but Livy also uses the word for the *pelte,* the small shield used by Greek skirmishing units (*peltasts*).

landam Tripolim Laconici agri, qui proximus finem Mega-
10 lopolitarum est, duxit, et magna vi pecorum hominumque
inde abrepta, priusquam a Gytheo tyrannus praesidium
agris mitteret, discessit.

11 Inde Tegeam exercitu contracto, concilioque eodem et
Achaeis et sociis indicto, in quo et Epirotarum et Acarna-
12 num fuere principes, statuit, quoniam satis et suorum[29] a
pudore maritimae ignominiae restituti animi et hostium
conterriti essent, ad Lacedaemonem ducere, eo modo uno
ratus ab obsidione Gythei hostem abduci posse. ad Caryas
13 primum in hostium terra posuit castra. eo ipso die
Gytheum expugnatum.[30] cuius rei ignarus Philopoemen
castra ad Barbosthenem—mons est decem milia passuum
14 ab Lacedaemone—promovit. et Nabis recepto Gytheo
cum expedito exercitu inde profectus, cum praeter Lacedaemonem raptim duxisset, Pyrrhi quae vocant castra
occupavit, quem peti locum ab Achaeis non dubitabat.
15 inde hostibus occurrit. obtinebant autem longo agmine
propter angustias viae prope quinque milia passuum; co-
gebatur agmen ab equitibus et maxima parte auxiliorum,
quod existimabat Philopoemen tyrannum mercennariis
militibus, quibus plurimum fideret, ab tergo suos adgres-
16 surum. duae res simul inopinatae perculerunt eum: una
praeoccupatus quem petebat locus, altera quod primo
agmini occurrisse hostem cernebat, ubi, cum per loca

[29] et suorum *Asc.*: essent testes suorum et *B*χ: essent . . . et
inter obelos Briscoe   [30] expugnatum *B*χ: expugnatum est *Mg*

---

[101] Cf. 34.26.9. In northern Laconia, but the site is uncertain
(possibly *Barr.* 58 D3 [Karyai]).   [102] Location unknown, but it
must date from Pyrrhus' attack on Sparta in 272 BC.

74

Tripolis in that part of Spartan territory next to the border of Megapolis. Here he seized a large number of livestock and men and left the area before the tyrant could send aid for the country districts from Gytheum.

He then assembled his forces at Tegea and convened in the city a meeting of the Achaeans and their allies, at which the leaders both of the Epirotes and of the Acarnanians were also present. Since his own men's confidence had now been restored after the shame of their naval fiasco and the enemy were also in a state of panic, he determined at this meeting to march on Sparta, considering this the only way that the enemy could be drawn away from the siege of Gytheum. His first encampment in enemy territory was at Caryae;[101] and on that very same day Gytheum was taken. Philopoemen, unaware of this, moved his camp forward to Barbosthenes (a mountain ten miles distant from Sparta.) As for Nabis, after recovering Gytheum he set off from the town with a force of light infantry, marched swiftly past Sparta and seized a place called The Camp of Pyrrhus,[102] in no doubt that it was the Achaeans' objective. From there he advanced to meet his enemy. They, because of the narrowness of the road, were in a long column stretching nearly five miles; the rear was brought up by cavalry and by most of the auxiliary troops because Philopoemen believed the tyrant would attack his force from behind with his mercenaries, in whom he had the most confidence. But two concomitant and unexpected circumstances threw him off balance. The first was that the position for which he was making had already been taken; and the second was that he could see that the enemy had come to meet his column head-on. Since his

confragosa iter esset, sine levis armaturae praesidio signa
ferri non videbat posse.

28. Erat autem Philopoemen praecipuae in ducendo
agmine locisque capiendis sollertiae atque usus, nec belli
tantum temporibus sed etiam in pace ad id maxime ani-
2 mum exercuerat. ubi iter quopiam faceret et ad difficilem
transitu saltum venisset, contemplatus ab omni parte loci
naturam, cum solus iret secum ipse agitabat animo, cum
3 comites haberet ab his quaerebat, si hostis eo loco apparuisset, quid si a fronte, quid si ab latere hoc aut illo, quid
si ab tergo adoriretur capiendum consilii foret: posse in-
structos derecta[31] acie, posse inconditum agmen et tan-
4 tummodo aptum viae occurrere. quem locum ipse captu-
rus esset cogitando aut quaerendo exsequebatur, aut quot
armatis aut quo genere armorum—plurimum enim interesse—usurus; quo impedimenta, quo sarcinas, quo turbam inermem reiceret; quanto ea aut quali praesidio cus-
5 todiret; et utrum pergere qua coepisset ire via an eam qua
6 venisset repetere melius esset; castris quoque quem locum caperet, quantum munimento amplecteretur loci,
qua opportuna aquatio, qua pabuli lignorumque copia esset; qua postero die castra moventi tutum maxime iter,
7 quae forma agminis esset. his curis cogitationibusque ita

[31] derecta *H.J.M*: directa *B*: recta χ

path lay over rough terrain, he could not see how any advance could be made without light-armed cover.

28. Philopoemen, however, was a man of extraordinary ingenuity and experience in leading a marching army and selecting positions, and he had trained himself in this in times of peace as well as war. Whenever he was making a journey anywhere and had reached a defile where passage was difficult, he would examine the lie of the land from every angle. He would mull over with himself when he was traveling alone, or ask his companions when he had people with him, what strategy should be employed if an enemy appeared in that particular spot—what strategy if the enemy attacked head-on, or on one flank or the other, or at the rear. The enemy, he hypothesized, could be met with the men in a regular battle line or grouped as a column that was not in battle order and was suited only for marching. By reflecting on the problem or by posing questions he would try to work out what vantage point he would seize, or how many soldiers he would employ or (a most important consideration) what kind of weapons. He would investigate where to put equipment and baggage, where to position the crowd of noncombatants, and what size and what sort of guard to use to protect them. He would ask if it was preferable to continue along the path on which he had started or to retrace his steps; what site he should choose for a camp and how great an area he should enclose with its palisade; where there was a suitable water supply, and where quantities of food and wood were to be found; where lay the safest route when he struck camp the next day and how his column should be organized. Philopoemen had preoccupied himself with such problems and reflections from his early years, to the point that in a situ-

ab ineunte aetate animum agitaverat ut nulla ei nova in tali
re cogitatio esset.

8   Et tum omnium primum agmen constituit; dein Cretenses auxiliares et quos Tarentinos vocabant equites, bi-
nos secum trahentes equos, ad prima signa misit, et iussis
equitibus subsequi super torrentem unde aquari possent

9 rupem occupavit. eo impedimenta omnia et calonum turbam conlectam armatis circumdedit, et pro natura loci
castra communivit; tabernacula statuere in aspretis et

10 inaequabili solo difficile erat. hostes quingentos passus
aberant. ex eodem rivo utrique cum praesidio levis armaturae aquati sunt; et priusquam, qualia in[32] propinquis
castris solent, contraheretur certamen, nox intervenit:
postero die apparebat pugnandum pro aquatoribus circa
riuum esse. nocte in valle a conspectu hostium aversa
quantam multitudinem locus occulere poterat condidit
caetratorum.

29. Luce orta Cretensium levis armatura et Tarentini
equites super torrentem proelium commiserunt. Telemnastus Cretensis popularibus suis, equitibus Lycortas

2 Megalopolitanus praeerat. Cretenses et hostium auxiliares
equitumque idem genus, Tarentini, praesidio aquatoribus
erant. aliquamdiu dubium proelium fuit, ut eodem ex arte

---

[32] in $B\chi$: *del.* Duker: tam *Weiss.*

---

[103] On Philopoemen's "practical self-training," cf. also Plut.
Phil. 4.5–6.   [104] This is a type of cavalry, not where it came
from. While they are referred to elsewhere (cf. 29.1–2 below,
37.40.13), only here do they have two horses each.

[105] Probably the Telemnastus named by Polybius (29.4.8) as
ambassador to Antiochus.

ation of this kind there was nothing that he had not considered.[103]

On this occasion he first of all set the column in order, and he next sent up to the front his Cretan auxiliaries and the cavalry that they called Tarentine,[104] all of them taking a pair of horses with them. Then, ordering the regular cavalry to follow, he seized a rock on the banks of a stream from which they could provision themselves with water. There, gathering together all the equipment and camp followers, he placed an armed guard around them and established a camp as well as the nature of the terrain permitted—setting up tents on rough and uneven ground was a difficult matter. The enemy was half a mile away. Both sides, under the protection of some light infantry, drew water from the same stream, but before battle could be joined (the natural consequence when camps lie close together) night fell. It was clear that they would have to fight close to the riverbank the following day to defend their respective water bearers. During the night Philopoemen stationed in a valley out of the enemy's view as large a group of *peltasts* as the place could conceal.

29. At dawn the Cretan light infantry and the Tarentine cavalry opened the fighting on the banks of the stream. The Cretan Telemnastus[105] was in command of his compatriots, the Megapolitan Lycortas[106] of the cavalry. On the enemy side, too, there were Cretan auxiliaries and the same kind of cavalry—Tarentine—providing cover for the water bearers. For some time the battle remained in

[106] The Achaean cavalry commander (*hipparchos*) and Polybius' father.

3 utraque hominum genere et armis paribus. procedente
certamine et numero vicere tyranni auxiliares, et quia ita
praeceptum a Philopoemene praefectis erat ut modico
edito proelio in fugam inclinarent, hostemque ad locum
insidiarum pertraherent. effuse secuti fugientes per
convallem plerique et volnerati et interfecti sunt, prius-
4 quam occultum hostem viderent. caetrati ita, quantum
latitudo vallis patiebatur, instructi sederant ut facile per
5 intervalla ordinum fugientes suos acciperent. consurgunt
deinde ipsi integri recentes instructi; in hostes inordinatos
effusos, labore etiam et volneribus fessos, impetum fa-
6 ciunt. nec dubia victoria fuit. extemplo terga dedit tyranni
miles, et haud paulo concitatiore cursu quam secutus erat
fugiens ad castra est compulsus; multi caesi captique in
7 ea fuga sunt. et in castris quoque foret trepidatum, ni
Philopoemen receptui cani iussisset, loca magis confragosa et quacumque temere processisset iniqua quam
hostem metuens.

8   Inde et ex fortuna pugnae et ex ingenio ducis coniec-
tans in quo tum is pavore esset, unum de auxiliaribus spe-
9 cie transfugae mittit ad eum, qui pro comperto adferret
Achaeos statuisse postero die ad Eurotan amnem, qui
prope ipsis adfluit moenibus, progredi, ut intercluderent
iter, ne aut tyrannus cum vellet receptum ad urbem habe-

doubt, since the same class of troops and similar weapons were found on both sides. As the fight progressed the tyrant's auxiliaries got the upper hand since they were numerically superior, and Philopoemen's officers had also been ordered by him to put up only a halfhearted fight and then turn to flight and draw the enemy to the spot where the ambush was set. Nabis' men were in complete disorder as they chased the fugitives along the valley and several were wounded or killed before they caught sight of the concealed enemy. The peltasts had remained immobile, deployed in such a way (as far as the width of the valley permitted) that they could easily take in their fleeing comrades between their ranks. Then they themselves rose up, fresh, vigorous and in formation; and they attacked an enemy that was disordered and dispersed, and also exhausted from fatigue and wounds. There was no uncertainty about the victory. The tyrant's men immediately turned tail and were driven back to camp in a flight not much less speedy than their earlier pursuit. Many were cut down or captured in the rout, and there would have been panic in the camp, too, had not Philopoemen ordered the retreat to be sounded; he feared the broken terrain and uneven ground through which he had recklessly advanced more than he did the enemy.

Then, surmising from the outcome of the battle, and the temperament of the enemy leader, the state of alarm the man must then be in, Philopoemen sent one of his auxiliaries to him, posing as a deserter, to report as a certainty that the Achaeans had decided to advance the next day to the River Eurotas, which flows close to the very walls of Sparta. Their aim, he was to say, was to block the tyrant's path so that he would have no way of retreating to

81

10   ret, aut commeatus ab urbe in castra portarentur, simul et
temptaturos si quorum animi sollicitari ad defectionem a
11   tyranno possent. non tam fidem dictis perfuga fecit quam
perculso metu relinquendi castra causam probabilem
12   praebuit. postero die Pythagoram cum auxiliaribus et
equitatu stationem agere pro vallo iussit: ipse tamquam in
aciem cum robore exercitus egressus, signa ocius ferri ad
urbem iussit.

    30. Philopoemen postquam citatum agmen per angus-
tam et proclivem viam duci raptim vidit, equitatum omnem et Cretensium auxiliares in stationem hostium quae
2   pro castris erat emittit. illi ubi hostes adesse et a suis se
desertos viderunt, primo in castra recipere se conati sunt:
3   deinde postquam instructa acies tota Achaeorum admovebatur, metu ne cum ipsis castris caperentur, sequi suorum
agmen aliquantum praegressum insistunt.

4   Extemplo caetrati Achaeorum in castra impetum faciunt et diripiunt;[33] ceteri ad persequendos hostes ire pergunt. erat iter tale per quod vix tranquillum ab hostili
5   metu agmen expediri posset. ut vero ad postremos proelium ortum est, clamorque terribilis ab tergo paventium
ad prima signa est perlatus, pro se quisque armis abiectis
6   in circumiectas itineri silvas diffugiunt, momentoque temporis strage armorum saepta via est, maxime hastis, quae
pleraeque adversae[34] cadentes velut vallo obiecto iter

        [33] et diripiunt *Mg*: *om. B*χ: et ea diripiunt *Gron.*
        [34] adversae *B*χ: transversae *Duker*

the city when he wished or of having supplies brought from the city to his camp; and it was also to test his men's sympathies, in hopes that some could be induced to defect from the tyrant. It proved less a matter of the deserter carrying conviction with his story as his giving the terror-stricken man a plausible excuse for abandoning camp. The following day he commanded Pythagoras to stand guard with the auxiliaries and cavalry before the rampart; then he himself left with the main body of his army as if for battle, but ordered a swift advance toward the city.

30. On seeing the swiftly moving column being hurried along the steep and narrow road, Philopoemen sent forth all his cavalry and the Cretan auxiliaries to charge the enemy soldiers stationed before the camp. When these men saw that their enemies were approaching and that they themselves had been abandoned by their comrades, they first tried to retreat into the camp. Then, when the entire Achaean line began bearing down on them in battle formation, they, from fear that they might be taken along with their camp, proceeded to follow their compatriots' column, which was already some way ahead.

The Achaean peltasts immediately attacked and pillaged the camp, and the rest of their men went off in pursuit of the enemy. The road was such that it could hardly be negotiated by a column of men even if there were no fear of an enemy; but when fighting broke out at the rear and a spine-chilling cry from the panic-stricken men behind reached those at the front they all threw down their weapons and scattered in flight into the woods bordering the road. In a trice the way was barred by a pile of weaponry, spears for the most part, the majority of which fell point backward and blocked the road with a virtual

7 impediebant. Philopoemen utcumque possent instare et
persequi auxiliaribus iussis—utique enim equitibus haud
facilem futuram fugam—ipse gravius agmen via paten-
8 tiore ad Eurotan amnem deduxit. ibi castris sub occasum
solis positis, levem armaturam, quam ad persequendum
reliquerat hostem, opperiebatur. qui ubi prima vigilia
venerunt, nuntiantes tyrannum cum paucis ad urbem
penetrasse, ceteram multitudinem inermem toto sparsam
vagari saltu, corpora curare eos iubet.

9 Ipse ex cetera copia militum qui, quia priores in castra
venerant, refecti et cibo sumpto et modica quiete erant
delectos, nihil praeter gladios secum ferentes, extemplo
educit et duarum portarum itineribus quae Pharas quaeque Barbosthenem ferunt eos instruxit, qua ex fuga recep-
10 turos sese hostes credebat. nec eum opinio fefellit. nam
Lacedaemonii, quoad lucis superfuit quicquam, deviis
callibus medio saltu recipiebant se; primo vespere, ut lu-
mina in castris hostium conspexere, e regione[35] eorum
11 occultis semitis se tenuerunt; ubi praegressi ea sunt,[36] iam
tutum rati in patentes vias descenderunt. ibi excepti ab
insidente hoste passim ita multi caesi captique sunt ut vix
12 quarta pars de toto exercitu evaserit. Philopoemen, incluso tyranno in urbem, insequentes dies prope triginta

[35] e regione *ed. Rom.*: regione *Bχ*

[36] praegressi ea sunt *Bχ*: ea sunt praegressi *Mg*: praetergressi
ea sunt *EmgPmg*: ea sunt praetergressi *Pluygers*

---

[107] An odd statement: Livy does not explain how the spears all
fell point backward to block the Achaean advance, and he may
again have misunderstood Polybius, whose account is missing
here.

palisade.[107] Philopoemen told his auxiliaries to press on and continue the pursuit as best they could—flight would not be easy, he said, especially for the cavalry—and he himself took the heavier-armed troops to the River Eurotas by a more open road. There he pitched camp just before sunset, and proceeded to wait for the light infantry that he had left behind to pursue the enemy. These arrived at the time of the first watch, bringing word that the tyrant had made it back to the city with a few of his soldiers but that the remaining horde of his men had scattered and were wandering unarmed throughout the woods. Philopoemen told them to take food and rest.

The others, since they had arrived earlier in the camp, had already taken nourishment and a short rest to recuperate. Philopoemen immediately led out a select group of them, carrying only swords, and positioned them on roads leading from two of the city gates toward Pharae and Barbosthenes respectively—he thought that this was the way the enemy would return after their flight. And he was not wrong in his assessment. While some light remained, the Spartans made their way back along remote trails in the heart of the forest. Then, after evening fell and they caught sight of the lights in the enemy camp, they avoided the area where they were by following concealed paths; and after they passed the camp, and thought all was safe, they went down to the open roads. There they were intercepted at many points by their enemy who was lying in wait for them and they were killed or taken prisoner in such great numbers that scarcely a quarter of the whole army escaped. With the tyrant confined to the city, Philopoemen spent nearly all of the thirty days that followed

vastandis agris Laconum absumpsit, debilitatisque ac
13 prope fractis tyranni viribus domum rediit, aequantibus
eum gloria rerum Achaeis imperatori Romano, et quod ad
Laconum bellum attineret, praeferentibus etiam.

31. Dum inter Achaeos et tyrannum bellum erat, legati
Romanorum circuire sociorum urbes, solliciti ne Aetoli
2 partis alicuius animos ad Antiochum avertissent. mini-
mum operae in Achaeis adeundis consumpserunt, quos,
quia Nabidi infesti erant, ad cetera quoque satis fidos cen-
3 sebant esse. Athenas primum, inde Chalcidem, inde in
Thessaliam iere, adlocutique concilio frequenti Thessalos
4 Demetriadem iter flexere. eo Magnetum concilium indictum est. accuratior ibi habenda oratio fuit, quod pars principum alienati Romanis totique Antiochi et Aetolorum
5 erant, quia cum reddi obsidem filium Philippo adlatum
esset stipendiumque impositum remitti, inter cetera vana
adlatum erat Demetriadem quoque ei reddituros Roma-
6 nos esse. id ne fieret, Eurylochus princeps Magnetum
factionisque eius quidam omnia novari Aetolorum Antio-
7 chique adventu malebant. adversus eos ita disserendum
erat ne timorem vanum iis demendo spes incisa Philippum
abalienaret, in quo plus ad omnia momenti quam in

---

108 Cf. Just. *Epit*. 31.3.4: "Philopoemen's courage was so con-
spicuous that he merited comparison, in the view of all, with the
Roman general Flamininus." Plutarch, in fact, pairs the biogra-
phies of the two men.

laying waste the countryside of the Spartans, and returned home only when the tyrant's power had been weakened and almost broken. The Achaeans now ranked him equal with the Roman commander in the glory of his achievements, and even above him as far as the Spartan campaign was concerned.[108]

31. While the war between the Achaeans and the tyrant was in progress, the Roman commissioners were making the rounds of the allies' cities, concerned that the Aetolians might have induced a number to join Antiochus. They made very little effort to approach the Achaeans, thinking that as they were on hostile terms with Nabis they could also be confidently relied upon in all other matters. They went to Athens first, then Chalcis, and then Thessaly, and after addressing the Thessalians in a crowded assembly they turned off to Demetrias, where a council of the Magnesians had been called. There they had to be somewhat more diplomatic in their language as some of the leading Magnesians had turned against the Romans and were wholeheartedly supporting Antiochus and the Aetolians. This was because when news was brought that Philip's son, who was a hostage, was being returned to him, and that the indemnity imposed on him was being waived, a number of false rumors had arisen, including one that the Romans were also going to restore Demetrias to him. Rather than have this happen, Eurylochus, one of the leading Magnesians, and some of his supporters preferred to see a complete change in the situation now that the Aetolians and Antiochus were on the scene. The arguments employed against these people had to be such as to allay their groundless fears but not alienate Philip by destroying his hopes—he was in all respects more important

8 Magnetibus esset. illa tantum commemorata, cum totam
Graeciam beneficio libertatis obnoxiam Romanis esse,
9 tum eam civitatem praecipue; ibi enim non praesidium
modo Macedonum fuisse sed regiam exaedificatam, ut
10 praesens semper in oculis habendus esset dominus; ceterum nequiquam ea facta, si Aetoli Antiochum in Philippi
regiam adducerent et novus et incognitus pro vetere et
experto habendus rex esset.
11 Magnetarchen summum magistratum vocant; is tum
Eurylochus erat, ac potestate ea fretus negavit dissimulan-
dum sibi et Magnetibus esse quae fama volgata de red-
denda Demetriade Philippo foret: id ne fieret, omnia et
12 conanda et audenda Magnetibus esse. et inter dicendi
contentionem inconsultius evectus proiecit tum quoque
specie liberam Demetriadem esse, re vera omnia ad nu-
13 tum Romanorum fieri. sub hanc vocem fremitus variantis
multitudinis fuit partim adsensum partim indignationem
dicere id ausum eum; Quinctius quidem adeo exarsit ira
ut manus ad caelum tendens deos testes ingrati ac perfidi
14 animi Magnetum invocaret. hac voce perterritis omnibus,
Zeno ex principibus unus, magnae cum ob eleganter ac-
tam vitam auctoritatis tum quod semper Romanorum
haud dubie partis fuerat, ab Quinctio legatisque aliis flens
15 petit ne unius amentiam civitati adsignarent: suo quem-

88

than the Magnesians. Thus all that was said was the following: that the whole of Greece was indebted to the Romans' for the gift of liberty, and that state especially so; for not only had a Macedonian garrison been installed there but a palace had also been built to ensure that the people had their master ever-present before their eyes. However, what had been done served no purpose if the Aetolians installed Antiochus in Philip's palace and if the people of Demetrias had to recognize a king who was both new and unfamiliar to them instead of the old one whom they knew.

"Magnetarch" is the title the Magnesians give their chief magistrate. At that time it was Eurylochus and, confident in its authority, he declared that neither he nor other Magnesians should feign ignorance of the rumor circulating about Demetrias being restored to Philip. The Magnesians, he said, should try anything and face any risk to prevent that happening. And, carried into indiscretion in the fervor of his address, Eurylochus tossed out the comment that even at that moment Demetrias might look free but that in fact everything was being done in accordance with the will of the Romans. At these words there was muttering in various parts of the crowd, some expressing agreement and others anger that he had dared make such a comment. Quinctius was so beside himself with rage that, raising his hands to heaven, he called the gods to witness the ingratitude and perfidy of the Magnesians. All were struck with terror by these words and one of the leading citizens, Zeno, a man of considerable influence both because he led a decent life and because his support of the Romans had always been beyond question, tearfully begged Quinctius and the other commissioners not to attribute one person's lunacy to the whole state; a man be-

que periculo furere. Magnetas non libertatem modo sed omnia quae hominibus sancta caraque sint T. Quinctio et
16 populo Romano debere: nihil quemquam ab dis immortalibus precari posse quod non Magnetes ab illis haberent, et in corpora sua citius per furorem saevituros quam ut Romanam amicitiam violarent.

32. Huius orationem subsecutae multitudinis preces sunt; Eurylochus ex concilio itineribus occultis ad portam
2 atque inde protinus in Aetoliam profugit. iam enim, et id magis in dies, Aetoli defectionem nudabant, eoque ipse forte tempore Thoas princeps gentis, quem miserant ad Antiochum, redierat inde Menippumque secum adduxe-
3 rat regis legatum. qui, priusquam concilium iis daretur, impleverant omnium aures terrestres navalesque copias commemorando: ingentem vim peditum equitumque ve-
4 nire, ex India elephantos accitos, ante omnia, quo maxime credebant moveri multitudinis animos, tantum aduehi auri ut ipsos emere Romanos posset.
5 Apparebat quid ea oratio in concilio motura esset; nam et venisse eos et quae agerent omnia legatis Romanis defe-
6 rebantur; et quamquam prope abscisa spes erat, tamen non ab re esse Quinctio visum est sociorum aliquos legatos interesse ei concilio, qui admonerent Romanae societatis Aetolos, qui vocem liberam mittere adversus regis lega-
7 tum auderent. Athenienses maxime in eam rem idonei visi

---

109 Thoas: cf. 12.4 above and note, but there has been no mention of a mission to Antiochum (referred to again at 36.26.1).
110 For Menippus, cf. 34.57.6–59.8.

haved crazily at his own risk, he said. The people of Magnesia were indebted to Titus Quinctius and the Roman people not only for their liberty but for everything that human beings hold sacred and dear; and there was nothing that anyone could ask of the immortal gods that the Magnesians did not have from them. Sooner would they furiously lacerate their own bodies than violate their treaty with Rome.

32. Zeno's words were followed by entreaties from the crowd. Eurylochus fled from the council, making for the city gate by some backstreets and then heading straight for Aetolia. For by now the Aetolians were revealing their rebellious intentions and doing so more and more every day; and it so happened that at that very time Thoas, a leader of that people whom they had sent to Antiochus, had returned from his mission,[109] and had brought with him Menippus, a representative of the king.[110] Before these men were granted an audience, they had filled everybody's ears with reports of land and sea forces, saying that a mighty host of infantry and cavalry was on its way, that elephants had been sent for from India and above all—something by which they thought the crowd would be most impressed—that as much gold was being brought as could buy the Romans themselves.

What effect such words was going to have in the council was clear (for everything about the men's arrival and activities was being relayed to the Roman commissioners). Although hope was all but cut off, Quinctius still thought it worthwhile for some representatives of the allies to attend that meeting to remind the Aetolians of their alliance with Rome and dare to speak out freely against the king's envoy. The Athenians seemed best suited for this, both

sunt et propter civitatis dignitatem et vetustam societatem
cum Aetolis. ab iis Quinctius petit ut legatos ad Panaeto-
licum concilium mitterent.

8   Thoas primus in eo concilio renuntiavit legationem.
Menippus post eum intromissus optimum fuisse omnibus
qui Graeciam Asiamque incolerent ait integris rebus Phi-
9 lippi potuisse intervenire Antiochum: sua quemque habiturum fuisse, neque omnia sub nutum dicionemque Ro-
10 manam perventura. "nunc quoque" inquit, "si modo vos
quae incohastis consilia constanter perducitis ad exitum,
poterit dis iuvantibus et Aetolis sociis Antiochus quamvis
inclinatas Graeciae res restituere in pristinam dignitatem.
11 ea autem in libertate posita est, quae suis stat viribus, non
ex alieno arbitrio pendet."

12   Athenienses, quibus primis post regiam legationem
dicendi quae vellent potestas facta est, mentione omni
regis praetermissa, Romanae societatis Aetolos merito-
rumque in universam Graeciam T. Quincti admonuerunt:
13 ne temere eam nimia celeritate consiliorum everterent;
consilia calida et audacia prima specie laeta, tractatu dura,
eventu tristia esse. legatos Romanos, et in iis T. Quinc-
14 tium, haud procul inde abesse; dum integra omnia essent,
verbis potius de iis quae ambigerentur disceptarent quam
Asiam Europamque ad funestum armarent bellum.

because of the regard in which their state was held and also because of their long-standing alliance with the Aetolians. Quinctius accordingly asked them to send ambassadors to the Panaetolian council.

At the council, Thoas opened the proceedings with a report on his embassy. Menippus, introduced after him, declared that it would have been best for all who lived in Greece and Asia if Antiochus could have intervened when Philip's power was still intact: then each would have retained what was his and everything would not have been subject to the approval and authority of Rome. "Even now," he continued, "if you just resolutely carry through to the end the policies you have embarked upon, Antiochus will, with the help of the gods and with the Aetolians as his allies, still be able to restore the fortunes of Greece to their former level of respect, however far they have declined. But this respect depends on freedom, and freedom that stands through its own strength and does not depend on the will of another."

The Athenians, who were first after the king's ambassadors to be permitted to speak their minds, avoided all mention of the king, and simply reminded the Aetolians of their alliance with Rome and the advantages conferred on all Greece by Titus Quinctius. They cautioned the Aetolians against recklessly destroying that alliance with plans too hastily conceived; hotheaded and foolhardy decisions looked appealing at first, they said, but were difficult to execute and dire in their outcome. The Roman commissioners, Titus Quinctius included, were not far distant and, while the whole situation remained unchanged, they should discuss any contentious issues with them rather than arm Asia and Europe for a deadly conflict.

LIVY

33. Multitudo avida novandi res Antiochi tota erat, et ne admittendos quidem in concilium Romanos censebant; principum maxime seniores auctoritate obtinuerunt ut

2 daretur iis concilium. hoc decretum Athenienses cum ret-
3 tulissent, eundum in Aetoliam Quinctio visum est: aut enim moturum aliquid aut omnes homines testes fore penes Aetolos culpam belli esse, Romanos iusta ac prope necessaria sumpturos arma.

4 Postquam ventum est eo, Quinctius in concilio orsus a principio societatis Aetolorum cum Romanis et quotiens ab iis fides mota foederis esset, pauca de iure civitatium
5 de quibus ambigeretur disseruit: si quid tamen aequi se habere arbitrarentur, quanto esse satius Romam mittere
6 legatos, seu disceptare seu rogare senatum mallent, quam populum Romanum cum Antiocho, lanistis Aetolis, non sine magno motu generis humani et pernicie Graeciae dimicare? nec ullos prius cladem eius belli sensuros quam
7 qui movissent. haec nequiquam velut vaticinatus Romanus.

Thoas deinde ceterique factionis eiusdem, cum ad-
8 sensu omnium auditi, pervicerunt ut ne dilato quidem concilio et absentibus Romanis decretum fieret, quo ac-cerseretur Antiochus ad liberandam Graeciam disceptan-
9 dumque inter Aetolos et Romanos. huic tam superbo de-creto addidit propriam contumeliam Damocritus praetor

---

111 Latin *lanistis.* This is a distinctly Roman metaphor that almost certainly did not appear in Polybius. A *lanista* was a man-ager of a troop of gladiators. The Romans and Antiochus are here billed as the fighters, and the Aetolians as the *lanistae,* who super-vise the fight but take no risks themselves.

94

33. The mass of those present were eager for change and totally committed to Antiochus, and they voted against even admitting the Romans to their assembly. It was mostly the older men among their leading citizens who by their influence ensured that they be given a hearing. When the Athenians reported this decision, Quinctius thought he should go to Aetolia. Either he would effect some change in the situation or all people would be witnesses that blame for the war lay with the Aetolians and that the Romans would be taking up arms with justice and almost from necessity.

When he arrived there Quinctius began his address in the council with an account of the beginnings of the Aetolian-Roman alliance and of how often the Aetolians had reneged on their treaty obligations, and then he dealt briefly with the rights of the city-states that were at issue. If these thought they had a fair claim, he said, how much better it was to send envoys to Rome, whether to argue their case or petition the senate, than to see the Roman people in a fight with Antiochus with the Aetolians as its promoters[111]—a struggle that would have serious repercussions for all humanity and spell ruin for Greece. And, he added, none would face the destruction of that war sooner than those who had brought it on. This prophetic utterance of the Roman was in vain.

Thoas and the others in his camp were heard next, to universal applause, and they managed to get a decree passed—without even adjourning the council or waiting for the Romans to absent themselves—by which Antiochus was to be called on to liberate Greece and arbitrate between the Aetolians and the Romans. To this high-handed decree the Aetolian magistrate Damocritus added

eorum; nam cum id ipsum decretum posceret eum Quinc-
10 tius, non veritus maiestatem viri, aliud in praesentia quod
magis instaret praevertendum sibi esse dixit: decretum
responsumque in Italia brevi castris super ripam Tiberis
11 positis daturum. tantus furor illo tempore gentem Aetolorum, tantus magistratus eorum cepit.

34. Quinctius legatique Corinthum redierunt; † inde ut
quaeque de Antiocho nihil †[37] per se ipsi moti et sedentes
2 exspectare adventum viderentur regis, concilium quidem
universae gentis post dimissos Romanos non habuerunt,
per apocletos autem—ita vocant sanctius consilium: ex de-
lectis constat viris—id agitabant quonam modo in Graecia
res novarentur.

3   Inter omnes constabat in civitatibus principes et optimum quemque Romanae societatis esse et praesenti statu
gaudere, multitudinem et quorum res non ex sententia
4 ipsorum essent omnia novare velle. Aetoli consilium cum
rei tum[38] spei quoque non audacis modo sed etiam im-
pudentis ceperunt, Demetriadem Chalcidem Lacedae-
5 monem occupandi. singuli in singulas principes missi
sunt, Thoas Chalcidem, Alexamenus Lacedaemonem,
6 Diocles Demetriadem. hunc exsul Eurylochus, de cuius
fuga causaque fugae ante dictum est, quia reditus in pa-

---

[37] *locus desperatus*: *post* ut *lac. indic. Weiss.*: inde ut quaeque
de Antiocho adferrentur excipiebant. Aetoli ne nihil *McDonald*;
vid. Briscoe, comm. 2.195.

[38] cum rei tum *M. Müller*: uno die *Bχ*: non dico rei, sed
Madvig

---

[112] The insult would later come back to haunt Damocritus and
the Aetolians (cf. 36.24.12).

[113] The text seems irremediably corrupt at this point.

his own personal insult. For when Quinctius asked him for the text of the decree, Damocritus, with no regard for the dignity of the man, said that for the moment he had to attend to more urgent business, but that he would soon give him the decree and his answer, in Italy, from a camp pitched on the banks of the Tiber.[112] Such was the madness that seized the Aetolian people and their magistrates at that time.

34. Quinctius and the commissioners returned to Corinth. To appear to be doing nothing themselves †about Antiochus†[113] and to be quietly awaiting the king's arrival, they held no plenary meeting of the people after dismissing the Romans. However, by means of their *apocleti* (this is what they call their inner council, which is composed of select individuals) they did consider how revolution could be fomented in Greece.

It was generally agreed that the leading citizens and all aristocrats[114] in the city-states were for the Roman alliance and happy with the status quo, while the masses and those dissatisfied with their circumstances wanted radical change. The Aetolians formulated a plan that was not merely bold but downright brazen in its ambition, to wit seizing Demetrias, Chalcis[115] and Sparta. Their leading men were sent out individually to the individual cities: Thoas to Chalcis, Alexamenus to Sparta, and Diocles to Demetrias.[116] Diocles was aided by the exiled Eurylochus (whose flight, and the reason for it, was related above)

---

[114] The Latin here (*optimum quemque*) refers to high socioeconomic class but also clearly implies political conservativism.

[115] Two of Philip's "fetters of Greece" (cf. 16.12 note, above).

[116] Thoas: 12.4 note, above; Alexamenus was *strategos* in 197/6; Diocles is otherwise unknown.

7 triam nulla alia erat spes, adiuvit. litteris Eurylochi admo-
niti, propinqui amicique et qui eiusdem factionis erant
liberos et coniugem eius cum sordida veste, tenentes velamenta supplicum, in contionem frequentem accierunt,[39]
singulos universosque obtestantes ne insontem indemna-
8 tum consenescere in exsilio sinerent. et simplices homines
misericordia et improbos seditiososque immiscendi res
tumultu Aetolico spes movit, et pro se[40] quisque revocari
iubebant.

9 His praeparatis Diocles cum omni equitatu—et erat
tum praefectus equitum—specie reducentis exsulem hos-
pitem profectus, die ac nocte ingens iter emensus, cum
milia sex ab urbe abesset, luce prima tribus electis turmis,
cetera multitudine equitum subsequi iussa, praecessit.
10 postquam portae adpropinquabat, desilire omnes ex equis
iussit et loris ducere equos, itineris maxime modo solutis
ordinibus, ut comitatus magis praefecti videretur quam
11 praesidium. ibi una ex turmis ad portam relicta ne excludi
subsequens equitatus posset, media urbe ac per forum
manu Eurylochum tenens, multis occurrentibus gratulan-
12 tibusque, domum deduxit. mox equitum plena urbs erat
et loca opportuna occupabantur; tum in domos missi qui
principes adversae factionis interficerent. ita Demetrias
Aetolorum facta est.

[39] in contionem . . . accierunt *Madvig*: *sic, sed* acciverunt *M.
Müller*: contionem . . . adierunt *BχMg**

[40] et pro se *Mg*: pro se *Bχ*: ita pro se *M. Müller*

---

[117] Latin *velamenta:* the emblems of a suppliant, usually an
olive branch wrapped in wool.

because he had no hope otherwise of returning to his homeland. Eurylochus' relatives, friends and partisans, briefed in a letter from him, brought his children and his wife into a crowded assembly in clothes of mourning and carrying the olive branches of suppliants;[117] and they begged those present, as individuals and as a body, not to allow a man to grow old in exile when he was innocent and had not been condemned. The naive were moved by compassion, scoundrels and subversives by the hope of stirring up trouble with an uprising spearheaded by the Aetolians; and all, for their own reasons, demanded the recall of Eurylochus.

These preparations made, Diocles set out with all the cavalry (he was the cavalry commander at that time), ostensibly on the mission to bring his exiled friend back home. He covered an enormous amount of ground, traveling day and night, and when he was six miles from the city he went ahead at daybreak with three crack squadrons, ordering the main body of cavalrymen to follow behind. After approaching the gate, he told all his men to dismount, lead their horses by the reins and not keep ranks, as if they were on a journey more than anything else so that they would seem to be simply the commander's escort rather than an armed force. He then left one of the squadrons there so the cavalrymen who were following could not be shut out and, taking Eurylochus by the hand, conducted him through the town center and forum to his home, as crowds of people rushed up and congratulated him. Soon the city was full of horsemen and the key points were occupied; men were then sent into the houses to put to death the leaders of the opposing party. So it was that Demetrias fell to the Aetolians.

35. Lacedaemone non urbi vis adferenda sed tyrannus
2 dolo capiendus erat; quem spoliatum maritimis oppidis
ab Romanis, tunc intra moenia etiam Lacedaemonis ab
Achaeis compulsum qui occupasset occidere, eum totius
3 gratiam rei apud Lacedaemonios laturum. causam mittendi ad eum habuerunt quod fatigabat precibus ut auxilia
4 sibi, cum illis auctoribus rebellasset, mitterentur. mille
pedites Alexameno dati sunt et triginta delecti ex iuventute equites. iis a praetore Damocrito in consilio arcano
5 gentis, de quo ante dictum est, denuntiatur ne se ad bellum Achaicum aut rem ullam quam sua quisque opinione
praecipere posset crederent missos esse: quidquid Alexamenum res monuisset subiti consilii capere, ad id, quamvis inopinatum temerarium audax, oboedienter exsequen-
dum parati essent, ac pro eo acciperent tamquam ad id
unum agendum missos ab domo se scirent.
6 Cum his ita praeparatis Alexamenus ad tyrannum venit, quem adveniens extemplo spei implevit: Antiochum
7 iam transisse in Europam, mox in Graecia fore, terras maria armis viris completurum; non cum Philippo rem esse
creditoros Romanos; numerum iniri peditum equitumque
ac navium non posse; elephantorum aciem conspectu ipso
8 debellaturam. Aetolos toto suo exercitu paratos esse venire Lacedaemonem, cum res poscat, sed frequentes ar-

---

118 As the meeting of the privy council had taken place earlier
(34.2, above), Adam (ad loc.) observes that the pluperfect tense
would have been more appropriate in the Latin here.

119 Their leader (cf. 34.5, above).

35. At Sparta the plan was not to apply force to the city but to catch the tyrant by subterfuge. He had been stripped of his coastal towns by the Romans and at that moment was confined within the walls of Sparta by the Achaeans; and the man who was first to assassinate him would presumably earn gratitude from the Lacedaemonians for the deed. The Aetolians had good reason for sending men to Nabis because he had been plaguing them with entreaties for him to be sent help since, he said, it was at their instigation that he had recommenced hostilities. Alexamenus was given 1,000 infantry and 30 cavalrymen, handpicked from the young men of Aetolia. They were briefed by the praetor Damocritus in the privy council of the nation[118] (referred to above) and instructed not to assume that their mission was the Achaean war or anything else that each might deduce for himself. Whatever emergency plan the circumstances might prompt Alexamenus[119] to adopt, they must be prepared to carry it through obediently, however surprising, adventurous, or audacious it may be, and accept that this was the sole objective for which they had been sent from home.

The men thus prepared, Alexamenus came with them to the tyrant and his arrival immediately filled the man with hope. Antiochus had already crossed to Europe and would soon be in Greece, Alexamenus told him, and he would fill land and sea with armaments and soldiers. The Romans were going to understand that it was not a Philip they were dealing with; the number of Antiochus' infantry and cavalry was incalculable and the mere sight of his line of elephants would end the war. The Aetolians were ready to come to Sparta with their entire army when the situation called for it, he said, but they had wanted to demon-

9 matos ostendere advenienti regi voluisse. Nabidi quoque
et ipsi[41] faciendum esse ut quas haberet copias non sineret
sub tectis marcescere otio, sed educeret et in armis decur-
rere cogeret, simul animos acueret et corpora exerceret.

10 consuetudine leviorem laborem fore, et comitate ac benignitate ducis etiam non iniucundum fieri posse.

Educi inde frequenter ante urbem in campum ad Eu-

11 rotan amnem coepere. satellites tyranni media fere in acie
consistebant; tyrannus cum tribus summum equitibus,
inter quos plerumque Alexamenus erat, ante signa vecta-

12 batur, cornua extrema invisens; in dextro cornu Aetoli
erant, et qui ante auxiliares tyranni fuerant et qui venerant

13 mille cum Alexameno. fecerat sibi morem Alexamenus
nunc cum tyranno inter paucos ordines circumeundi mo-

14 nendique eum quae in rem esse videbantur, nunc in dextrum cornu ad suos adequitandi, mox inde, velut imperato

15 quod res poposcisset, recipiendi[42] ad tyrannum. sed quem
diem patrando facinori statuerat, eo paulisper cum ty-

16 ranno vectatus cum ad suos concessisset, tum equitibus ab
domo secum missis "agenda" inquit "res est, iuvenes, au-
dendaque quam me duce impigre exsequi iussi estis.
parate animos dextras, ne quis in eo quod me viderit fa-

17 cientem cesset. qui cunctatus fuerit et suum consilium

---

41 Nabidi quoque et ipsi *B*χ: nam id quoque ipsi *Mg*: Nabidi
quoque ipsi *Madvig*: Nabidi et ipsi *vel* Nabidi quoque *M. Müller*:
Nabidi quoque id ipsum *H.J.M*

42 recipiendi *B*χ: recipiendi se *ed. Rom.*

strate the strength of their troops to the king when he arrived. Nabis himself should also take steps not to allow the troops under his command to languish in idleness in their barracks; he should lead them out and make them undertake military exercises, sharpening their spirit and at the same time training their bodies. The toil would become lighter through practice and might even be rendered not unpleasant by their commander's geniality and kindness.

After that the soldiers began to be brought out on a regular basis to the plain before the city, beside the River Eurotas. The tyrant's bodyguards would stand at about the middle of the line; and the tyrant himself would ride before the standards, inspecting the far ends of the wings, with at most three cavalrymen accompanying him, Alexamenus usually being one. The Aetolian troops would be on the right wing, both those that had been earlier serving as the tyrant's auxiliary troops and the thousand that had come with Alexamenus. Alexamenus had now made a practice of going around a few of the ranks with the tyrant and giving him seemingly useful advice. He would then ride over to his men on the right wing and presently return to the tyrant after apparently issuing some order that the circumstances required. But, on the day that he had fixed for bringing off the coup, he rode with the tyrant only briefly before going over to his own men. He then addressed the cavalrymen who had been sent from home with him: "My young warriors, the action that you were ordered to execute with energy under my command is now to be done and dared. Prepare your hearts and hands so that no one hangs back from what he sees me do. Anyone faltering or following his own course instead of mine must

meo interponet, sciat sibi reditum ad penates non esse."
horror cunctos cepit et meminerant cum quibus mandatis
exissent.

18   Tyrannus ab laevo cornu veniebat. ponere hastas
equites Alexamenus iubet et se intueri: conligit et ipse
animum confusum tantae cogitatione rei. postquam adpropinquabat, impetum facit et transfixo equo tyrannum
19   deturbat, iacentem equites confodiunt; multis frustra in
loricam ictibus datis tandem in nudum corpus volnera pervenerunt, et priusquam a media acie succurreretur exspiravit.

36. Alexamenus cum omnibus Aetolis citato gradu ad
2   regiam occupandam pergit. corporis custodes, cum in
3   oculis res gereretur, pavor primo cepit; deinde, postquam
abire Aetolorum agmen videre, concurrunt ad relictum
tyranni corpus, et spectatorum turba ex custodibus vitae
4   mortisque ultoribus est facta. nec movisset se quisquam si
extemplo positis armis vocata in contionem multitudo fuisset et oratio habita tempori conveniens, frequentes inde
5   retenti in armis Aetoli sine iniuria cuiusquam; sed ut opor-
tuit in consilio fraude coepto, omnia in maturandam per-
6   niciem eorum qui fecerant sunt acta. dux regia inclusus
diem ac noctem in scrutandis thesauris tyranni absumpsit;
Aetoli velut capta urbe quam liberasse videri volebant in
praedam versi.

---

120 This seems to be the same misunderstanding of Polybius'
Greek as noted at 33.8.13, with Livy taking the Greek καταβάλ-
λειν to mean "lay down" instead of "lower."

know that for him there is to be no going home." Horror seized them all and they remembered the orders with which they had left home.

The tyrant was now returning from the left wing. Alexamenus told his horsemen to put down their spears[120] and keep their eyes on him, and even he braced himself, disconcerted as he was by the thought of such a great deed ahead of him. When Nabis approached, he attacked and unseated the tyrant by running his horse through, and the cavalrymen stabbed him as he lay on the ground. Though many of their blows fell ineffectually on his cuirass, eventually their thrusts got through to his exposed body, and before help could be brought from the middle of the line, he breathed his last.

36. Alexamenus now moved at a rapid pace with all the Aetolians to seize the palace. When the coup was taking place before their eyes, Nabis' bodyguards were at first panic-stricken; then, after seeing the Aetolian column leave, they ran to the tyrant's forsaken corpse and the men duty bound to defend him in life and avenge his death became merely a crowd of spectators. No one would have taken action if the populace had been immediately called to an assembly, with all weapons laid aside, and if a speech had been delivered appropriate to the occasion, with a large force of Aetolians kept in arms but with nobody injured. Instead, as was only right in a project begun with treachery, everything that was done combined to hasten the downfall of those guilty of the deed. Their leader spent a day and a night cooped up in the palace rummaging through the tyrant's treasures, and the Aetolians turned to looting as if they had captured the city that they wished to appear to have liberated.

7 Simul indignitas rei, simul contemptus animos Lacedaemoniis ad coeundum fecit. alii dicere exturbandos Aetolos et libertatem, cum restitui videretur interceptam, repetendam; alii, ut caput agendae rei esset, regii generis

8 aliquem in speciem adsumendum. Laconicus eius stirpis erat puer admodum, eductus cum liberis tyranni. eum in equum imponunt et armis arreptis Aetolos vagos per ur-

9 bem caedunt. tum regiam invadunt; ibi Alexamenum cum paucis resistentem obtruncant. Aetoli circa Chalcioecon—Mineruae aereum est templum—congregati caeduntur;

10 pauci armis abiectis pars Tegeam pars Megalen polin perfugiunt; ibi comprensi a magistratibus sub corona venierunt.

37. Philopoemen, audita caede tyranni, profectus

2 Lacedaemonem cum omnia turbata metu invenisset, evocatis principibus et oratione habita qualis habenda Alexameno fuerat, societati Achaeorum Lacedaemonios adiu-

3 nxit, eo etiam facilius quod ad idem forte tempus A. Atilius cum quattuor et viginti quinqueremibus ad Gytheum accessit.

4 Iisdem diebus circa Chalcidem Thoas per Euthymidam principem, pulsum opibus eorum qui Romanae so-

---

121 Not recorded as a Spartan name, and it is possible that Livy has again misunderstood Polybius, who may have simply been referring to a "Spartan boy" (Λακωνικός).

122 "Athena of the Brazen House," the temple where some two-and-a-half centuries earlier Pausanias had been confined, left to starve. and then removed just before he expired.

123 Literally, "sold under the wreath/chaplet." Slaves wore a garland of flowers when put up for sale.

106

The enormity of their conduct and at the same time the contempt felt for them gave the Lacedaemonians the courage to take concerted action. Some said they should drive out the Aetolians and reclaim the liberty that was cut off just when it seemed to be being restored, others that they should take some member of the royal family as their figurehead so as to have a leader for their enterprise. There was one Laconicus,[121] a mere boy, who was of that family and had been brought up with the tyrant's children. They put him on a horse, took up their weapons and massacred the Aetolians as they drifted through the city. Next they stormed the palace and there killed Alexamenus when he resisted with a few of his men. The Aetolians congregated around Chalcioecus—the bronze temple of Minerva[122]—but were cut down; only a few threw down their arms and escaped either to Tegea or Megalopolis. There they were arrested by the magistrates and auctioned off as slaves.[123]

37. On hearing of the tyrant's death, Philopoemen set off for Sparta where he found everything full of confusion and panic. He summoned the leading citizens and giving the kind of address that Alexamenus should have given brought the Spartans into the Achaean league, which he did all the more easily because Aulus Atilius[124] happened to reach Gytheum at that same time with twenty-four quinqueremes.

At Chalcis during that same period Thoas had nothing like the success that had attended Eurylochus' taking of Demetrias. He had been assisted by Euthymidas, a prom-

---

[124] A. Atilius Serranus (60); cf. 20.10, above, for his fleet assignment.

5 cietatis erant, post T. Quincti legatorumque adventum, et
Herodorum, Cianum mercatorem sed potentem Chalcide
propter divitias, praeparatis ad proditionem iis qui Euthy-
midae factionis erant, nequaquam eandem fortunam qua
6 Demetrias per Eurylochum occupata erat habuit. Euthymidas ab Athenis—eum domicilio delegerat locum—Thebas primum hinc Salganea processit, Herodorus ad Thro-
7 nium. inde haud procul in Maliaco sinu duo milia peditum
Thoas et ducentos equites, onerarias leves ad triginta
habebat. eas cum sescentis peditibus Herodorus traicere
8 in insulam Atalanten iussus, ut inde, cum pedestres copias
adpropinquare iam Aulidi atque Euripo sensisset, Chalci-
9 dem traiceret; ipse ceteras copias nocturnis maxime itineribus quanta poterat celeritate Chalcidem ducebat.

38. Micythio et Xenoclides,[43] penes quos tum summa
rerum pulso Euthymida Chalcide erat, seu ipsi per se sus-
picati seu indicata re, primo pavidi nihil usquam spei nisi
2 in fuga ponebant; deinde postquam resedit terror et prodi
et deseri non patriam modo sed etiam Romanorum socie-
3 tatem cernebant, consilio tali animum adiecerunt. Sacrum
anniversarium eo forte tempore Eretriae Amarynthidis
Dianae erat, quod non popularium modo sed Carystiorum
4 etiam coetu celebratur. eo miserunt qui orarent Ere-

----

[43] Xenoclides *Ald.*: Enoclides *Ba*: Enochides χ

----

[125] Salganeus lay just west of the Euripus (*Barr.* 55 F4), Thronium just south of the Malian Gulf (55 D3 Thronion).

[126] Island of Atalante: *Barr.* 55 E3; Aulis and Euripus: F4.

[127] Amarynthos lay east of Eretria (*Barr.* 57 B3), Carystus to
the southeast (C3 Karystos).

inent citizen who, after the arrival of Titus Quinctius and the commissioners, had been driven out of the city by the authority wielded by the group supporting the Roman alliance and by Herodorus, a merchant from Cius, influential in Chalcis because of his wealth. With their help he had primed the supporters of Euthymidas to betray the city to him. Euthymidas went from Athens (which he had chosen as his place of residence) first to Thebes and then to Salganeus, while Herodorus proceeded to Thronium.[125] Not far from there, in the Malian Gulf, Thoas had 2,000 infantry, 200 cavalry and about 30 light cargo vessels. Herodorus was instructed to take the ships together with 600 infantry over to the island of Atalante so that he could cross from there to Chalcis when he found out that the land forces were approaching Aulis and Euripus.[126] Thoas himself proceeded to take the rest of the troops as quickly as he could to Chalcis, marching mostly at night.

38. Micythio and Xenoclides, with whom supreme authority at Chalcis then lay after Euthymidas' expulsion, either themselves suspected what was happening or had the plot betrayed to them. At first they panicked, and placed no hope in any course of action other than flight. Then, when their terror subsided and they came to see that it was not only their country but also the alliance with Rome that was being abandoned, they turned their attention to the following plan. The annual festival of Diana of Amarynthis happened to be taking place in Eretria at that time and this is celebrated not only by local devotees but also by crowds of people from Carystus.[127] Micythio and Xenoclides sent men to the festival to beg the Eretrians

trienses Carystiosque ut et suarum fortunarum, in eadem
insula geniti, misererentur, et Romanam societatem respi-
5 cerent: ne sinerent Aetolorum Chalcidem fieri; Euboeam
habituros, si Chalcidem habuissent; graves fuisse Macedonas dominos, multo minus tolerabiles futuros Aetolos.
6 Romanorum maxime respectus civitates movit, et virtutem nuper in bello et in victoria iustitiam benignitatemque
expertas. itaque quod roboris in iuventute erat utraque
civitas armavit misitque.
7 Iis tuenda moenia Chalcidis oppidani cum tradidissent,
ipsi omnibus copiis transgressi Euripum ad Salganea po-
8 suerunt castra. inde caduceator primum deinde legati ad
Aetolos missi, percunctatum quo suo dicto factove socii
9 atque amici ad se oppugnandos venirent. respondit Thoas,
dux Aetolorum, non ad oppugnandos sed ad liberandos ab
10 Romanis venire sese: splendidiore nunc eos catena sed
multo graviore vinctos esse quam cum praesidium Macedonum in arce habuissent. se vero negare Chalcidenses
11 aut servire ulli aut praesidio cuiusquam egere. ita digressi
ex conloquio legati ad suos; Thoas et Aetoli, ut qui spem
12 omnem in eo ut improviso opprimerent habuissent, ad
iustum bellum oppugnationemque urbis mari ac terra
13 munitae haudquaquam pares, domum rediere. Euthymidas postquam castra popularium ad Salganea esse profec-
14 tosque Aetolos audivit, et ipse a Thebis Athenas rediit; et

and Carystians to have compassion on their misfortunes—
they were, after all, born on the same island—and also to
respect the Roman alliance. They asked them not to allow
Chalcis to fall to the Aetolians, who would possess all
Euboea if they possessed Chalcis. The Macedonians had
been severe taskmasters, they said, but the Aetolians
would be much harder to bear. It was respect for the Romans that carried most weight with the two states, which
had recently seen both their valor in war and their fairness
and generosity in victory. Both states therefore armed and
sent all their best men of military age.

After entrusting the defense of their walls to these
troops, the citizens of Chalcis themselves crossed the
Euripus with all their forces and encamped at Salganeus.
From there first a herald and then ambassadors were sent
to the Aetolians to ask what they had said or done to make
their allies and friends come to attack them. The leader of
the Aetolians, Thoas, replied that they were coming not to
attack them but to liberate them from the Romans; they
were now bound with fetters that were more ornate but
much heavier than when they had had a Macedonian garrison in their citadel, he said. The Chalcidians, however,
declared that they were slaves to no one, and needed no
one's protection. With that the ambassadors left the meeting and returned to their people. Thoas and the Aetolians
had placed all their hopes on taking them with a surprise
attack and since they were in no position to mount a conventional campaign and invest a city that had land and sea
defenses they returned home. On hearing that his countrymen were encamped at Salganeus and that the Aetolians had left, Euthymidas himself also returned from
Thebes to Athens. Herodorus, who had for a number of

Herodorus cum per aliquot dies intentus ab Atalante signum nequiquam exspectasset, missa speculatoria nave ut quid morae esset sciret, postquam rem omissam ab sociis vidit, Thronium unde venerat repetit.

39. Quinctius quoque his auditis, ab Corintho veniens
2 navibus, in Chalcidico Euripo Eumeni regi occurrit. placuit quingentos milites praesidii causa relinqui Chalcide
3 ab Eumene rege, ipsum Athenas ire. Quinctius, quo profectus erat, Demetriadem contendit, ratus Chalcidem liberatam momenti aliquid apud Magnetas ad repetendam
4 societatem Romanam facturam, et ut praesidii aliquid esset suae partis hominibus, Eunomo praetori Thessalorum scripsit ut armaret iuventutem, et Villium[44] ad Demetriadem praemisit ad temptandos animos, non aliter nisi pars aliqua inclinaret ad respectum pristinae societatis rem
5 adgressurus. Villius quinqueremi nave ad ostium portus est invectus. eo multitudo Magnetum omnis cum se effudisset, quaesivit Villius utrum ad amicos an ad hostes
6 venisse se mallent. respondit Magnetarches Eurylochus ad amicos venisse eum, sed abstineret portu et sineret Magnetas in concordia et libertate esse, nec per conloquii
7 speciem multitudinem sollicitaret. altercatio inde non sermo fuit, cum Romanus ut ingratos increparet Magnetas imminentesque praediceret clades, multitudo obstreperet nunc senatum nunc Quinctium accusando. ita inrito in-

---

44 Villium *Fr. 2*: Iulium *ed. Rom.*: om. Bχ

---

128 This is the first mention of Eumenes' presence in Greece.
129 He was Thessalian *strategos* for only the last four months of 193/2.
130 Magnetarch: cf. 31.11, above.

days been eagerly but vainly awaiting a signal from Atalante, sent out a spy vessel to ascertain what was delaying matters, and after he saw that the operation had been abandoned by the allies he too headed back to Thronium, whence he had come.

39. When Quinctius, coming from Corinth by sea, also heard of this, he met King Eumenes in the Euripus of Chalcis.[128] It was there decided that 500 men should be left at Chalcis by King Eumenes to form a garrison and that the king himself should proceed to Athens. Quinctius continued to Demetrias, for which he had set out. He believed that the liberation of Chalcis would, to some extent, favorably dispose the Magnesians toward resuming their alliance with Rome and, to ensure that his supporters there had some protection, he wrote to the praetor of the Thessalians, Eunomus,[129] asking him to put his fighting men under arms. He also sent Villius ahead to Demetrias to sound out the sentiments of the people, intending to take no action unless some were in favor of respecting the old alliance. Villius sailed to the harbor mouth in a quinquereme; and when all the Magnesians poured out in a mass to the spot, he asked them whether they preferred that he had come to friends or to enemies. The Magnetarch[130] Eurylochus replied that he had come to friends, but that he should keep away from the harbor and allow the Magnesians to live in harmony and liberty and not use the pretext of a meeting to inflame the masses. It then became a slanging match rather than a discussion, with the Roman berating the Magnesians as ingrates and predicting imminent disaster, and the Magnesian populace, in an uproar, hurling accusations at the senate at one moment and at Quinctius the next. Accordingly, his initiative a fail-

8 cepto Villius ad Quinctium sese recepit. at Quinctius nuntio ad praetorem misso ut reduceret domum copias, ipse navibus Corinthum rediit.

40. Abstulere me velut de spatio Graeciae res immixtae Romanis, non quia ipsas operae pretium esset perscribere, sed quia causae cum Antiocho fuerunt belli.

2 Consulibus designatis—inde namque deverteram—L. Quinctius et Cn. Domitius consules in provincias profecti

3 sunt, Quinctius in Ligures, Domitius adversus Boios. Boii quieverunt, atque etiam senatus eorum cum liberis et praefecti cum equitatu—summa omnium mille et quin-

4 genti—consuli dediderunt sese. ab altero consule ager Ligurum late est vastatus castellaque aliquot capta, unde non praeda modo omnis generis cum captivis parta, sed recepti quoque aliquot cives sociique qui in hostium potestate fuerant.

5 Eodem hoc anno Vibonem colonia deducta est ex senatus consulto plebique scito. tria milia et septingenti pe-

6 dites ierunt, trecenti equites; triumviri deduxerunt eos Q. Naevius M. Minucius M. Furius Crassipes;[45] quina dena iugera agri data in singulos pedites sunt, duplex equiti. Bruttiorum proxime fuerat ager; Bruttii ceperant de Graecis.

---

[45] Crassipes *Fr. 1*: Crassus *Bχ*

---

[131] That is, the Thessalian "praetor" (*strategos*) Eunomus.

[132] The inconsistency between Livy's account here and at 22.3–4 above (where the consuls have already left for their provinces) probably results from his following and failing to reconcile two different annalistic sources (see Introduction to vol. IX, xxvi–xxx).   [133] Vibo Valentia, in Calabria, earlier called Hipponion by the Greeks (*Barr.* 46 D4).

ure, Villius beat a retreat to Quinctius. Quinctius then sent a message to the praetor[131] ordering him to take his forces home, and Quinctius himself returned to Corinth with his fleet.

40. These events where Greek and Roman history converge have taken me off course, as it were, not because the narration of them was worthwhile of itself but because they were the causes of the war with Antiochus.

When the new consuls had been designated (which was where I began my digression), the consuls Lucius Quinctius and Gnaeus Domitius left for their provinces, Quinctius going to the Ligurians, and Domitius against the Boii.[132] The Boii remained pacified, and even their senate together with their children and their cavalry commanders together with their troops surrendered to the consul, a total of 1,500 people. The Ligurian farm lands were plundered far and wide by the other consul and several fortresses were captured. Not only was there booty of all kinds forthcoming from them, and captives along with it, but a number of Roman citizens and allies who had been in the hands of the enemy were also recovered.

In this same year a colony was established at Vibo[133] following a decree of the senate and its ratification by the plebs. Three thousand, seven hundred infantry and 300 cavalry went there and the triumvirs Quintus Naevius, Marcus Minucius and Marcus Furius Crassipes were its commissioners. Infantrymen were each given fifteen *iugera* of land and a cavalryman twice that amount. The land had most recently belonged to the Bruttii, and the Bruttii had taken it from the Greeks.

7 Romae per idem tempus duo maximi fuerunt terrores, diutinus alter sed segnior: terra dies duodequadraginta movit. per totidem dies feriae in sollicitudine ac metu
8 fuere; triduum eius rei causa supplicatio habita est. ille non pavor vanus sed vera multorum clades fuit: incendio a foro bovario orto diem noctemque aedificia in Tiberim versa arsere tabernaeque omnes cum magni pretii mercibus conflagraverunt.

41. Iam fere in exitu annus erat, et in dies magis fama[46]
2 de bello Antiochi et cura patribus crescebat; itaque de provinciis designatorum magistratuum, quo intentiores
3 essent omnes, agitari coeptum est. decrevere ut consulibus Italia et quo senatus censuisset—eam esse bellum adversus Antiochum regem omnes sciebant—provinciae
4 essent; cuius ea sors esset quattuor milia peditum civium Romanorum et trecenti equites, sex milia socium Latini
5 nominis cum quadringentis equitibus sunt decreta. eorum dilectum habere L. Quinctius consul iussus, ne quid moraretur quo minus consul novus quo senatus censuisset extemplo proficisci posset.
6 Item de provinciis praetorum decretum est,[47] prima ut sors duae urbanaque et inter cives ac peregrinos iurisdictio esset, secunda Bruttii, tertia classis, ut navigaret quo

---

46 magis fama *Holk. Lips.*: magna fama *B*χ: et fama *Mg*: fama *Weiss.*: magis et fama *Madvig*
47 est χ: *om. B*

---

134 See 8.4 and note, above.
135 The Roman cattle market, which lay between the Tiber and the Velabrum (Richardson 162–64, with fig. 37).
136 For the formula cf. 20.7 and note, above.

In this same period there were two very terrifying incidents at Rome, one lasting longer than the other but less dangerous. There were earth tremors for thirty-eight days. For the same number of days business was suspended in an atmosphere of anxiety and fear, and a three-day period of supplication[134] was held because of the phenomenon. The other was no false alarm but meant actual destruction for many people. A fire broke out in the Forum Boarium,[135] the buildings along the bank of the Tiber burned for a day and a night, and all the shops in the district went up in flames along with their valuable merchandise.

41. The year was now almost at its end and every day talk of war with Antiochus was growing, as were the concerns of the senators. Accordingly, the assignment of provinces to the newly elected magistrates began to be mooted so that these could all apply themselves more diligently to them. The senators decided that the provinces for the consuls should be Italy and "wherever the senate decided"[136]—and everyone knew that that meant the war against King Antiochus. The troop allocation for the consul allotted this area was 4,000 infantrymen and 300 cavalry from the Roman citizenry, plus 6,000 infantry and 400 cavalry from the allies and holders of Latin rights. The consul Lucius Quinctius was instructed to raise these troops so that there would be nothing to delay the new consul's immediate departure for whatever destination the senate voted for him.

A decision was also made on the provinces of the praetors. The first was to be a twofold jurisdiction, city affairs and citizen-foreigner affairs; the second was Bruttium; the third the fleet (which was to sail wherever the senate de-

senatus censuisset, quarta Sicilia, quinta Sardinia, sexta
7 Hispania ulterior. imperatum praeterea L. Quinctio consuli est ut duas legiones civium Romanorum novas conscriberet, et socium ac Latini nominis viginti milia peditum et
octingentos equites. eum exercitum praetori cui Bruttii
provincia evenisset decreverunt.

8   Aedes duae Iovis eo anno in Capitolio dedicatae sunt;
voverat L. Furius Purpureo praetor Gallico bello unam,
9 alteram consul; dedicavit Q. Marcius Ralla duumvir. iudi-
cia in faeneratores eo anno multa severe sunt facta, accu-
santibus privatos aedilibus curulibus M. Tuccio et P. Iunio
10 Bruto. de multa damnatorum quadrigae inauratae in Capitolio positae et in cella Iovis supra fastigium aediculae
duodecim clipea inaurata; et iidem porticum extra portam
Trigeminam inter lignarios fecerunt.

42. Intentis in apparatum novi belli Romanis ne ab
2 Antiocho quidem cessabatur. tres eum civitates tenebant,
Zmyrna et Alexandria Troas et Lampsacus, quas neque vi
expugnare ad eam diem poterat neque condicionibus in
amicitiam perlicere, neque ab tergo relinquere traiciens
3 ipse in Europam volebat. tenuit eum et de Hannibale
deliberatio. et primo naves apertae quas cum eo missurus
4 in Africam fuerat moratae sunt; deinde an omnino mitten-
dus esset consultatio mota est, maxime a Thoante Aetolo,

---

137 Public projects were frequently financed from fines collected by the aediles: cf. Oakley 4.259–61.
138 The "timber market," or possibly "carpenters' quarter"
(*inter lignarios*), is not mentioned elsewhere. On the Porta Trigemina, cf 10.12 note, above.   139 Smyrna (mod. Izmir):
Barr. 56 E5; Alexandria Troas: C2; Lampsacus: 57 E1.
140 Cf. 34.60.5, where, however, the ships are decked.

cided); the fourth Sicily; the fifth Sardinia; and the sixth Farther Spain. The consul Lucius Quinctius was also ordered to raise two new legions of Roman citizens and 20,000 infantry and 800 cavalry from the allies and those with Latin rights. The senate decreed that this army was for the praetor to whom the province of Bruttium should fall.

Two temples of Jupiter were dedicated on the Capitol that year. Lucius Furius Purpureo had promised them in vows, one as praetor in the Gallic War, the second as consul; and the duumvir Quintus Marcius Ralla dedicated them. Many harsh judgments were passed on usurers that year when the curule aediles Marcus Tuccius and Publius Iunius Brutus brought charges against private citizens. From the fines imposed on those found guilty gilded four-horse chariots were installed on the Capitol, and twelve gilded shields placed in the inner chapel of the temple of Jupiter above the pediment.[137] The same aediles also had a portico built outside the Porta Trigemina in the timber market.[138]

42. While the Romans were focused on preparations for the new war, there was no easing up on Antiochus' side, either. Three city-states were holding him back—Smyrna, Alexandria Troas and Lampsacus[139]—and up to that time he had been unable to take them by assault, or inveigle them into an alliance by offering terms; and he did not want to leave them to his rear when he was crossing into Europe. He was also detained by the question of Hannibal. First, there was a delay with the open-decked ships that Antiochus had been going to send to Africa with him,[140] and then there had been questions raised, principally by Thoas the Aetolian, over whether Hannibal should

qui omnibus in Graecia tumultu completis Demetriadem
5 adferebat in potestate esse, et quibus mendaciis de rege,
multiplicando verbis copias eius, erexerat multorum in
6 Graecia animos, iisdem et regis spem inflabat: omnium
votis eum accersi; concursum ad litora futurum, unde classem regiam prospexissent. hic idem ausus de Hannibale
7 est movere sententiam prope iam certam regis. nam neque dimittendam partem navium a classe regia censebat,
neque si mittendae naves forent, minus quemquam ei
8 classi quam Hannibalem praeficiendum. exsulem illum et
Poenum esse, cui mille in dies nova consilia vel fortuna
9 sua vel ingenium possit facere, et ipsam eam gloriam belli
qua velut dote Hannibal concilietur nimiam in praefecto
regio esse. regem conspici, regem unum ducem unum
10 imperatorem videri debere. si classem si exercitum amittat Hannibal, idem damni fore ac si per alium ducem amittantur; si quid prospere eveniat, Hannibalis eam non
11 Antiochi gloriam fore; si vero universo bello vincendi
Romanos fortuna detur, quam spem esse sub rege victurum Hannibalem, uni subiectum, qui patriam prope non
12 tulerit? non ita se a iuventa eum gessisse, spe animoque
complexum orbis terrarum imperium, ut in senectute
13 dominum laturus videatur. nihil opus esse regi duce Han-

---

141 This was, of course, true (cf. 34.6–11, above).

be sent at all. Thoas brought the news that there was total chaos in Greece, and that Demetrias was in Antiochus' hands;[141] and just as he had raised the expectations of many in Greece with lies about the king and by inflating the numbers of Antiochus' forces in his reports, so now he was using the same routine to build up the king's hopes. Everyone was praying for Antiochus to come, he said, and there would be a rush to the shores from which they sighted the royal fleet. This same fellow even made so bold as to challenge the king's decision on Hannibal, by now almost settled in his mind. He recommended that the king not detach a number of ships from the royal fleet, and added that if ships had to be sent the last man to be put in command of that fleet should be Hannibal. He was an exile and a Carthaginian, a man whose fortunes or character could conjure up for him a thousand new schemes a day. In addition, his military reputation, which, like a woman's dowry, made Hannibal an attractive proposition, was too great for a mere officer of the king. It was the king who should have center stage, the king who should be seen as the sole admiral and sole commander. If Hannibal lost a fleet or an army, the damage would be the same as if they were lost by another general; in the event of success, however, the glory would be Hannibal's, not Antiochus.' In fact, if they were granted the good fortune of defeating the Romans in the war as a whole, what hope was there of Hannibal, who had scarcely tolerated the authority of his native land, living under a king, subject to one man? His behavior from his early years, with hopes and ambitions embracing worldwide supremacy, had not been such as to suggest that he would in his old age tolerate a master. The king had no need of Hannibal as a commander, but he

nibale; comite et consiliario eodem ad bellum uti posse.
14 modicum fructum ex ingenio tali neque gravem neque
inutilem fore: si summa petantur, et dantem et acci-
pientem praegravatura.

43. Nulla ingenia tam prona ad invidiam sunt quam
eorum qui genus ac fortunam suam animis non aequant,
2 quia virtutem et bonum alienum oderunt. extemplo consilium mittendi Hannibalis, quod unum in principio belli
utiliter cogitatum erat, abiectum est. Demetriadis maxime
defectione ab Romanis ad Aetolos elatus, non ultra dif-
3 ferre profectionem in Graeciam constituit. priusquam solveret naves, Ilium a mari escendit ut Mineruae sacrificaret. inde ad classem regressus proficiscitur quadraginta
tectis navibus apertis sexaginta, et ducentae onerariae
cum omnis generis commeatu bellicoque alio apparatu
4 sequebantur. Imbrum primo insulam tenuit; inde Scia-
thum traiecit; ubi conlectis in alto quae dissipatae erant
5 navibus, ad Pteleum primum continentis venit. ibi Eurylochus ei Magnetarches principesque Magnetum ab Demetriade occurrerunt; quorum frequentia laetus die postero
in portum urbis navibus est invectus, copias haud procul
6 inde exposuit. decem milia peditum fuere et quingenti
equites, sex elephanti, vix ad Graeciam nudam occupandam satis copiarum, nedum ad sustinendum Romanum
bellum.
7 Aetoli, postquam Demetriadem venisse Antiochum

142 Sacrifices to Minerva (Athena) were made at Troy by Xerxes before he crossed to Greece in 480 (Hdt. 7.43.2) and by Alexander on his Persian campaign (Arr. 1.11.7). Scipio would do
the same two years later (37.37.2–3).

143 Imbros: *Barr.* 57 D1; Sciathos: B2; Pteleon: A2.

could use him as a courtier and adviser for the war. A limited employment of such talent would not be harmful or unprofitable, but if the greatest services were requested of the man they would be detrimental to both the giver and the receiver.

43. No temperaments are as susceptible to jealousy as those of people whose character does not measure up to their pedigree or station, because they hate excellence and quality in another. The project of sending Hannibal—the one sound idea produced at the start of the war—was immediately abandoned. Encouraged especially by Demetrias' defection to the Aetolians from the Romans, Antiochus decided to delay no longer his advance into Greece. Before setting sail, he went inland from the coast to Ilium to sacrifice to Minerva.[142] Then, rejoining his fleet, he set off with 40 decked and 60 open-decked ships; and 200 transport vessels, carrying all manner of provisions as well as military equipment, followed behind. He first put in at the island of Imbros and crossed from there to Sciathos. When he had brought together the vessels that had been scattered at sea he sailed on to Pteleum,[143] his first landfall on the mainland. There the Magnetarch Eurylochus and leading Magnesians came from Demetrias to meet him. Delighted to see their great numbers, he sailed with his fleet into the harbor of their city the following day and disembarked his forces not far from there. These comprised 10,000 infantry, 500 cavalry, and 6 elephants—an armament barely sufficient to take possession of an undefended Greece and much less sustain a war with Rome.

On receiving the report that Antiochus had reached Demetrias, the Aetolians convened an assembly and

adlatum est, concilio indicto decretum quo accerserent
8 eum fecerunt. iam profectus ab Demetriade rex, quia ita
decreturos sciebat, Phalara in sinum Maliacum processe-
9 rat. inde decreto accepto Lamiam venit, exceptus ingenti
favore multitudinis cum plausibus clamoribusque et quibus aliis laetitia effusa volgi significatur.

44. In concilium ut ventum est, aegre[48] a Phaenea praetore principibusque aliis introductus silentio facto dicere
2 orsus rex. prima eius oratio fuit excusantis quod tanto
3 minoribus spe atque opinione omnium copiis venisset: id
suae impensae erga eos voluntatis maximum debere indi-
cium esse, quod nec paratus satis ulla re, et tempore ad
navigandum immaturo, vocantibus legatis eorum haud
gravate obsecutus esset, credidissetque cum se vidissent
Aetoli, omnia vel in se uno posita praesidia existimaturos
4 esse. ceterum eorum quoque se quorum exspectatio des-
tituta in praesentia videatur spem abunde expleturum;
5 nam simul primum anni tempus navigabile praebuisset
mare, omnem se Graeciam armis viris equis, omnem oram
6 maritimam classibus completurum, nec impensae nec labori nec periculo parsurum, donec depulso cervicibus
eorum imperio Romano liberam vere Graeciam atque in
7 ea principes Aetolos fecisset. cum exercitibus commeatus
quoque omnis generis ex Asia venturos: in praesentia cu-

---

[48] aegre *hic Mg*, *ante* facto *Damsté*: om. Bχ

---

144 Phalara (tentatively) and Lamia: *Barr.* 57 A3.
145 Pro-Roman former *strategos* of the Aetolians (198/7). He
had tried to reach a settlement with Rome, and had commanded
the Aetolian troops supporting the Romans at Cynoscephalae

passed a decree inviting him to join them. By now the king had left Demetrias, because he knew the Aetolians would pass the decree, and had advanced to Phalara on the Malian Gulf. After receiving the decree, he came from there to Lamia,[144] where he was given a very warm welcome by the populace, with clapping and cheering and other displays of extravagant rejoicing typical of the common herd.

44. When he came to the assembly, the king was with difficulty ushered in by the praetor Phaeneas[145] and the other leading Aetolians, and when silence was obtained he began to speak. His address started with an apology for having come with forces so much smaller than everybody had been hoping for and expecting. That, he said, should be taken as the best testimony to the strength of his goodwill toward them: unprepared in all respects and at an unseasonable time for sailing, he had promptly acceded to the appeal of their envoys and had believed that when the Aetolians saw him they would consider that in him alone lay all they needed for their protection. Nevertheless, he would amply fulfill the hopes of those whose expectations seemed temporarily frustrated. For as soon as the early part of the year made the sea navigable he would fill the whole of Greece with arms, men, and horses and the entire coastline with his fleets; and he would spare no expense and shirk no effort or danger until, by removing Roman domination from their shoulders, he had made Greece truly free and the Aetolians leaders within it. Provisions of all kinds would also come from Asia with his

(33.3.9). This is his second term of office. The king was presumably ushered in "with difficulty" because of the crowd.

rae esse Aetolis debere ut copia frumenti suis et annona
tolerabilis rerum aliarum suppeditetur.

45. In hanc sententiam rex cum magno omnium ad-
2 sensu locutus discessit. post discessum regis inter duos
principes Aetolorum Phaeneam et Thoantem contentio
3 fuit. Phaeneas reconciliatore pacis et disceptatore de iis
quae in controversia cum populo Romano essent utendum
4 potius Antiocho censebat quam duce belli: adventum eius
et maiestatem ad verecundiam faciendam Romanis vim
maiorem habituram quam arma. multa homines, ne bellare necesse sit, voluntate remittere quae bello et armis
5 cogi non possint. Thoas negare paci studere Phaeneam
sed discutere apparatum belli velle, ut taedio et impetus
relanguescat regis et Romani tempus ad comparandum
6 habeant; nihil enim aequi ab Romanis impetrari posse,
totiens legationibus missis Romam, totiens cum ipso
Quinctio disceptando, satis expertum esse, nec nisi abscisa
7 omni spe auxilium Antiochi imploraturos fuisse. quo celerius spe omnium oblato non esse elanguescendum, sed
orandum potius regem ut quoniam, quod maximum fuerit,
ipse vindex Graeciae venerit, copias quoque terrestres
8 navalesque accersat. armatum regem aliquid impetratu-
rum: inermem non pro Aetolis modo sed ne pro se quidem
9 ipso momenti ullius futurum apud Romanos. haec vicit
sententia, imperatoremque regem appellandum censue-

armies, he said, but for the moment the Aetolians should see to it that his men were furnished with grain supplies and other commodities at a reasonable price.

45. After speaking to this effect and receiving loud applause from all, the king departed; and following his departure an argument broke out between two of the principal Aetolians, Phaeneas and Thoas. Phaeneas was of the view that, rather than have Antiochus as commander in chief in war, they should use him to restore peace and arbitrate their differences with the Roman people. His coming and his regal presence, said Phaeneas, would have more force than armed might in winning the Romans' respect. To avoid having to go to war, men freely make many concessions that could not be wrung from them by war and force of arms he said. Thoas claimed that Phaeneas was not really eager for peace but merely wished to obstruct preparations for war; he wanted the king's drive to peter out through ennui and the Romans to have time to prepare. Experience had shown clearly enough, he said, after all their delegations to Rome and all the discussions with Quinctius himself, that no justice could be obtained from the Romans—they would not have asked for Antiochus' help had not all hope been cut off for them! This help had now been offered them sooner than anyone had expected and they must not slacken their efforts; rather, because the king had come to them in person as the champion of Greece—the most important point—they should beg him also to send for his land and sea forces. In arms the king would get some results; unarmed he would have no influence at all to further the Aetolian cause, or even his own interests, with the Romans. This was the view that prevailed and they voted that the king should be appointed

runt, et triginta principes cum quibus, si qua vellet, consultaret delegerunt.

46. Ita dimisso concilio, multitudo omnis in suas civitates dilapsa est; rex postero die cum apocletis eorum
2 unde bellum ordiretur consultabat. optimum visum est Chalcidem, frustra ab Aetolis nuper temptatam, primum adgredi, et celeritate magis in eam rem quam magno
3 conatu et apparatu opus esse. itaque cum mille peditibus rex, qui Demetriade[49] secuti erant, profectus per Phocidem est, et alio itinere principes Aetoli, iuniorum paucis evocatis, ad Chaeroniam occurrerunt et decem constratis
4 navibus secuti sunt. rex, ad Salganea castris positis, navibus ipse cum principibus Aetolorum Euripum traiecit; et cum haud procul portu egressus esset, magistratus quoque Chalcidensium et principes ante portam processerunt.
5 pauci utrimque ad conloquium congressi sunt. Aetoli magnopere suadere ut salua Romanorum amicitia regem quo-
6 que adsumerent socium atque amicum; neque enim eum inferendi belli sed liberandae Graeciae causa in Europam traiecisse, et liberandae re, non verbis et simulatione,
7 quod fecissent Romani. nihil autem utilius Graeciae civitatibus esse quam utramque complecti amicitiam; ita enim ab utriusque iniuria tutas alterius semper praesidio et fi-
8 ducia fore. nam si non recepissent regem, viderent quid

---

[49] Demetriade *Bχ*: eum Demetriade *ed. Med. 1478*: ab Demetriade *Fr. 2*

---

[146] Cf. 34.2, above.

commander in chief; and they then chose thirty leading Aetolians whom he could consult on any matter he wished.

46. With the council thus adjourned, the assembled members all dispersed to their various city-states; and the next day the king began consultation with their *apocleti*[146] on where hostilities should begin. It seemed best to start with an attack on Chalcis, object of the recent unsuccessful attempt by the Aetolians, and for that it was speed that was needed rather than a powerful drive and extensive preparations. The king therefore set off through Phocis with a thousand infantry that had come with him from Demetrias; and the Aetolian leaders, calling up a few of their young soldiers, took another route, met him at Chaeronea and followed him with ten decked ships. After pitching camp at Salganeus, the king crossed the Euripus with his ship together with his leaders of the Aetolians. When he disembarked not far from their port, the Chalcidian magistrates and leading citizens came out before the city gate. A small number from both sides met to parley. The Aetolians made a serious effort to persuade the Chalcidians to accept the king as their ally and friend while also preserving their alliance with Rome. He had crossed to Europe not to make war, they said, but in order to make the liberation of Greece a genuine liberation and not one that was all talk and show as the Romans had done. In fact, he said, there was nothing more advantageous for the city-states of Greece than to espouse both friendships; in this way they would always be assured of protection against aggression by the one through the support and loyalty of the other. For they should also consider the immediate consequences of not receiving the king, when Roman

patiendum iis extemplo foret, cum Romanorum procul auxilium, hostis Antiochus, cui resistere suis viribus non possent, ante portas esset.

9 Ad haec Micythio, unus ex principibus, mirari se dixit ad quos liberandos Antéiochus relicto regno suo in Euro-
10 pam traiecisset; nullam enim civitatem se in Graecia nosse quae aut praesidium habeat, aut stipendium Romanis pendat, aut foedere iniquo adligata quas nolit leges patia-
11 tur; itaque Chalcidenses neque vindice libertatis ullo egere, cum liberi sint, neque praesidio, cum pacem eius-
12 dem populi Romani beneficio et libertatem habeant. amicitiam regis non aspernari nec ipsorum Aetolorum. id primum eos pro amicis facturos, si insula excedant atque
13 abeant; nam ipsis certum esse non modo non recipere moenibus, sed ne societatem quidem ullam pacisci nisi ex auctoritate Romanorum.

47. Haec renuntiata regi ad naves ubi restiterat cum essent, in praesentia—neque enim iis venerat copiis ut vi agere quicquam posset—reverti Demetriadem placuit.
2 ibi, quoniam primum vanum inceptum evasisset, consultare cum Aetolis rex quid deinde fieret. placuit Boeotos Achaeos Amynandrum regem Athamanum temptare.
3 Boeotorum gentem aversam ab Romanis iam inde a Brachylli[50] morte et quae secuta eam fuerant censebant;
4 Achaeorum Philopoemenem principem aemulatione glo-

[50] Brachy(i)lli *Bχ*: Brachyllae *Sig.*

---

147 Athamania, in the southeast of Epirus (*Barr.* 55 A2), became independent of Epirus about 230. Its king, Amynander, a relative of Scerdilaedas, had been instrumental in arranging the Peace of Phoenice in 205.   148 Cf. 33.28.1–29.12.

assistance was far off and Antiochus, whom they could not resist with their own forces, stood at their gates as an enemy.

In reply Micythio, one of their leading citizens, said he wondered for whose liberation it was that Antiochus had left his realm and crossed to Europe; for there was not a single state in Greece that he was aware of that had a garrison, paid tribute to Rome, or endured laws it did not want through the obligations of a one-sided treaty. The people of Chalcis therefore needed no one to champion their freedom, as they were free, and no protection since, thanks to the same Roman people, they had peace and their freedom. They were not rejecting friendship with the king or with the Aetolians themselves. The first thing they could do as friends, he said, would be to quit their island and withdraw; for the Chalcidians were determined not only not to welcome them within their walls, but not even to conclude any alliance without the approval of the Romans.

47. This was reported to the king at the ships, where he had remained, and for the moment—for he had not come with sufficient troops to be able to take forceful action—he decided to return to Demetrias. There, since their first endeavor had come to nothing, the king conferred with the Aetolians on what should be done next. They decided to approach the Boeotians, the Achaeans and Amynander, the Athamanian king.[147] They thought that the Boeotian people had been hostile to the Romans ever since the death of Brachylles and what followed it,[148] and they believed that Philopoemen, the leading Achaean,

riae in bello Laconum infestum invisumque esse Quinctio
5 credebant. Amynander uxorem Apamam, filiam Alexandri
cuiusdam Megalopolitani, habebat, qui, se oriundum a
magno Alexandro ferens, filiis duobus Philippum atque
6 Alexandrum et filiae Apamam nomina imposuerat; quam
regiis[51] inclutam nuptiis maior e fratribus Philippus secu-
7 tus in Athamaniam fuerat. hunc forte ingenio vanum Aetoli et Antiochus impulerant in spem Macedoniae regni,
quod is vere regum stirpis esset, si Amynandrum Athama-
8 nesque Antiocho coniunxisset; et ea vanitas promissorum
non apud Philippum modo sed etiam apud Amynandrum
valuit.

48. In Achaia legatis Antiochi Aetolorumque coram T.
2 Quinctio Aegii datum est concilium. Antiochi legatus prior
quam Aetoli est auditus. is, ut plerique quos opes regiae
alunt, vaniloquus maria terrasque inani sonitu verborum
3 complevit: equitum innumerabilem vim traici Hellesponto in Europam, partim loricatos, quos cataphractos
vocant, partim sagittis ex equo utentes, et a quo nihil satis
4 tecti sit, averso refugientes equo certius figentes. his

---

51 regiis *ed. Rom.*: regis Bχ

---

149 Cf. 30.12–13 above and note.

150 Greek Apame. The name remained in the families of Alexander's successors after Apame, daughter of the Bactrian chieftain Spitamenes, was married to Alexander's companion Seleucus
at Susa in 324 (Arr. *Anab.* 7.4.6).

151 Literally, "he filled the seas and lands with the empty
sound of his words."   152 Soldiers wearing mail breastplates
(κατάφρακτος, mail-clad): cf. *OLD* s.v. *cataphractus*.

was ill disposed to, and hated by, Quinctius because they had been rivals for glory in the Spartan campaign.[149] As for Amynander, he had a wife, Apama, daughter of a certain Alexander of Megalopolis who, claiming descent from Alexander the Great, had given the names Philip and Alexander to his two sons, and Apama[150] to his daughter. The daughter had gained fame through her royal marriage and her elder brother Philip had followed her to Athamania. This man happened to be an egotistical character and the Aetolians and Antiochus had led him to hopes of gaining the throne of Macedon—he was, indeed, of royal stock, they said—if he brought Amynander and the Athamanians to join Antiochus. And these empty promises of theirs proved effective not only with Philip but with Amynander, too.

48. In Achaea, the delegations from Antiochus and the Aetolians were granted a hearing at a council in the presence of Titus Quinctius at Aegium. Antiochus' ambassador was heard before the Aetolians. Like most who are sustained by a king's resources, the man blustered, making out with empty rhetoric that seas and lands would be filled with troops.[151] A countless force of horsemen was being transported to Europe by way of the Hellespont, he said. Some of these were men wearing breastplates, the so-called *cataphracti*;[152] others were warriors who shot arrows from horseback and—something against which there is no effective defense—found their mark more accurately when they had turned their horses in flight.[153] Even if the

[153] The famed "Parthian shot" was a stock theme in Roman literature after Crassus' disastrous defeat at Carrhae in 53 BC.

equestribus copiis quamquam vel totius Europae exerci-
5 tus in unum coacti obrui possent, adiciebat multiplices
copias peditum et nominibus quoque gentium vix fando
auditis terrebat, Dahas Medos Elymaeosque et Cadusios
6 appellans; navalium vero copiarum, quas nulli portus capere in Graecia possent, dextrum cornu Sidonios et Tyrios,
sinistrum Aradios et ex Pamphylia Sidetas tenere, quas
gentes nullae unquam nec arte nec virtute navali ae-
7 quassent. iam pecuniam iam alios belli apparatus referre
supervacaneum esse: scire ipsos abundasse auro semper
regna Asiae. itaque non cum Philippo nec Hannibale rem
futuram Romanis, principe altero unius civitatis, altero
Macedoniae tantum regni finibus incluso, sed cum magno
8 Asiae totius partisque Europae rege. eum tamen, quamquam ab ultimis orientis terminis ad liberandam Graeciam
veniat, nihil postulare ab Achaeis in quo fides eorum adversus Romanos, priores socios atque amicos, laedatur;
9 non enim ut secum adversus eos arma capiant, sed ut neu-
tri parti sese coniungant petere. pacem utrique parti, quod
medios deceat amicos, optent: bello se non interponant.
10 Idem ferme et Aetolorum legatus Archidamus petiit[52]
ut, quae facillima et tutissima esset, quietem praestarent,

---

[52] peti⟨i⟩t *Fr. 1*: petit χ: peti *B*

---

[154] All four are middle-eastern peoples, but the Medes stand
out as being well-known in Greco-Roman literature and certainly
not "barely heard in conversation." They are, moreover, missing
from the list in Flamininus' reply (49.8, below), and Briscoe
(2.212) wonders whether the word should be deleted.

[155] From Arados, an island town off the Phoenician coast
(*Barr.* 68 A4), and Side, on the Pamphylian coast (*Barr.* 65 F4).

armies of all Europe were brought together, they could be crushed by these cavalry forces, said the ambassador—but even so he kept adding to the list of infantry forces and tried to intimidate his audience with the names of races barely heard in conversation, citing "the Dahae," "the Medes," "the Elymaeans," and "the Cadusians."[154] Then there were the naval forces that no harbors in Greece could possibly contain: on the right wing Sidonians and Tyrians, on the left Aradians and Sidetans[155] from Pamphylia, races that no others had ever matched in skill or naval prowess. It was unnecessary by now to talk of money or other resources for the war, he said—the Achaeans themselves knew that the kingdoms of Asia had always been awash with gold. So the Romans would be dealing not with a Philip or a Hannibal—one the leader of a single city-state, the other limited merely to the territory of the kingdom of Macedonia—but with the great king of all Asia and part of Europe. Even so, although he was coming from the farthest bounds of the East to liberate Greece, he made no demand on the Achaeans by which their loyalty to the Romans, their earlier allies and friends, would be compromised. He was not asking them to take up arms with him against the Romans but simply to join neither side. They should wish for peace for both parties, as was appropriate for friends standing between the two, and not take part in the war.

The request of Archidamus, the representative of the Aetolians,[156] was much the same, namely that the Achae-

---

[156] He was three times *strategos* of the league and led the Aetolian troops under Flamininus at Cynoscephalae in 197. Here he appears as leader of the anti-Roman faction.

spectatoresque belli fortunarum alienarum eventum sine
11 ullo discrimine rerum suarum opperirentur. provectus
deinde est intemperantia linguae in maledicta nunc
communiter Romanorum, nunc proprie ipsius Quincti,
12 ingratos appellans et exprobrans non victoriam modo de
Philippo virtute Aetolorum partam sed etiam salutem,
13 ipsumque et exercitum sua opera servatos. quo enim illum
unquam imperatoris functum officio esse? auspicantem
immolantemque et vota nuncupantem sacrificuli uatis
modo in acie vidisse, cum ipse corpus suum pro eo telis
hostium obiceret.

49. Ad ea Quinctius coram quibus magis quam apud
quos verba faceret dicere Archidamum rationem habuisse:
2 Achaeos enim probe scire Aetolorum omnem ferociam in
verbis non in factis esse, et in conciliis magis contionibus-
3 que quam in acie apparere; itaque parui Achaeorum exis-
timationem, quibus notos esse se scirent, fecisse; legatis
4 regis et per eos absenti regi eum se iactasse. quod si quis
antea ignorasset quae res Antiochum et Aetolos coniunxisset, ex legatorum sermone potuisse apparere: mentiendo
in vicem iactandoque vires quas non haberent, inflasse
vana spe atque inflatos esse.

---

157 A general took the auspices (divination by various means;
cf. *OLD* s.v. *auspicium,* Levene 3–4) before commencing a campaign or committing himself to battle.

158 Polybius (18.21.5) gives Archidamus (spelled "Archeda-
mus"), Eupolemus (also an Aetolian), and two Roman tribunes
credit for effective action at Cynoscephalae, but does not mention
this.

ans should remain at peace, the easiest and safest course; watching the conflict, they should wait to see how the fortunes of others turned out without putting their own at risk. Then his outspokenness ran away with him as he descended to insulting the Romans in general at one point and Quinctius himself specifically at another. The Romans were ungrateful, he said, and he sneeringly claimed that not only their victory over Philip but even their survival was achieved through the courage of the Aetolians, that it was by them that Quinctius himself and his army had been saved. What duty of a commander had Quinctius ever discharged, he asked. He had seen him in the battlefield taking the auspices,[157] making offerings and uttering vows like some little priest at sacrifice, while he himself was throwing his body in the way of the enemy's weapons on his behalf.[158]

49. In reply Quinctius commented that Archidamus had taken into account those present at his address more than those at whom the address was directed. For, he said, Achaeans were well aware that all the pugnacity of Aetolians lay in talk, not action, and was more to be observed in their meetings and assemblies than on the battlefield. Thus Archidamus had not been much concerned with the opinion of the Achaeans, aware as he was that he and the Aetolians were well known to them—it was to the king's envoys, and through them to the absent king, that his ranting had been directed. If anyone had been unaware earlier of what it was that had brought Antiochus and the Aetolians together, it could have been easily seen in what their delegates said. By lying to each other, and boasting of strength that they did not possess they had managed to fill each other with groundless expectations.

5   "Dum hi ab se victum Philippum, sua virtute protectos Romanos, et quae modo audiebatis, narrant vos ceterasque civitates et gentes suam sectam esse secuturos, rex contra peditum equitumque nubes iactat et consternit ma-
6 ria classibus suis. est autem res simillima cenae Chalcidensis hospitis mei, et hominis boni et sciti conuivatoris, apud quem solstitiali tempore comiter accepti cum miraremur
7 unde illi eo tempore anni tam varia et multa venatio, homo non qua[53] isti sunt gloriosus renidens condimentis ait varietatem illam et speciem ferinae carnis ex mansueto sue
8 factam." hoc dici apte in copias regis, quae paulo ante iactatae sint, posse; varia enim genera armorum et multa nomina gentium inauditarum, Dahas[54] et Cadusios et Elymaeos, Syros omnes esse, haud paulo mancipiorum melius propter servilia ingenia quam militum genus.
9   "Et utinam subicere vestris oculis, Achaei, possem concursationem regis magni ab Demetriade nunc Lamiam
10 in concilium Aetolorum, nunc Chalcidem: videretis vix duarum male plenarum legiuncularum instar in castris regis, videretis regem nunc mendicantem prope frumen-
11 tum ab Aetolis quod militi admetiatur, nunc mutuas pecu-

---

[53] non qua *Asc. (1510)*: non quam *Bχ*: numquam *a*: non quam ut *Mg*: non quantum *Weiss*.
[54] Dahas *ed. Rom.*: Dacas *Bφ*: Datas *ψ* et *Bχ*: et Medos et *ed. Rom.*

---

[159] That is, the delegates from Antiochus and the Aetolians.
[160] Plutarch (*Flam.* 17.4) also cites this anecdote in connection with Antiochus' troops, so it presumably originates with Polybius. In the same chapter he also cites Flamininus' comparison of the Peloponnese with the tortoise (*Flam.* 17.2; cf. Livy 36.32.6–

"These men maintain that it was by them that Philip was defeated and by their courage that the Romans were protected," Quinctius continued. "And, as you heard just now, they say that you and the other states and peoples will subscribe to their views. The king, on the other hand, boasts of his 'clouds of infantry and cavalry' and covers the seas with his fleets! This is very much like a dinner party hosted by a Chalcidian friend of mine, a good man and a refined dining companion. It was the summer solstice and we were given a cordial welcome at his home, but we expressed our surprise at where he had been able to find such a variety and abundance of game at that time of year. The man, not boastful as those men are,[159] smiled and said that all those different meats that looked like wild game were, thanks to the seasonings, actually made from domesticated pig. This, said Quinctius, could be appropriately said of the king's troops, the subject of the boasting just now. The different kinds of arms, the many names of nations one had never heard of—Dahae, Cadusians, and Elymaeans—these were all only Syrians, who made much better slaves than soldiers because of their servile nature.[160]

"And, Achaeans," he continued, "I wish that I could set before your eyes the picture of this great king running from Demetrias, at one time to the council of the Aetolians at Lamia, at another to Chalcis. In the king's camp you would see what was barely the equivalent of two undermanned little legions, and you would see the king practically begging the Aetolians for grain to distribute to his

8), so this sort of anecdote may be typical of Flamininus' discourse.

nias faenore in stipendium quaerentem, nunc ad portas
Chalcidis stantem et mox, inde exclusum, nihil aliud quam
Aulide atque Euripo spectatis in Aetoliam redeuntem.
male crediderunt et Antiochus Aetolis et Aetoli regiae
12 vanitati; quo minus vos decipi debetis, sed expertae potius
13 spectataeque Romanorum fidei credere. nam quod optimum esse dicunt, non interponi vos bello, nihil immo tam
alienum rebus vestris est; quippe sine gratia sine dignitate
praemium victoris eritis."

50. Nec absurde adversus utrosque respondisse visus
est, et facile erat orationem apud faventes aequis auribus
2 accipi. nulla enim nec disceptatio nec dubitatio fuit quin
omnes eosdem genti Achaeorum hostes et amicos quos
populus Romanus censuisset iudicarent, bellumque et
3 Antiocho et Aetolis nuntiari iuberent. auxilia etiam quo
censuit Quinctius, quingentorum militum Chalcidem
4 quingentorum Piraeum extemplo miserunt. erat enim
haud procul seditione Athenis res, trahentibus ad Antiochum quibusdam spe largitionum venalem pretio multitudinem, donec ab iis qui Romanae partis erant Quinctius
est accitus, et accusante Leonte quodam Apollodorus auctor defectionis damnatus atque in exsilium est eiectus.

5 Et ab Achaeis quidem cum tristi responso legatio ad
regem rediit; Boeoti nihil certi responderunt: cum Antio-

troops, or requesting a loan (at interest) for their pay, or standing at the gates of Chalcis and then, shut out of the city, returning to Aetolia, having done no more than take a look at Aulis and Euripus! They both made a mistake, Antiochus in trusting the Aetolians, and the Aetolians in believing the king's empty promises. All the more reason for you not to be taken in. Instead, you should trust to the good faith of the Romans, which you have already experienced and put to the test. For the course that they claim is the best, namely nonintervention in the war—nothing, in fact, is so contrary to your best interests. Earning no gratitude and no consideration, you will become the prize of the victor."

50. Quinctius' response to the two delegations seemed to be on the mark and his speech, delivered before supporters, was readily accepted by willing ears. There was no debate or hesitation; the participants unanimously voted that the Achaean people would regard as their enemies and their friends those whom the Roman people had themselves judged as such, and they authorized war to be declared on Antiochus and the Aetolians. Furthermore, they immediately sent auxiliaries to the destinations specified by Quinctius, 500 fighting men to Chalcis and 500 to Piraeus. For there was almost a state of civil war at Athens where, with the prospect of enrichment, some were trying to win over the common people, who are easily bought. Eventually, Quinctius was sent for by the pro-Roman faction, and Apollodorus, the man responsible for the disaffection, was condemned and driven into exile, on charges brought by a certain Leon.

The delegation returned to the king from the Achaeans with the unfavorable reply, and the Boeotians gave no

141

chus in Boeotiam venisset, tum quid sibi faciendum esset
se deliberaturos esse.

6   Antiochus cum ad Chalcidis praesidium et Achaeos et
Eumenem regem misisse audisset, maturandum ratus ut
7 et praevenirent sui, et venientes, si possent, exciperent,
Menippum cum tribus ferme milibus militum et cum[55]
omni classe Polyxenidan mittit, ipse paucos post dies sex
milia suorum militum et ex ea copia quae Lamiae repente
8 conligi potuit non ita multos Aetolos ducit. Achaei quingenti et ab Eumene rege modicum auxilium missum, duce
Xenoclide Chalcidensi, nondum obsessis itineribus tuto
9 transgressi Euripum, Chalcidem pervenerunt. Romani
milites, quingenti ferme et ipsi, cum iam Menippus castra
ante Salganea ad Hermaeum, qua transitus ex Boeotia in
10 Euboeam insulam est, haberet, venerunt. Micythio erat
cum iis, legatus ab Chalcide ad Quinctium ad id ipsum
11 praesidium petendum missus. qui postquam obsessas ab
hostibus[56] fauces vidit, omisso ad Aulidem itinere Delium
convertit, ut inde in Euboeam transmissurus.

    51. Templum est Apollinis Delium, imminens mari;
quinque milia passuum ab Tanagra abest; minus quattuor

55 cum Bχ: om. Mg
56 obsessas ab hostibus χ: ab hostibus obsessas B

---

161 Menippus was his ambassador to Rome in 193 (34.57.6–
59.7) and this year to the Aetolians (32.2–33.11, above).

162 An exiled Rhodian who as the admiral of the king's fleet
would have a large role in the Romans' war with Antiochus; cf.
36.8.1, 41.7ff.; 37.8.3, 10–13, 26–30.

163 For Xenoclides and Micythio (below), the loyal supporters
of Rome in Chalcis, cf. 38.1–2, above.

definite answer—they would consider what course to take only when Antiochus came to Boeotia, they said.

When Antiochus was told that both the Achaeans and King Eumenes had sent troops to garrison Chalcis, he thought he should move quickly so that his men could reach the city first and also, if possible, surprise the enemy on their arrival. He sent Menippus[161] off with about 3,000 soldiers and Polyxenidas[162] with the entire fleet, and a few days later himself led to Chalcis 6,000 of his own men and a rather small number of Aetolians taken from a force that could be quickly raised at Lamia. Since the roads had not yet been blockaded, the 500 Achaeans and a small auxiliary force sent by King Eumenes safely crossed the Euripus, led by Xenoclides[163] the Chalcidian, and reached Chalcis. The Roman soldiers, who also numbered about 500 themselves, arrived at a time when Menippus already had his camp set up before Salganeus near the shrine of Hermes, the crossing point from Boeotia to the isle of Euboea. With them was Micythio,[164] who had been sent as an envoy from Chalcis to Quinctius to request these very reinforcements, and when he saw the pass was held by the enemy he abandoned the march toward Aulis and headed instead for Delium, intending to cross to Euboea from there.

51. Delium[165] is a temple of Apollo that overlooks the sea. It is five miles from Tanagra, and by sea the crossing

[164] He and Xenoclides were Chalchis' two most powerful men (cf. 38.1, above), though Livy does not give their official position.

[165] Town on the northeast coast of Boeotia (*Barr.* 55 F4) famous for the Boeotian defeat of the Athenians in 424.

2 inde milium in proxima Euboeae est mari traiectus. ubi et
   in fano lucoque ea religione et eo iure sancto quo sunt
   templa quae asyla Graeci appellant, et nondum aut indicto
3 bello aut ita commisso ut strictos gladios aut sanguinem
   usquam factum audissent, cum per magnum otium milites
   alii ad spectaculum templi lucique versi, alii in litore
4 inermes vagarentur, magna pars per agros lignatum pabu-
   latumque dilapsa esset, repente Menippus palatos passim
   adgressus † eos †[57] cecidit, ad quinquaginta vivos cepit;
   perpauci effugerunt, in quibus Micythio parva oneraria
5 nave exceptus. ea res Quinctio Romanisque sicut iactura
   militum molesta, ita ad ius inferendi Antiocho belli adiecisse aliquantum videbatur.
6   Antiochus admoto ad Aulidem exercitu, cum rursus
   oratores partim ex suis partim Aetolos Chalcidem misisset
   qui eadem illa quae nuper cum minis gravioribus agerent,
   nequiquam contra Micythione et Xenoclide tendentibus
7 facile tenuit ut portae sibi aperirentur. qui Romanae partis
   erant sub adventum regis urbe excesserunt.
      Achaeorum et Eumenis milites Salganea tenebant, et
   in Euripo castellum Romani milites pauci custodiae causa
8 loci communiebant. Salganea Menippus, rex ipse castellum Euripi oppugnare est adortus. priores Achaei et Eu-

---

[57] eos *Bχ*: *numerum corruptum esse vid. Crév.*: ccc *Madvig*:
eorum ccc *Walsh*

---

[166] "Inviolate" (ἄσυλα).

[167] "them" translates the manuscript reading, but it is clearly
a corruption of the number killed in the attack (around three
hundred).

to the closest parts of Euboea is less than four miles. The Romans were in the shrine and its grove (which are venerable and sacrosanct, enjoying the same religious status as the temples that the Greeks call "asyla"[166]); war had not yet been declared, nor had there been any military brush serious enough to bring reports of swords drawn or blood shed in any quarter; and the soldiers were very much at ease as they wandered about, some visiting the temple and the grove, others strolling unarmed on the beach, while a large number had slipped off to gather firewood and food in the countryside. Suddenly Menippus attacked the widely scattered force, killed †them†[167] and took fifty alive. A very small number made good their escape, including Micythio, who was rescued by a small merchant vessel. While the incident was distressing for Quinctius and the Romans because of the loss of manpower it entailed, it did at the same time seem to have provided some further justification for opening hostilities against Antiochus.

Antiochus now moved his army up to Aulis. He then once more sent spokesmen—a number of his own men and a number of Aetolians—to Chalcis, to raise the same issues as had been recently discussed, but with more serious threats added; and despite opposition from Micythio and Xenoclides, he easily attained his object of having the gates opened to him. The members of the pro-Roman party left the city at the approach of the king.

The troops of the Achaeans and Eumenes now held Salganeus, and a few Roman soldiers proceeded to build a fortress on the Euripus to defend the spot. Menippus then began an assault on Salganeus, and the king himself on the fortress on the Euripus. The Achaeans and

145

menis milites, pacti ut sine fraude liceret abire, praesidio
9   excesserunt; pertinacius Romani Euripum tuebantur. hi
quoque tamen cum terra marique obsiderentur et iam
machinas tormentaque adportari viderent, non tulere
obsidionem.

10   Cum id, quod caput erat Euboeae, teneret rex, ne ceterae quidem insulae eius urbes imperium abnuerunt;
magnoque principio sibi orsus bellum videbatur, quod
tanta insula et tot opportunae urbes in suam dicionem
venissent.

Eumenes' men were the first to abandon their defensive position, striking a bargain that allowed them to depart in safety, but the Romans were more resolute in defending the Euripus. However, facing a blockade by land and sea, and seeing the engines and slings being brought up, they too failed to withstand the siege.

Since the king now held what was the most important position of Euboea, the other cities of the island did not reject his authority either. He felt that he had made a successful start to the war, seeing that such a large island and so many strategically positioned cities had come into his hands.

LIBRI XXXV PERIOCHA

P. Scipio Africanus, legatus ad Antiochum missus Ephesi cum Hannibale, qui se Antiocho adiunxerat, conlocutus est ut, si fieri posset, metum ei, quem ex populo R. conceperat, eximeret. inter alia cum quaereret quem fuisse maximum imperatorem Hannibal crederet, respondit Alexandrum, Macedonum regem, quod parva manu innumerabiles exercitus fudisset quodque ultimas oras, quas visere supra spem humanam esset, peragrasset. quaerenti deinde, quem secundum poneret, Pyrrhum, inquit, castra metari primum docuisse, ad hoc neminem loca elegantius cepisse, praesidia disposuisse. exsequenti quem tertium diceret, semet ipsum dixit. ridens Scipio: quidnam tu diceres, inquit, si me vicisses? Tunc vero me, inquit, et ante Alexandrum et ante Pyrrhum et ante alios posuissem.

Inter alia prodigia, quae plurima fuisse traduntur, bovem Cn. Domitii cos. Locutam: Roma cave tibi, refertur.

SUMMARY OF BOOK XXXV

Sent as an ambassador to Antiochus, Publius Scipio Africanus conversed with Hannibal (who had attached himself to Antiochus) with the aim of removing from him, if it could be done, the fear of the Roman people that he had developed. When, among other things, he asked Hannibal who he thought had been the greatest general, Hannibal replied Alexander, king of the Macedonians, because with a small number of men he had routed innumerable armies and because he had traveled to the farthest shores, visiting which lay beyond human expectations. When Scipio next asked him whom he placed second he said Pyrrhus: he was the man who had first shown how to lay out a camp, and in addition no one had shown such skill in choosing locations and stationing troops. To the further question of whom he declared third Hannibal replied himself. With a smile, Scipio said: "And what would you say if you had defeated me?" "Well, then, in that case," he replied, "I would have placed myself ahead of Alexander, Pyrrhus, and all the others."

Among the prodigies that occurred (which are reported to have been numerous), it is claimed that an ox belonging to the consul Gnaeus Domitius said "Rome, watch out for yourself."

Nabis, Lacedaemoniorum tyrannus, incitatus ab Aetolis, qui et Philippum et Antiochum ad inferendum bellum
populo R. sollicitabant, a populo R. descivit, sed bello
adversus Philopoemenen, Achaeorum praetorem, gesto
ab Aetolis interfectus est. Aetoli quoque ab amicitia populi
Romani defecerunt. cum societate iuncta Antiochus, Sy-
riae rex, bellum Graeciae intulisset, complures urbes
occupavit, inter quas Chalcidem et totam Euboeam. res
praeterea in Liguribus gestas et adparatum belli ab Antiocho continet.

Nabis, tyrant of the Lacedaemonians, abandoned the Roman people, incited to do so by the Aetolians, who were urging both Philip and Antiochus to open hostilities against the Roman people, but he was killed by the Aetolians in the war fought against Philolopoemen, praetor of the Achaeans. The Aetolians also abandoned their alliance with the Roman people. When, forming a pact with the Aetolians, Antiochus king of Syria launched a war against Greece, he seized numerous cities, including Chalcis and all of Euboea. The book also contains operations conducted among the Ligurians and Antiochus' preparations for war.

LIBER XXXVI

1. P. Cornelium Cn. f. Scipionem et M'. Acilium Gla-
2 brionem consules, inito magistratu, patres priusquam de
provinciis agerent res divinas facere maioribus hostiis iusserunt in omnibus fanis in quibus lectisternium maiorem
partem anni fieri solet, precarique quod senatus de novo
bello in animo haberet, ut ea res senatui populoque Ro-
3 mano bene ac feliciter eveniret. ea omnia sacrificia laeta
fuerunt, primisque hostiis perlitatum est, et ita haruspices
responderunt, eo bello terminos populi Romani propa-
4 gari, victoriam ac triumphum ostendi. haec cum renun-

---

1 P. Cornelius (30) Scipio Nasica, son of Cn. Cornelius Scipio
Calvus (killed in Spain in 212) and cousin of Scipio Africanus. He
was especially noted for having been chosen as the best citizen to
receive the statue of Cybele (the Magna Mater) in Rome from
Pessinus in Asia Minor in 204 (cf. 35.10.9 and note, and 29.14.5–
14). He had served in Spain with distinction as praetor in 194. M'.
Acilius (35) Glabrio, a *novus homo* who rose to the consulship,
was tribune of the plebs in 201 and praetor in 196. He would
distinguish himself in the war with Antiochus. For the election of
the two, cf. 35.24.5.

2 Sacrificial animals were either unweaned (*lactantes*) or full-
grown (*maiores*). The looming war with Antiochus merited the
full-grown animals.

BOOK XXXVI

1. The consuls Publius Cornelius Scipio, son of Gnaeus Cornelius, and Manius Acilius Glabrio[1] had started their term of office when the senate instructed them to see to offering sacrifices before attending to the question of their provinces. They were to use full-grown victims[2] and sacrifice at all the shrines in which the *lectisternium*[3] was normally practiced for most of the year; and they were also to offer prayers asking that the new war that the senate had in mind might have a prosperous and successful outcome for the senate and people of Rome. All the sacrifices proved auspicious, a favorable omen was obtained with the first victims, and the *haruspices*[4] replied that the bounds of the Roman people would be extended by the war and that victory and a triumph were presaged. When

---

[3] Of Greek origin, and first recorded in 399 BC, the *lectisternium* was a ritual banquet for the gods put on to secure their favor, at first in periods of disease but later also in time of war. Figures of the gods were set out on couches and meals set before them in front of their temples. These perpetual *lectisternia*, however (cf. also 42.30.8), seem to be restricted to this period. Cf. *OLD* s.v. *lectisternium.*

[4] Priests of divination, originally Etrurian, especially connected with the interpretation of the entrails of sacrificial animals.

tiata essent, solutis religione animis patres rogationem ad populum ferri iusserunt, vellent iuberentne cum Antiocho
5 rege, quique eius sectam secuti essent, bellum iniri; si ea perlata rogatio esset, tum si ita videretur consulibus, rem integram ad senatum referrent.

6 P. Cornelius eam rogationem pertulit; tum senatus decrevit ut consules Italiam et Graeciam provincias sortirentur; cui Graecia evenisset, ut praeter eum numerum militum quem L. Quinctius consul in eam provinciam ex
7 auctoritate senatus scripsisset imperassetue, ut eum exercitum acciperet quem M. Baebius praetor anno priore ex
8 senatus consulto in Macedoniam traiecisset; et extra Italiam permissum ut si res postulasset, auxilia ab sociis ne supra quinque milium numerum acciperet. L. Quinctium
9 superioris anni consulem legari ad id bellum placuit. alter consul, cui Italia provincia evenisset, cum Boiis iussus bellum gerere utro exercitu mallet ex duobus quos superiores consules habuissent, alterum ut mitteret Romam, eaeque urbanae legiones essent paratae quo senatus censuisset.

2. His ita in senatu, incerto ad id[1] quae cuius provincia foret, decretis, tum demum sortiri consules placuit. Acilio
2 Graecia Cornelio Italia evenit. certa deinde sorte senatus

---

[1] incerto ad id *Koch*: ad id *Bχ*: haud ad id *Madvig*: intento ad id *Weiss*.

---

[5] The formula used when the senators set before the popular assembly the decision to go to war (or make peace): cf. 21.17.4, 30.43.2, 33.25.6, etc.   [6] Cf. 35.41.5.

[7] M. Baebius Tamphilus (44), later consul in 181; for his crossing from Brundisium to Epirus: 35.24.7.   [8] Flamininus and Cn. Domitius Ahenobarbus (18) (*MRR* 350).

this was reported the senators' minds were freed from religious obligations and they issued orders for the question to be formally put to the people whether it was their wish and command[5] that war be initiated with Antiochus and those who had followed his lead. Should the motion be passed, the consuls, if they agreed, were to refer the entire matter back to the senate.

Publius Cornelius carried the motion, and then the senate decreed that the consuls should proceed to sortition for the provinces of Italy and Greece. The one drawing Greece was to command the troops that Lucius Quinctius had as consul enrolled or conscripted for the province on senatorial authority,[6] in addition to the army that the praetor Marcus Baebius had taken across to Macedonia the previous year, in accordance with a senatorial decree.[7] He was also permitted to take auxiliary forces from the allies outside Italy, if the situation warranted, but no more than 5,000 men. It was further decided that the previous year's consul, Lucius Quinctius, should be sent to the war as a legate. The other consul, to whom Italy fell as his province, was ordered to conduct the war against the Boii with whichever army he preferred of the two that the previous consuls[8] had commanded. The other army he was to send to Rome to form the city legions,[9] and these were to be ready to move to wherever the senate decided.

2. These decisions were taken in the senate while it was still undecided which consul would have which command, but eventually it was determined that the consular sortition should be held. Greece fell to Acilius and Italy to

[9] Legions stationed in Rome to meet emergencies.

consultum factum est, quod populus Romanus[2] duellum
iussisset esse cum rege Antiocho, quique sub imperio eius
essent, ut eius rei causa supplicationem imperarent consules, utique M'. Acilius consul ludos magnos Iovi voveret
3 et dona ad omnia pulvinaria. id votum in haec verba,
praeeunte P. Licinio pontifice maximo, consul nuncupavit:
"si duellum, quod cum rege Antiocho sumi populus iussit,
id ex sententia senatus populique Romani confectum erit,
4 tum tibi, Iuppiter, populus Romanus ludos magnos dies
decem continuos faciet, donaque ad omnia pulvinaria
5 dabuntur de pecunia quantam senatus decreverit. quis-
quis magistratus eos ludos quando ubique faxit, hi ludi
recte facti donaque data recte sunto." supplicatio inde ab
duobus consulibus edicta per biduum fuit.

6   Consulibus sortitis provincias, extemplo et praetores
sortiti sunt. M. Iunio Bruto iurisdictio utraque evenit, A.
Cornelio Mammulae Bruttii, M. Aemilio Lepido Sicilia, L.
Oppio Salinatori Sardinia, C. Livio Salinatori classis, L.
Aemilio Paullo Hispania ulterior.

---

2 quod populus Romanus $B\psi$ ϕmg: quo tempore ϕ: quod
populus Romanus eo tempore *ed. Rom.*

---

10 Cf. 35.8.3 and note.

11 That is, a *lectisternium*.

12 As Walsh ad loc. notes, Livy's citation of the vow in full
reveals the importance he attaches to religious observance.

13 The law was the original sphere of the praetors, the praetor
urbanus handling citizens' cases, and the praetor peregrinus
those involving noncitizens. When urgent matters required that
one praetor serve in another area, the other might be required to
take on such a "double jurisdiction."

Cornelius. Then, the sortition decided, a senatorial decree was passed to the effect that, inasmuch as the Roman people had ruled that there was war with King Antiochus and those under his command, the consuls should declare a supplication[10] for success therein and the consul Manius Acilius should make a vow of great games to Jupiter, and of gifts at all the couches of the gods.[11] That vow, dictated by the *pontifex maximus* Publius Licinius, the consul pronounced publicly as follows: "As regards the war that the people have ordered undertaken with King Antiochus, should this be concluded as the senate and people of Rome desire, then the Roman people shall celebrate great games for ten successive days in your honor, Jupiter, and gifts shall be presented at all the couches, the amount of funding being at the discretion of the senate. Whichever magistrate celebrates these games, and whenever and wherever he does so, let it be deemed that the games have been duly celebrated and the gifts duly presented."[12] After this, a two-day period of supplication was proclaimed by the two consuls.

The consular sortition of provinces completed, the praetors immediately drew lots for theirs. The double jurisdiction[13] fell to Marcus Iunius Brutus, Bruttium to Aulus Cornelius Mammula, Sicily to Marcus Aemilius Lepidus,[14] Sardinia to Lucius Oppius Salinator, the fleet to Gaius Livius Salinator and Farther Spain to Lucius Aemilius Paullus.

[14] M. Aemilius Lepidus (68): curule aedile (193), praetor this year, consul 187 and again in 175, and censor in 179.

7   His ita exercitus decreti: A. Cornelio novi milites, conscripti priore anno ex senatus consulto a L. Quinctio consule, dati sunt, iussusque tueri omnem oram circa Tarentum

8   Brundisiumque. L. Aemilio Paullo in ulteriorem Hispaniam, praeter eum exercitum quem a M. Fulvio proconsule accepturus esset, decretum[3] ut novorum militum tria milia duceret et trecentos equites, ita ut in iis duae partes socium Latini nominis, tertia civium Romanorum esset. idem supplementi ad C. Flaminium, cui imperium

9   prorogabatur, in Hispaniam citeriorem est missum.

10   M. Aemilius Lepidus ab L. Valerio, cui successurus esset,

11   simul provinciam exercitumque accipere iussus; L. Valerium, si ita videretur, pro praetore in provincia retinere et provinciam ita dividere ut una ab Agrigento ad Pachynum esset, altera a Pachyno Tyndareum; eam maritimam oram

12   L. Valerius viginti navibus longis custodiret. eidem praetori mandatum ut duas decumas frumenti exigeret; id ad mare comportandum devehendumque in Graeciam curaret.

13   idem L. Oppio de alteris decumis exigendis in Sardinia imperatum; ceterum non in Graeciam sed Romam id

14   frumentum portari placere. C. Livius praetor, cui classis evenerat, triginta navibus paratis traicere in Graeciam primo quoque tempore iussus, et ab Atilio naves accipere.

[3] decretum *B*χ: decretum est *Mg*

---

15 Cf. 35.7.5 note.

16 For M. Aemilius Lepidus, cf. 35.10.11.

17 L. Valerius (350) Tappo; cf. 35.23.8 and note.

18 *Barr.* 47: Agrigentum, D4; Pachynus, G5; Tyndaris, G2.

To these men the armies were officially distributed as follows: Aulus Cornelius was given the new recruits conscripted the previous year by the consul Lucius Quinctius in compliance with a decree of the senate, and he was instructed to protect the entire coastline around Tarentum and Brundisium. For Farther Spain, Lucius Aemilius Paullus, in addition to the army he was to assume from the proconsul Marcus Fulvius, was further authorized by decree to take there 3,000 new infantry and 300 cavalry, two thirds of whom were to be allies and men with Latin rights[15] and one third Roman citizens. Gaius Flaminius, whose *imperium* was prorogued, was sent the same supplementary force for service in Hither Spain. Marcus Aemilius Lepidus[16] was instructed to take over both the province and its army from Lucius Valerius,[17] whom he was to succeed. If Lepidus agreed, he was to retain Lucius Valerius as propraetor in the province, which he should divide in two, one section running from Agrigentum to Pachynus, and the other from Pachynus to Tyndaris[18] (and Lucius Valerius should protect the coastline of the latter section with 20 warships). The same praetor was also ordered to commandeer two tithes of grain, and see to its being transported to the sea and then ferried to Greece. Lucius Oppius was given the same order with respect to a second set of two tithes in Sardinia, only in this case it was decided that the grain should be taken not to Greece but Rome. The praetor Gaius Livius, to whom the fleet had been allotted, was instructed to prepare thirty ships and cross to Greece at the earliest possible moment. There he was to assume command of the ships that had been under

15 veteres naves, quae in navalibus erant, ut reficeret et armaret, M. Iunio praetori negotium datum est, et in eam classem socios navales libertinos legeret.

3. Legati terni in Africam ad Carthaginienses et in Numidiam ad frumentum rogandum, quod in Graeciam portaretur, missi, pro quo pretium solveret populus Roma-

2 nus. adeoque in apparatum curamque eius belli civitas

3 intenta fuit ut P. Cornelius consul ediceret, qui senatores essent quibusque in senatu sententiam dicere liceret, quique minores magistratus essent, ne quis eorum longius ab urbe Roma abiret quam unde eodem[4] die redire posset, neve uno tempore quinque senatores ab urbe Roma abessent.

4 In comparanda impigre classe C. Livium praetorem contentio orta cum colonis maritimis paulisper tenuit.

5 nam cum cogerentur in classem, tribunos plebi appellarunt; ab iis ad senatum reiecti sunt. senatus, ita ut ad unum omnes consentirent, decrevit vacationem rei navalis eis

6 colonis non esse. Ostia et Fregenae et Castrum Novum et Pyrgi et Antium et Tarracina et Minturnae et Sinuessa fuerunt quae cum praetore de vacatione certarunt.[5]

7 Consul deinde M'. Acilius ex senatus consulto ad col-

[4] eodem *Fügner*: eo *Bχ*
[5] certarunt *Holk. 353*: certarent *B*: certaverunt *χ*

---

[19] A. Atilius Serranus (60): praetor 192 and 173, consul 170. Cf. 34.54.3. He is to be a major figure in the war with Antiochus.
[20] That is, those not yet formally admitted to the senate by the censors but who had held offices that made them eligible for membership.

Atilius.[19] The praetor Marcus Iunius was assigned the task of repairing and equipping the old vessels in the dockyards, and he was to enlist freedmen as sailors to man that fleet.

3. Envoys were sent to Africa—three to the Carthaginians and three also to Numidia—to ask for grain, which was to be transported to Greece (and for which the Roman people would pay). So absorbed was the community in arrangements and preparation for the war that the consul Publius Cornelius issued an edict relating to all senators, all those with the right to vote in the senate,[20] and all minor magistrates: no one was to go so far from the city of Rome that he could not return on the same day, and five senators were not to be absent from the city at the same time.[21]

The praetor Gaius Livius was now busily engaged in assembling a fleet but an argument that arose with members of the maritime colonies briefly distracted him. Being pressed into service in the fleet, these men appealed to the plebeian tribunes and by them their case was referred to the senate. The senate then decided, with complete unanimity, that the colonists should have no exemption from naval duty. The colonies in dispute with the praetor over the exemptions were Ostia, Fregenae, Castrum Novum, Pyrgi, Antium, Terracina, Minturnae, and Sinuessa.[22]

The consul Manius Acilius, following a decree of the

[21] This is the first mention of such a restriction; for a similar emergency measure enacted later, cf. 43.11.4–5.

[22] Towns on the coast of Latium: *Barr.* 44 A1–E3.

legium fetialium rettulit, ipsine utique regi Antiocho indi-
ceretur bellum, an satis esset ad praesidium aliquod eius
8 nuntiari;[6] et num Aetolis quoque separatim indici iuberent
bellum, et num prius societas et amicitia eis renuntianda
9 esset quam bellum indicendum. fetiales responderunt iam
ante sese, cum de Philippo consulerentur, decrevisse nihil
10 referre ipsi coram an ad praesidium nuntiaretur; amicitiam renuntiatam videri, cum legatis totiens repetentibus
11 res nec reddi nec satisfieri aequum censuissent; Aetolos
ultro sibi bellum indixisse, cum Demetriadem, sociorum
12 urbem, per vim occupassent, Chalcidem terra marique
oppugnatum issent, regem Antiochum in Europam ad bellum populo Romano inferendum traduxissent.
13   Omnibus iam satis comparatis, M'. Acilius consul edixit
ut quos L. Quinctius milites conscripsisset et quos sociis
nominique Latino imperasset, quos secum in provinciam
ire oporteret, et tribuni militum legionis primae et tertiae,
14 ut ii omnes Brundisium idibus Maiis convenirent. ipse
ante diem quintum nonas Maias paludatus urbe egressus
est. per eosdem dies et praetores in provincias profecti
sunt.

4. Sub idem tempus legati ab duobus regibus, Philippo

---

[6] nuntiari *Kreyssig*: nuntiaret *B*: nuntiare χ

---

[23] See further *OCD* s.v. *fetiales*. Priests, twenty in number,
whose area of expertise was the declaration of wars and the making and observation of treaties, on which they advised to the
senate.   [24] Cf. 31.8.2–3.   [25] Cf. 35.34.5–11.
[26] Cf. 35.37.4–38.13, 46.2–13, 51.6–7.   [27] Cf 35.7.5 note.
[28] Latin *paludamentum:* a cloak fastened with a brooch at the
shoulder worn by generals on active service.

senate, then consulted the college of *fetiales*,[23] asking whether the declaration of war should be delivered to Antiochus in person or whether it sufficed for an announcement to be made at one of his military outposts. He also asked if the *fetiales* enjoined a separate declaration of war for the Aetolians and whether the alliance and friendship with them should be formally renounced before that declaration was made. The *fetiales* replied that they had already given their decision (when they were consulted about Philip)[24] that it was immaterial whether the declaration was made directly to the person or to a military outpost. As for the friendship, that was evidently renounced because, they said, they had decided that despite repeated demands made by Roman ambassadors no restitution or equitable compensation had been made. The Aetolians had themselves declared war on the Romans when they forcefully occupied Demetrias,[25] a city of their allies, launched an attack by land and sea on Chalcis,[26] and brought King Antiochus over to Europe to make war on the Roman people.

All the preparations now satisfactorily completed, the consul Manius Acilius issued a proclamation for a general mobilization at Brundisium on May 15th of those troops that Lucius Quinctius had enlisted or requisitioned from the allies and holders of Latin rights[27]—that is, the troops that were to go with him to his province—as well as the military tribunes of the first and third legions. Acilius himself set out from the city wearing his general's cloak[28] on May 3rd, and the praetors also left for their provinces at about the same date.

4. It was around this same time that ambassadors came to Rome from two kings, Philip and King Ptolemy of

et Ptolomaeo Aegypti rege, Romam venerunt, Philippo
pollicente[7] ad bellum auxilia et pecuniam et frumentum;
2 ab Ptolomaeo mille pondo auri, viginti milia[8] pondo ar-
3 genti allata. nihil eius acceptum; gratiae regibus actae; et
cum uterque se cum omnibus copiis in Aetoliam venturum
belloque interfuturum polliceretur, Ptolomaeo id remis-
4 sum; Philippi legatis responsum gratum eum senatui populoque Romano facturum si M'. Acilio consuli non de-
fuisset.
5 Item ab Carthaginiensibus et Masinissa rege legati
venerunt. Carthaginienses tritici modium quingenta[9] milia hordei quingenta ad exercitum, dimidium eius Romam
6 apportaturos polliciti: id ut ab se munus Romani acciperent, petere sese; et classem suo sumptu comparaturos,
7 et stipendium, quod pluribus pensionibus in multos annos
8 deberent, praesens omne daturos; Masinissae legati quingenta milia modium tritici trecenta hordei ad exercitum in
Graeciam, Romam trecenta milia modium tritici ducenta
quinquaginta hordei, equites quingentos elephantos tri-
9 ginta regem ad M'. Acilium consulem missurum. de frumento utrisque responsum ita usurum eo populum Romanum si pretium acciperent; de classe Carthaginiensibus
remissum, praeterquam si quid navium ex foedere de-

---

[7] Philippo pollicente . . . mille *Mg*: pollicentes . . . etiam mille
Bχ   [8] viginti milia *ψAE Gel.*: viginti *BP*: ducenta quin-
quaginta duo *Mg*   [9] modium quingenta *M. Müller*: modium
Bχ: *lac. post* modium *Weiss. (1862)*

---

[29] In response to the request made to the Carthaginians and
Numidians (3.1, above).
[30] Under the treaty of 201 (cf. 30.37.5, Polyb. 15.18.7, App.

164

Egypt. Philip promised to supply reinforcements, money and grain for the war effort, and from Ptolemy there arrived 1,000 pounds of gold and 20,000 pounds of silver. None of this was accepted; the kings were both thanked for their offers; and both also made a pledge to come to Aetolia with all their forces and participate in the war. Ptolemy was excused from this, and Philip's envoys were given the answer that the senate and people of Rome people would be grateful if he simply did not withhold his assistance from the consul Manius Acilius.

Envoys also came from the Carthaginians and King Masinissa.[29] The Carthaginians gave an undertaking to bring 500,000 measures of wheat and 500,000 of barley to the army and half that amount to Rome. They were asking the Romans to accept this as a gift from them, they said, adding that they would also put together a fleet at their own expense and discharge in full with a single payment the indemnity that they were under obligation to pay in several installments over a number of years.[30] The envoys of Masinissa promised that their king would send 500,000 measures of wheat and 300,000 of barley to the army in Greece, 300,000 measures of wheat and 250,000 of barley to Rome, and 500 cavalry plus 30 elephants to the consul Manius Acilius. With respect to the grain, the answer given to both parties was that the Roman people would avail themselves of the offer if the parties accepted payment. With regard to the fleet, the Carthaginians' offer was declined except for such ships as they owed under their treaty, and in the matter of money the response was

Pun. 54) it was ten thousand talents over fifty years. Cf. Walbank 2.470.

berent; de pecunia item responsum nullam ante diem accepturos.

5. Cum haec Romae agebantur, Chalcide Antiochus, ne cessaret per hibernorum tempus, partim ipse sollicitabat civitatium animos mittendis legatis, partim ultro ad eum veniebant, sicut Epirotae communi gentis consensu et

2 Elei e Peloponneso venerunt. Elei auxilium adversus Achaeos petebant, quos post bellum non ex sua sententia indictum Antiocho primum civitati suae arma inlaturos

3 credebant.[10] mille iis pedites cum duce Cretensi Euphane sunt missi.

Epirotarum legatio erat minime in partem ullam liberi aut simplicis animi; apud regem gratiam initam volebant

4 cum eo ut caverent ne quid offenderent Romanos, petebant enim ne se temere in causam deduceret, expositos adversus Italiam pro omni Graecia et primos impetus

5 Romanorum excepturos; sed si ipse posset terrestribus navalibusque copiis praesidere Epiro, cupide eum omnes Epirotas et urbibus et portibus suis accepturos; si id non posset, deprecari ne se nudos atque inermes Romano

6 bello obiceret. hac legatione id agi apparebat ut sive, quod magis credebant, abstinuisset Epiro, integra sibi omnia apud exercitus Romanos essent, conciliata satis apud re-

7 gem gratia, quod accepturi fuissent venientem, sive venisset, sic quoque spes veniae ab Romanis foret, quod non

[10] credebant *Harl. 2671*: *om.* Bχ

---

[31] The Carthaginians appear to be trying to maintain good relations with the Romans after Hannibal's flight to Antiochus in 195, and the Romans to be keeping them at arm's length.

likewise that the Romans would accept none before the due date.[31]

5. While this was taking place in Rome, Antiochus was at Chalcis. Not to remain idle during the wintertime, he was looking for support among the city-states himself by sending embassies to a number of them; others were coming to him of their own initiative, the Epirotes, for instance, who came with the support of all their people, and the Eleans from the Peloponnese. The Eleans were seeking his help against the Achaeans who, they believed, after declaring war on Antiochus against their wishes, would attack their city-state first. They were sent a thousand infantry under the leadership of the Cretan Euphanes.

The embassy from Epirus was not at all forthright or honest in any regard; they wished to win the king's favor while also taking care not to offend the Romans. They asked that Antiochus not drag them heedlessly into the dispute since their position opposite Italy and at the forefront of Greece meant that they would face the first onset of the Romans. If, however, the king could protect Epirus with his land and sea forces, they said, all the Epirotes would eagerly welcome him in their cities and ports. If he could not, then they entreated him not to expose them, unprotected and vulnerable as they were, to a war with Rome. The rationale for sending this embassy was evident. If, as they were inclined to believe, Antiochus avoided Epirus, their whole situation with regard to the Roman armies would be unchanged, while they would have gained the king's goodwill because they would have been ready to receive him had he come. On the other hand, should he come, they could also hope for indulgence from the Romans because, not anticipating help from

167

exspectato longinquo ab se auxilio praesentis viribus suc-
8 cubuissent. huic tam perplexae legationi quia non satis in
promptu erat quid responderet, legatos se missurum ad
eos dixit, qui de iis quae ad illos seque communiter per-
tinerent loquerentur.

6. In Boeotiam ipse profectus est, causas in speciem
irae adversus Romanos eas quas ante dixi habentem,
Brachylli[11] necem et bellum a Quinctio Coroneae propter
2 Romanorum militum caedes inlatum, re vera per multa
iam saecula publice privatimque labante egregia quondam
disciplina gentis, et multorum eo statu qui diuturnus esse
sine mutatione rerum non posset.

3 Obviam effusis undique Boeotiae principibus Thebas
venit. ibi in concilio gentis, quamquam et ad Delium,
impetu in praesidium Romanum facto, et ad Chalcidem
4 commiserat nec parvis nec dubiis principiis bellum, tamen
eandem orationem exorsus[12] qua in conloquio primo ad
Chalcidem quaque per legatos in concilio Achaeorum
usus erat, ut amicitiam secum institui, non bellum indici
5 Romanis postularet. neminem quid ageretur fallebat; decretum tamen sub leni verborum praetexto pro rege adversus Romanos factum est.

6 Hac quoque gente adiuncta Chalcidem regressus,

11 Bracchylli *Weiss.*: Bracchili *B*χ: Brachyllae *Sig.*
12 exorsus *B*χ: est exorsus *Kreyssig*: exorsus est *Duker*

---

32 For the murder of Brachylles: 33.27.8–28.15; Coronea:
33.29.6–9.
33 Livy contrasts the Boeotians of the early second century BC
with those of Epaminondas' day, nearly two centuries earlier.
34 Delium: 35.51.1–5; Chalcis: 35.51.6–10.

them at such a distance, they would simply have buckled before the might of an enemy on the spot. Not having a ready response to an embassy with such a complex agenda, Antiochus stated that he would send a delegation to them to discuss the matters that were of common concern to them and him.

6. Antiochus himself left for Boeotia, which had the pretexts for resentment toward the Romans that I gave above, namely the assassination of Brachylles and Quinctius' assault on Coronea in retaliation for the massacre of Roman soldiers.[32] In fact, however, the discipline for which this people was once noted had already been in decline for many generations in both public and private life and many were in circumstances that could not long be maintained without political upheaval.[33]

Antiochus met the state's leading citizens, who streamed out from all over Boeotia when he came to Thebes. He had clearly established that he was at war by significant and incontrovertible initiatives both at Delium, with his attack on the Roman garrison, and at Chalcis;[34] but there, in the council of the Boeotian people, he nevertheless opened with the same remarks that he had employed in his first address at Chalcis and, through his representatives, in the council of the Achaeans: he was asking that a treaty of friendship be established with him, not that war be declared on the Romans. He left no one under any illusion as to what was really at issue but a decree was passed, couched in inoffensive language supporting the king and unfavorable to the Romans.

Having also won over this people, Antiochus returned

praemissis inde litteris ut Demetriadem convenirent principes Aetolorum, cum quibus de summa rerum delibe-
7 raret, navibus eo ad diem indictum concilio venit. et
Amynander, accitus ad consultandum ex Athamania, et
Hannibal Poenus, iam diu non adhibitus, interfuit ei con-
8 silio. consultatum de Thessalorum gente est, quorum
9 omnibus qui aderant voluntas temptanda videbatur. in eo
modo diversae sententiae erant, quod alii extemplo agendum, alii ex hieme, quae tum ferme media erat, differen-
10 dum in veris principium, et alii[13] legatos tantummodo
mittendos, alii cum omnibus copiis eundum censebant,
terrendosque metu si cunctarentur.

7. Cum circa hanc fere consultationem disceptatio
omnis verteretur, Hannibal nominatim interrogatus sententiam in universi belli cogitationem regem atque eos qui
2 aderant tali oratione avertit. "si ex quo traiecimus in Graeciam adhibitus essem in consilium, cum de Euboea deque
Achaeis et de Boeotia agebatur, eandem sententiam dixis-
3 sem quam hodie, cum de Thessalis agitur, dicam. ante
omnia Philippum et Macedonas in societatem belli qua-
4 cumque ratione censeo deducendos esse. nam quod ad
Euboeam Boeotosque et Thessalos attinet, cui dubium est
quin—ut quibus nullae suae vires sint, praesentibus adu-

13 et alii *Bχ*: alii *Holk. 345*

---

35 For Amynander and the Athamanians, cf. 35.47.2–8.
36 Appian (*Syr.* 14) also reports the speech of Hannibal, which
suggests that Polybius included it at this point (cf. Walsh 36.82–83
for a comparison of the speeches in Livy and Appian). It also occurs in Justin (*Epit.* 31.5.2–9, in indirect speech, as usual), but its
thrust is very different, focusing entirely on an attack on Italy.

to Chalcis. From there he sent ahead letters instructing the Aetolian leaders to assemble at Demetrias so that he could discuss with them the general strategy for the war, and he arrived by ship on the day fixed for the meeting. Amynander, summoned from Athamania to take part in the deliberations,[35] also attended the conference, as did Hannibal the Carthaginian, who had long been excluded from discussions. The issue under consideration was the Thessalian people, whose inclinations all present felt should be sounded out. Opinions diverged only over modalities. Some urged immediate action and others that they postpone matters from the winter, which was then about halfway through, until the start of spring. Some voted that only an embassy be sent, and others that they go in full force and intimidate them with threats if they hesitated.

7. The discussion was focused almost entirely on this issue, but Hannibal, when invited by name to state his opinion, brought the king and all present to think about the war in general with the following speech:[36] "Had I been invited to your deliberations from the time that we first crossed to Greece, when discussion centered on Euboea, the Achaeans and Boeotia, I would have given you the same opinion that I shall give today when the subject is the Thessalians. Before anything else, I think that, above all, Philip and the Macedonians must be brought into a military alliance. For can there be any doubt about Euboea, the Boeotians and the Thessalians? Having no strength of their own, they are always ingratiating themselves with powers close at hand; and they will use that

171

lando semper, quem metum in consilio habeant, eodem ad
5 impetrandam veniam utantur—simul ac Romanum exercitum in Graecia viderint, ad consuetum imperium se
avertant, nec iis noxiae futurum sit quod cum Romani
procul abessent, vim tuam praesentis exercitusque tui experiri noluerint?

6 "Quanto igitur prius potiusque est Philippum nobis
coniungere quam hos? cui, si semel in causam descenderit,
nihil integri futurum sit, quique eas vires adferat quae non
accessio tantum ad Romanum esse bellum, sed per se ip-
7 sae nuper sustinere potuerint Romanos. hoc ego adiuncto—absit verbo invidia—qui dubitare de eventu pos-
sim, cum quibus adversus Philippum valuerint Romani, iis
8 nunc fore videam ut ipsi oppugnentur? Aetoli, qui Philippum, quod inter omnes constat, vicerunt, cum Philippo
9 adversus Romanos pugnabunt; Amynander atque Athamanum gens, quorum secundum Aetolos plurima fuit
10 opera in eo bello, nobiscum stabunt; Philippus tum te
quieto totam molem sustinebat belli; nunc duo maximi
reges Asiae Europaeque viribus adversus unum populum,
ut meam utramque fortunam taceam, patrum certe aetate
ne uni quidem Epirotarum regi parem—qui quid tandem
erit[14] vobiscum comparatus?—geretis bellum.

11 "Quae igitur res mihi fiduciam praebet coniungi nobis
Philippum posse? una, communis utilitas, quae societatis

---

[14] erit χMg: om. B: erat Madvig

---

[37] Pyrrhus, of course. Walsh (36.84) suggests that the example
comes from Livy himself, not Polybius, "to contrast rhetorically
with the looming strength of the two kings and their allies."

same faintheartedness that they demonstrate in their policy decisions to gain pardon for their actions. As soon as they see a Roman army in Greece, they will turn to the imperial power to which they are accustomed; nor will it harm them at all that, when the Romans were far off, they were unwilling to tackle you and your army's power, which were on the spot.

"So how much more urgent and important is it to bring Philip rather than these people onto our side? The moment he has espoused our cause, he would have no way out and would bring with him a strength that would not merely be extra support for the Roman war but one that was recently able to withstand the Romans all on its own. With him enlisted, how can I doubt the outcome (forgive me for saying it!) when I see the Romans themselves will be under attack from the very men with whose aid they achieved success against Philip. It was the Aetolians, everybody agrees, who defeated Philip, and they will be fighting alongside Philip against the Romans. Amynander and the Athamanian people, whose contributions in that war were the greatest after the Aetolians', will be standing with us. You were then a nonparticipant and Philip bore the whole weight of the war. This time you, the two greatest kings, will fight a war employing the strength of Asia and Europe against one people, and a people who (not to speak of my mixed fortunes against them) could not, at least in the days of our fathers, show themselves a match even for one king of Epirus[37]—and how will he possibly stand comparison with you?

"What then makes me confident that Philip can be brought to join us? First of all, common interest, that strongest bond in an alliance; and, secondly, the assur-

12 maximum vinculum est; altera, auctores vos, Aetoli. vester enim legatus hic Thoas, inter cetera quae ad exciendum in Graeciam Antiochum dicere est solitus, ante omnia hoc semper adfirmavit, fremere Philippum et aegre pati sub
13 specie pacis leges servitutis sibi impositas. ille quidem ferae[15] bestiae vinctae aut clausae et refringere claustra cupienti regis iram verbis aequabat. cuius si talis animus est, solvamus nos eius vincula et claustra refringamus, ut erumpere diu coercitam iram in hostes communes possit.
14 quod si nihil eum legatio nostra moverit, at nos, quoniam nobis eum adiungere non possumus, ne hostibus nostris
15 ille adiungi possit caveamus. Seleucus filius tuus Lysimachiae est; qui si eo exercitu quem secum habet per Thraciam proxima Macedoniae coeperit depopulari, facile ab auxilio ferendo Romanis Philippum ad sua potissimum tuenda avertet.
16 "De Philippo meam sententiam habes; de ratione universi belli quid sentirem, iam ab initio non ignorasti. quod si tum auditus forem, non in Euboea Chalcidem captam et castellum Euripi expugnatum Romani, sed Etruriam Ligurumque et Galliae Cisalpinae oram bello ardere, et qui maximus iis terror est, Hannibalem in Italia esse au
17 dirent, nunc quoque accersas censeo omnes navales terrestresque copias; sequantur classem onerariae cum commeatibus; nam hic sicut ad belli munera pauci sumus, sic
18 nimis multi pro inopia commeatuum. cum omnis tuas con-

---

[15] ferae *Gel.*: ut ferae *Bχ*

---

[38] Cf. 35.18.6, but the comparison is there made by Alexander of Acarnania.

ances you have given, Aetolians. For your representative here, Thoas, used to have a number of things to say in favor of inducing Antiochus to come to Greece, but the reason that he always emphasized before all others was that Philip was foaming at the mouth and incensed that the terms imposed on him, ostensibly peace terms, reduced him to serfdom. Thoas compared the enraged king to a wild beast chained or caged and longing to burst its bonds.[38] If such are his feelings, let us untie his shackles and break his chains so that he can let his long-restrained fury burst forth against our common enemy. But if our delegation fails to persuade him, let us at least make sure that, even if we cannot enlist him in our cause, he cannot be enlisted by our enemies. Your son Seleucus is at Lysimachia. If he advances through Thrace with the army that he has with him and proceeds with raids on the adjacent areas of Macedonia, he will easily make Philip turn from bringing assistance to the Romans to defending his own possessions, his highest priority.

"You have my thoughts on Philip and from the very beginning you have not been unaware of my opinion on the strategy for the war as a whole. Had I been listened to then, the Romans would not now be hearing of the capture of Chalcis in Euboea and the storming of a fortress on the Euripus; no, they would be hearing of Etruria, the coast of Liguria and Cisalpine Gaul being engulfed in the flames of war, and—their greatest dread—of Hannibal present in Italy. Now, too, I think you should send for all your land and sea forces and have transports follow the fleet loaded with supplies. For our numbers here are small for all the operations of the war but too large for the meager provisions at our disposal. When you have brought together all

175

traxeris vires, divisa classe partem Corcyrae in statione
19 habebis, ne transitus Romanis liber ac tutus pateat, partem ad litus Italiae quod Sardiniam Africamque spectat
traicies; ipse cum omnibus terrestribus copiis in Bullinum
20 agrum procedes; inde Graeciae praesidebis, et speciem
Romanis traiecturum te praebens, et si res poposcerit,
traiecturus. haec suadeo, qui ut non omnis peritissimus
sim belli, cum Romanis certe bellare bonis malisque meis
21 didici. in quae consilium dedi, in eadem nec infidelem nec
segnem operam polliceor. di adprobent eam sententiam
quae tibi optima visa fuerit."

8. Haec ferme Hannibalis oratio fuit; quam laudarunt
magis in praesentia qui aderant quam rebus ipsis exsecuti
sunt; nihil enim eorum factum est, nisi quod ad classem
2 copiasque accersendas ex Asia Polyxenidam misit. legati
Larisam ad concilium Thessalorum sunt missi, et Aetolis
Amynandroque dies ad conveniendum cum exercitu[16]
Pheras est dictus; eodem et rex cum suis copiis confestim
3 venit. ubi dum opperitur Amynandrum atque Aetolos,
Philippum Megalopolitanum cum duobus milibus hominum ad legenda ossa Macedonum circa Cynoscephalas,
4 ubi debellatum erat cum Philippo, misit, sive ab ipso,
quaerente sibi commendationem ad Macedonum gentem

---

[16] cum exercitu *Gron.*: exercitui *Bχ*

---

[39] The reference is probably to the land around the town of
this name in Epirus, a few miles inland (*Barr.* 49 B3). This is
clearly a defensive measure to counter any Roman force crossing
from Brundisium.   [40] An exiled Rhodian who was admiral of
the king's fleet.   [41] Son of the Alexander of Megalopolis who
claimed descent from Alexander the Great: cf. 35.47.5–8.

your forces, split your fleet and keep part on patrol off Corcyra to deny the Romans a free and secure crossing. The rest you should send over to that part of the Italian coastline facing Sardinia and Africa. You personally should move forward with all your land forces into the territory of Byllis;[39] from there you will stand guard over Greece and at the same time give the Romans the impression that you are going to cross—and, if circumstances require it, you will do so. These are my recommendations. I may not be an expert in every kind of warfare, but I have at least learned from my successes and failures how to fight the Romans. For prosecuting the strategy that I have suggested I promise support that lacks neither loyalty nor energy, and may the gods show their favor on whichever proposal you find the best."

8. Such was the tenor of Hannibal's remarks, for which his audience expressed immediate praise without following up with action. Apart from Antiochus sending Polyxenidas[40] to fetch his fleet and his land forces from Asia, not one of the recommendations was implemented. Envoys were sent to the council of the Thessalians at Larisa, and a date was set for the Aetolians and Amynander to assemble with the army at Pherae; and the king came here post haste with his troops. While Antiochus was waiting there for Amynander and the Aetolians, he sent Philip of Megalopolis[41] with 2,000 men to gather up the bones of the Macedonians at Cynoscephalae, the site of the decisive battle with Philip. He had perhaps been advised to do this by the Megapolitan, who wished to ingratiate himself with the Macedonian people and generate resentment to-

et invidiam regi, quod insepultos milites reliquisset, moni-
tus, sive ab insita regibus vanitate ad consilium specie
5 amplum re inane animo adiecto. tumulus est in unum
ossibus, quae passim strata erant, coaceruatis factus, qui
nullam gratiam ad Macedonas, odium ingens ad Philip-
6 pum movit. itaque qui ad id tempus fortunam esset habiturus in consilio, is extemplo ad M. Baebium proprae-
torem misit, Antiochum in Thessaliam impetum fecisse; si
videretur ei, moveret ex hibernis; se obviam processurum,
ut quid agendum esset consultarent.

9. Antiocho ad Pheras iam castra habenti, ubi con-
iunxerant ei se Aetoli et Amynander, legati ab Larisa venerunt, quaerentes quod ob factum dictumue Thessalorum
2 bello lacesseret eos, simul orantes ut remoto exercitu per
3 legatos, si quid ei videretur, secum disceptaret. eodem
tempore quingentos armatos duce Hippolocho Pheras in
praesidium miserunt; ii exclusi aditu, iam omnia itinera
obsidentibus regiis, Scotusam se receperunt.

4 Legatis Larisaeorum rex clementer respondit non belli
faciendi, sed tuendae et stabiliendae libertatis Thessalo-
5 rum causa se Thessaliam intrasse. similia his qui cum Pheraeis ageret missus; cui nullo dato responso, Pheraei ipsi
legatum ad regem principem civitatis Pausaniam mise-
6 runt. qui cum haud dissimilia iis, ut in causa pari, quae pro

---

42 That is, Philip had planned on waiting to see how things
turned out before deciding what action to take himself.
43 Nine miles west of Pherae (*Barr.* 55 D2: Skotoussa).

ward their king for having left his soldiers unburied, or else it was the natural vanity of royalty that turned the king's thoughts to a scheme that looked impressive but was in fact futile. A mound was formed by bringing together bones strewn around the area, but this engendered no feelings of gratitude among the Macedonians and provoked deep resentment toward Philip. The result was that the man who was up to that point going to let fortune guide his policy[42] now, on the spur of the moment, sent a message to the propraetor Marcus Baebius to inform him that Antiochus had attacked Thessaly; that Baebius should, if he thought fit, move from his winter quarters; and that Philip would advance to meet him to discuss what should be done.

9. Antiochus was now encamped at Pherae, where the Aetolians and Amynander had joined him. Here envoys came from Larisa asking him what the Thessalians had done or said to make him open hostilities against them, and to appeal to him to withdraw his army and conduct discussions with them through ambassadors on whatever he thought pertinent. (At the same time the people of Larisa sent 500 soldiers under Hippolochus to protect Pherae but, denied access since the king's troops now blocked all the roads, they fell back to Scotusa.[43])

The king gave the envoys of the people of Larisa a mild response: he had entered Thessaly not to make war, but to protect and consolidate the liberty of the Thessalians. A messenger was also sent to make a similar declaration to the people of Pherae, but they gave him no reply and sent their chief magistrate, Pausanias, to the king as their spokesman. Pausanias presented arguments not unlike those made in the conference at the strait of Euripus on

Chalcidensibus in conloquio ad Euripi fretum dicta erant,
7 quaedam etiam ferocius egisset, rex etiam atque etiam
deliberare eos iussos ne id consilii caperent cuius, dum in
futurum nimis cauti et providi essent, extemplo paeniteret, dimisit.

8 Haec renuntiata Pheras legatio cum esset, ne paulum
quidem dubitarunt quin pro fide erga Romanos quidquid
9 fors belli tulisset paterentur. itaque et hi summa ope parabant se ad urbem defendendam, et rex ab omni parte
10 simul oppugnare moenia est adgressus, et ut qui satis
intellegeret—neque enim dubium erat—in eventu eius
urbis positum esse quam primam adgressus esset aut
sperni deinde ab universa gente Thessalorum aut timeri
se, omnem undique terrorem obsessis iniecit.

11 Primum impetum oppugnationis satis constanter sustinuerunt; deinde cum multi propugnantes caderent aut
12 volnerarentur, labare animi coeperunt. revocati deinde
castigationibus[17] principum ad perseverandum in proposito, relicto exteriore circulo muri, deficientibus iam copiis
in interiorem partem urbis concesserunt, cui brevior orbis
munitionis circumiectus erat; postremo victi malis, cum
timerent ne vi captis nulla apud victorem venia esset,
dediderunt sese.

13 Nihil inde[18] moratus, rex quattuor milia armatorum,
dum recens terror esset, Scotusam misit. nec ibi mora

---

[17] castigationibus *Mg*: castigatione χ: castigationes *B*
[18] inde *B*χ: deinde *Mg**

---

[44] Made there by the Chalcidian Micythio, who stated that
protection was unnecessary, as the Romans had granted them
peace and independence (35.46.9–11).

behalf of the people of Chalcis,[44] who were in similar circumstances, and some he made even more emphatically.
The king let the Larisans go only after bidding them consider the matter very, very carefully so they would not
adopt a policy which, being too cautious and careful for
the long-term, they might immediately regret.

When the results of this embassy were reported at
Pherae, the people had not the slightest doubt but that
they should from loyalty to the Romans face whatever the
fortunes of war might bring. They therefore proceeded to
devote all their energy to defending their city, and the king
mounted an attack on their walls from every direction at
once. He also well realized—for it was indubitably true—
that, this being the first city he had attacked, whether he
would be met with derision or fear by the entire Thessalian people would depend on the outcome. He therefore
inflicted every form of intimidation at all points on the
beleaguered inhabitants.

The initial thrust of the attack the Pheraeans withstood
with a firm resolve; then, when many of the defenders
were killed or wounded, their spirit began to weaken. Inspired once more to stick to their resolve by the rebukes
of their officers, they abandoned the outer encircling wall,
their forces being too thin to hold it, and withdrew to the
inner part of the town, which had a defense work of shorter
circumference. Eventually, crushed by their adversities,
and frightened that there would be no mercy from the
victor if they were taken by force, they capitulated.

Without any delay, the king sent 4,000 soldiers from
there to Scotusa while the panic was still fresh. There was
no delay with the surrender there, either, since the Scotu-

LIVY

14 deditionis est facta, cernentibus Pheraeorum recens
exemplum, qui quod pertinaciter primo abnuerant, malo
domiti tandem fecissent; cum ipsa urbe Hippolochus
15 Larisaeorumque deditum est praesidium. dimissi ab rege
inviolati omnes, quod eam rem magni momenti futuram
rex ad conciliandos Larisaeorum animos credebat.

10. Intra decimum diem quam Pheras venerat his perfectis, Crannonem profectus cum toto exercitu primo
2 adventu cepit. inde Cierium et Metropolim et iis circum-
iecta castella recepit; omniaque iam regionis eius praeter
3 Atragem[19] et Gyrtonem in potestate erant. tunc adgredi
Larisam constituit, ratus vel terrore ceterarum ex-
pugnatarum, vel beneficio praesidii dimissi, vel exemplo
tot civitatium dedentium sese non ultra in pertinacia man-
4 suros. elephantis agi ante signa terroris causa iussis, quadrato agmine ad urbem incessit, ut incerti fluctuarentur
animi magnae partis Larisaeorum inter metum praesen-
tem hostium et verecundiam absentium sociorum.

5 Per eosdem dies Amynander cum Athamanum iuventute occupat Pelinnaeum, et Menippus, cum tribus milibus peditum Aetolorum et ducentis equitibus in Per-
rhaebiam profectus, Malloeam et Chyretias[20] vi cepit, et[21]
6 depopulatus est agrum Tripolitanum. his raptim peractis,

[19] Atragem *Bekker*: Atracem *Mg*: ad regem *Bχ*
[20] Chyretias *Asc.*: Cyret(c)hias *Bχ*: Cyretias *Fr. 1*
[21] et depopulatus *Weiss.*: depopulatus *Bχ*

[45] Some twelve miles southwest of Larissa: *Barr.* 55 C1 (Krannon).   [46] *Barr.* 55 C2 (Kierion); B2 (Metropolis); C1 (Atrax);
D1 (Gyrton).
[47] *Barr.* 55 C1 (Pelinnaion, Malloia, Chyretiai); B–C1 (Per-

182

sans reflected on the recent example of the people of Pherae, who had been ultimately forced by adversity into doing what they had at first obstinately refused to do. Hippolochus and the Larisan garrison were surrendered along with the city itself. All were released unharmed by the king because he believed that the gesture would be of great importance for winning the hearts and minds of the people of Larisa.

10. These successes had been achieved within ten days of Antiochus' arrival at Pherae and, setting off for Crannon[45] with his whole army, he took it immediately on his arrival. After this he seized Cierium and Metropolis, and the surrounding forts, and by now everything in the region was under his control except Atrax and Gyrton.[46] He then decided to attack Larisa, thinking its inhabitants would not continue their obstinate resistance, either from fear after his storming of the other cities or from gratitude for his release of their garrison or because of the example of all the other states that had voluntarily surrendered. Ordering elephants to be driven before the standards to intimidate the foe, he marched on the city in battle formation, with the result that the feelings of most of the inhabitants of Larisa wavered between fear of the enemy before them and shame at letting down their absent allies.

During those same days Amynander seized Pelinnaeum with his Athemanian troops; and Menippus set off into Perrhaebia with 3,000 Aetolian infantry and 200 cavalry, took Malloea and Chyretiae by force, and laid waste the farmland of Tripolis.[47] These objectives swiftly at-

raibia). The Tripolis comprised the towns of Azoros (*Barr.* 55 C1), Pythion and Doliche (50 B4).

Larisam ad regem redeunt; consultanti quidnam agendum
7 de Larisa esset supervenerunt. ibi in diversum sententiae
tendebant, aliis vim adhibendam et non differendum cen-
sentibus quin operibus ac machinis simul undique moenia
adgrederetur urbis sitae in plano, aperto et[22] campestri
8 undique aditu, aliis nunc vires urbis nequaquam Pheraeis
conferendae memorantibus, nunc hiemem et tempus anni
nulli bellicae rei, minime obsidioni atque oppugnationi
9 urbium aptum. incerto regi inter spem metumque legati a
Pharsalo, qui ad dedendam urbem suam forte venerant,
animos auxerunt.

10 M. Baebius interim, cum Philippo in Dassaretiis congressus, Ap. Claudium ex communi consilio ad praesidium
Larisae misit, qui per Macedoniam magnis itineribus in
11 iugum montium, quod super Gonnos est, pervenit. oppidum Gonni viginti milia ab Larisa abest, in ipsis faucibus
12 saltus quae Tempe appellantur situm. ibi castra metatus
latius quam pro copiis et plures quam quot satis in usum
erant ignes cum accendisset, speciem quam quaesierat
hosti fecit, omnem ibi Romanum exercitum cum rege Phi-
13 lippo esse. itaque hiemem instare[23] apud suos causatus,
rex unum tantum moratus diem, ab Larisa recessit et
Demetriadem rediit, Aetolique et Athamanes in suos re-

---

[22] aperto et *Duker*: apert(a)e *Bχ*
[23] instare *Voss.*: stare *Bχ*: obstare *Duker*: *inter obelos Briscoe*

---

[48] The Aetolians had claimed this city as theirs (33.13.6–12,
33.34.7), but though nominally free after Flamininus' settlement
of 194 it had come under Roman control.
[49] In southeast Illyria: *Barr.* 49 C3 (Dassaretis).
[50] Ap. Claudius Pulcher (294). Legate of Flamininus against

tained, they returned to the king at Larisa and found him
considering what should be done about the town. In that
meeting opinions were divided. Some suggested that they
use force and not delay making a simultaneous assault on
the city walls from all directions with siege works and
engines, since the town lay on a plain, exposed and easily
approachable over level ground on every side. Others observed at one moment that the strength of this city was of
a very different order from that of the Pheraeans, at another and that it was now winter, a time of year not suitable
for any military activity and least of all for besieging and
assaulting cities. The king was wavering between hope and
fear when delegates, who had chanced to arrive from
Pharsalus to surrender their city,[48] raised his spirits.

Meanwhile, Marcus Baebius met Philip in the land of
the Dassareti,[49] and following a plan drafted together with
him sent Appius Claudius[50] to defend Larisa. Claudius
traversed Macedonia with forced marches, and reached
the crest of the mountains overlooking Gonni. The town
of Gonni lies twenty miles from Larisa, right at the entrance of the pass called Tempe.[51] There, by laying out a
camp of proportions greater than his forces warranted,
and lighting more fires than they really needed,[52] he gave
the enemy the impression he had sought to give, namely
that the entire Roman army was present there along with
King Philip. As a result, the king made the excuse of the
onset of winter to his men and, waiting only one day, left
Larisa and returned to Demetrias, while the Aetolians and

Nabis in 195 (34.28.10), he was praetor in 188 or 187 (cf. *MRR*
367 n. 1) and consul in 185.   [51] *Barr.* 55 C1.   [52] A well-
known stratagem: cf. Frontin. *Str.* 1.1.7, 1.1.9, 1.5.22, 2.12.4.

14 ceperunt se fines. Appius etsi, cuius rei causa missus erat,
solutam cernebat obsidionem, tamen Larisam ad confir-
15 mandos in reliquum sociorum animos descendit; duplex-
que laetitia erat, quod et hostes excesserant finibus, et
intra moenia praesidium Romanum cernebant.

11. Rex Chalcidem a Demetriade profectus, amore
captus virginis Chalcidensis, Cleoptolemi filiae, cum pa-
2 trem primo adlegando, deinde coram ipse rogando fatigas-
set, invitum se gravioris fortunae condicioni inligantem,
tandem impetrata re tamquam in media pace nuptias celebrat,[24] et reliquum hiemis, oblitus quantas simul duas res
suscepisset, bellum Romanum et Graeciam liberandam,
omissa omnium rerum cura, in conviviis et vinum sequen-
tibus voluptatibus, ac deinde ex fatigatione magis quam
3 satietate earum in somno traduxit. eadem omnes praefectos regios, qui ubique, ad Boeotiam maxime, praepositi
4 hibernis erant, cepit luxuria; in eandem et milites effusi
sunt, nec quisquam eorum aut arma induit, aut stationem
aut vigilias servavit, aut quicquam quod militaris operis
5 aut muneris esset fecit. itaque principio veris, cum per
Phocidem Chaeroneam, quo convenire omnem undique

---

[24] celebrat α: celebrabat Bχ

---

[53] The episode is found in Polybius and elsewhere (cf. Walbank 3.75). Cleoptolemus, otherwise unknown, is described by
Polybius as a leading man of Chalcis (20.8.3). Whether there was
a reason for Antiochus' marriage other than infatuation (he was
fifty and had perhaps already repudiated Laodice, daughter of
Mithridates II of Pontus) is unclear. The winter of debauchery
described here appears at least exaggerated, if not "clearly false"
(Walbank 3.76).   [54] Livy's geography is strange here, as the

Athamanians withdrew to their respective territories. Although Appius could see that the siege had been raised—the purpose of his mission—he nevertheless went down to Larisa to give the allies reassurance for the future. These had two reasons to feel happy: the enemy had left their lands and they could also see a Roman garrison within their walls.

11. The king left Demetrias for Chalcis and there fell in love with a young Chalcidian woman, the daughter of Cleoptolemus.[53] He kept badgering the father, first sending intermediaries and then presenting his suit in person. Cleoptolemus was averse to involvement in a marriage at a level too uncomfortable for him but Antiochus finally had his way and celebrated a wedding, as though peace were established all around. Forgetting the importance of the two causes that he had taken up together, namely the war with Rome and the liberation of Greece, he abandoned responsibility for everything and spent the rest of the winter in dinner parties and the pleasures that accompany drinking, and then in sleeping, exhausted by these activities rather than sated with them. All the king's officers put in charge of winter quarters everywhere, but especially Boeotia, fell victim to the same excesses. Even the rank and file abandoned themselves to the same ways; none put on armor, did guard duty, kept the night watch, or performed any of the regular military duties or responsibilities. Thus, at the start of spring, when Antiochus came through Phocis to Chaeronea,[54] where he had or-

king goes westward from Chalcis (*Barr.* 55 F4) to Chaeronea (D4) via Phocis (C4), which is west of Chaeronea. He has again probably misunderstood Polybius.

exercitum iusserat, venisset, facile animadvertit nihilo
severiore disciplina milites quam ducem hibernasse.

6   Alexandrum inde Acarnana et Menippum Macedonem
Stratum Aetoliae copias ducere iussit; ipse, Delphis sacri-

7 ficio Apollini facto, Naupactum processit. consilio principum Aetoliae habito via quae praeter Calydonem et Lysimachiam fert ad Stratum[25] suis, qui per Maliacum sinum

8 veniebant, occurrit. ibi Mnasilochus princeps Acarnanum,
multis emptus donis, non ipse solum gentem regi con-
ciliabat, sed Clitum[26] etiam praetorem, penes quem tum

9 summa potestas erat, in suam sententiam adduxerat. is
cum Leucadios, quod Acarnaniae caput est, non facile ad
defectionem posse cerneret impelli propter metum Romanae classis, quae cum Atilio quaeque[27] circa Cephalla-

10 niam erat, arte eos est adgressus. nam cum in concilio
dixisset tuenda mediterranea Acarnaniae esse, et omnibus
qui arma ferrent exeundum ad Medionem et Thyrreum,

11 ne ab Antiocho aut Aetolis occuparentur, fuere qui dicerent nihil attinere omnes tumultuose concitari, satis

[25] ad Stratum *ed. Rom.*: Astratum *Bχ*
[26] Clitum *Bχ*: Clytum *ed. Rom.*
[27] quaeque *Weiss.*: quae *Bχ*: quaeve *ed. Rom.*

[55] *Barr.* 55 A3.   [56] Calydon: *Barr.* 55 B4; Lysimachia:
A3. Livy's geography is again haywire. If the army starts at Chaeronea (D4) and meets Antiochus between these towns, it goes
nowhere near the Malian Gulf (D3). Manuelian ad loc. suggests
(perhaps giving Livy too much credit) that these troops were
reinforcements brought over to Greece by Polyxenides (cf. 8.1,
15.1), who may have landed in the Malian Gulf and were now en
route to link up with the main force.

dered his entire army to muster from their various quarters, he easily noticed that the men had spent the winter under no stricter discipline than had their commander in chief.

Antiochus ordered Alexander the Acarnanian and Menippus the Macedonian to lead the troops from there to Stratus in Aetolia;[55] and after sacrificing to Apollo at Delphi he himself advanced to Naupactus. He held a meeting of the Aetolian chieftains and then met his men, who were coming along the Malian Gulf, on the road that leads to Stratus by way of Calydon and Lysimachia.[56] There, a leading Acarnanian, Mnasilochus, who had been bought with numerous bribes, was not only using his own influence to gain the support of the people for the king but had also won over to his point of view the praetor Clitus,[57] who held the highest office at the time. Since Clitus could see that the Leucadians, whose city was the capital of Acarnania,[58] could not easily be incited to defection because of their fear of the Roman fleet that was with Atilius and lay off Cephallania, he set out to trick them. He declared in council that the interior of Acarnania needed protection and that all who could bear arms should march out to Medion and Thyrreum[59] to prevent their capture by Antiochus or the Aetolians. There were some, however, who argued that a general levy conducted in panic was inadvis-

---

[57] As usual in Greek contexts, "praetor" here represents *strategos*. Clitus is otherwise unknown.

[58] Leucas, on the island of the same name (*Barr.* 54 C4).

[59] *Barr.* 54 D4 (Medion); C4 (Thyrreion).

esse quingentorum hominum praesidium. eam iuventutem nactus, trecentis Medione ducentis Thyrrei in praesidio positis, id agebat ut pro obsidibus futuri venirent in
potestatem regis.

12. Per eosdem dies legati regis Medionem venerunt;
quibus auditis cum in contione quidnam respondendum

2 regi esset consultaretur, et alii manendum in Romana societate alii non aspernandam amicitiam regis censerent,

3 media visa est Cliti sententia eoque accepta, ut ad regem
mitterent legatos, peterentque ab eo ut Medionios super

4 tanta re consultare in concilio Acarnanum pateretur. in
eam legationem Mnasilochus et qui eius factionis erant de
industria coniecti, clam missis qui regem admovere copias

5 iuberent, ipsi terebant tempus. itaque vixdum iis egressis
legatis[28] Antiochus in finibus et mox ad portas erat, et
trepidantibus qui expertes proditionis fuerant, tumultuo-
seque iuventutem ad arma vocantibus, ab Clito et Mnasi-

6 locho in urbem est inductus; et aliis sua voluntate adfluen-
tibus, metu coacti etiam qui dissentiebant ad regem
convenerunt. quos placida oratione territos cum permul-
sisset, ad spem volgatae clementiae aliquot populi Acarnaniae defecerunt.

7 Thyrreum a Medione profectus est, Mnasilocho eodem et legatis praemissis. ceterum detecta Medione fraus

---

[28] iis (h(i)is ϕ) egressis legatis $B\phi$: egressis legatis ψ: iis egressis *Gron.*

able and that a force of 500 men would suffice. On taking charge of such a troop of young men, Clitus stationed a garrison of 300 at Medion and 200 at Thyrreum and took steps to have them fall into the king's hands, to serve as hostages later on.

12. In this same period envoys of the king came to Medion. After they were granted an audience and the question of the reply to be given to Antiochus was discussed in council, some were of the opinion that they should remain faithful to the alliance with Rome, others that they should not reject the king's overtures of friendship. The position advocated by Clitus seemed the middle course and was therefore adopted: that they send an embassy to the king and ask him to allow the people of Medion to discuss such an important matter in the council of the Acarnanians. Mnasilochus and supporters of his cause were deliberately included in this embassy and they sent secret messages to the king to ask him to bring up his forces; and then they simply played for time. Thus the delegation had barely left when Antiochus was in their country and soon at their gates. Those having no part in the treachery panicked and, in consternation, called the soldiers to arms; and meanwhile Antiochus was let into the city by Clitus and Mnasilochus. Some flocked to him of their own volition and even those unsympathetic to him were driven by fear to join the king. He allayed their fears with conciliatory words and a number of the peoples of Acarnania went over to him, their hopes aroused by his widely publicized clemency.

Antiochus left Medion for Thyrreum, sending Mnasilochus and some envoys ahead to the town. However, the treachery at Medion had been brought to light and this

191

8 cautiores non timidiores Thyrreenses fecit; dato enim
haud perplexo responso, nullam se novam societatem nisi
ex auctoritate imperatorum Romanorum accepturos, por-
9 tis[29] clausis armatos in muris disposuerunt. et peroppor-
tune ad confirmandos Acarnanum animos Cn. Octavius
missus a Quinctio, cum praesidium et paucas naves ab A.
Postumio, qui ab Atilio legato Cephallaniae praepositus
10 fuerat, accepisset, Leucadem venit, implevitque spei socios M'. Acilium consulem iam cum legionibus mare traie-
11 cisse et in Thessalia castra Romana esse. hunc rumorem
quia similem veri tempus anni maturum iam ad navigandum faciebat, rex, praesidio Medione imposito et in quibusdam aliis Acarnaniae oppidis, Thyrreo abscessit et per
Aetoliae ac Phocidis urbes Chalcidem rediit.

13. Sub idem tempus M. Baebius et Philippus rex, iam
ante per hiemem in Dassaretiis congressi, cum Ap. Claudium, ut obsidione Larisam eximeret, in Thessaliam mi-
2 sissent, quia id tempus rebus gerendis immaturum erat, in
hiberna regressi, principio veris coniunctis copiis in Thes-
3 saliam descenderunt. in Acarnania tum Antiochus erat.
advenientes Philippus Malloeam Perrhaebiae, Baebius
Phacium est adgressus; quo primo prope impetu capto,
4 Phaustum[30] eadem celeritate capit. inde Atragem cum se
recepisset, Chyretias[31] hinc et Ericium[32] occupat, prae-

29 portis *B*: portisque *χ*
30 Phaustum *BψEP*: Plaustum *A*: Phaestum *Sig.*
31 Chyretias *Mg*: Cyrethias *Bχ*: Cyretias *Fr. 1*
32 Eritic(t)ium *Bχ*: Erit(c)ium *a*

60 Probably rather of a flotilla transferred to him by Atilius and
now operating off the island.

made the people of Thyrreum more wary, not more fearful. Giving the king the forthright answer that they would accept no fresh alliance without the authorization of the Roman generals, they shut their gates and placed armed guards on the walls. Very opportunely, Gnaeus Octavius arrived in Leucas to bolster the resolution of the Acarnanians, filling the allies with hopes that Manius Acilius had already crossed the sea with his legions and that there was a Roman camp established in Thessaly. (Octavius had been sent by Quinctius and had received a body of troops and a few ships from Aulus Postumius, who had been put in charge of Cephallenia[60] by the legate Atilius.) Since this rumor was made plausible by the fact that it was now a seasonable time of year for sailing, the king installed a garrison at Medion and certain other towns of Acarnania, left Thyrreum and returned to Chalcis by way of the cities of Aetolia and Phocis.

13. Marcus Baebius and King Philip had already met in the wintertime in the land of the Dassareti (at the time when they had sent Appius Claudius into Thessaly to raise the siege of Larisa)[61] but because it was still too early in the year for military operations they had returned to their winter quarters. Now, at the beginning of spring, they joined forces and came down into Thessaly (at that point Antiochus was in Acarnania). On their arrival, Philip assaulted Malloea in Perrhaebia and Baebius attacked Phacium. Capturing Phacium with his first onslaught, Baebius just as quickly took Phaustus. Turning back to Atrax from there, he next seized Chyretiae and Ericinium and, after

---

[61] 10.10, above. For the towns in this chapter, cf. *Barr.* 55 A-B-C 1–2, though several are unlocated/unlisted.

sidiisque per recepta oppida dispositis Philippo rursus
5 obsidenti Malloeam se coniungit. sub adventum Romani
exercitus seu ad metum virium seu ad spem veniae cum
dedidissent sese, ad ea recipienda oppida quae Athamanes
6 occupaverant uno agmine ierunt. erant autem haec: Aeginium, Ericinium, Gomphi, Silana, Tricca, Meliboea, Pha-
7 loria. inde Pelinnaeum, ubi Philippus Megalopolitanus
cum quingentis peditibus et equitibus quadraginta in
praesidio erat, circumsidunt, et priusquam oppugnarent,
mittunt ad Philippum qui monerent ne vim ultimam expe-
8 riri vellet. quibus ille satis ferociter respondit vel Romanis
vel Thessalis se crediturum fuisse, in Philippi se pot-
9 estatem commissurum non esse. postquam apparuit vi
agendum, quia videbatur et Limnaeum eodem tempore
oppugnari posse, regem ad Limnaeum ire placuit, Baebius
restitit ad Pelinnaeum oppugnandum.

14. Per eos forte dies M'. Acilius consul, cum viginti[33]
milibus peditum duobus milibus equitum quindecim elephantis mari traiecto, pedestres copias Larisam ducere
tribunos militum iussit; ipse cum equitatu Limnaeum ad
2 Philippum venit. adventu consulis deditio sine cuncta-
tione est facta, traditumque praesidium regium et cum iis
3 Athamanes. ab Limnaeo Pelinnaeum consul proficiscitur.
ibi primi Athamanes tradiderunt sese, deinde et Philippus
4 Megalopolitanus; cui decedenti praesidio cum obvius
forte fuisset Philippus rex, ad ludibrium regem eum con-

[33] viginti *Par. Lat. 14360,* decem *B*χ

---

[62] On the Roman troop numbers for the war with Antiochus,
see Briscoe 2.37–38 and Walsh 36.92.

placing garrisons throughout the captured towns, rejoined Philip who was again besieging Malloea. At the approach of the Roman army, the inhabitants of Malloea capitulated, either fearing the enemy's strength or hoping for clemency, and the two leaders went ahead in a single column to recover the towns that the Athamanians had seized. (The towns were: Aeginium, Ericinium, Gomphi, Silana, Tricca, Meliboea and Phaloria.) The two next surrounded Pelinnaeum, where Philip of Megalopolis was commanding a garrison of 500 infantry and 40 cavalry, and before assaulting it they sent a delegation to Philip to caution him against resisting to the last. He made the truculent reply to them that he would have entrusted himself to either the Romans or the Thessalians but he would not put himself in King Philip's hands. It was clear that force had to be employed and, because it seemed that an attack on Limnaeum could be made at the same time, it was decided that the king should proceed to Limnaeum, and Baebius stayed behind for the assault on Pelinnaeum.

14. It so happened that at about this time the consul Manius Acilius, who had now completed his sea crossing with 20,000 infantry, 2,000 cavalry, and 15 elephants,[62] ordered the military tribunes to lead his infantry to Larisa, and he himself came to Philip at Limnaeum with the cavalry. At the consul's approach the town surrendered without hesitation and the king's garrison was delivered to him and the Athamanians with it. From Limnaeum the consul set off to Pelinnaeum. There the Athamanians were the first to surrender and after them Philip of Megalopolis, whom King Philip happened to meet as he was leaving the

salutari iussit, ipse congressus fratrem haud sane decoro
5 maiestati suae ioco appellavit. deductus inde ad consulem
custodiri iussus,[34] et haud ita multo post in vinculis Romam missus. cetera multitudo Athamanum aut militum
Antiochi regis, quae in praesidiis deditorum per eos dies
oppidorum fuerat, Philippo tradita regi est; fuere autem
6 ad tria[35] milia hominum. consul Larisam est profectus, ibi
de summa belli consultaturus. in itinere ab Cierio et Me-
tropoli legati tradentes urbes suas occurrerunt.
7 Philippus, Athamanum praecipue captivis indulgenter
habitis, ut per eos conciliaret gentem, nactus spem Athamaniae potiundae, exercitum eo duxit, praemissis in civi-
8 tates captivis. et illi magnam auctoritatem apud populares
habuerunt, clementiam erga se regis munificentiamque
9 commemorantes, et Amynander, cuius praesentis maies-
tas aliquos in fide continuisset, veritus ne traderetur Philippo iam pridem hosti et Romanis merito tunc propter
defectionem infensis, cum coniuge ac liberis regno excessit Ambraciamque se contulit; ita Athamania omnis in ius
dicionemque Philippi concessit.
10 Consul ad reficienda maxime iumenta, quae et navigatione et postea itineribus fatigata erant, paucos Larisae

[63] Philip mocks the Megalopolitan for his claim that he was
descended from Alexander the Great (cf. 35.47.5).

[64] *Barr.* 55 C2 (Kierion); B2 (Metropolis).

[65] Ambracia in Epirus (*Barr.* 54 C3) was earlier Pyrrhus' capital. It had recently fallen to Aetolia, so that Amynander could
expect a welcome there.

garrison. To poke fun at him, he ordered him to be hailed as king,[63] and he himself approached him and addressed him as "brother," a quip truly inappropriate to his royal station. The man was then brought before the consul, orders were issued for him to be kept under guard, and shortly afterward he was sent to Rome in irons. The horde of remaining prisoners—Athamanians or soldiers of King Antiochus who had garrisoned the towns that surrendered in that period—was delivered to King Philip; they numbered some 3,000 men. The consul then set off for Larisa to hold discussions there on general strategy for the war. On the journey he was met by delegations from Cierium and Metropolis,[64] offering their cities' surrender.

Philip was especially indulgent with the Athamanian prisoners of war in order to win the support of their people through them; and having conceived the hope of gaining control of Athamania, he now led his army there after first sending ahead the prisoners to their city-states. The prisoners did have a profound influence on their compatriots with their talk of the king's clemency toward them and his openhandedness. Amynander's commanding presence might perhaps have kept some loyal had he remained; but, frightened that he would be delivered to Philip, an enemy of long standing, and to the Romans, justly angry with him because of his desertion, he left the kingdom with his wife and children and went to Ambracia.[65] Thus all Athamania fell under Philip's authority and control.

The consul waited a few days at Larisa, mainly to revive the pack animals, which were exhausted from the sea voyage and the land journeys that followed, and then he set

moratus dies, velut renovato modica quiete exercitu,
11 Crannonem est progressus. venienti Pharsalus et Scotusa
et Pherae quaeque in eis praesidia Antiochi erant dedun-
tur. ex iis, interrogatis qui manere secum vellent, mille
volentes Philippo tradit, ceteros inermes Demetriadem
12 remittit. Proernam inde recepit et quae circa eam castella
erant. ducere tum porro in sinum Maliacum coepit. adpro-
pinquanti faucibus super quas siti Thaumaci sunt, deserta
urbe iuventus omnis armata silvas et itinera insedit, et in
13 agmen Romanum ex superioribus locis incursavit. consul,
primo missis[36] qui ex propinquo conloquentes deterrerent
eos a tali furore, postquam perseverare in incepto vidit,
tribuno cum duorum signorum militibus circummisso,
interclusit ad urbem iter armatis vacuamque eam cepit.
14 tum clamore ab tergo captae urbis audito, refugientium
15 undique ex silvis insidiatorum caedes facta est. ab Thaumacis altero die consul ad Spercheum amnem pervenit,
inde Hypataeorum agros vastavit.

15. Cum haec agebantur, Chalcide erat Antiochus, iam
tum cernens nihil se ex Graecia praeter amoena Chalcide
hiberna et infames nuptias petisse. tunc Aetolorum vana
2 promissa incusare et Thoantem, Hannibalem vero non ut
prudentem tantum virum, sed prope vatem omnium quae

---

36 missis *Gron.*: missi *Bχ*: mittere *Mg*: misit *Madvig*

---

66 *Barr.* 55 C1 (Krannon).

67 Proerna and Thaumaci (Thaumakoi) *Barr.* 55 C2. At
32.4.3–6, Livy praises the view from Thaumaci and derives the
name from the Greek "thauma" (miracle).

68 River Spercheios, Hypata: *Barr.* 55 C3.

69 For Thoas, cf. 35.12.4 note.

off for Crannon[66] with an army he judged restored after its brief repose. While he was on his way, Pharsalus, Scotusa and Pherae, along with the garrisons of Antiochus stationed in them, surrendered to him. Acilius asked which of the prisoners chose to remain with him, and handed over to Philip 1,000 who volunteered to do so; the rest he sent, disarmed, to Demetrias. He next took Proerna and its surrounding strongholds. Then he began to march toward the Malian Gulf. As he was approaching the gorge above which Thaumaci[67] lies, all the men of military age armed themselves, left the town, took up positions for ambush in the woods and along the roads, and from the higher ground made attacks on the Roman column. At first the consul sent intermediaries to speak to them face to face in order to dissuade them from such madness; but seeing them determined to continue what they had started, he sent a tribune with the soldiers of two maniples to make their way around them, closed off access to the city to the enemy soldiers, and captured it when it was left undefended. Then, hearing the shouting from the captured city to their rear, the men in ambush fled in all directions from the woods and were slaughtered. The next day the consul came from Thaumaci to the River Spercheus, and then raided the farmlands of Hypata.[68]

15. While this was going on, Antiochus was at Chalcis, by now already coming to see that all he had gained from Greece was a winter pleasantly spent in Chalcis and a disreputable marriage. He then started to complain about the Aetolians' empty promises and about Thoas,[69] but he was full of admiration for Hannibal, not merely as a man of sound judgment but almost as a prophet of all that was taking place at that time. Nevertheless, not to ruin his

tum evenirent admirari. ne tamen temere coepta segnitia
insuper everteret, nuntios in Aetoliam misit, ut omni con-
3 tracta iuventute convenirent Lamiam; et ipse eo decem
milia fere peditum, ex iis qui postea venerant ex Asia ex-
4 pleta, et equites quingentos duxit. quo cum aliquanto pauciores quam unquam antea convenissent, et principes tantummodo cum paucis clientibus essent, atque ii dicerent
omnia sedulo ab se facta ut quam plurimos ex civitatibus
5 suis evocarent—nec auctoritate nec gratia nec imperio
adversus detractantes militiam valuisse—destitutus undique et ab suis, qui morabantur in Asia, et ab sociis, qui ea
in quorum spem vocaverant non praestabant, intra saltum
Thermopylarum sese recepit.
6   Id iugum, sicut Appennini dorso Italia dividitur, ita
7 mediam Graeciam dirimit. ante saltum Thermopylarum
in septentrionem versa Epirus et Perrhaebia et Magnesia
et Thessalia est, et Phthiotae Achaei et sinus Maliacus;
8 intra fauces ad meridiem vergunt Aetoliae pars maior et
Acarnania, et cum Locride Phocis, et Boeotia, adiunc-
taque insula Euboea et excurrente in altum velut promun-

---

70 The numbers are confirmed by Appian, *Syr.* 17.

71 Latin *clientes*. As often, Livy here imports a Roman term
that he thinks is roughly equivalent to a foreigner's rank or status.
A *cliens* was a free person who provided services for a (rich) patron (*patronus*) in return for help and protection in time of need
(cf. *OCD* s.v. *cliens*).

72 Livy's geography is notoriously wobbly and his comparison
of the Apennines with the mountain range at Thermopylae is
absurd. Having no personal acquaintance with the area, he prob-

reckless endeavor further by inactivity, he sent messengers to Aetolia instructing the Aetolians to mobilize all their fighting men and assemble at Lamia, and he himself led to that city about 10,000 infantry (their number having been augmented by troops that had subsequently arrived from Asia) and 500 cavalry.[70] The Aetolians who assembled here did so in considerably smaller numbers than on any previous occasion and only their leading men and a few dependents[71] were present. They claimed they had done their best to call out as many as possible from their communities but neither their influence nor their standing nor their authority had carried any weight with those refusing to serve. Antiochus was thus left deserted everywhere—both by his own men, who were malingering in Asia, and by his allies, who were not providing the support that they had led him to expect when they had asked him to come—and he fell back within the pass of Thermopylae.

As Italy is divided by the chain of the Apennines, so the mountain range here splits Greece in two.[72] Before the pass of Thermopylae are Epirus, Perrhaebia, Magnesia and Thessaly, as well as Phthiotic Achaea and the Malian Gulf, all of them to the north. On this side of the defile, to the south, lie most of Aetolia, Acarnania, and Phocis together with Locris, and Boeotia with its adjoining island, Euboea; and lying behind these are the land of Attica (on

ably again misconstrues Polybius, who must have described it (cf. App. *Syr.* 17). He perhaps felt that its fame as the site of the famous battle of the "three hundred Spartans" with the Persians in 480 called for some geographical excursus.

9 turio Attica terra, sita ab tergo, et[37] Peloponnesus. hoc
iugum, ab Leucade[38] et mari ad occidentem verso per
Aetoliam ad alterum mare orienti obiectum tendens, ea
aspreta rupesque interiectas habet ut non modo exercitus
sed ne expediti quidem facile ullas ad transitum calles
10 inveniant. extremos ad orientem montes Oetam vocant,
quorum quod altissimum est Callidromon appellatur, in
cuius valle ad Maliacum sinum vergente iter est non latius
11 quam sexaginta passus. haec una militaris via est, qua tra-
12 duci exercitus, si non prohibeantur, possint. ideo Pylae et
ab aliis, quia calidae aquae in ipsis faucibus sunt, Thermopylae locus appellatur, nobilis Lacedaemoniorum adversus Persas morte magis memorabili quam pugna.

16. Haudquaquam pari tum animo Antiochus intra
portas loci eius castris positis munitionibus insuper saltum
2 impediebat, et cum duplici vallo fossaque et muro etiam,
qua res postulabat, ex multa copia passim iacentium lapi-
3 dum permunisset omnia, satis fidens nunquam ea vim
Romanum exercitum facturum, Aetolos ex quattuor milibus—tot enim convenerant—partim ad Heracleam prae-
4 sidio obtinendam, quae ante ipsas fauces posita est, partim
Hypatam mittit, et Heracleam haud dubius consulem op-

---

[37] sita ab tergo et *Bχ*: *del* et *Crév.*: et sita ab tergo *M. Müller*:
sita ab tergo est *H.J.M*   [38] Leucade *Bχ*: Leucate *Harl. 2671*

---

[73] Oeta sometimes refers, as here, to the whole range, including Mt. Knemis (*Barr.* 55 C–D3). Callidromon is just southeast
of Thermopylae (D3: Kallidromon).

[74] Literally, "Hot Gates." Pylae: "Gates."

[75] Probably the upcoming battle (though Walsh *ad loc.* thinks
the "natural meaning" is the battle of 480 BC).

a kind of promontory jutting out to sea) and the Peloponnese. The range extends from Leucas and the western sea through Aetolia to the other sea that lies to the east and at points has terrain so craggy and precipitously steep that it is not easy for lightly equipped men, much less an army, to find paths affording a way across. The mountains at the eastern extremity they call Oeta, and the highest of them is named Callidromon.[73] In the Callidromon valley, at the point where it slopes down to the Malian Gulf, there is a passage no more than sixty paces wide. This is the only road suitable for an army, a point where forces could be led though if there is no opposition. For that reason the place is called Pylae—Thermopylae[74] by others, because there are hot springs within the pass itself—and it is famous for the deaths of the Spartans in the struggle against Persia, deaths more renowned than the engagement.[75]

16. It was with feelings not at all like theirs[76] that Antiochus now encamped within the "Gates"[77] of the place and also proceeded to block the pass with fortifications. He protected the entire position with a double rampart, a ditch and, where required, even a wall made of the numerous stones lying around the area. Then, confident that the Roman army would never force its way through there, he sent off the 4,000 Aetolians who had congregated there, some to garrison Heraclea, which lay right before the pass, and others to Hypata.[78] He was convinced that the consul

[76] That is, of Leonidas and his three hundred Spartans.

[77] There were in fact three such "gates" in the pass, and Antiochus made his stand at the eastern one.

[78] Heraclea (*Barr.* 55 C3) was a Spartan foundation, dating to 426, sometimes referred to as Heraclea in Trachis to distinguish it from other towns with the same name. Hypata: *Barr.* 55 C3.

pugnaturum, et iam multis nuntiantibus circa Hypatam omnia evastari.

5   Consul, depopulatus Hypatensem primo deinde Heracleensem agrum, inutili utrobique auxilio Aetolorum, in ipsis faucibus prope fontes calidarum aquarum adversus regem posuit castra. Aetolorum utraeque manus Heracleam sese incluserunt.

6   Antiochum, cui priusquam hostem cerneret satis omnia permunita et praesidiis obsaepta videbantur, timor incessit ne quas per imminentia iuga calles inveniret ad
7 transitum Romanus; nam et Lacedaemonios quondam ita a Persis circuitos fama erat, et nuper Philippum ab iisdem
8 Romanis; itaque nuntium Heracleam ad Aetolos mittit, ut hanc saltem sibi operam eo bello praestarent, ut vertices circa montium occuparent obsiderentque, ne qua transire
9 Romani possent. hoc nuntio audito dissensio inter Aetolos orta est. pars imperio parendum regis atque eundum censebant, pars subsistendum Heracleae ad utramque for-
10 tunam, ut sive victus ab consule rex esset, in expedito haberent integras copias ad opem propinquis ferendam civitatibus suis, sive vinceret, ut dissipatos in fugam Roma-
11 nos persequerentur. utraque pars non mansit modo in sententia sua, sed etiam exsecuta est consilium: duo milia Heracleae substiterunt; duo trifariam divisa Callidromum et Rhoduntiam et Tichiunta—haec nomina cacuminibus sunt—occupavere.

---

79 Persians/Spartans: Hdt. 7.215–28; Romans/Philip (at the River Aous): 32.11.1–12.10.

80 *Barr.* 55 D3.

would attack Heraclea, and in addition many reports were already coming in that all the lands around Hypata were being laid waste.

The consul first razed the fields of Hypata and then those of Heraclea, the Aetolians providing no effective assistance to either, and he encamped within the pass itself, close to the hot springs and facing the king. The two Aetolian forces barricaded themselves in at Heraclea.

Before he set eyes on his enemy, Antiochus had thought the entire position well enough fortified and secured by his guard posts. Now, however, the fear gripped him that the Romans would discover some paths over the hills dominating the pass that would let them through; for it was said that this was how the Spartans had once been encircled by the Persians and, more recently, Philip by these same Romans.[79] He therefore sent a message to the Aetolians at Heraclea asking them at least to do him this one service in this war, namely to seize and occupy the mountain tops in the vicinity to prevent the Romans from crossing them. When the message was received, an argument arose among the Aetolians. Some thought they should accede to the king's request and go, others that they should remain at Heraclea ready to respond to either outcome: should the king be defeated by the consul, they would have fresh troops at their disposal to bring aid to their own cities nearby; and, if he were victorious, they could chase the Romans when they scattered in flight. Both groups not only remained firm in their own opinions but also acted on them. Two thousand stayed on at Heraclea; 2,000 formed three divisions and seized Callidromus, Rhoduntia, and Tichius, as the mountain peaks are called.[80]

17. Consul postquam insessa superiora loca ab Aetolis
vidit, M. Porcium Catonem et L. Valerium Flaccum consulares legatos cum binis milibus delectorum peditum ad
castella Aetolorum, Flaccum in Rhoduntiam et Tichiunta,
2 Catonem in Callidromum mittit. ipse, priusquam ad hostem copias admoveret, vocatos in contionem milites paucis est adlocutus.

"Plerosque omnium ordinum, milites, inter vos esse
video, qui in hac eadem provincia T. Quincti ductu auspi-
3 cioque militaveritis. Macedonico bello inexsuperabilior
4 saltus ad amnem Aoum fuit quam hic; quippe portae sunt
hae, et unus inter duo maria clausis omnibus velut natu-
ralis transitus est; munitiones et locis opportunioribus
tunc fuerunt et validiores impositae; exercitus hostium ille
et numero maior et militum genere aliquanto melior;
5 quippe illic Macedones Thracesque et Illyrii erant, fero-
cissimae omnes gentes, hic Syri et Asiatici Graeci sunt,
6 vilissima genera hominum et servituti nata; rex ille belli-
cosissimus et exercitatus iam inde ab iuventa finitimis
Thracum atque Illyriorum et circa omnium accolarum
7 bellis, hic, ut aliam omnem vitam sileam, is est qui cum ad
inferendum populo Romano bellum ex Asia in Europam

---

81 The consuls for 195: M. Porcius Cato (9), the famous Cato
the Censor, a leading figure in Rome in the first half of the second
century; and L. Valerius Flaccus (173), Cato's patron at the start
of his career. The two were partners not only in the consulship
but later also in the censorship (184).

82 The conventional prebattle speech now follows. Whether
such a speech occurred in Polybius is uncertain (it does not occur
in Appian's *Syriaca*).

17. When he saw that the heights were held by the Aetolians, the consul sent Marcus Porcius Cato and Lucius Valerius Flaccus, his legates of consular rank,[81] each with 2,000 elite infantrymen, against the fortified positions of the Aetolians, Flaccus to Rhoduntia and Tichius, and Cato to Callidromus. Before moving his troops ahead against the enemy, Acilius himself summoned the men to a meeting and briefly addressed them:[82]

"Men: I see among you a large number of soldiers of all ranks who fought in this same province under the leadership and auspices of Titus Quinctius. In the Macedonian war, the pass at the River Aous[83] was more difficult to negotiate than this. For here there are these gates and, with the whole terrain blocked, only one naturally formed passageway, as it were, between the two seas. On that occasion the defenses of the enemy were more favorably situated for them and more firmly established. That enemy army was numerically superior and considerably better in the quality of its soldiers; for there were Macedonians there, and Thracians and Illyrians, all highly aggressive peoples, and here there are Syrians and Asiatic Greeks, the dregs of humanity, born for slavery.[84] That king who faced us was a great warrior, one trained from boyhood in wars against Thracian and Illyrian neighbors and all the other peoples in the region. In this king you have a man who, to say nothing of the rest of his record, has, after crossing from Asia to Europe to make war on the

[83] For the battle at the Aous and Philip's position, cf 32.5.8–6.8.   [84] A commonplace in Roman writers; cf. 38.17.10–16, where their weakness is attributed to the enervating effect of the climate of the eastern peoples.

transisset, nihil memorabilius toto tempore hibernorum gesserit quam quod amoris causa ex domo privata et ob-
8   scuri etiam inter populares generis uxorem duxit, et novus maritus, velut saginatus nuptialibus cenis, ad pugnam processit.

"Summa virium speique eius in Aetolis fuit, gente vanissima et levissima,[39] ut vos prius experti estis, nunc
9   Antiochus experitur. nam nec frequentes convenerunt[40] nec contineri in castris potuerunt, et in seditione ipsi inter sese sunt, et cum Hypatam tuendam Heracleamque deposcissent, neutram tutati refugerunt in iuga montium, pars Heracleae incluserunt sese.

10   "Rex ipse confessus nusquam aequo campo non modo congredi se ad pugnam audere, sed ne castra quidem in aperto ponere, relicta omni ante se regione ea quam se
11   nobis ac Philippo ademisse gloriabatur, condidit se intra rupes, ne ante fauces quidem saltus, ut quondam Lacedaemonios fama est, sed intra penitus retractis castris; quod quantum interest ad timorem ostendendum, an mu-
12   ris urbis alicuius obsidendum sese incluserit? sed neque Antiochum tuebuntur angustiae, nec Aetolos vertices illi quos ceperunt. satis undique provisum atque praecautum est ne quid adversus vos in pugna praeter hostis esset.

13   "Illud proponere animo vestro debetis, non vos pro Graeciae libertate dimicare tantum, quamquam is quoque

---

[39] levissima *Mg*: ingratissima *Bχ*
[40] frequentes convenerunt *Mg*: venerunt frequentes *Bχ*

---

[85] While romantic love may be involved in Roman marriage (cf. Treggiari 253–61), it was not generally considered by the ancients a good basis for it.

Roman people, done nothing throughout the entire winter more memorable than get married for love[85]—and to a woman from the household of a commoner and a family of no distinction even among her compatriots! And now the new bridegroom has come out to fight, virtually bloated with his wedding feasts!

"His greatest strength and hope lay in the Aetolians, a vain and fickle people, as you learned earlier and he is learning now. They have not come together in large numbers; they could not be made to stay in their camp; they squabble among themselves; and, after demanding that Hypata and Heraclea be defended, they have failed to defend either—they have fled to the mountain tops and some have barricaded themselves in Heraclea.

"The king himself has clearly acknowledged that he cannot even risk an encampment in the open, let alone commit himself to battle anywhere on level ground. He has abandoned all the area that lay before him, which he used to boast he had taken from us and from Philip, and has buried himself among the rocks. And he has done that not even at the opening to the pass, as they say the Spartans once did, but has brought his camp back into the depths of it. In terms of showing funk, what difference is there between this and shutting oneself up within some city's walls to face a siege? But a narrow pass is not going to protect Antiochus nor will the hilltops they seized protect the Aetolians. Enough care and precaution has been taken everywhere to ensure that you will have nothing against you in the battle but the enemy.

"This is what you should keep at the front of your minds. You are fighting not simply for the independence of Greece, a fine enterprise though that would also be—to

209

egregius titulus esset, liberatam[41] a Philippo ante nunc ab
Aetolis et ab Antiocho liberare, neque ea tantum in prae-
14 mium vestrum cessura quae nunc in regiis castris sunt, sed
illum quoque omnem apparatum qui in dies ab Epheso
exspectatur praedae futurum, Asiam deinde Syriamque et
omnia usque ad ortum solis ditissima regna Romano impe-
15 rio aperturos. quid deinde aberit quin ab Gadibus ad mare
rubrum Oceano fines terminemus, qui orbem terrarum
amplexu finit, et omne humanum genus secundum deos
16 nomen Romanum veneretur? in haec tanta praemia dig-
nos parate animos, ut crastino die bene iuvantibus dis acie
decernamus."

18. Ab hac contione dimissi milites, priusquam corpora
curarent, arma tela parant. luce prima, signo pugnae proposito, instruit aciem consul, arta fronte, ad naturam et
2 angustias loci. rex, postquam signa hostium conspexit, et
ipse copias educit. levis armaturae partem ante vallum in
primo locavit, tum Macedonum robur, quos sarisophorus[42] appellabant, velut firmamentum circa ipsas muni-
3 tiones constituit. his ab sinistro cornu iaculatorum sagit-
tariorumque et funditorum manum sub ipsis radicibus
montis posuit, ut ex altiore loco nuda latera hostium inces-
4 serent. ab dextro Macedonibus ad ipsum munimentorum

---

41 liberatam *ed. Rom.*: liberam *Bχ*   42 sarisophorus *Weiss.*,
Hertz: sarisophoros *Asc.*: sariphorus *Bχ*

---

86 The term in Latin can apply variously to the Red Sea, the
Indian Ocean, or the Persian Gulf. Here Livy is probably using it
simply to suggest the furthest reaches of the inhabited world.

87 "Sarissa-bearing." There may have been some men of
Macedonian origin resident in the Seleucid kingdom, but the

free now from the Aetolians and Antiochus a country that you earlier freed from Philip; and it is not only what can now be found in the king's camp that will fall to you as your prize—you will also have as your booty all the equipment that is expected any day now from Ephesus. After that you will open up to Roman rule Asia, Syria and all the wealthiest kingdoms stretching as far as the rising sun. How far shall we be then from having our empire, from Gades to the Red Sea,[86] limited only by the Ocean that embraces the world? How far shall we be from having all humanity revere the Roman name next only to the gods? Prepare your spirits, making them worthy of such great rewards, so that tomorrow, with heaven's gracious aid, we may decide the issue on the field of battle."

18. Dismissed from the assembly, and before taking food and rest, the men made ready their armor and weapons. At dawn the consul displayed the signal for battle and drew up his line with a narrow front to suit the naturally restricted features of the position. When he saw the standards of his enemy, the king also led out his forces. Some of the light infantry he deployed in the front line before the rampart and then, as his mainstay, he set his powerful "Macedonian" unit called the "sarisophori,"[87] around the actual defense works. To support these on the left flank he deployed a unit of javelin throwers, archers, and slingers right at the foot of the mountains, so they could put pressure on the unprotected flank of the enemy from the higher ground. To the right of the "Macedonians," where the fortifications actually terminated but where the posi-

term is perhaps applied here simply to men using Macedonian weapons. Only here is it found for the Seleucid phalanx.

finem, qua loca usque ad mare inuia palustri limo et uora-
ginibus claudunt, elephantos cum adsueto praesidio posuit, post eos equites, tum modico intervallo relicto ceteras copias in secunda acie.

5   Macedones pro vallo locati primo facile sustinebant
Romanos, temptantes ab omni parte aditus, multum adiu-
vantibus qui ex loco superiore fundis velut nimbum glan-
6 dis et sagittas simul ac iacula ingerebant; deinde, ut maior
nec iam toleranda vis hostium inferebat se, pulsi loco intra
munimenta subductis ordinibus concesserunt; inde ex
vallo prope alterum vallum hastis prae se obiectis fece-
7 runt. et ita modica altitudo valli erat ut et locum superiorem suis ad pugnandum praeberet, et propter longitudi-
8 nem hastarum subiectum haberet hostem. multi temere
subeuntes vallum transfixi sunt; et aut incepto inrito reces-
sissent aut plures cecidissent, ni M. Porcius ab iugo Calli-
dromi, deiectis inde Aetolis et magna ex parte caesis—
incautos enim et plerosque sopitos oppresserat—, super
imminentem castris collem apparuisset.

    19. Flacco non eadem fortuna ad Tichiunta et Rhodun-
tiam, nequiquam subire ad ea castella conato, fuerat.
2   Macedones quique alii in castris regiis erant primo,

tion was blocked by marshland and bogs (making it impassable right down to the sea), he deployed his elephants, with their usual keepers. To their rear he placed his cavalry and, a short distance behind, the rest of his troops in a second line.

The "Macedonians" stationed before the rampart at first would easily parry the attack of the Romans, who were at all points trying to make inroads, and they were greatly helped by the men with the slings on the higher ground who were hurling down a veritable shower of lead balls and arrows, and javelins, too. Then, as pressure from their enemy mounted to the point of becoming irresistible, they were dislodged from their position and, pulling back their ranks, retreated within their fortifications. There, from the rampart, they made what almost constituted a second rampart by extending their spears before them. In addition, the rampart was of such limited height that it offered Autiochus' men a higher location from which to fight and also enabled them, because of the length of their spears, to keep their enemy beneath them. Many who recklessly ventured up to the rampart were impaled by them, and the Romans would have withdrawn in failure or suffered heavier casualties had not Marcus Porcius driven the Aetolians down from the crest of Callidromon, killing most of them—he had taken them by surprise, many of them asleep—and appeared on the hill overlooking the camp.

19. (Flaccus had not had the same success at Tichius and Rhoduntia, having failed in his attempt to reach those strongholds.)

While all that was visible in the distance was a body of men on the march, the "Macedonians" and the others in

213

dum procul nihil aliud quam turba et agmen apparebat,
3 Aetolos credere, visa procul pugna, subsidio venire; ceterum, ut primum signaque et arma ex propinquo cognita
errorem aperuerunt, tantus repente pavor omnes cepit ut
4 abiectis armis fugerent. et munimenta sequentes impedie-
runt, et angustiae vallis per quam sequendi erant, et maxime omnium quod elephanti novissimi agminis erant, quos
5 pedes aegre praeterire, eques nullo poterat modo, timen-
tibus equis tumultumque inter se maiorem quam in proelio edentibus; aliquantum temporis et direptio castrorum
tenuit; Scarpheam tamen eo die consecuti sunt hostem.
6 multis in ipso itinere caesis captisque, non equis virisque
tantum, sed etiam elephantis, quos capere non potuerant,
7 interfectis, in castra reverterunt; quae temptata eo die
inter ipsum pugnae tempus ab Aetolis, Heracleam obtinentibus praesidio, sine ullo haud parum audacis incepti
effectu fuerant.

8   Consul, noctis insequentis tertia vigilia praemisso
equitatu ad persequendum hostem, signa legionum luce
9 prima movit. aliquantum viae praeceperat rex, ut qui non
ante quam Elatiae ab effuso constiterit cursu; ubi primum
reliquiis pugnaeque et fugae conlectis, cum perexigua
10 manu semiermium militum Chalcidem se recepit. Romanus equitatus ipsum quidem regem Elatiae adsecutus non

---

88 Horses' fear of the smell of elephants (and camels) is well
documented in the ancient sources, and they had to be specially
trained to face them. (For problems caused by this in the second
Punic War, cf. 21.55.7, 30.18.7.)

89 Scarphea: about three miles northwest of Thronium (*Barr.*
55 D3: Skarpheia). Cf. 33.3.6.

90 There were four watches during the hours of darkness,

the king's camp assumed that this was the Aetolians who, having seen the battle from afar, were coming to their aid. However, as soon as the standards and armor were recognized at close quarters, revealing their mistake, such panic suddenly seized them all that they threw down their weapons and fled. Both the defense works and the narrowness of the valley through which they had to be pursued impeded the pursuers, but the elephants bringing up the enemy rear did so most of all—infantrymen had difficulty getting past them and cavalrymen found it impossible because the horses took fright,[88] producing greater turmoil for their own side than they had in the battle. Ransacking the camp also took a certain amount of time; even so, on that day, they chased the enemy to Scarphea.[89] On the way they inflicted heavy casualties and took many prisoners, killing not only horses and men but also elephants that they had been unable to capture. They then returned to their camp. This had been attacked that day, while the battle was actually in progress, by the Aetolians of the garrison occupying Heraclea, but their ambitious enterprise had proved unsuccessful.

At the third watch[90] of the following night the consul sent his cavalry ahead to pursue the enemy, and at dawn moved his legions forward. The king had covered some distance as he had not halted his headlong flight before reaching Elatia. There he first brought together the survivors of the battle and the flight and then retreated to Chalcis with a mere handful of poorly armed soldiers. The Roman cavalry did not overtake the king himself at Elatia

each introduced by a bugle call, and the third was the favored time for clandestine operations.

est, magnam partem agminis aut lassitudine subsistentes aut errore, ut qui sine ducibus per ignota itinera fugerent,

11 dissipatos oppresserunt; nec praeter quingentos, qui circa regem fuerunt, ex toto exercitu quisquam effugit, etiam ex decem milibus militum quos[43] Polybio auctore traiecisse secum regem in Graeciam scripsimus, exiguus numerus;

12 quid si Antiati Valerio credamus, sexaginta milia militum fuisse in regio exercitu scribenti, quadraginta inde milia cecidisse, supra quinque milia capta cum signis militaribus

13 ducentis triginta? Romanorum centum quinquaginta in ipso certamine pugnae, ab incursu Aetolorum se tuentes non plus quinquaginta interfecti sunt.

20. Consule per Phocidem et Boeotiam exercitum ducente consciae defectionis civitates cum velamentis ante

2 portas stabant, metu ne hostiliter diriperentur. ceterum per omnes dies haud secus quam pacato agro sine vexatione ullius rei agmen processit, donec in agrum Coro-

3 neum ventum est. ibi statua regis Antiochi, posita in templo Mineruae Itoniae,[44] iram accendit, permissumque militi est ut circumiectum templo agrum popularetur; dein cogitatio animum subit cum communi decreto Boeotorum posita esset statua, indignum esse in unum Co-

---

43 quos φ: quod Bψa
44 Itoniae *Gron.*: *om.* Bχ: Itonaeae *Mg*

---

91 The number is also found in Appian (*Syr.* 20).

92 Cf. 35.43.6. On Polybius, see Introduction to vol. IX (LCL 295), xix–xxvi, lxxviii–lxxxii.

93 On Valerias Antias and his habit of inflating figures, see Introduction to vol. IX (LCL 295), xxvii–xxviii.

94 On the olive branches (*velamenta*), cf. 35.34.7 and note.

but they did catch most his column, men who had stopped from fatigue or become dispersed after losing their way (to be expected with people fleeing without guides on unfamiliar roads). In fact, from the entire army no one escaped, apart from 500 who were with the king,[91] a tiny fraction even of 10,000 soldiers, the number that I, following Polybius, gave above[92] as that which the king brought over to Greece with him. Imagine if we accept Valerius Antias' account[93] that there were 60,000 men in the king's army, that 40,000 of them lost their lives, and that more than 5,000 were captured, along with 230 military standards! One hundred and fifty of the Romans were killed actually fighting in the battle and no more than 50 defending themselves in the assault made by the Aetolians.

20. As the consul led his army through Phocis and Boeotia, the communities in the region, conscience-stricken over their defection and fearful of being plundered as enemies, stood before their gates with suppliant olive branches.[94] During all those days, however, the Roman column marched on just as if the countryside were pacified, and inflicted no damage at all until its arrival in the territory of Coronea. There a statue of King Antiochus that had been erected in the temple of Minerva Itonia[95] made tempers flare, and the soldiers were given leave to plunder the countryside around the temple. The thought then struck Acilius that savage reprisals against the territory of Coronea alone were unfair since the statue had been erected by a communal decision of the people of

---

[95] Athena Itonia, whose worship spread from Thessaly to other states, including Athens. Her most famous shrine was this one, at Coronea in Boeotia.

4 ronensem agrum saevire. revocato extemplo milite finis
populandi factus; castigati tantum verbis Boeoti ob ingra-
tum in tantis tamque recentibus beneficiis animum erga
Romanos.

5   Inter ipsum pugnae tempus decem naves regiae cum
praefecto Isidoro ad Thronium[45] in sinu Maliaco stabant.
eo gravis volneribus Alexander Acarnan, nuntius adversae
pugnae, cum perfugisset, trepidae inde recenti terrore
naves Cenaeum Euboeae petierunt. ibi mortuus sepultus-

6 que Alexander. tres, quae ex Asia profectae eundem portum tenuerunt, naves audita exercitus clade Ephesum
redierunt. Isidorus ab Cenaeo Demetriadem, si forte eo
deferret fuga regem, traiecit.

7   Per eosdem dies A. Atilius, praefectus Romanae classis, magnos regios commeatus iam fretum quod ad An-
drum insulam est praetervectos excepit; alias mersit alias

8 cepit naves; quae novissimi agminis erant cursum in Asiam
verterunt. Atilius, Piraeum—unde profectus erat—cum
agmine captivarum navium revectus, magnam vim frumenti et Atheniensibus et aliis eiusdem regionis sociis
divisit.

    21. Antiochus, sub adventum consulis a Chalcide pro-
fectus, Tenum primo tenuit, inde Ephesum transmisit.

2 consuli Chalcidem venienti portae patuerunt, cum adpro-
pinquante eo Aristoteles praefectus regis urbe excessisset.

3 et ceterae urbes in Euboea sine certamine traditae; pau-

---

45 ad Thronium *Mog*: ad Thorontum *Bφ*: Athorontum *ψ*

---

96 Thronion: *Barr.* 55 D3.

97 The former friend of Philip of Macedon, whom he left to
join the court of Antiochus (cf. 35.18.1).

Boeotia. The men were immediately recalled and the plundering was stopped. The Boeotians were merely reprimanded for their ingratitude toward the Romans after such great benefits had been so recently conferred on them.

During the very time that the battle had been in progress, ten of the king's ships, commanded by Isidorus, lay at anchor off Thronium[96] in the Malian gulf. Alexander the Acarnanian[97] came there in his flight, severely wounded, bringing news of the defeat; and the fleet, with the onset of fresh panic, headed for Cenaeum in Euboea.[98] Here Alexander died and was buried. Three ships that had sailed from Asia and put in at the same port returned to Ephesus on hearing of the defeat of their army. Isidorus then crossed from Cenaeum to Demetrias on the off chance that the flight might take the king there.

At about this same time the admiral of the Roman fleet, Aulus Atilius, intercepted a large convoy of provisions belonging to the king that had crossed the strait close to the island of Andros. He sank a number of the ships and captured others, and those at the rear of the line changed course for Asia. Atilius returned to Piraeus (whence he had set out) with his contingent of captured vessels and distributed large quantities of grain both to the Athenians and to other allies in the region.

21. Just before the consul's arrival, Antiochus set out from Chalcis and first made for Tenos and then crossed to Ephesus. On reaching Chalcis, the consul found the gates open since the king's prefect, Aristoteles, had left the city at his approach. The other cities of Euboea also capitu-

---

[98] At the northwest tip of Euboea (*Barr.* 55 D3 [Kenaion]).

cosque post dies,[46] omnibus perpacatis sine ullius noxa urbis, exercitus Thermopylas reductus, multo modestia post victoriam quam ipsa victoria laudabilior.

4 Inde consul M. Catonem, per quem quae gesta essent senatus populusque Romanus haud dubio auctore sciret,
5 Romam misit. is a Creusa—Thespiensium emporium est, in intimo sinu Corinthiaco retractum—Patras Achaiae petit; a Patris Corcyram usque Aetoliae atque Acarnaniae
6 litora legit, atque ita ad Hydruntem Italiae traicit. quinto die inde pedestri itinere Romam ingenti cursu pervenit. ante lucem ingressus urbem a porta ad praetorem M. Iunium iter intendit.

7 Is prima luce in senatum vocavit; quo L. Cornelius Scipio, aliquot diebus ante a consule dimissus, cum adveniens audisset praegressum Catonem in senatu esse,
8 supervenit exponenti quae gesta essent. duo inde legati iussu senatus in contionem sunt producti, atque ibi eadem quae in senatu de rebus in Aetolia gestis exposuerunt.

---

[46] paucosque post dies *Novák*: post paucosque post dies *Mg*: paucosque per dies *Bχ*

---

[99] Usually "Creusis" (cf. Paus. 9.32.1): *Barr.* 55 E4 (Kreusis).

[100] Citizens of Thespiae, the chief city of southern Boeotia (*Barr.* 55 E4), famous because of its proximity to Mt. Helicon and as a religious center.

[101] An Adriatic port (mod. Otranto), important for travel to and from Greece (*Barr.* 45 H4).

[102] L. Cornelius Scipio (337) Asiagenes, younger brother of Africanus, under whom he served in Spain, Sicily, and Africa (207–202). In 193 he had been praetorian governor of Sicily, and would be consul in 190.

lated without a struggle and a few days later, when peace had been restored everywhere without damage to any city, the army was brought back to Thermopylae—more praiseworthy for its moderation following the victory than for the victory itself.

From there, the consul dispatched Marcus Cato to Rome so the Roman senate and people could be informed of the events from a reliable source. Cato made for Patrae in Achaea, setting out from Creusa,[99] the commercial port of the Thespians[100] that lies deep in the Corinthian Gulf. From Patrae he passed along the coastline of Aetolia and Acarnania as far as Corcyra, and then crossed to Hydruntum[101] in Italy. Four days later, after an overland journey conducted at a headlong pace, he reached Rome. He entered the city before dawn and headed from the gate to the praetor Marcus Iunius.

Iunius summoned members to the senate at break of day. Lucius Cornelius Scipio[102] had been sent to Rome by the consul some days earlier and when told on his arrival that Cato had outpaced him[103] and was now in the senate; he came there to find Cato recounting what had transpired. The two legates were then brought before the popular assembly by order of the senate and there they gave the same report on events in Aetolia as they had given in the senate. A three-day period of supplication was de-

---

[103] There is a problem here, in that two messengers with the news of the victory were apparently sent, first Scipio, then Cato. On this, see Briscoe 2.252–53, and Walsh 36.100.

9   supplicatio in triduum decreta est et ut quadraginta hostiis
maioribus praetor, quibus dis ei videretur, sacrificaret.

10   Per eosdem dies et M. Fulvius Nobilior, qui biennio
ante praetor in Hispaniam erat profectus, ovans urbem est

11   ingressus; argenti bigati prae se tulit centum triginta milia
et extra numeratum duodecim milia pondo argenti, auri
pondo centum viginti septem.

22. Acilius consul ab Thermopylis Heracleam ad Aetolos praemisit, ut tunc saltem, experti regiam vanitatem,
resipiscerent, traditaque Heraclea cogitarent de petenda

2   ab senatu seu furoris sui seu erroris venia. et ceteras Graeciae civitates defecisse eo bello ab optime meritis Romanis; sed quia post fugam regis, cuius fiducia officio de-
cessissent, non addidissent pertinaciam culpae, in fidem

3   receptas esse; Aetolos quoque, quamquam non secuti sint
regem sed accersierint, et duces belli non socii fuerint, si
paenitere possint, posse et incolumes esse.

4   Ad ea cum pacati nihil responderetur, appareretque
armis rem gerendam, et rege superato bellum Aetolicum
integrum restare, castra ab Thermopylis ad Heracleam
movit, eoque ipso die, ut situm nosceret urbis ab omni
parte equo moenia est circumvectus.

---

104 On supplication cf. 35.8.3 note. Sacrificial victims were
divided by age into "unweaned" (*lactantes*) and "full-grown"
(*maiores*) animals, the latter being used for the more important
thanksgivings/crises.   105 A minor triumph granted to a
man not thought worthy of a full triumph. He entered Rome on
foot or on horseback, not in a chariot (cf. Beard passim, esp. 62–
63). Fulvius would go on to greater success as consul in 189, when
he successfully besieged Ambracia (38.4.1–9.9).

106 That is, the two-horse chariot usually found on the *denarius*, a silver coin originally worth ten asses (Lat. *deni* = ten).

creed, and the praetor was instructed to sacrifice 40 full-grown victims[104] to gods of his own choosing.

It was also at about this time that Marcus Fulvius Nobilior, who had set out for Spain two years earlier as praetor, entered the city in ovation.[105] He had 130,000 coins stamped with the *biga*[106] carried before him and, in addition to the coin, 12,000 pounds of silver and 127 pounds of gold.

22. From Thermopylae the consul Acilius sent a message to the Aetolians in Heraclea that now that they had experienced the king's incompetence they should finally come to their senses, deliver Heraclea and consider asking the senate to pardon what had been either an act of folly or an error of judgment on their part. The other states of Greece had, in that war, also broken faith with the Romans, who had deserved well of them,[107] said Acilius. They too had reneged on their duty from confidence in the king, but after his flight they had not added obstinacy to their guilt and had been taken back under Roman protection. As for the Aetolians, they had not *followed* the king but had actually invited him to Greece and been leaders and not just allies in the war; but even they could be out of harm's way if they could bring themselves to show remorse.

As there was no conciliatory response to these overtures, it was evident that military action was necessary and that, though the king was defeated, the Aetolian war was still to be fought. Acilius accordingly moved his camp from Thermopylae to Heraclea and on that very same day rode around the walls to examine the layout of the city on every side.

[107] Latin *ceteras* means *all* the others; Acilius exaggerates.

5   Heraclea sita est in radicibus Oetae montis, ipsa in
campo, arcem imminentem loco alto et undique praecipiti
6 habet. contemplatus omnia quae noscenda erant, quattuor
7 simul locis adgredi urbem constituit. a flumine Asopo, qua
et gymnasium est, L. Valerium operibus atque oppugnationi praeposuit; partem extra muros quae[47] fre-
quentius prope quam in urbe habitabatur, Ti.[48] Sempronio
8 Longo oppugnandam dedit; a sinu Maliaco, quae[49] aditum
haud facilem pars habebat, M. Baebium, ab altero amniculo,[50] quem Melana vocant, adversus Dianae templum
9 Ap. Claudium opposuit. horum magno certamine intra
paucos dies turres arietesque et alius omnis apparatus op-
10 pugnandarum urbium perficitur. et cum ager Heracle-
ensis, paluster omnis frequensque proceris arboribus,
benigne ad omne genus operum materiam suppeditabat,
11 tum, quia refugerant intra moenia Aetoli, deserta quae in
vestibulo urbis erant tecta in varios usus non tigna modo
et tabulas, sed laterem quoque et caementa et saxa variae
magnitudinis praebebant.
    23. Et Romani quidem operibus magis quam armis
urbem oppugnabant, Aetoli contra armis se tuebantur.

[47] partem . . . quae *Drak.* (partem qua extra muros *iam Gron.*):
om. Bχ: arcem . . . quae *Mg*

[48] Ti. *Sig.*: T. *Bχ*

[49] a sinu maliaco quae *Gel.*: et regionem Mellea (Mella *B*) *Bχ*:
e regione sinus Maliaci quae *Weiss.*

[50] amniculo *P Gel.*: anniculo ψ*AE*: angulo *B*: amnis latere *Mg*

[108] *Barr.* 55 C3.

[109] T. Sempronius Longus (67): praetor 196, consul 194. As

Heraclea lies at the foot of Mt Oeta;[108] it is in a plain itself but has a citadel that rises above it on a lofty elevation, sheer on all sides. After thoroughly reconnoitering its salient features, Acilius decided to attack the city at four points simultaneously. On the side of the River Asopus, where there is also a gymnasium, he put Lucius Valerius in charge of the siege works and the assault. The attack on the area outside the walls, which was almost more densely populated than the city itself, he entrusted to Tiberius Sempronius Longus.[109] On the side of the Malian Gulf, an area that did not afford easy access, he placed Marcus Baebius;[110] and on the side of the other small river called the Melas, and opposite the temple of Diana, he set Appius Claudius. Thanks to the keen competition between these men, the towers, battering rams and all the other machinery for besieging cities were completed in a matter of days. Moreover, the land around Heraclea, being all marshland, thickly forested with tall trees, offered a wealth of timber for every kind of construction; and in addition, because the Aetolians had sought refuge within their walls, the houses that they had abandoned at the entrance to the city provided not only beams and planks that could be put to various uses but also tiles, rubble[111] and rocks of various sizes.

23. The Romans were conducting their offensive against the city more by means of siege works than armed

consul he had, with his colleague Scipio Africanus, campaigned against the Boii and the Ligurians (34.46.4–48.1).

[110] M. Baebius Tamphilus (44): praetor 192 (cf.1.7, above), and later consul (181).

[111] Latin *caementa,* used for making a sort of concrete.

2 nam cum ariete quaterentur muri, non laqueis, ut solet, exceptos declinabant ictus, sed armati frequentes erumpebant,[51] quidam ignes etiam, quos aggeribus inicerent,

3 ferebant. fornices quoque in muro erant apti ad excurrendum, et ipsi, cum pro dirutis reficerent muros, crebriores eos, ut pluribus erumperetur in hostem locis, faciebant.

4 hoc primis diebus, dum integrae vires erant, et frequentes et impigre fecerunt, in dies deinde pauciores et segnius.

5 etenim cum multis urgerentur rebus, nulla eos res aeque ac vigiliae conficiebant, Romanis in magna copia militum succedentibus aliis in stationem aliorum, Aetolos propter paucitatem eosdem dies noctesque adsiduo labore urente.

6 per quattuor et viginti dies, ita ut nullum tempus vacuum dimicatione esset, adversus quattuor e partibus simul oppugnantem hostem nocturnus diurno continuatus labor est.

7 Cum fatigatos iam Aetolos sciret consul, et ex spatio[52] temporis et quod ita transfugae adfirmabant, tale consi-

8 lium init: media nocte receptui signum dedit, et ab oppugnatione simul milites omnes deductos usque ad ter-

9 tiam diei horam quietos in castris tenuit; inde coepta oppugnatio ad mediam rursus noctem perducta est, inter-

10 missa deinde usque ad tertiam diei horam. fatigationem rati esse causam Aetoli non continuandae oppugnationis,

[51] erumpebant *Gron.*: *om. B*χ: aderant *Weiss.*
[52] ex spatio *Novák*: expectatio *B*ψ: expectatione φ: ex ratione *Gel.*

---

[112] Nooses thrown over the front of the battering ram and then pulled sideways or upward to deflect it from its target.

assault, whereas the Aetolians relied on their weapons for their defense. When the walls were being shaken by the battering ram, they would not employ the usual tactic of deflecting the blows with lassos,[112] but would make repeated counterattacks in armed groups, some also carrying torches to throw on the siege works. There were, moreover, vaulted arches in the wall, well suited for making sorties, and when they were rebuilding their walls to replace what had been demolished they would fashion larger numbers of these so that forays against the enemy could be made in more places. In the early days of the siege, while their strength was intact, they did this in large numbers and with vigor, but as the days passed they did so in smaller numbers and less energetically. For, while they were under pressure in many respects, nothing sapped their strength as much as lack of sleep. The Romans, with their large array of troops, would replace each other on guard duty; but, because of their small numbers, the unremitting hardship that confronted the same men day and night was grinding down the Aetolians. For twenty-four days, with no time away from the conflict as they faced an enemy attacking them simultaneously on four fronts, the nightly struggle went on into the day.

The consul, aware that the Aetolians were now exhausted (he surmised it from the duration of the siege, and deserters also reported it), adopted the following plan. In the middle of the night he gave the signal to retreat and, after bringing back all his men from the assault at the one time, he kept them at ease in camp until the third hour of the day. Then the offensive was resumed and continued again until the middle of the night, when it was again suspended until the third hour of the day. The Aetolians

quae et ipsos adfecerat, ubi Romanis datum receptui signum esset, velut ipsi hoc[53] revocati pro se quisque ex stationibus decedebant, nec ante tertiam diei horam armati
in muris apparebant.

24. Consul cum nocte media intermisisset oppugnationem, quarta vigilia rursus ab tribus partibus summa vi
2 adgressus, ab una Ti.[54] Sempronium tenere intentos milites signumque exspectare iussit, ad ea[55] in nocturno tumultu unde clamor exaudiretur haud dubie ratus hostes
3 concursuros. Aetoli pars sopiti adfecta labore ac vigiliis
corpora ex somno moliebantur, pars vigilantes adhuc ad
4 strepitum pugnantium in tenebris currunt. hostes partim
per ruinas iacentis muri transcendere conantur, partim
scalis ascensus temptant, adversus quos undique ad opem
5 ferendam occurrunt[56] Aetoli. pars una, in qua aedificia
extra urbem erant, neque defenditur neque oppugnatur;
sed qui oppugnarent intenti signum exspectabant; defensor nemo aderat.

6   Iam dilucescebat cum signum consul dedit; et sine ullo
certamine partim per semirutos partim scalis[57] integros
muros transcendere. simul clamor, index capti oppidi, est
exauditus; undique Aetoli desertis stationibus in arcem

53 ipsi hoc φ: spe hac B: spe ac ψ: ipsi quoque hoc *ed. Rom.*
54 Ti. *Sig.*: T. *Mg*: *om. B*χ
55 ea *ed. Rom.*: eam *B*χ
56 occurrunt *B*χ: concurrunt *Mg*
57 per semirutos partim scalis *Weiss.*: per erutos partim scalis
per *Mg*: per semiruta partim scalis *Gel.*: *om. B*χ

113 This was the last watch of the night (cf. 19.8 note, above),
when the defenders were likely to be exhausted.

assumed that the reason for their not continuing the assault was the fatigue that had afflicted them, too, and when the signal was given for the Romans to retire, they would all leave their posts themselves as if they had also been recalled by it, and would not reappear in arms on the walls until the third hour of the day.

24. After discontinuing the assault at midnight, the consul once more at the fourth watch[113] mounted an all-out attack on three of the sides but ordered Tiberius Sempronius to hold his men at the ready on the one remaining side and await his signal. He was sure that in the confusion of the night the enemy would swiftly converge on the points from which shouting would be heard. Some of the Aetolians had been asleep and were now trying to rouse themselves from their slumber, physically drained as they were by their efforts and sleep deprivation; the others who were still awake ran in the dark toward the noise of the fighting. Some of their enemy were trying to clamber over the debris where the wall had collapsed while others were attempting to climb up with ladders, and the Aetolians rushed from all over the town to help repel them. Only one side, that where the buildings outside the city proper were situated, was neither being defended nor attacked; but men ready to attack were eagerly awaiting the signal and here there was no defender in place.

Dawn was already breaking when the consul gave the signal. Meeting no resistance, some of his men climbed over the half-demolished walls and others scaled with ladders those that were intact. At the same time, a shout was heard signaling the capture of the city and the Aetolians everywhere abandoned their posts and fled to the citadel.

7   fugiunt. oppidum victores permissu consulis diripiunt, non tam ab ira nec ab odio, quam ut miles, coercitus in tot receptis ex potestate hostium urbibus, aliquo tandem loco fructum victoriae sentiret.

8   Revocatos inde a medio ferme die milites cum in duas divisisset partes, unam radicibus montium circumduci ad rupem iussit, quae fastigio altitudinis par media valle velut

9   abrupta ab arce erat; sed adeo prope geminata cacumina eorum montium sunt ut ex vertice altero conici tela in arcem possint; cum dimidia parte militum consul, ab urbe escensurus[58] in arcem, signum ab iis qui ab tergo in rupem

10 evasuri erant exspectabat. non tulere qui in arce erant Aetoli primum eorum qui rupem ceperant clamorem, deinde impetum ab urbe Romanorum, et[59] fractis iam animis et nulla ibi praeparata re ad obsidionem diutius tole-

11 randam, utpote congregatis feminis puerisque et imbelli alia turba in arcem, quae vix capere nedum tueri multitudinem tantam posset. itaque ad primum impetum abiectis

12 armis dediderunt sese. traditus inter ceteros princeps Aetolorum Damocritus est, qui principio belli decretum Aetolorum, quo accersendum Antiochum censuerant, T. Quinctio poscenti responderat in Italia daturum, cum castra ibi Aetoli posuissent. ob eam ferociam maius victoribus gaudium traditus fuit.

---

[58] escensurus ψ: descensurus B: ascensurus φ: excessurus (ante consul) Mg

[59] et Holk.: ex Bχ

---

[114] 35.33.10. For Damocritus' fate, cf. 37.3.8, 46.5.

The victors pillaged the town with the consul's leave, given not from anger or animosity, but rather so that the soldiers, who had been held back in so many cities wrested from the enemy, might somewhere finally taste the fruits of victory.

It was some time after midday that Acilius recalled his soldiers and split them into two groups. One he ordered to be taken around the foot of the mountain to a rocky outcrop that was the same height as the citadel but more or less cut off from it by a ravine that lay between them. The tops of both eminences were, however, so close to each other that weapons could be hurled at the citadel from the other height. The consul was going to ascend the citadel from the city with the second party of soldiers, and he was waiting for a signal from the men who were to appear on the rocky outcrop to his rear. The Aetolians in the citadel could not, in the first place, endure the cheers of the men who had taken the outcrop nor, after that, the Roman attack from the city. Their spirit was now broken and no preparations had been made there for further resistance to the siege; for women, children and a host of other noncombatants had been herded into the citadel, which could barely contain (and much less protect) such a crowd. Thus, at the first onset, they threw down their arms and surrendered. Among those delivered to the Romans was Damocritus, the leading Aetolian who, at the start of the war, when Titus Quinctius asked for the decree of the Aetolians by which they had voted to bring Antiochus to Greece, had replied that he would give it to him in Italy when the Aetolians had established their camp there.[114] Damocritus' surrender was all the more pleasing to the victors because of that insolent remark.

25. Eodem tempore quo Romani Heracleam Philippus Lamiam ex composito oppugnabat, circa Thermopylas cum consule redeunte ex Boeotia, ut victoriam ipsi populoque Romano gratularetur, excusaretque quod morbo
2 impeditus bello non interfuisset, congressus. inde diversi
3 ad duas simul oppugnandas urbes profecti. intersunt septem milia ferme passuum; et quia Lamia cum posita est in tumulo, tum regionem maxime Oetae spectat, oppido quam breve intervallum videtur, et omnia in conspectu sunt.

4 Cum enixe, velut proposito certamine, Romani Macedonesque diem ac noctem aut in operibus aut in proeliis essent, hoc maior difficultas Macedonibus erat quod Romani aggere et vineis et omnibus supra terram operibus, subter Macedones cuniculis oppugnabant, et in asperis
5 locis silex saepe[60] inpenetrabilis ferro occurrebat. et cum parum procederet inceptum, per conloquia principum
6 oppidanos temptabat rex, ut urbem dederent, haud dubius quin si prius Heraclea capta foret, Romanis se potius quam sibi dedituri essent, suamque gratiam consul in
7 obsidione liberanda facturus esset. nec eum opinio est frustrata; confestim enim ab Heraclea capta nuntius venit, ut oppugnatione absisteret: aequius esse Romanos milites, qui acie dimicassent cum Aetolis, praemia victoriae ha-

---

[60] saepe *B*χ: poene *Mg*

---

[115] Possibly true, but it is more likely that he had been waiting to see how the first Roman encounter with Antiochus would turn out before he committed himself.

25. At the same time as the Romans were assaulting Heraclea, Philip was, as had been agreed, attacking Lamia. When the consul was returning from Boeotia, Philip had met him near Thermopylae to congratulate him and the Roman people on their victory and explain that he had been prevented by illness from taking part in the war against Antiochus.[115] They had then set off in different directions to make their assaults on the two cities at the same time. They are about seven miles apart and, as Lamia is situated on a hill and also has a clear view of the district about Oeta, the distance between the two seems very short indeed and the whole area can be clearly seen.

The Romans and Macedonians were exerting themselves day and night on the siege works or in battle as if they were in competition, but it was the Macedonians who faced the harder task. This was because the Romans were conducting their offensive with a mound, mantlets, and all kinds of siege works above ground, while the Macedonians were conducting theirs underground with tunnels, and in difficult spots they were confronted with flint that could barely be penetrated by iron. The operation making little headway, the king was parleying with the leading citizens of Lamia, trying to induce them to surrender the city; he was convinced that, if Heraclea were taken first, the Lamians would choose to surrender to the Romans rather than to him, and the consul would take the credit for raising the siege. Nor was he mistaken in his thinking. A message came from Heraclea right after its capture ordering him to abandon the siege—it was fairer for the Roman soldiers who had fought the Aetolians in the field to have the prizes of victory, he was told. He accordingly withdrew

233

8   bere. ita recessum ab Lamia est, et propinquae clade urbis
    ipsi ne quid simile paterentur effugerunt.

    26. Paucis priusquam Heraclea caperetur diebus Ae-
2   toli, concilio Hypatam coacto, legatos ad Antiochum mise-
    runt, inter quos et Thoas idem qui et antea missus est.
    mandata erant ut ab rege peterent primum ut ipse coactis
    rursus terrestribus navalibus copiis in Graeciam traiceret,
3   deinde, si qua ipsum teneret res, ut pecuniam et auxilia
    mitteret; id cum ad dignitatem eius fidemque pertinere,
4   non prodi socios, tum etiam ad incolumitatem regni, ne
    sineret Romanos vacuos omni cura, cum Aetolorum gen-
5   tem sustulissent, omnibus copiis in Asiam traicere. vera
    erant, quae dicebantur; eo magis regem moverunt. itaque
    in praesentia pecuniam, quae ad usus belli necessaria erat,
    legatis dedit; auxilia terrestria navaliaque adfirmavit mis-
6   surum. Thoantem unum ex legatis retinuit, et ipsum haud
    invitum morantem, ut exactor praesens promissorum ad-
    esset.

    27. Ceterum Heraclea capta fregit tandem animos
2   Aetolorum, et paucos post dies quam ad bellum renovan-
    dum acciendumque regem in Asiam miserant legatos,
    abiectis belli consiliis pacis petendae oratores ad consulem
3   miserunt. quos dicere exorsos consul interfatus, cum alia
    sibi praevertenda esse dixisset, redire Hypatam eos, datis
    dierum decem indutiis et L. Valerio Flacco cum iis misso,

---

116 The abandonment of the siege is odd, as the Romans do
not undertake it themselves, and Lamia did not fall until the next
year (37.5.3).   117 Cf. 35.12.4, 32.2 and notes.

118 Consul with M. Porcius Cato in 195. The two were now
consular legates (cf. 17.1, above).

from Lamia, and its inhabitants, thanks to the disaster that had befallen her neighboring city, escaped a like fate themselves.[116]

26. A few days before Heraclea was captured, the Aetolians held a council meeting at Hypata and sent an embassy to Antiochus that included the same Thoas who had also been sent earlier.[117] The envoys' instructions were to ask the king first of all to bring his land and sea forces together once more and cross to Greece in person; then, if anything was holding him back, they were to ask him to send money and military assistance. Not letting down his allies was important for his dignity and honor, they were to say; but ensuring that the Romans, relieved of all concerns after they had destroyed the Aetolian people, should not cross to Greece with all their forces was also important for the security of his realm. Their observations were correct and thus impressed the king all the more. So, as a temporary measure, he gave the envoys the moneys required to defray the costs of the war and promised that he would send them both land and naval reinforcements. Of the ambassadors he detained only Thoas, and Thoas had no objection to staying behind, so as to be present as overseer of the king's commitments.

27. However, the capture of Heraclea finally broke the Aetolians' spirit; and few days after sending the embassy to Asia to recommence hostilities and bring over the king they abandoned their plans for war and sent spokesmen to the consul to sue for peace. The spokesmen had begun their address when the consul interrupted them, saying that other things that required his attention first. He bade them return to Hypata, granting them a ten-day truce. He sent with them Lucius Valerius Flaccus[118] and instructed

235

iussit eique quae secum acturi fuissent exponere, et si qua
4 vellent alia. Hypatam ut est ventum, principes Aetolorum
apud Flaccum concilium habuerunt, consultantes quo-
5 nam agendum modo apud consulem foret. parantibus iis
antiqua iura foederum ordiri meritaque in populum Ro-
6 manum, absistere iis Flaccus iussit quae ipsi violassent ac
rupissent; confessionem iis culpae magis profuturam et
totam in preces orationem versam; nec enim in causa ipsorum, sed in populi Romani clementia spem salutis positam
7 esse; et se suppliciter agentibus iis adfuturum[61] et apud
consulem et Romae in senatu; eo quoque enim mittendos
8 fore legatos. haec una via omnibus ad salutem visa est, ut
in fidem se permitterent Romanorum; ita enim et illis
violandi supplices verecundiam se imposituros, et ipsos
nihilo minus suae potestatis fore, si quid melius fortuna
ostendisset.

28. Postquam ad consulem ventum est, Phaeneas, legationis princeps, longam orationem et varie ad mitigandam
iram victoris compositam ita ad extremum finivit ut diceret Aetolos se suaque omnia fidei populi Romani permit-
2 tere. id consul ubi audivit, "etiam atque etiam videte,"
inquit "Aetoli, ut ita permittatis." tum decretum Phaeneas,
in quo id diserte scriptum erat, ostendit.

---

[61] se . . . adfuturum *Gel.*: agentibus iis profuturum *Bχ*

---

[119] That is, Acilius.
[120] Polybius (20.10) explains that to the Romans this meant
unconditional surrender, which (as is clear from the rest of this
chapter) was not the Aetolians' interpretation. Cf. Walbank 3.79.
[121] The former pro-Roman *strategos* who was at the meeting
of Flamininus and Philip at Nicaea (32.32.11–34.3) and later
commanded the Aetolian troops at Cynoscephalae (33.3.9).

them to lay before Flaccus the matters they were going to discuss with him[119] and any other issues they wished to raise. On reaching Hypata, the leading Aetolians held a meeting in Flaccus' presence at which they discussed how they should handle matters with the consul. They were preparing to lead off with old treaty rights and the services they had rendered the Roman people, but Flaccus told them to steer clear of compacts that they themselves had violated and broken. An admission of culpability and an address turning entirely on appeals for mercy would benefit them more, he said, for their hopes for safety lay not in the strength of their case but in the clemency of the Roman people; if they adopted a supplicatory demeanor, he would help them both before the consul and in the senate at Rome (for they would have to send a delegation there, too). It seemed to all present that this was the only road to safety, namely entrusting themselves to the good faith of the Romans.[120] In this way they would make the Romans feel ashamed about maltreating suppliants, and they would also have no less control over their own fate if fortune offered something better.

28. When the Aetolians appeared before the consul, Phaeneas,[121] the head of the delegation, launched into a long disquisition composed with various turns of speech designed to soothe the victor's anger and finally concluded by saying that the Aetolians entrusted themselves and all their possessions to the good faith of Roman people. When he heard this, the consul said: "Men of Aetolia, consider very, very carefully your surrender on such terms." Phaeneas thereupon showed him the decree in which the Aetolian decision was clearly worded.

3   "Quando ergo" inquit "ita permittitis, postulo ut mihi
Dicaearchum civem vestrum et Menestam Epirotam"—
Naupactum is cum praesidio ingressus ad defectionem
compulerat—"et Amynandrum cum principibus Athamanum, quorum consilio ab nobis defecistis, sine mora de-
4   datis." prope dicentem interfatus Phaeneas Romanum
"non in servitutem" inquit "sed in fidem tuam nos tradidi-
mus, et certum habeo te imprudentia labi qui nobis im-
5   peres quae moris Graecorum non sint." ad ea consul "nec
hercule" inquit "magnopere nunc curo quid Aetoli satis ex
more Graecorum factum esse censeant, dum ego more
Romano imperium inhibeam in deditos modo decreto
6   suo, ante armis victos; itaque, ni propere fit quod impero,
vinciri vos iam iubebo."

   Adferri catenas et circumsistere lictores iussit. tum
fracta Phaeneae ferocia Aetolisque aliis est, et tandem
7   cuius condicionis essent senserunt, et Phaeneas se quidem
et qui adsint Aetolorum scire facienda esse quae imperen-
tur dixit, sed ad decernenda ea concilio Aetolorum opus
8   esse; ad id petere ut decem dierum indutias daret. petente
Flacco pro Aetolis indutiae datae, et Hypatam reditum
est. ubi cum in consilio delectorum, quos apocletos vocant, Phaeneas et quae imperarentur et quae ipsis prope
9   accidissent exposuisset, ingemuerunt quidem principes

122 In entrusting themselves to Glabrio's good faith (*fides*), the
Aetolians assumed they were putting themselves under his protection and would be treated as suppliants. For Glabrio it meant
unquestioned surrender.
123 Cf. 35.34.2 and note.

238

"Well, then, since you surrender on these terms," said the consul, "I demand that you immediately hand over to me your fellow citizen Dicaearchus, the Epirote Menestas (this man had gone into Naupactus with a garrison and forced the town to rebel), and Amynander along with the leading Athamanians on whose advice you defected from us." Phaeneas, almost interrupting the Roman as he spoke, replied: "What we did was to entrust ourselves to your good faith, not put ourselves in slavery, and I am sure your mistake in giving us orders not in accord with Greek convention was just a thoughtless slip on your part." To this the consul's rejoinder was: "Good God, I really do not much care what Aetolians consider to have been done in accordance with Greek convention. I, following Roman convention, am asserting my authority over men who just now surrendered to me by their own decree after being earlier defeated in war.[122] So, if my order is not swiftly carried out, I shall have you clapped in irons."

He then gave instructions for chains to be brought and for the lictors to stand around the Aetolian delegation. With that, the truculence of Phaeneas and the other Aetolians was broken and they finally became aware of their predicament. Phaeneas declared that he and the other Aetolians present knew that they had to carry out the orders but, he said, a meeting of the Aetolian council was needed to ratify the conditions, and for that he was requesting that Acilius grant them a ten-day truce. Flaccus supported the Aetolians' request, the truce was accorded, and the envoys returned to Hypata. There in a meeting of the select committee they call the *apocleti*,[123] Phaeneas gave an account of the orders they had received and the fate that had almost overtaken them. The Aetolian leaders

239

condicioni suae, parendum tamen victori censebant et ex
omnibus oppidis convocandos Aetolos ad concilium.

29. Postquam vero coacta omnis multitudo eadem illa
audivit, adeo saevitia imperii atque indignitate exasperati
animi sunt, ut si in pace fuissent, illo impetu irae concitari
2 potuerint ad bellum. ad iram accedebat et difficultas
eorum quae imperarentur—quonam modo enim utique
3 regem Amynandrum se tradere posse?—, et spes forte
oblata, quod Nicander eo ipso tempore ab rege Antiocho
veniens implevit exspectatione vana multitudinem terra
marique ingens parari bellum.

4 Duodecimo is die quam conscenderat navem in Aetoliam, perfecta legatione rediens, Phalara in sinu Maliaco
5 tenuit. inde Lamiam pecuniam cum devexisset, ipse cum
expeditis prima vespera inter Macedonum Romanaque
castra medio agro, dum Hypatam notis callibus petit, in
stationem incidit Macedonum, deductusque ad regem est
6 nondum convivio dimisso. quod ubi nuntiatum est, velut
hospitis non hostis adventu motus Philippus accumbere
7 eum epularique iussit, atque inde dimissis aliis, solum
retentum, ipsum quidem de se timere quicquam vetuit,
8 Aetolorum prava consilia atque in ipsorum caput semper
recidentia accusavit, qui primum Romanos deinde Antio-
9 chum in Graeciam adduxissent. sed praeteritorum, quae

bemoaned their situation but nevertheless decided that the victor must be obeyed and that the Aetolian people must be summoned from all their towns to a general assembly.

29. However, when the whole crowd came together and heard that same report, they were so incensed at the severity of the commands and the humiliation involved that, had they been at peace, they could have been pushed into war by the intensity of their anger. In addition to their anger, there was also the problem of executing the orders (for how on earth could they possibly deliver King Amynander?) and of a hope that chanced to arise when Nicander, coming from King Antiochus at that very time, filled the masses with the erroneous expectation of a huge war being set in motion on land and sea.

Nicander had completed his mission and, returning to Aetolia, he put in at Phalara on the Malian Gulf, eleven days after he had first embarked. From there he brought Antiochus' money to Lamia, and was later heading for Hypata with a retinue of light-armed men over paths that he knew when, early in the evening, he stumbled upon a Macedonian outpost in the countryside between the Macedonian and Roman camps and was brought to the king, who had not yet terminated his dinner party. When the man's arrival was reported, Philip, reacting as if a guest, not an enemy, had come, bade Nicander recline and take dinner and, keeping him behind after sending off the other guests, told him not to have any fears for his safety. He then reproached the Aetolians for their ill-conceived plans (which always backfired on them) in bringing into Greece first the Romans and after them Antiochus. But he would forget the past, he said, which it was easier to criti-

10 magis reprehendi quam corrigi possint, oblitum se non facturum ut insultet adversis rebus eorum; Aetolos quoque finire tandem adversus se odia debere, et Nicandrum
11 privatim eius diei quo servatus a se foret meminisse. ita datis qui in tutum eum prosequerentur, Hypatam Nicander consultantibus de pace Romana supervenit.

30. M'. Acilius vendita aut concessa militi circa Heracleam praeda, postquam nec Hypatae pacata consilia esse, et Naupactum concurrisse Aetolos, ut inde totum impe-
2 tum belli sustinerent, audivit, praemisso Ap. Claudio cum quattuor milibus militum ad occupanda iuga, qua difficiles
3 transitus montium erant, ipse Oetam escendit, Herculique sacrificium fecit in eo loco quem Pyram, quod ibi mortale corpus eius dei sit crematum, appellant. inde toto exercitu profectus reliquum iter satis expedito agmine
4 fecit; ut ad Coracem ventum est—mons est altissimus inter Callipolim et Naupactum—, ibi et iumenta multa ex agmine praecipitata cum ipsis oneribus sunt et homines
5 vexati; et facile apparebat quam cum inerti hoste res esset, qui tam impeditum saltum nullo praesidio, ut clauderet
6 transitum, insedisset. tum quoque vexato exercitu ad Naupactum descendit, et uno castello adversus arcem posito ceteras partes urbis divisis copiis pro situ moenium cir-

---

124 The former hero, by now a god, had been transported to Olympus; and Oeta was traditionally the site of his cremation. Pyra (Πυρά) means "Funeral Pyre."
125 Korax and Kallipolis: *Barr.* 55 C3.

cize than rectify, and would not behave in such a way as to be scoffing at their adversity. The Aetolians should also finally bring their animosity toward him to an end and Nicander for his part ought to keep in mind that present day on which his life had been saved by Philip. The king then gave him men to escort him to a safe zone and Nicander arrived at Hypata to find the Aetolians discussing the peace with Rome.

30. Manius Acilius sold off or turned over to his men the booty taken around Heraclea. He then heard that the decisions taken at Hypata were not in favor of peace, and that the Aetolians had speedily assembled at Naupactus, which they intended using as a base from which to bear the full brunt of the war. He thereupon sent Appius Claudius ahead with 4,000 men to seize the heights, where crossing the mountains was difficult, while he himself climbed Oeta and sacrificed to Hercules at the place called Pyra, so named because it was where the mortal body of the god was cremated.[124] Setting off from there with the entire army, he completed the rest of the journey relatively smoothly. When they reached Corax, a towering mountain between Callipolis[125] and Naupactus, a large number of pack animals plummeted from the train, along with their loads, and the men also found themselves in difficulty. The lack of enterprise in the enemy they were facing was readily apparent, as they had not occupied such a difficult pass with any sort of force to block a crossing. Even as it was the army experienced some distress before Acilius descended to Naupactus. There he established a single fort opposite the citadel and laid siege to the other areas of the city, dividing his troops as the layout of its

cumsedit. nec minus operis laborisque ea oppugnatio quam Heracleae habuit.

31. Eodem tempore et Messene in Peloponneso ab Achaeis, quod concilii eorum recusaret esse, oppugnari

2 coepta est. etenim duae[62] civitates, Messene et Elis, extra

3 concilium Achaicum erant; cum Aetolis sentiebant. Elei tamen post fugatum ex Graecia Antiochum legatis Achaeorum lenius responderant: dimisso praesidio regio cogita-

4 turos se quid sibi faciendum esset; Messenii, sine responso

5 dimissis legatis, moverant bellum, trepidique rerum suarum, cum iam ager effuso exercitu passim ureretur castraque prope urbem poni viderent, legatos Chalcidem ad T. Quinctium, auctorem libertatis, miserunt, qui nuntiarent Messenios Romanis non Achaeis et aperire portas et dedere urbem paratos esse.

6 Auditis legatis extemplo profectus Quinctius a Megalopoli ad Diophanen praetorem Achaeorum misit, qui extemplo reducere eum a Messene exercitum et venire ad

7 se iuberet. dicto paruit Diophanes, et soluta obsidione expeditus ipse praegressus agmen circa Andaniam, parvum oppidum inter Megalopolim Messenenque posi-

8 tum, Quinctio occurrit; et cum causas oppugnationis exponeret, castigatum leniter, quod tantam rem sine auctoritate sua conatus esset, dimittere exercitum iussit nec pacem

9 omnium bono partam turbare. Messeniis imperavit ut

---

62 etenim duae *ed. Rom.*: et duae *Bχ*: duae *Holk. 345*

---

126 *Strategos* in 192/1. He had earlier tried to invade Sparta with Flamininus, but Philopoemen arrived in the city before them and shut them out (Plut. *Phil.* 16.2).

127 About five miles north of Messene: *Barr.* 58 B3.

fortifications required. And the operation against this town involved no less effort and hardship than at Heraclea.

31. At this same time the siege of Messene in the Peloponnese was also begun by the Achaeans because it refused to join their league. In fact, two states, Messene and Elis, remained outside the Achaean league, their sympathies lying with the Aetolians. After Antiochus had been chased from Greece, however, the Eleans had been more restrained in their response to the Achaean delegates, telling them that if the king's garrison were removed, they would then consider what action to take. The Messenians had simply dismissed the delegates without a response and opened hostilities. Then, fearing for their situation when their lands were burned in many places by a wide-ranging army and they saw a camp being set up near the city, they sent envoys to Titus Quinctius, the architect of their freedom, in Chalcis to report that the Messenians were prepared to open their gates and surrender their city to the Romans but not to the Achaeans.

After hearing the envoys, Quinctius set out immediately and from Megalopolis sent a messenger to the Achaean praetor, Diophanes,[126] to order him to withdraw his army from Messene immediately and come to him. Diophanes obeyed the order, raised the siege and, traveling light ahead of his column, met Quinctius near Andania, a small town situated between Megalopolis and Messene.[127] When Diophanes explained the reasons for the siege, Quinctius gently reprimanded him for having embarked on such an important venture without his approval and then told him to demobilize his army and not upset a peace that had been settled to everyone's benefit. The

exsules reducerent et Achaeorum concilii essent; si qua
haberent de quibus aut recusare aut in posterum caveri
10   sibi vellent, Corinthum ad se venirent; Diophanen concilium Achaeorum extemplo sibi praebere iussit.

   Ibi de Zacyntho intercepta per fraudem insula questus,
11   postulavit ut restitueretur Romanis. Philippi Macedonum
regis Zacynthus fuerat; eam mercedem Amynandro dederat, ut per Athamaniam ducere exercitum in superiorem
partem Aetoliae liceret, qua expeditione fractis animis
12   Aetolos compulit ad petendam pacem. Amynander Philippum Megalopolitanum insulae praefecit; postea per bellum quo se Antiocho adversus Romanos coniunxit, Philippo ad munera belli revocato, Hieroclen Agrigentinum
successorem misit.

   32. Is post fugam ab Thermopylis Antiochi Amynan-
drumque a Philippo Athamania pulsum, missis ultro ad
Diophanen praetorem Achaeorum nuntiis, pecunia pactus
2   insulam Achaeis tradidit. id praemium belli suum esse
aequum censebant Romani: non enim M'. Acilium consulem legionesque Romanas Diophani et Achaeis ad Ther-
3   mopylas pugnasse. Diophanes adversus haec interdum
purgare sese gentemque, interdum de iure facti disserere.
4   quidam Achaeorum et initio eam se rem aspernatos testa-

---

   128 Zacynthus (*Barr.* 1 H3), captured by Philip in 217, had
been taken by M. Valerius Laevinus in 211 (26.24.15) but subsequently retaken by Philip, perhaps in 207.
   129 The expedition took place in 207, and the peace between
Philip and the Aetolians was concluded the following year.
   130 On Amynander and Philip of Megalopolis, cf. 35.47.5–8
and 14.4–5, above.   131 Cf. 14.9, above.

people of Messene he commanded to recall their exiles and join the Achaean league, adding that they should come to him at Corinth if there were terms to which they wished to object or regarding which they wanted safeguards for the future; and he ordered Diophanes to give him an immediate audience at the council of the Achaeans.

There Quinctius protested against the treacherous seizure of the island of Zacynthus,[128] and demanded that it be restored to the Romans. Zacynthus had belonged to King Philip of Macedon, and Philip had ceded it to Amynander so he would allow him to take his army through Athamania into the upper reaches of Aetolia—the expedition by which he had broken the spirit of the Aetolians and forced them to sue for peace.[129] Amynander put Philip of Megalopolis[130] in charge of the island; but later, during the war in which Amynander joined Antiochus against the Romans, he recalled Philip for military duties and sent Hierocles of Agrigentum to succeed him.

32. After Antiochus fled from Thermopylae, and Amynander was driven from Athamania by Philip,[131] Hierocles on his own initiative sent messengers to Diophanes, praetor of the Achaeans, and after a financial settlement with him ceded the island to the Achaeans. The Romans believed that it was rightly theirs as a prize of war; for, they said, it was not for Diophanes and the Achaeans that the consul Manius Acilius and the Roman legions had fought at Thermopylae. In response to this, Diophanes sometimes tried to justify himself and his people and sometimes questioned the legality of the action. Some Achaeans declared that they had objected to the business from the beginning and now reproached their praetor for his

247

bantur, et tunc pertinaciam increpitabant[63] praetoris;
auctoribusque iis decretum est ut T. Quinctio ea res per-
5 mitteretur. erat Quinctius sicut adversantibus asper, ita, si
cederes, idem placabilis. omissa igitur[64] contentione vocis
voltusque "si utilem" inquit "possessionem eius insulae
censerem Achaeis esse, auctor essem senatui populoque
6 Romano ut eam vos habere sinerent;[65] ceterum sicut tes-
tudinem, ubi conlecta in suum tegumen est, tutam ad
omnes ictus video esse, ubi exserit partes aliquas, quod-
7 cumque nudavit obnoxium atque infirmum habere, haud
dissimiliter vos, Achaei, clausos undique mari, quae intra
8 Peloponnesi sunt terminos, ea et iungere vobis et iuncta
tueri facile, simul aviditate plura amplectendi hinc exce-
datis, nuda vobis omnia quae extra sint, et exposita ad
9 omnes ictus esse." adsentienti omni concilio, nec Diophane ultra tendere auso, Zacynthus Romanis traditur.

33. Per idem tempus Philippus rex, proficiscentem
consulem ad Naupactum percunctatus si se interim quae
defecissent ab societate Romana urbes recipere vellet,
2 permittente eo ad Demetriadem copias admovit, haud
3 ignarus quanta ibi tum turbatio esset. destituti enim ab
omni spe, cum desertos se ab Antiocho, spem nullam in
Aetolis esse cernerent, dies noctesque aut Philippi hostis
adventum aut infestiorem etiam, quo iustius irati erant,
Romanorum exspectabant.

[63] increpitabant *Mg*: increpabant *Bχ*
[64] igitur *Mg*: *om. Bχ*
[65] sinerent *Pa*: sineret *BAE*: sinere ψ

[132] Plutarch (*Flam.* 17.2) also quotes this tortoise simile,
which presumably comes from Polybius; cf also 35.49.7 note.

intransigence. At their suggestion it was decided that the matter be referred to Titus Quinctius. While Quinctius was hard on people who opposed him, he was also easily appeased if one deferred to him. So, with all intensity removed from his voice and expression, he said: "If I considered the possession of this island to be in the interests of the Achaeans, I would recommend to the senate and people of Rome that they let you keep it. But you are like the tortoise.[132] When it is completely withdrawn into its shell, I observe that it is secure against all attacks; but when it puts forth some of its limbs, whatever it has left exposed is vulnerable and weak. Similarly, I see that you, men of Achaea, enclosed as you are on all sides by the sea, can easily annex all that lies within the bounds of the Peloponnese and easily protect it once annexed; but as soon as you overstep those bounds through greed for further acquisitions, you would find everything outside them unprotected and exposed to all manner of attack." The entire meeting agreed and since Diophanes did not dare continue his opposition Zacynthus was ceded to the Romans.

33. In this same period, when the consul was setting out for Naupactus, King Philip asked him if he wished him in the meantime to recover those cities that had abandoned the Roman alliance. When the consul agreed, Philip moved his forces ahead to Demetrias, well aware of the chaos reigning in the town at the time. The people there had lost all hope. They could see they had been abandoned by Antiochus, and that there was no prospect of help from the Aetolians; and day and night they were awaiting the arrival of their enemy Philip or—even more dangerous in that their anger was more justified—the arrival of the Romans.

249

4   Turba erat ibi incondita regiorum, qui primo pauci in praesidio relicti, postea plures, plerique inermes, ex proelio adverso fuga delati, nec virium nec animi satis ad
5 obsidionem tolerandam habebant; itaque praemissis a Philippo, qui[66] spem impetrabilis veniae ostendebant, re-
6 sponderunt patere portas regi. ad primum eius ingressum principum quidam urbe excesserunt, Eurylochus mortem sibi conscivit. Antiochi milites—sic enim pacti erant—per Macedoniam Thraciamque, prosequentibus Macedonibus
7 ne quis eos violaret, Lysimachiam deducti sunt. erant et paucae naves Demetriade, quibus praeerat Isidorus; eae quoque cum praefecto suo dimissae sunt. inde Dolopiam et Aperantiam et Perrhaebiae quasdam civitates recipit.

34.   Dum haec a Philippo geruntur, T. Quinctius recepta Zacyntho ab Achaico concilio Naupactum traiecit,
2 quae iam per duos menses—et iam prope excidium erat—oppugnabatur, et si capta vi foret, omne nomen ibi Aeto-
3 lorum ad internecionem videbatur venturum. ceterum quamquam merito iratus erat Aetolis, quod solos obtrectasse gloriae suae, cum liberaret Graeciam, meminerat, et nihil auctoritate sua motos esse cum, quae tum maxime
4 acciderant[67] casura praemonens, a furioso incepto eos

---

66 qui *ed. Rom.*: quia Bχ   67 acciderant α (*Holk. Esc. Voss.*): acciderat Bχ: accidebant *vel* acciderent *Madvig*

---

133 That is, Antiochus' soldiers.

134 The former Magnetarch (35.31.6), who had welcomed the Syrians into the city (35.43.5).   135 Cf. 20.5–6, above.

136 Dolopia: *Barr.* 55 B2; Perrhaebia: B–C1 (Perraibia). Aperantia: an area southwest of Dolopia, its boundaries uncertain (cf. Walbank 3.85; not identified in *Barr.*)   137 33.11.4–9, 12.3–4.

There was in Demetrias an unruly crowd of the king's soldiers.[133] At first only a few had been left in the garrison, but later more had been brought there in flight after the defeat, most of them unarmed, and they had neither the strength nor the spirit to face a siege. Thus, when men sent ahead by Philip indicated that the soldiers could hope for mercy, they replied that the gates were open to the king. When Philip first entered, a number of the leading citizens left the city and Eurylochus[134] committed suicide. The soldiers of Antiochus were taken through Macedonia and Thrace to Lysimachia—such was the agreement they had made—with a Macedonian escort to prevent anyone from doing them harm. There were also a few ships at Demetrias under the command of Isidorus,[135] and these were also allowed to leave together with their admiral. After that Philip recovered Dolopia, Aperantia and a number of cities of Perrhaebia.[136]

34. While Philip was thus employed, Titus Quinctius, after gaining Zacynthus, left the Achaean council and crossed to Naupactus. This had already been under siege for two months—and was now on the verge of collapse—and if it were taken by storm it seemed that the entire Aetolian nation would face extinction there. Quinctius was justifiably incensed with the Aetolians; he remembered that they were the only people to have disparaged his glorious achievement when he was liberating Greece[137] and that they had been swayed not one bit by his authority when he tried to deter them from their mad undertaking

deterreret, tamen sui maxime operis esse credens nullam
gentem liberatae ab se Graeciae funditus everti, obambu-
5 lare muris, ut facile nosceretur ab Aetolis, coepit. confestim a primis stationibus cognitus est, volgatumque per
omnes ordines Quinctium esse. itaque concursu facto
undique in muros, manus pro se quisque tendentes, con-
sonante clamore nominatim Quinctium orare ut opem
6 ferret ac servaret. et tum quidem, quamquam moveretur
his vocibus, manu tamen abnuit quicquam opis in se esse;
7 ceterum postquam ad consulem venit, "utrum fefellit"[68]
inquit "te, M'. Acili, quid agatur, an cum satis peruideas,
nihil id magnopere ad summam rem pertinere censes?"

8   Erexerat exspectatione consulem; et "quin expromis"
inquit, "quid rei sit?" tum Quinctius "ecquid vides te devicto Antiocho in duabus urbibus oppugnandis tempus
terere, cum iam prope annus circumactus sit imperii tui,
9 Philippum autem, qui non aciem non signa hostium vidit,
non solum urbes sed tot iam gentes, Athamaniam Perrhae-
biam Aperantiam Dolopiam, sibi adiunxisse, et victoriae
tuae praemium te militesque tuos nondum duas urbes,
10 Philippum tot gentes Graeciae habere? atqui non tantum
interest nostra Aetolorum opes ac vires minui, quantum
non supra modum Philippum crescere."

    35. Adsentiebatur his consul; sed pudor, si inrito in-
cepto abscederet obsidione, occurrebat. tota inde Quinc-

---

68 fefellit *Mg*: fallit *B*χ

by warning them that they would face the consequences that had just then overtaken them. Even so, believing that after liberating Greece he had a special responsibility to ensure that none of its peoples should be totally destroyed, he proceeded to walk about the walls so that he could be easily recognized by the Aetolians. He was immediately spotted by the guards of the first outposts and word spread throughout the ranks that Quinctius was present. There was therefore a rush to the walls from all quarters, the people all stretching out their hands and with a chorus of cries begging Quinctius by name to bring help and rescue them. He was moved to pity by these appeals but at the time he simply indicated with a gesture of his hand that he could not help. When he came to the consul, however, he said: "Have you failed to see what is going on, Manius Acilius? Or do you fully realize it but think it does not greatly bear upon the interests of the state?"

He had piqued the curiosity of the consul, who replied: "Why not explain what you mean?" Quinctius then said: "Do you realize that since defeating Antiochus you have been wasting your time besieging two cities when the year of your *imperium* is almost over, while Philip, who has not set eyes on a battlefield or enemy standards, has annexed not merely cities but a whole host of nations—Athamania, Perrhaebia, Aperantia, and Dolopia? Do you see that, as your prize of victory, you and your men do not yet have two cities and Philip has all those nations of Greece? And yet it is not so much in our interest to have the Aetolians' strength and resources curtailed as it is to see that Philip's power does not grow inordinately."

35. The consul agreed with this; but he felt ashamed at the prospect of abandoning the siege without having

2 tio res permissa est. is rursus ad eam partem muri qua
paulo ante vociferati Aetoli fuerant redit.[69] ibi cum impensius orarent ut misereretur gentis Aetolorum, exire aliquos
3 ad se iussit. Phaeneas ipse principesque alii extemplo
egressi sunt. quibus provolutis ad pedes "fortuna" inquit
4 "vestra facit ut et irae meae et orationi temperem. eveve-
runt quae praedixi eventura, et ne hoc quidem reliqui
vobis est, ut indignis accidisse ea videantur; ego tamen,
sorte quadam nutriendae Graeciae datus, ne ingratis qui-
5 dem bene facere absistam. mittite oratores ad consulem,
qui indutias in tantum[70] temporis petant ut mittere legatos
Romam possitis, per quos senatui de vobis permittatis; ego
6 apud consulem defensor deprecatorque vobis adero." ita
ut censuerat Quinctius fecerunt, nec aspernatus est consul
legationem; indutiisque in diem certam datis, qua legatio
renuntiari ab Roma posset, soluta obsidio est et exercitus
in Phocidem missus.

7   Consul cum T. Quinctio ad Achaicum concilium Aegium traiecit. ibi de Eleis et de exsulibus Lacedaemoniorum restituendis actum est;[71] neutra perfecta res, quia
suae gratiae reservari exsulum causam[72] Achaei, Elei per
se ipsi quam per Romanos maluerunt Achaico contribui
8 concilio. Epirotarum legati ad consulem venerunt, quos

[69] redit *BAP*: reddit *EHolk*: redi *ψ*: rediit *Par.*

[70] in tantum *Drak.*: tantum *BφVL*: tanti *N*

[71] est *Weiss.*: et *Bχ*

[72] exsulum causam *Madvig*: eam *BψGel.*: ea *φ*: eam causam
Rossbach: hanc causam *Walsh*

achieved his objective. The decision was then left entirely to Quinctius. He went back once more to that part of the wall where the Aetolians had called out to him a little earlier. When they now appealed to him more urgently to pity the Aetolian people, he bade a number of them come out to him. Phaeneas himself and other leading Aetolians immediately came forth. They flung themselves at his feet and Flamininus said to them: "Your unfortunate plight obliges me to temper both my anger and my words to you. What I said would happen *has* happened and you are not even left the consolation of appearing to be undeserving victims. Nevertheless, as I have by some stroke of fate been appointed to take care of Greece, I shall not withhold my services even from ingrates. Send spokesmen to the consul to request a truce long enough for you to be able to send to Rome ambassadors through whom you can put your case to the senate. I shall be at the consul's side to defend your interests and intercede for you." They followed Quinctius' advice, and the consul did not reject their petition. A truce was accorded until a fixed day by which the report from the embassy could be brought back from Rome; and the siege was raised and the army sent back to Phocis.

The consul then crossed with Titus Quinctius to the Achaean Council in Aegium. There deliberations centered on the Elians and the repatriation of the Spartan exiles. Neither issue was resolved because the Achaeans preferred the case of the exiles to be shelved until they could win the credit for it, while the Elians preferred their induction into the Achaean League to be their own responsibility rather than brought about through Roman mediation. Ambassadors came to the consul from the

non sincera fide in amicitia fuisse satis constabat; militem tamen nullum Antiocho dederant; pecunia iuvisse eum insimulabantur; legatos ad regem ne ipsi quidem misisse

9 infitiabantur. iis petentibus ut in amicitia pristina esse liceret, respondit consul se utrum hostium an pacatorum eos

10 numero haberet nondum scire; senatum eius rei iudicem fore; integram se causam eorum Romam reicere; indutias ad id dierum nonaginta dare.

11 Epirotae Romam missi senatum adierunt. iis magis quae non fecissent hostilia referentibus quam purgantibus ea de quibus arguebantur, responsum datum est quo veniam impetrasse non causam probasse videri possent.

12 Et Philippi regis legati sub idem tempus in senatum introducti, gratulantes de victoria. iis petentibus ut sibi sacrificare in Capitolio donumque ex auro liceret ponere in aede Iovis optimi maximi, permissum ab senatu. cen-

13 tum pondo coronam auream posuerunt. non responsum solum benigne regis legatis est, sed filius quoque Philippi Demetrius, qui obses Romae erat, ad patrem reducendus

14 legatis datus est. bellum quod cum Antiocho rege in Graecia gestum est a M'. Acilio consule hunc finem habuit.

36. Alter consul P. Cornelius Scipio, Galliam provin-

---

138 "Golden crown" is often not to be taken literally; the Greek word for "crown" (στέφανος, *corona* in Latin) is also used of a gift of precious metal (Walbank 3.86, Oakley 2.359–60). Here, however, it could possibly be a gift of a heavy crown.

139 This had been part of the treaty that ended the Second Macedonian War (33.30.10). Cf. also 34.52.9 for Demetrius' appearance in Rome, and Books 39–40 for his later career and tragic end.

Epirotes who, it was quite clear, had not been completely loyal in their adherence to their treaty. They had, however, supplied Antiochus with no troops; they were accused of having given him financial aid; and they themselves did not even deny that they had sent ambassadors to the king. When they asked to be allowed to remain in their earlier alliance, the consul replied that he was not yet sure whether to consider them enemies or people at peace with Rome, a matter on which the senate would decide. He was referring their case in its entirety to Rome, he said, and for that he was granting them a ninety-day truce.

The Epirotes who were sent to Rome approached the senate but, since their defense rested more on the listing of hostile acts that they had *not* committed rather than on clearing themselves of the charges against them, the response they were given could be seen as their having gained a pardon rather than having successfully substantiated their case.

At about this same time envoys from King Philip were also brought before the senate, offering congratulations on the Roman victory. When they requested permission to offer sacrifice in the Capitol and set a gift of gold in the temple of Jupiter Optimus Maximus, their request was granted by the senate. They then made a dedication of a golden crown[138] weighing a hundred pounds. The king's envoys were not only given a courteous response but were also presented with Demetrius (Philip's son, who had been a hostage at Rome[139]) to be taken back to his father. Thus ended the war against King Antiochus that was fought in Greece by the consul Manius Acilius.

36. The other consul, Publius Cornelius Scipio (who had been allotted Gaul as his province) had promised

ciam sortitus, priusquam ad bellum quod cum Boiis gerendum erat proficisceretur, postulavit ab senatu ut pecunia sibi decerneretur ad ludos, quos praetor in Hispania
2 inter ipsum discrimen pugnae vovisset. novum atque
iniquum postulare est visus; censuerunt ergo quos ludos
sine senatus consulto ex sua unius sententia vovisset, eos
vel de manubiis, si quam pecuniam ad id reservasset, vel
3 sua ipse impensa faceret. eos ludos per dies decem P. Cornelius fecit.

Per idem fere tempus aedes Matris Magnae Idaeae
dedicata est, quam deam is P. Cornelius advectam ex Asia
P. Cornelio Scipione, cui postea Africano fuit cognomen,
4 P. Licinio consulibus in Palatium a mari detulerat. locave-
rant aedem faciendam ex senatus consulto M. Livius C.
Claudius censores M. Cornelio P. Sempronio consulibus;
tredecim annis postquam locata erat dedicavit eam M.
Iunius Brutus, ludique ob dedicationem eius facti, quos
primos scaenicos fuisse Antias Valerius est auctor, Megalesia appellatos.

---

140 This is Scipio Nasica (cf. 1.1 note, above), and the battle
and vow date to 193 (cf. 35.1.8–12).   141 The refusal of state
funds for the games has been interpreted as an indication of
hostility in the senate toward the Scipio family at this time.

142 That is in 205 BC, Scipio Africanus' first consulship, in
which his colleague was P. Licinius Crassus Dives (69).

143 P. Cornelius (30) Scipio Nasica. For Scipio and the Idaean
mother goddess, cf. 35.10.9 and note, and 29.14.6–14.

144 On the problems of the dating here, cf. Briscoe 2.274–75.

some games in a vow at the crucial stage of a battle during his praetorship in Spain.[140] Now, before departing for the war that he was to fight against the Boii, he requested of the senate that funds for these games be voted to him. The request was deemed irregular and unreasonable; and the senators decreed that, since he had made a vow to hold the games on his own initiative and without senatorial authorization, he should finance them from any moneys he had kept back for that purpose from his spoils or else from his own resources.[141] These games were held by Publius Cornelius over a ten-day period.

At about the same time the temple of the Magna Mater Idaea was dedicated. This goddess had been brought from Asia during the consulship of Publius Cornelius Scipio (who was subsequently given the *cognomen* Africanus) and of Publius Licinius,[142] and had been escorted from the coast to the Palatine by the Publius Cornelius under discussion.[143] Construction of the temple had been contracted out, in accordance with a senatorial decree, by the censors Marcus Livius and Gaius Claudius in the consulship of Marcus Cornelius and Publius Sempronius.[144] Thirteen years after the awarding of the contract, it was dedicated by Marcus Iunius Brutus, and games were put on to celebrate its dedication. These, the first games with dramatic performances according to Valerius Antias, were called the *Megalesia*.[145]

[145] In fact, the earliest presentation of drama seems to have taken place in 240, when Livius Andronicus presented a comedy or a tragedy at the *Ludi Romani,* and Antias may simply have referred to the earliest dramatic performance at the *Megalesia,* first held in 204 but with drama staged first in 194 (cf. 34.54.3).

5 Item Iuventatis aedem in circo maximo C. Licinius
6 Lucullus duumvir dedicavit. voverat eam sedecim annis
   ante M. Livius consul, quo die Hasdrubalem exercitumque eius cecidit; idem censor eam faciendam locavit M.
7 Cornelio P. Sempronio consulibus. huius quoque dedican-
   dae causa ludi facti, et eo omnia cum maiore religione
   facta quod novum cum Antiocho instabat bellum.

   37. Principio eius anni quo haec agebantur,[73] iam pro-
   fecto ad bellum M'. Acilio, manente adhuc Romae P. Cor-
2 nelio consule, boves duos domitos in Carinis per scalas
   pervenisse in tegulas aedificii proditum memoriae est. eos
   vivos comburi cineremque eorum deici in Tiberim harus-
3 pices iusserunt. Tarracinae et Amiterni nuntiatum est
   aliquotiens lapidibus pluvisse, Menturnis aedem Iovis et
   tabernas circa forum de caelo tactas esse, Volturni in ostio
4 fluminis duas naves fulmine ictas conflagrasse. eorum prodigiorum causa libros Sibyllinos ex senatus consulto decemviri cum adissent, renuntiaverunt ieiunium instituen-
5 dum Cereri esse, et id quinto quoque anno servandum; et

---

[73] agebantur *hic Briscoe*: *post* consule (consulis *AE*) *Bχ*

---

[146] M. Livius Salinator (33), who defeated Hannibal's brother
at the River Metaurus in 207 (cf. 27.48.9–49.4, where, however,
there is no mention of Livius' vow).   [147] In 204; the censors
were Salinator and C. Claudius Nero (246).

[148] Located between the Esquiline and Caelian hills, the Carinae became a very fashionable neighborhood, especially in the
late Republic (Pompey had a house there, which subsequently
belonged to Mark Antony [Vell. 2.77.1]). Cf. Richardson 71–72.
   [149] Cf. 1.3 note, above.   [150] Tarracina: *Barr.* 44 D3;
Amiternum: 42 E4; Minturnae, Volturnum: 44 E3.

Furthermore, the duumvir Gaius Licinius Lucullus dedicated the temple of Juventas in the Circus Maximus. This temple Marcus Livius had promised in a vow as consul sixteen years earlier, on the day when he cut Hasdrubal and his army to pieces,[146] and he also, as censor, contracted out the work for the temple, in the consulship of Marcus Cornelius and Publius Sempronius.[147] Games were also held to commemorate this dedication and the entire event was celebrated with all the greater attention to ritual because of the threat of the new war with Antiochus.

37. At the start of the year when these events were taking place, and at a point when Manius Acilius had already left for the war and the consul Publius Cornelius was still in Rome, it is recorded that two domesticated oxen climbed the stairs to the tiled roof of a building in the Carinae.[148] The *haruspices*[149] ordered the oxen to be burned alive and their ashes thrown into the Tiber. There were reports that stones had fallen as rain on a number of occasions at Tarracina and Amiternum; that the temple of Jupiter and shops around the forum had been struck by lightening at Minturnae; and that two ships had been consumed by fire after being struck by lightning in the river mouth at Volturnum.[150] In view of these prodigies, the decemvirs consulted the Sibylline books on a directive from the senate,[151] and reported that a fast should be instituted in honor of Ceres, to be held every fifth year.

---

[151] The *decemviri sacris faciundis* (cf. 35.9.5 note) gave the senate (and individuals) advice on religious matters, especially prodigies. In the more ominous cases of such divine manifestations, they were instructed to consult the Sibylline Books.

ut novendiale sacrum fieret et unum diem supplicatio esset; coronati supplicarent; et consul P. Cornelius quibus dis quibusque hostiis edidissent decemviri sacrificaret.

6 placatis dis nunc votis rite solvendis nunc prodigiis expiandis, in provinciam proficiscitur consul, atque inde Cn. Domitium proconsulem dimisso exercitu Romam decedere iussit; ipse in agrum Boiorum legiones induxit.

38. Sub idem fere tempus Ligures, lege sacrata coacto exercitu, nocte improviso castra Q. Minuci proconsulis

2 adgressi sunt. Minucius usque ad lucem intra vallum militem instructum tenuit, intentus ne qua transcenderet

3 hostis munimenta. prima luce duabus simul portis eruptionem fecit. nec primo impetu, quod speraverat, Ligures

4 pulsi sunt; duas amplius horas dubium certamen sustinuere; postremo, cum alia atque alia agmina erumperent, et integri fessis succederent ad pugnam, tandem Ligures, inter cetera etiam vigiliis confecti, terga dederunt. caesa supra quattuor milia hostium; ex Romanis sociisque minus trecenti perierunt.

5 Duobus fere post mensibus P. Cornelius consul cum

6 Boiorum exercitu signis conlatis egregie pugnavit. duodetriginta milia hostium occisa Antias Valerius scribit, capta tria milia et quadringentos, signa militaria centum viginti

---

152 Cn. Domitius Ahenobarbus (18), consul 192.

153 A seemingly Italic practice (cited by Livy also for the Etruscans, Samnites, Volsci, and Aequi) by which anyone failing to enlist for service was to forfeit his life and property to a god (see further Oakley 4.392–98).

154 Q. Minucius (65) Thermus, praetor 196, consul 193.

155 On Valerius Antias, see Introduction to vol. IX (LCL 295), 14–15. He is often cited for the unreliability of his numbers.

There was also to be a nine-day period of sacrifice and one day of supplication, with garlands worn for the supplication, and the consul Publius Cornelius was to sacrifice to such gods and with such animals as the decemvirs should stipulate. The gods were placated both by the appropriate fulfillment of vows and by the expiation of the prodigies, and the consul then left for his province. Here he ordered the proconsul, Gnaeus Domitius,[152] to demobilize his army, leave the province and return to Rome; he himself took his legions into the territory of the Boii.

38. About this same time, the Ligurians raised an army under their "sacred law,"[153] and launched a surprise attack at night on the camp of the proconsul Quintus Minucius.[154] Minucius kept his men drawn up in battle formation within the rampart until daybreak, intent on ensuring that the enemy not cross his fortifications at any point. At dawn he made a simultaneous counterattack through two of the camp gates. The Ligurians were not routed at the first charge as he had hoped, and for more than two hours they kept the outcome of the battle in doubt. However, as company after company came rushing out and fresh soldiers replaced the weary at the front, the Ligurians, worn out by lack of sleep as well as everything else, finally turned tail. More than 4,000 of the enemy were cut down and of the Romans and their allies fewer than 300 lost their lives.

Some two months later the consul Publius Cornelius fought an outstanding pitched battle against an army of the Boii. Valerius Antias[155] recounts that 28,000 of the enemy were killed, 3,400 taken prisoner, and 124 military

quattuor, equos mille ducentos triginta, carpenta ducenta
quadraginta septem; ex victoribus mille quadringentos
7 octoginta quattuor cecidisse. ubi ut in numero scriptori
parum fidei sit, quia in augendo eo non alius intemperan-
tior est, magnam tamen victoriam fuisse apparet, quod et
castra capta sunt et Boii post eam pugnam extemplo dediderunt sese, et quod supplicatio eius victoriae causa decreta ab senatu victimaeque maiores caesae.

39. Per eosdem dies M. Fulvius Nobilior ex ulteriore
2 Hispania ovans urbem est ingressus. argenti transtulit
duodecim milia pondo, bigati argenti centum triginta milia,[74] auri centum viginti septem pondo.

3 P. Cornelius consul, obsidibus a Boiorum gente accep-
tis, agri parte fere dimidia eos multavit, quo, si vellet,
4 populus Romanus colonias mittere posset. inde Romam ut
ad triumphum haud dubium decedens exercitum dimisit,
5 et adesse Romae ad diem triumphi iussit; ipse postero die
quam venit, senatu in aedem Bellonae vocato, cum de
rebus ab se gestis disservisset, postulavit ut sibi trium-
6 phanti liceret urbem invehi. P. Sempronius Blaesus tribunus plebis non negandum Scipioni sed differendum honorem triumphi censebat: bella Ligurum Gallicis semper

---

[74] milia *Drak.*: om. Bχ

---

156 Supplication and full-grown animals: cf. 21.9 note, above.
157 On ovation, cf. 21.10 above and note.   158 This repeats
almost verbatim 21.10–11 above and can perhaps be attributed
to carelessness on Livy's part. The *bigae* (sometimes *biga*) was the
two-horse chariot usually found on the *denarius,* a silver coin
originally worth ten asses (Lat. *deni* = ten).   159 The temple of
Bellona lay near the Circus Flaminius (cf. Richardson 57–58, with

standards, 1,230 horses and 247 wagons captured, while 1,484 of the victors fell in the action. Little trust can be placed in this author where numbers are concerned because no one is more extravagant than he in inflating them; but it is clear that this was a great victory—the camp was captured, the Boii surrendered immediately after the battle, and a supplication for the victory was decreed by the senate and full-grown animals sacrificed.[156]

39. At about this same time Marcus Fulvius Nobilior, returning from Farther Spain, entered the city in ovation.[157] He carried in his procession 12,000 lbs of silver, 130,000 silver coins stamped with the *biga* and 127 lbs of gold.[158]

After taking hostages from the tribe of the Boii, the consul Publius Cornelius confiscated about half of their lands so the Roman people could send colonies there if they so wished. Leaving then for Rome for the triumph he was sure was coming, he demobilized his troops and ordered them to appear in Rome on the day of the triumph. The day after his arrival in the city, Cornelius convened the senate in the temple of Bellona,[159] gave an account of his achievements, and requested permission to ride into the city in triumph. The tribune Publius Sempronius Blaesus proposed that Scipio not be refused the honor of a triumph but that it be deferred. Wars fought with the Ligurians, he explained, were invariably connected with

fig. 17 [p. 65]), outside the *pomerium*. As a triumphing general did not cross the *pomerium* until granted his triumph (see, however, Beard 204–5), it was often used for meetings of the senate to consider requests for one. Nasica had clearly also decided the date of the triumph that he was sure was coming.

iuncta fuisse; eas inter se gentes mutua ex propinquo ferre
7 auxilia. si P. Scipio devictis acie Boiis aut ipse cum victore
exercitu in agrum Ligurum transisset, aut partem copiarum Q. Minucio misisset, qui iam tertium ibi annum dubio
8 detineretur bello, debellari cum Liguribus potuisse; nunc
ad triumphum frequentandum deductos esse milites, qui
egregiam navare operam rei publicae potuissent, possent
etiam si senatus quod festinatione triumphi praetermissum
9 esset, id restituere differendo triumpho vellet. iuberent
consulem cum legionibus redire in provinciam, dare operam ut Ligures subigantur. nisi illi cogantur in ius iudi-
ciumque populi Romani, ne Boios quidem quieturos; aut
10 pacem aut bellum utrobique habenda. devictis Liguribus
paucos post menses proconsulem P. Cornelium, multorum exemplo qui in magistratu non triumphaverunt, tri-
umphaturum esse.

40. Ad ea consul neque se Ligures provinciam sortitum
esse ait, neque cum Liguribus bellum gessisse, neque
2 triumphum de iis postulare; Q. Minucium confidere brevi
subactis iis meritum triumphum postulaturum atque im-
3 petraturum esse; se de Gallis Boiis postulare triumphum,
quos acie vicerit castris exuerit, quorum gentem biduo
post pugnam totam acceperit in deditionem, a quibus

those fought with the Gauls: the tribes, being so close, brought assistance to each other. The war with the Ligurians could have been finished off if, after defeating the Boii in battle, Publius Scipio had either himself passed into Ligurian territory with his victorious army or had dispatched some of his forces to Quintus Minucius, who had already been pinned down there for two years in an inconclusive war. As it was, Scipio's men had been withdrawn from the field to make up the numbers at his triumph, when they could have rendered sterling service to the state—and could still do if, by deferring the triumph, the senate were prepared to restore the situation that had been let slip by Scipio's impatience for that triumph. They should, he continued, instruct the consul to return to his province with his legions and concentrate his efforts on subjugating the Ligurians. Unless these were forced to accept the authority and jurisdiction of the Roman people, even the Boii would not remain at peace—it had to be either peace or war in both cases. After defeating the Ligurians, Publius Cornelius would celebrate his triumph a few months later as proconsul, following the example of many who had not celebrated their triumph during their term of office.

40. In reply, the consul observed that the province he had been allotted had not been the Ligurians, that he had not been at war with the Ligurians, and that it was not over them that he was requesting the triumph. He was sure that Quintus Minucius would soon vanquish them and would request and be granted a well-deserved triumph. As for himself, his petition was for a triumph over the Gallic Boii. He had defeated them in battle, stripped them of their camp, and two days after the battle had accepted the sur-

4 obsides abduxerit, pacis futurae pignus. verum enimvero illud multo maius esse, quod tantum numerum Gallorum occiderit in acie quod cum tot milibus[75] certe Boiorum
5 nemo ante se imperator pugnaverit. plus partem dimidiam ex quinquaginta milibus hominum caesam, multa milia
6 capta; senes puerosque Boiis superesse. itaque id quemquam mirari posse, cur victor exercitus, cum hostem in provincia neminem reliquisset, Romam venerit ad cele-
7 brandum consulis triumphum? quorum militum si et in alia provincia opera uti senatus velit, utro tandem modo promptiores ad aliud periculum novumque laborem ituros credat, si persoluta eis sine detractatione prioris periculi laborisque merces sit, an si spem pro re ferentes dimittant,
8 iam semel in prima spe deceptos? nam quod ad se attineat, sibi gloriae in omnem vitam illo die satis quaesitum esse quo se virum optimum iudicatum ad accipiendam matrem
9 Idaeam misisset senatus. hoc titulo, etsi nec consulatus nec triumphus addatur, satis honestam honoratamque P. Scipionis Nasicae imaginem fore.
10 Universus senatus non ipse modo ad decernendum triumphum consensit, sed etiam tribunum plebis auctori-
11 tate sua compulit ad remittendam intercessionem. P. Cornelius consul triumphavit de Boiis.

[75] quod cum tot Bχ: quod cum *Holk. Esc.*: quot cum *Holk. 353.*

---

160 Cf. 1.1 note, above.

161 Polybius notes that portrait masks (*imagines*) of important men were kept in the atrium of the family home (cf. Walbank 1.738–40). They were worn by actors at public sacrifices and family funerals (*OCD* s.v. *imagines*).

render of the entire tribe and taken hostages from them to secure future peace. But, in fact, there was a much more important point: he had in the field killed a huge number of Gauls, and certainly no general before him had faced in battle so many thousands of Boii. Of their 50,000 men more than half had been killed, and many thousands taken prisoner—the Boii were left with only old men and children. Could anyone be surprised, then, at a victorious army coming to Rome to celebrate the consul's triumph when it had left no enemy in the province? And suppose the senate wished to avail itself of the services of these soldiers in another province as well. Which of the two ways of dealing with them did the senators think would make them readier to face another danger and fresh hardship? Was it if they were given the recompense without equivocation for the danger and hardship already faced or if, instead, the senators sent them off only with hopes rather than tangible rewards when they had already been deceived in their initial hopes? As far as he himself was concerned, he had acquired enough glory to last a lifetime on the day that the senate, judging him the best man, had sent him to welcome the Idaean mother.[160] With that title, even if neither his consulship nor a triumph were added to it, the death mask[161] of Publius Scipio Nasica would be honorable and honored enough.

To a man the senate not only agreed to accord Scipio the triumph but also wielded its authority to make the tribune of the plebs withdraw his objection. The consul Publius Cornelius then triumphed over the Boii.

In eo triumpho Gallicis carpentis arma signaque et
spolia omnis generis travexit, et vasa aenea Gallica et cum
captivis nobilibus equorum quoque captorum gregem tra-
12   duxit. aureos torques transtulit mille quadringentos septuaginta unum, ad hoc auri pondo ducenta quadraginta
septem, argenti infecti factique in Gallicis vasis, non in-
fabre suo more factis, duo milia trecenta quadraginta
pondo, bigatorum nummorum ducenta triginta quattuor
13   milia.[76] militibus qui currum secuti sunt centenos vicenos
quinos asses divisit, duplex centurioni, triplex equiti.

14   Postero die, contione advocata, de rebus ab se gestis et
de iniuria tribuni bello alieno se inligantis, ut suae victoriae fructu se fraudaret, cum disseruisset, milites exauc-
toratos dimisit.

41. Dum haec in Italia geruntur, Antiochus Ephesi
securus admodum de bello Romano erat, tamquam non
transituris in Asiam Romanis; quam securitatem ei magna
pars amicorum aut per errorem aut adsentando faciebat.
2   Hannibal unus, cuius eo tempore vel maxima apud regem
auctoritas erat, magis mirari se aiebat quod non iam in
3   Asia essent Romani quam venturos dubitare; propius esse
ex Graecia in Asiam quam ex Italia in Graeciam traicere,
et multo maiorem causam Antiochum quam Aetolos esse;
neque[77] mari minus quam terra pollere Romana arma. iam

---

[76] milia *H.J.M*: *om. Bχ*
[77] neque *ed. Camp.*: neque enim *Bχ*: neque etiam *J. Gron.*

In that triumphal procession Scipio had arms, standards and spoils of all kinds carried on Gallic carts, and he also had on display Gallic vases made of bronze and a herd of captured horses along with highborn captives. He had 1,471 gold torques carried along, plus 247 pounds of gold, 2,340 lbs of silver, some unwrought and some in the form of Gallic vases, not inelegantly crafted in the Gallic style, and 234,000 coins stamped with the *biga*. To each of the soldiers who followed his chariot Scipio gave 125 asses, double that amount to a centurion, and triple to a cavalryman.

The next day Scipio convened an assembly of his men and spoke about his achievements and the insulting conduct of the tribune who was trying to make him responsible for a war that was not his concern in order to cheat him of the rewards of his victory. He then gave the men their discharge from service and dismissed them.

41. While these events were taking place in Italy, Antiochus was at Ephesus,[162] quite unconcerned about the war with Rome since he assumed the Romans would not cross to Asia. This assurance was given him by most of his friends, who were either mistaken or simply wished to humor him. Only Hannibal, whose influence with the king was at its peak at the time, demurred, saying he was surprised that the Romans were not in Asia already rather than doubtful that they would come. It was a shorter crossing from Greece to Asia than from Italy to Greece, and Antiochus was a much more important target than the Aetolians; furthermore, Roman arms were no less powerful on the sea than on land. A Roman fleet had long been

---

[162] The narrative picks up here from 20.8, above.

4 pridem classem circa Maleum esse; audire sese nuper
novas naves novumque imperatorem rei gerendae causa
5 ex Italia venisse; itaque desineret Antiochus pacem sibi
ipse spe vana facere. in Asia et de ipsa Asia brevi terra
marique dimicandum ei cum Romanis esse, et aut imperium adimendum orbem terrarum adfectantibus, aut ipsi
6 regnum amittendum. unus vera et providere et fideliter
praedicere visus. itaque ipse rex navibus quae paratae in-
structaeque erant Chersonesum petit, ut ea loca, si forte
7 terra venirent Romani, praesidiis firmaret; ceteram classem Polyxenidam parare et deducere iussit; speculatorias
naves ad omnia exploranda circa insulas dimisit.

42. C. Livius praefectus Romanae classis, cum quinquaginta navibus tectis profectus ab Roma Neapolim, quo
ab sociis eius orae convenire iusserat apertas naves quae
2 ex foedere debebantur, Siciliam inde petit fretoque Mes-
sanam praetervectus, cum sex Punicas naves ad auxilium
missas accepisset et ab Reginis Locrisque et eiusdem iuris
sociis debitas exegisset naves, lustrata classe ad Lacinium,
altum petit.
3 Corcyram, quam primam Graeciae civitatium adiit,

---

163 Cape Malea, the tip of the southeastern promontory of
Laconia (*Barr.* 58 E5).

164 C. Livius Salinator (29), praetor in 202 and later consul in
188 (cf. *MRR* 365 for his career). He would now play a major role
as fleet commander (cf. 2.6, above) in the war.

165 The Thracian Chersonese (*Barr.* 51 G4).

166 A promontory southeast of Croton (*Barr.* 46 F3). The ceremony involved the sacrifice of an animal, whose raw internal
organs were thrown in the sea (cf. 29.27.5).

stationed off Malea,[163] he added, and he was told that fresh ships and a fresh commander[164] had recently arrived from Italy to direct operations. Antiochus should therefore abandon any illusions he might have of peace for himself. He would shortly have to fight the Romans on land and sea and do so in Asia and for Asia itself. And he must either wrest power from them as they strove for worldwide dominion or else lose his own kingdom. Hannibal alone seemed to have clear foresight and to give forthright warnings of what was to come. And so the king made for the Chersonese[165] himself, with such ships as were ready and fitted out, in order to secure the area with garrisons in case the Romans came by land. He ordered Polyxenidas to fit out and launch the rest of the fleet, and sent spy vessels around the islands to conduct a thorough reconnaissance.

42. The commander of the Roman fleet, Gaius Livius, set off from Rome with 50 decked ships bound for Naples, the rallying point he had ordered for the open-decked ships that the allies on that coastline were obliged to provide under their treaty. He then made for Sicily. He went through the strait past Messana, took charge of six Carthaginian ships that had been sent to assist him, and requisitioned from Rhegium and Locri, and from other allies of the same treaty-standing, the ships due from them. Then, after a purification ceremony for the fleet at Lacinium,[166] he put out to sea.

When he arrived at Corcyra,[167] his first port of call

---

[167] Corcyra (mod. Corfu) had surrendered to Rome in the first Illyrian War (229–228) and had been the Roman naval base of operations against Philip V (31.22.4, 47.2; 32.14.7).

cum venisset, percunctatus de statu belli—necdum enim
omnia in Graecia perpacata erant—et ubi classis Romana
4 esset, postquam audivit circa Thermopylarum saltum in
statione consulem ac regem esse, classem Piraei stare,
maturandum ratus omnium rerum causa, pergit protinus
5 navigare Peloponnesum. Samen Zacynthumque, quia partis Aetolorum maluerant esse, protinus depopulatus, Maleum petit, et prospera navigatione usus paucis diebus
6 Piraeum ad veterem classem pervenit. ad Scyllaevm Eumenes rex cum tribus navibus occurrit, cum Aeginae diu
incertus consilii fuisset, utrum ad tuendum rediret regnum—audiebat enim Antiochum Ephesi navales terrestresque parare copias—, an nusquam abscederet ab
7 Romanis, ex quorum fortuna sua penderet. a Piraeo A.
Atilius, traditis successori quinque et viginti navibus tec-
8 tis, Romam est profectus. Livius una et octoginta constratis navibus, multis praeterea minoribus, quae aut apertae
rostratae aut sine rostris speculatoriae erant, Delum traiecit.

43. Eo fere tempore consul Acilius Naupactum oppugnabat. Livium Deli per aliquot dies—et est vento-
sissima regio inter Cycladas, fretis alias maioribus alias
2 minoribus divisas—adversi venti tenuerunt. Polyxenidas,
certior per dispositas speculatorias naves factus Deli stare
3 Romanam classem, nuntios ad regem misit. qui, omissis

---

168 Promontory at the tip of the Argolid (*Barr.* 58 F3).
169 Cf. 30.6 and 34.1, above.

among the Greek states, he made inquiries about the progress of the war—for peace had not yet been established everywhere in Greece—and the location of the Roman fleet. When he heard that the consul and the king were dug in near the pass of Thermopylae and that the fleet was riding at anchor in Piraeus, he felt that in view of everything he should take speedy action, and he immediately proceeded to set sail for the Peloponnese. He straightway plundered Same and Zacynthus because they had chosen to side with the Aetolians, then made for Malea and, a few days later, after a smooth voyage, reached the old fleet in Piraeus. At Scyllaeum[168] King Eumenes met him with three ships. He had waited a long time on Aegina, uncertain what to do, whether to return to defend his own realm (as he was receiving reports of Antiochus preparing naval and land forces at Ephesus) or not move anywhere away from the Romans, on whose fortunes his own depended. Aulus Atilius then transferred command of 25 decked ships to his successor, and left Piraeus for Rome. Livius thereupon crossed to Delos with 81 decked ships as well as a large number of smaller vessels, which were either open-decked galleys with beaks or reconnaissance ships without beaks.

43. At about that time the consul Acilius was engaged in the siege of Naupactus.[169] Livius was detained for several days at Delos by headwinds—in fact, the area around the Cyclades is particularly windy because of the straits that separate them, quite wide in some places, narrower in others. Polyxenidas received intelligence from reconnaissance vessels posted in different areas that the Roman fleet was riding at anchor at Delos and he sent messengers to the king. Antiochus abandoned his operations in the

quae in Hellesponto agebat, cum rostratis navibus, quantum adcelerare poterat, Ephesum redit et consilium extemplo habuit, faciendumne periculum navalis certaminis
4 foret. Polyxenidas negabat cessandum et utique prius confligendum quam classis Eumenis et Rhodiae naves
5 coniungerentur Romanis; ita numero non ferme impares futuros se, ceteris omnibus superiores, et celeritate na-
6 vium et varietate auxiliorum. nam Romanas naves cum ipsas inscite factas immobiles esse, tum etiam, ut quae in
7 terram hostium veniant, oneratas commeatu venire; suas autem, ut pacata omnia circa se relinquentes, nihil praeter militem atque arma habituras. multum etiam adiuturam notitiam maris terrarumque et ventorum, quae omnia ignaros turbatura hostes essent.

8   Movit omnes auctor consilii, qui et re consilium exsecuturus erat. biduum in apparatu morati, tertio die centum[78] navibus, quarum septuaginta tectae ceterae apertae, minoris omnes formae erant, profecti Phocaeam
9 petierunt. inde, cum audisset adpropinquare iam Romanam classem, rex, quia non interfuturus navali certamini erat, Magnesiam, quae ad Sipylum est, concessit ad ter-

---

[78] centum *B*χ: ducentis *Sig*.

---

170 The number of ships here is a problem. Appian (*Syr.* 22) gives it as 200; hence, Sigonius' proposed emendation (see textual note). However, since Polyxenides has just said that his ships and those of the Romans would be "roughly equal in numbers" and no large Syrian fleet appears in the ensuing battles (cf. 37.23.5, 30.2), the manuscript reading is likely to be correct.

Hellespont and, taking his beaked ships, returned with all possible speed to Ephesus and immediately held a council of war to discuss whether to risk a naval engagement. Polyxenidas kept saying that they should not delay and that they should certainly take on the enemy before Eumenes' fleet and the Rhodian vessels joined up with the Romans. In this way, he said, they would be roughly equal numerically but in all other respects superior, in the speed of their ships as well as the range of auxiliary forces at their disposal. For, he continued, the maneuverability of the Roman vessels was poor because of their inferior construction, but in addition they were coming laden with supplies since they were entering enemy territory. Their own ships, on the other hand, leaving peaceful surroundings all around them, would be carrying only fighting men and weaponry. Their knowledge of the sea, the coastline and the winds would also be of great help, said Polyxenidas, while these things would all pose problems for the enemy, who lacked such knowledge.

The man proposing this strategy, who would also be the one putting it into action, convinced them all. After spending two days on preparations, they set sail on the third with 100 ships[170]—70 decked and the rest open-decked, and all of quite small dimensions—and headed for Phocaea.[171] When he heard that the Roman fleet was now approaching, the king left there because he did not intend taking part in the sea battle and withdrew to Magnesia-near-

---

[171] The most northerly of the Ionian cities of Asia Minor (*Barr.* 57 E3). The Phocaeans were great traders who established colonies on the Mediterranean coast of France (e.g., Massilia [Marseille]) and Spain (e.g., Emporion).

10 restres copias comparandas; classis ad Cissuntem portum
Erythraeorum, tamquam ibi aptius exspectatura hostem,
contendit.

11 Romani, ubi primum aquilones—ii namque per aliquot
dies tenuerant—ceciderunt, ab Delo Phanas, portum Chiorum in Aegaeum mare versum, petunt; inde ad urbem
circumegere naves, commeatuque sumpto Phocaeam tra-
12 iciunt. Eumenes Elaeam ad suam classem profectus, paucis post inde diebus cum quattuor et viginti navibus tectis
apertis pluribus paulo Phocaeam ad Romanos parantes
13 instruentesque se ad navale certamen rediit. inde centum
quinque tectis navibus apertis ferme quinquaginta profecti, primo aquilonibus transversis cum urgerentur in
terram, cogebantur tenui agmine prope in ordinem singulae naves ire; deinde, ut lenita paulum vis venti est, ad
Corycum portum, qui super Cissuntem est, conati sunt
traicere.

44. Polyxenidas, ut adpropinquare hostes allatum est,
occasione pugnandi laetus, sinistrum ipse cornu in altum
extendit, dextrum cornu praefectos navium ad terram
explicare iubet, et aequa fronte ad pugnam procedebat.
2 quod ubi vidit Romanus, vela contrahit malosque inclinat,
et simul armamenta componens opperitur insequentes
3 naves. iam fere triginta in fronte erant; quibus ut aequaret
laevum cornu, dolonibus erectis altum petere intendit,
iussis qui sequebantur adversus dextrum cornu prope ter-

---

172 *Barr.* 56 E4. It was to be the site of the decisive battle
between Rome and Antiochus.   173 Location of Cissus unknown; Erythrae: *Barr.* 56 C5.   174 Phanae: *Barr.* 56 B5

175 Location of the port is unknown, but presumably it was
close to Mt. Korykos (*Barr.* 56 D5).

Sipylus[172] to assemble his land forces. The fleet hastened on to Cissus, a port of the Erythraeans,[173] which was thought a more favorable place to await the enemy.

As soon as the north winds died down (they had kept up for several days), the Romans set sail from Delos to Phanae, a Chian port facing the Aegean Sea.[174] From there they brought their ships round to the city and after taking on provisions crossed to Phocaea. Eumenes set off to join his own fleet at Elaea. He returned to Phocaea a few days later with 24 decked ships and a few more open-decked vessels and rejoined the Romans who were now preparing and equipping themselves for the forthcoming naval battle. They set sail from there with 105 decked and some 50 open-decked ships and at first were driven landward by northerly winds blowing across their bow, by which the ships were forced to proceed in a narrow column, almost in single file. Then, as the force of the wind abated a little, they attempted to cross to the port of Corycus,[175] which lies above Cissus.

44. When he was brought the news that the enemy was approaching, Polyxenidas was happy at having the chance to fight. He himself extended his left wing toward the open sea and ordered his ships' captains to deploy the right toward the shore; and he then advanced to do battle with a level front. Seeing this, the Roman admiral furled his sails, lowered his masts and, stowing the tackle, awaited the ships coming up behind. There were now about 30 ships in his front line and, to make it extend as far as the enemy's left wing, he put up the foresails and proceeded toward the open sea, ordering those following behind to turn their prows toward the enemy right wing close to the

4   ram proras derigere. Eumenes agmen cogebat; ceterum, ut demendis armamentis tumultuari primum coeptum est, et ipse quanta maxime celeritate potest concitat naves.

5   Iam omnibus in conspectu erant. duae Punicae naves antecedebant Romanam classem, quibus obviae tres fue-
6   runt regiae naves; et, ut in numero impari, duae regiae unam circumsistunt, et primum ab utroque latere remos detergunt, deinde transcendunt armati et deiectis caesis-
7   que propugnatoribus navem capiunt; una, quae pari Marte concurrerat, postquam captam alteram navem vidit, prius-quam ab tribus simul circumveniretur, retro ad classem
8   refugit. Livius, indignatione accensus, praetoria nave in hostes tendit. adversus quem[79] eadem spe duae quae Pu-nicam unam navem circumvenerant cum inferrentur, de-mittere remos in aquam ab utroque latere remiges stabi-liendae navis causa iussit, et in advenientes hostium naves
9   ferreas manus inicere, et ubi pugnam pedestri similem fecissent, meminisse Romanae virtutis nec pro viris du-cere regia mancipia. haud paulo facilius quam ante duae unam, tunc una duas naves expugnavit cepitque.

10   Et iam classes quoque undique concurrerant, et passim
11   permixtis navibus pugnabatur. Eumenes, qui extremus[80] commisso certamine advenerat, ut animadvertit laevum cornu hostium ab Livio turbatum, dextrum ipse, ubi aequa pugna erat, invadit.

[79] quem $B\chi$: quam *ed. Ven. 1495*
[80] extremus *Mg*: *om.* $B\chi$

shore. Eumenes was bringing up the rear but as soon as the scramble to stow the tackle began he also had his ships advance with all possible speed.

They were now visible to all the enemy ships. Two Punic vessels were at the forefront of the Roman fleet, and these were met by three of the king's. Because of the disparity in numbers, two of the king's ships closed in on one of the Carthaginians'. First they sheared off her oars on both sides, and then armed men climbed aboard, threw off or killed the defenders, and captured the vessel. The other ship, which had been fighting on equal terms, saw that her partner had been captured and beat a retreat back to the fleet before she could be surrounded by the three at the same time. Livius, roused to indignation, headed into the enemy with the flagship. The two that had beset the single Carthaginian craft now bore down on him, hoping to repeat their success, whereupon Livius ordered the rowers to lower their oars into the water on both sides to stabilize the ship and to hurl grappling irons onto the oncoming enemy vessels. Then, when they had thus made the battle similar to one on land, he told them to remember Roman courage and not consider the king's serfs as men. On this occasion, the single ship defeated and captured the two with much greater ease than the two had previously taken the one.

By now the fleets had engaged in all sectors and the battle raged everywhere as the ships became entangled with each other. Eumenes had arrived last, after the battle had started, and when he saw the enemy left wing reduced to confusion by Livius he himself attacked the right where the struggle was evenly matched.

45. Neque ita multo post primum ab laevo cornu fuga coepit. Polyxenidas enim, ut virtute militum haud dubie se superari vidit, sublatis dolonibus effuse fugere intendit; mox idem et qui prope terram cum Eumene contraxerant
2 certamen fecerunt. Romani et Eumenes, quoad sufficere remiges potuerunt et in spe erant extremi agminis vexandi,
3 satis pertinaciter secuti sunt. postquam celeritate navium, utpote levium, suas commeatu onustas eludi frustra tendentes viderunt, tandem abstiterunt, tredecim captis navi-
4 bus cum milite ac remige, decem demersis. Romanae classis una Punica navis, in primo certamine ab duabus circumventa, periit.

Polyxenidas non prius quam in portu Ephesi fugae fi-
5 nem fecit. Romani eo die unde[81] egressa regia classis erat manserunt; postero die hostem persequi intenderunt. medio fere in cursu obviae fuere iis quinque et viginti tectae
6 Rhodiae naves cum Pausistrato praefecto classis. his adiunctis Ephesum hostem persecuti, ante ostium portus acie instructa steterunt. postquam confessionem victis satis
7 expresserunt, Rhodii et Eumenes domos dimissi; Romani Chium petentes, Phoenicuntem primum portum Erythraeae[82] praetervecti, nocte ancoris iactis, postero die in

81 unde (inde E) Bχ: Cyssunte, unde Crév.
82 Erythreae Briscoe: Rithreo B: Erithreo φ: Eritreo ψ Voss.: Erythreae terrae Fr. 2

176 Pausistratus, now the Rhodian naval commander, had earlier commanded the Rhodian land forces against Philip V (33.18.1–2).
177 Phoenicus remains unlocated; Erythrae: Barr. 56 C5.

45. Not much later the flight began, on the left flank first. For Polyxenidas, seeing that he was unquestionably outclassed in the courage of the fighting men, raised his foresails and proceeded with a headlong flight; and soon those who had engaged with Eumenes close to shore followed suit. The Romans and Eumenes made a determined pursuit for as long as the rowers could keep going and had some hope of harassing the vessels at the rear. But when they saw that their ships, weighed down with supplies, were being outrun by the speed of those of the enemy (which were lighter than theirs) and that their efforts were in vain, they finally abandoned the chase, having captured thirteen ships, complete with marines and rowers, and having sunk ten. The only loss in the Roman fleet was the one Carthaginian vessel that had been beset by the two ships at the start of the battle.

Polyxenidas did not terminate his flight until he reached the harbor of Ephesus. The Romans spent that day in the port from which the king's fleet had sailed out, and on the next they set off in pursuit of the enemy. Roughly half way into the voyage they were joined by twenty-five decked Rhodian ships with their commander, Pausistratus.[176] Taking these along with them, they pursued the enemy to Ephesus, where they rode at anchor before the harbor mouth drawn up in battle formation. After they had satisfactorily wrung from the conquered an admission of defeat, the Rhodians and Eumenes were sent home. Heading for Chios, the Romans first sailed past Phoenicus, a port of Erythrae,[177] anchored at night, and the next day crossed to the island, and the city of Chios itself. After a

283

insulam ad ipsam urbem traiecerunt. ubi paucos dies re-
8 mige maxime reficiendo morati, Phocaeam tramittunt. ibi
relictis ad praesidium urbis quattuor quinqueremibus, ad
Canas classis venit; et cum iam hiemps appeteret, fossa
valloque circumdatis naves subductae.

9 Exitu anni comitia Romae habita, quibus creati sunt
consules L. Cornelius Scipio et C. Laelius—Africanum
intuentibus cunctis—ad finiendum cum Antiocho bellum.
postero die praetores creati M. Tuccius, L. Aurunculeius,
Cn. Fulvius, L. Aemilius, P. Iunius, C. Atinius Labeo.

few days stay, mostly to restore the strength of the rowers, they crossed to Phocaea. Leaving four quinqueremes there to protect the city, the fleet proceeded to Canae; and since winter was approaching, the ships were pulled ashore and surrounded with a ditch and a rampart.[178]

At the end of the year elections were held at Rome. Lucius Cornelius Scipio and Gaius Laelius[179] were elected consuls—the eyes of all were on Africanus—to finish the war with Antiochus. The next day the following were elected praetors: Marcus Tuccius, Lucius Aurunculeius, Gnaeus Fulvius, Lucius Aemilius, Publius Iunius, and Gaius Atinius Labeo.

---

[178] Canae (Kane: *Barr.* 56 D3) lies in Pergamene territory, and so the fleet is under Attalid protection.

[179] Both had close ties to Scipio Africanus. On Lucius Scipio (Asiagenes), Africanus' brother, cf. 21.7 note, above. On Laelius, cf. 35.10.3 note.

LIBRI XXXVI PERIOCHA

Acilius Glabrio cos. Antiochum ad Thermopylas Philippo
rege adiuvante victum Graecia expulit idemque Aetolos
subegit. P. Cornelius Scipio Nasica cos. aedem Matris
Deum, quam ipse in Palatium intulerat, vir optimus a senatu iudicatus, dedicavit. idemque Boios Gallos victos in
deditionem accepit, de his triumphavit. praeterea navalia
certamina prospera adversus praefectos Antiochi regis
referuntur.

SUMMARY OF BOOK XXXVI

The consul Acilius Glabrio defeated Antiochus at Thermopylae with the assistance of King Philip and drove him from Greece; and he also brought the Aetolians into submission. The consul Publius Cornelius Scipio Nasica dedicated the temple of the mother of the gods, whom he had himself brought to the Palatine, having been judged by the senate the best person to do this. He also defeated the Gallic Boii, accepted their surrender, and celebrated a triumph over them. In addition, there is an account of successful naval battles fought against the officers of King Antiochus.

LIBER XXXVII

1. L. Cornelio Scipione C. Laelio consulibus nulla prius
secundum religiones acta in senatu res est quam de Aetolis. et legati eorum institere, quia brevem indutiarum
diem habebant, et ab T. Quinctio, qui tum Romam ex
2 Graecia redierat, adiuti sunt. Aetoli, ut quibus plus in
misericordia senatus quam in causa spei esset, suppliciter
egerunt, veteribus benefactis nova pensantes maleficia.
3 ceterum et praesentes interrogationibus undique senatorum, confessionem magis noxae quam responsa exprimen-
tium, fatigati sunt, et excedere curia iussi magnum certa-
4 men praebuerunt. plus ira quam misericordia in causa
eorum valebat, quia non ut hostibus[1] modo, sed tamquam
indomitae et insociabili genti suscensebant.
5   Per aliquot dies cum certatum esset, postremo neque
dari neque negari pacem placuit; duae condiciones iis la-
tae sunt: vel senatui liberum arbitrium de se permitterent,

---

[1] hostibus χ: hostes B

[1] These included a nine-day supplication for Livius' victory
off Corycus (36.44.1–45.4), not mentioned by Livy but found in
Polybius (21.2.1).
[2] Cf. 36.27.8–28.7, where the Aetolians clearly misunderstood
the expression "to entrust themselves to the good faith of the
Romans," by which the Romans meant unconditional surrender.

BOOK XXXVII

1. When Lucius Cornelius Scipio and Gaius Laelius entered their consulship, the very first piece of business arising in the senate after the religious observances[1] was the Aetolian question. The Aetolian delegates were pressing for action because the day marking the end of the truce was at hand, and they were also supported by Titus Quinctius, who had by then returned to Rome from Greece. Since they placed more hope in the compassion of the senate than the strength of their case, the Aetolians adopted a suppliant attitude, trying to compensate for their recent offenses with their former services. But while they were in the house they were on all sides plied with questions from the senators, who were trying to squeeze out of them an admission of guilt rather than answers; and when they were ordered to withdraw from the senate house, they became the subject of vigorous debate. Anger prevailed over compassion in their case because the senators were furious with them not just as enemies but as a wild people incapable of alliance.

When the dispute had lasted some days the decision finally reached was that the Aetolians should be neither granted nor refused peace. They were offered two options: either put themselves entirely in the senate's hands,[2]

vel mille talentum darent eosdemque amicos atque inimi-
6 cos haberent. exprimere cupientibus quarum rerum in se
arbitrium senatui permitterent, nihil certi responsum est.
ita infecta pace dimissi, urbe eodem die, Italia intra quindecim dies excedere iussi.

7 Tum de consulum provinciis coeptum agi est. ambo
Graeciam cupiebant. multum Laelius in senatu poterat. is,
cum senatus aut sortiri aut comparare inter se provincias
consules iussisset, elegantius facturos dixit si iudicio pa-
8 trum quam si sorti eam rem permisissent. Scipio, responso
ad hoc dato cogitaturum quid sibi faciendum esset, cum
fratre uno locutus iussusque ab eo permittere audacter
senatui, renuntiat collegae facturum se quod is censeret.
9 cum res aut nova aut vetustate exemplorum memoriae iam
exoletae relata exspectatione certaminis senatum erexis-
set, P. Scipio Africanus dixit si L. Scipioni fratri suo pro-
10 vinciam Graeciam decrevissent, se legatum[2] iturum. haec
vox magno adsensu audita sustulit certamen; experiri libe-
bat utrum plus regi Antiocho in Hannibale victo an in
victore Africano consuli legionibusque Romanis auxilii
foret; ac prope omnes Scipioni Graeciam Laelio Italiam
decreverunt.

---

[2] se legatum *B*χ: se ei legatum *Duker*; se legatum ei *Weiss*.

---

[3] A thousand talents was Philip V's indemnity after the second
Macedonian War (33.30.7), and that huge amount, together with
the obligation to side with Rome against Antiochus, would prove
too much for the Aetolians to accept.

[4] This passage has aroused much dispute since, according to
Cicero (*Phil.* 11.17), Laelius wants the command but Lucius
draws the province by sortition. The senate then wants to give it

or else pay a thousand talents and accept the same friends and enemies as the Romans.[3] The Aetolians wanted clarification of the areas in which they would be in the senate's hands but were given no clear answer. They were therefore sent off without a peace settlement and ordered to leave the city that same day and Italy within fifteen days.

Discussion of the consuls' provinces then began. Both wanted Greece; and Laelius had great influence in the senate. When the senate instructed the consuls either to proceed to sortition or come to an agreement on the provinces, he said the consuls would be better advised to leave the matter to the judgment of the senators than to a lottery. Scipio, after replying that he would reflect on the course he should take, then discussed the question with his brother, and with him alone. Told by his brother that he could confidently leave the matter to the senate, he reported to his colleague that he would accept his suggestion. This was a novel procedure or else one based on precedents long forgotten and it had piqued the interest of the senators, who were now expecting a contest. Then Publius Scipio Africanus declared that, if the senators formally assigned the province of Greece to his brother, Lucius Scipio, he would go there as his legate. This statement, which was received with great approval, ended the contest. The senate wished to put to the test which of the two had the more solid support, Antiochus in the defeated Hannibal or the consul and the Roman legions in his conqueror, Africanus. Their decision to assign Greece to Scipio and Italy to Laelius was almost unanimous.[4]

to Laelius but is dissuaded by Africanus. For further discussion, see Briscoe 2.291.

2. Praetores inde provincias sortiti sunt, L. Aurunculeius urbanam, Cn. Fulvius peregrinam, L. Aemilius Regillus classem, P. Iunius Brutus Tuscos, M. Tuccius Apuliam et Bruttios, C. Atinius Siciliam.

2 Consuli deinde cui Graecia provincia decreta erat ad eum exercitum quem a M'. Acilio—duae autem legiones erant—accepturus esset in supplementum addita peditum civium Romanorum tria milia equites centum, et so-

3 cium Latini nominis quinque milia equites ducenti; et adiectum ut cum in provinciam venisset, si e re publica

4 videretur esse, exercitum in Asiam traiceret. alteri consuli totus novus exercitus decretus, duae legiones Romanae et socium Latini nominis quindecim milia peditum equites sescenti.

5 Exercitum ex Liguribus Q. Minucius—iam enim confectam provinciam scripserat et Ligurum omne nomen in deditionem venisse—traducere in Boios et P. Cornelio

6 proconsuli tradere iussus, ex agro quo victos bello multaverat Boios deducenti. duae[3] urbanae legiones, quae priore anno conscriptae erant, M. Tuccio praetori datae, et

[3] deducenti. duae *Madvig*: deducendae Bχ: deductae *ed. Rom.*: deducenti H.J.M

5 Cf. 36.45.9 for their election.

6 On the expression "allies . . . Latin rights," cf. 35.7.5 note.

7 This is Quintus Minucius (65) Thermus. For his victory over the Ligurians, cf. 36.38.1–4.

8 Publius Cornelius (30) Nasica, consul for 191; for his expropriation of the Boian land, cf. 36.39.3.

2. The praetors then proceeded to their provincial sortition.[5] Lucius Aurunculeius received the urban jurisdiction and Gnaeus Fulvius that over foreigners. Lucius Aemilius Regillus received the fleet, Publius Junius Brutus Etruria, Marcus Tuccius Apulia and Bruttium, and Gaius Atinius Sicily.

The consul who had been assigned Greece as his province was then allocated as a supplementary force—in addition to the army that he was to assume from Manius Acilius (that is, two legions)—3,000 infantry and 100 cavalry of Roman citizens, plus 5,000 infantry and 200 cavalry from the allies and those with Latin rights.[6] It was further decided that he should take his army across to Asia when he reached his province, if that seemed to be in the state's best interests. The other consul was assigned a completely fresh army composed of two Roman legions, plus 15,000 infantry and 600 cavalry from the allies and those with Latin rights.

As Quintus Minucius had written to say that his provincial responsibility had now been fulfilled, and that the entire Ligurian nation had capitulated,[7] he was instructed to take his army from Liguria to the land of the Boii and turn it over to the proconsul Publius Cornelius, who was conducting the Boii from the lands that he had confiscated from them after their defeat in the war.[8] To hold Apulia and Bruttium, the praetor Marcus Tuccius was given the two urban legions[9] that had been raised the previous year,

[9] "Urban legions," kept in reserve in or near Rome, were often made up of older soldiers and fresh recruits.

socium ac Latini nominis peditum quindecim milia et
7 equites sescenti, ad Apuliam Bruttiosque obtinendos. A.
Cornelio superioris anni praetori, qui Bruttios cum exercitu obtinuerat, imperatum si ita consuli videretur, ut
legiones in Aetoliam traiectas M'. Acilio traderet, si is
8 manere ibi vellet; si Acilius redire Romam mallet, ut A.
Cornelius cum eo exercitu in Aetolia remaneret. C. Ati-
nium Labeonem provinciam Siciliam exercitumque a M.
Aemilio accipere placuit, et in supplementum scribere ex
ipsa provincia, si vellet, peditum duo milia et centum
9 equites. P. Iunius Brutus in Tuscos exercitum novum, legionem unam Romanam et decem milia socium ac Latini
10 nominis scribere et quadringentos equites; L. Aemilius,
cui maritima provincia erat, viginti naves longas et socios
navales a M. Iunio praetore superioris anni accipere iussus, et scribere ipse mille navales socios duo milia peditum; cum iis navibus militibusque in Asiam proficisci et
11 classem a C. Livio accipere. duas Hispanias Sardiniamque
obtinentibus prorogatum in annum imperium est et idem
12 exercitus decreti. Siciliae Sardiniaeque binae eo[4] anno de-
cumae frumenti imperatae; Siculum omne frumentum in
Aetoliam ad exercitum portari iussum, ex Sardinia pars
Romam pars in Aetoliam, eodem quo Siculum.

[4] eo *Bχ*: eaeque proximae *Mg*: aeque ac proximo *Madvig*: eo
quoque *Weiss*.

---

[10] A. Cornelius (258) Mammula; for his election as praetor for
191, cf. 35.24.6.   [11] M. Aemilius Lepidus (68): cf. 35.10.11
and note, 36.2.10.
[12] C. Livius Salinator (29); cf. 32.16.3, and, for his naval activities, 36.42–45.

as well as 15,000 infantry and 600 cavalry of the allies and those with Latin rights. Aulus Cornelius,[10] praetor the previous year, who had held Bruttium with an army, was ordered to take his legions over to Aetolia, if such was the consul's pleasure, and transfer them to Manius Acilius, if he wished to remain there. If Acilius preferred to return to Rome, then Aulus Cornelius was to remain in Aetolia with the army. It was further decided that Gaius Atinius Labeo should take over from Marcus Aemilius[11] the province of Sicily and its army and, if he wished, raise from the province itself a supplementary force of 2,000 infantry and 100 cavalry. Publius Junius Brutus was instructed to raise a fresh army for service against the Etruscans—one Roman legion, and 10,000 infantry and 400 cavalry of the allies and those with Latin rights. Lucius Aemilius, holder of the maritime jurisdiction, was directed to take over from the previous year's praetor, Marcus Junius, 20 warships with their crews, and to enlist 1,000 sailors and 2,000 infantry himself. With these ships and fighting men he was to set off for Asia and assume command of the fleet from Gaius Livius.[12] The governors of the two Spains and Sardinia saw their commands prorogued for a year and the same armies assigned to them. Two tithes of grain were requisitioned from both Sicily and Sardinia that year;[13] and orders were issued for all the Sicilian grain to be taken to the army in Aetolia, while that from Sardinia was to go to partly to Rome and partly, like the Sicilian, to Aetolia.

[13] Two tithes had been taken from both for the first time in 191 (cf. 36.2.12), hence Madvig's proposed emendation "as in the previous year" (aeque ac proximo).

3. Priusquam consules in provincias proficiscerentur,
2 prodigia per pontifices procurari placuit. Romae Iunonis
Lucinae templum de caelo tactum erat, ita ut fastigium
valuaeque deformarentur; Puteolis pluribus locis murus
3 et porta fulmine icta et duo homines exanimati; Nursiae
sereno satis constabat nimbum ortum; ibi quoque duos
liberos homines exanimatos; terra apud se pluvisse Tuscu-
lani nuntiabant, et Reatini mulam in agro suo peperisse.

4 Ea procurata, Latinaeque instauratae, quod Laurenti-
5 bus carnis⁵ quae dari debet data non fuerat. supplicatio
quoque earum religionum causa fuit quibus dis decemviri
6 ex libris ut fieret ediderunt. decem ingenui decem vir-
gines, patrimi omnes matrimique, ad id sacrificium adhi-
biti, et decemviri nocte lactentibus rem divinam fecerunt.
7 P. Cornelius Scipio Africanus, priusquam proficisceretur,
fornicem in Capitolio adversus viam qua in Capitolium
escenditur cum signis septem auratis et equis duobus et
marmorea duo labra ante fornicem posuit.

8 Per eosdem dies principes Aetolorum tres et quadraginta, inter quos Damocritus et frater eius erant, ab duabus cohortibus missis a M'. Acilio Romam deducti et in

---

⁵ carnis χ, *Prisc. GL* 2.208: carinis *B*: pars carnis *Madvig*

---

14 On the Mons Cispius on the Esquiline, cf. Richardson 87
and fig. 75 (p. 349).

15 A Sabine town (mod. Norcia in the province of Perugia):
Barr. 42 E3.

16 Tusculum: *Barr.* 44 C2; Reate: 42 D4.

17 Laurentes is marked as a coastal district of Latium by *Barrington* (43 B3), and there is no town of Laurentum (cf. Ogilvie

3. It was decided that the prodigies should be expiated by the pontiffs before the consuls left for their provinces. In Rome the temple of Juno Lucina[14] had been struck by lightning so violently that its roof and doors were warped; in Puteoli the city wall as well as a gate were struck by lightning at several points and two men were killed. At Nursia[15] it was well documented that there had been a sudden downpour on a clear day and that there, too, two free men were killed. The people of Tusculum reported showers of earth on their lands, and the Reatini that a mule had given birth in theirs.[16]

These prodigies were expiated, and the Latin Festival was repeated because the Laurentes[17] had not been given the meat due to them. Because of these divine manifestations, a supplication was also offered to deities specified by the decemvirs after they consulted the Books.[18] Ten freeborn boys and ten girls, all with living fathers and mothers, were employed for the sacrifice, and the decemvirs offered up unweaned animals by night. Before he left, Publius Cornelius Scipio Africanus set up an arch on the Capitol facing the road that leads up to it, with seven gilded figures and two equestrian statues; and before the arch he placed two marble basins.

At this time forty-three of the Aetolians' leading men, including Damocritus and his brother, were brought to Rome by two cohorts sent out by Manius Acilius, and they

on Livy 1.1.10). Its main town is Lavinium, and the reference here is probably to that town's inhabitants.

[18] On supplication cf. 35.8.3 note; on *decemviri* and the (Sibylline) Books, cf. 35.9.5 note.

lautumias coniecti sunt. cohortes inde ad exercitum redire
9 L. Cornelius consul iussit. legati ab Ptolomaeo et Cleopatra regibus Aegypti, gratulantes quod M'. Acilius consul
10 Antiochum regem Graecia expulisset, venerunt, adhortan-
tesque ut in Asiam exercitum traicerent: omnia perculsa
metu non in Asia modo sed etiam in Syria esse; reges
11 Aegypti ad ea quae censuisset senatus paratos fore. gratiae
regibus actae; legatis munera dari iussa in singulos quater-
num milium aeris.

4. L. Cornelius consul, peractis quae Romae agenda
erant, pro contione edixit ut milites quos ipse in supplementum scripsisset quique in Bruttiis cum A. Cornelio pro
praetore essent, ut hi omnes idibus Quinctilibus Brundi-
2 sium convenirent. item tres legatos nominavit, Sex. Digi-
tium L. Apustium C. Fabricium Luscinum, qui ex ora
maritima undique naves Brundisium contraherent; et
omnibus iam paratis paludatus ab urbe est profectus.
3 ad quinque milia voluntariorum, Romani sociique, qui
emerita stipendia sub imperatore P. Africano habebant,
praesto fuere exeunti consuli et nomina dederunt.
4 Per eos dies quibus est profectus ad bellum consul,
ludis Apollinaribus, ante diem quintum idus Quinctiles
caelo sereno interdiu obscurata lux est, cum luna sub

---

19 Stone quarries on the Capitoline hill that served as a prison
and were purportedly named after the quarries in Syracuse that
were also so used (Richardson 234).

20 The king and queen are Ptolemy V Epiphanes and Antiochus' daughter Cleopatra I, who, as Briscoe (2.295) notes, "must
have had mixed feelings" about this.

21 Latin *paludamentum:* cf. 36.3.14 note.

298

were thrown into the Lautumiae.[19] The consul Lucius Cornelius then ordered the cohorts to return to the army. There also arrived from Ptolemy and Cleopatra, king and queen of Egypt, ambassadors offering congratulations on the consul Manius Acilius' expulsion of King Antiochus from Greece and urging the senators to send an army across to Asia.[20] Because of the panic, there was total chaos not just in Asia but also in Syria, they said, and the rulers of Egypt would be ready to comply with any decision of the senate. The king and queen were thanked and instructions were issued for the ambassadors to be given 4,000 asses each.

4. After completing what needed to be done in Rome, the consul Lucius Cornelius gave instructions, before an assembly, for all his men—the supplementary troops that he had himself enrolled and those who were in Bruttium with the propraetor Aulus Cornelius—to muster at Brundisium on July 15th. He also appointed three legates, Sextus Digitius, Lucius Apustius and Gaius Fabricius Luscinus, to bring together at Brundisium ships from all along the coast. His preparations now complete, he set out from the city in his military cloak.[21] About 5,000 volunteers, Romans and allies, who had completed their service under the command of Publius Africanus, presented themselves to the consul as he was leaving and enlisted for further duty with him.

The consul set out for the campaign on July 11th, during the Games of Apollo,[22] and at that time the light faded during the day when the sky was clear, as the moon passed

---

[22] Instituted in 212 in honor of Apollo as the averter of disease, the festival became an annual event after 211.

5 orbem solis subisset. et L. Aemilius Regillus, cui navalis
provincia evenerat, eodem tempore profectus est. L. Au-
runculeio negotium ab senatu datum est ut triginta quinqueremes viginti triremes faceret, quia fama erat Antiochum post proelium navale maiorem classem aliquanto
reparare.

6 Aetoli, postquam legati ab Roma rettulerunt nullam
spem pacis esse, quamquam omnis ora maritima eorum
quae in Peloponnesum versa est depopulata ab Achaeis
7 erat, periculi magis quam damni memores, ut Romanis
intercluderent iter, Coracem occupaverunt montem; neque enim dubitabant ad oppugnationem Naupacti eos
8 principio veris redituros esse. Acilio, quia id exspectari
sciebat, satius visum est inopinatam adgredi rem et La-
9 miam oppugnare; nam et a Philippo prope ad excidium
adductos esse, et tunc eo ipso, quod nihil tale timerent,
10 opprimi incautos posse. profectus ab Elatia primum in
hostium terra circa Spercheum amnem posuit castra; inde
nocte motis signis prima luce corona moenia est adgressus.

5. Magnus pavor ac tumultus, ut in re improvisa, fuit.
constantius tamen quam quis facturos crederet, in tam
subito periculo, cum viri propugnarent feminae tela omnis
generis saxaque in muros gererent, iam multifariam scalis
2 appositis urbem eo die defenderunt. Acilius signo receptui dato suos in castra medio ferme die reduxit; et tunc

---

23 An eclipse dated to March 14, 190 (July 11 on the pre-Julian
calendar, which was almost four months out of alignment). On
the dislocation of the Roman calendar, cf. Briscoe 2.17–26).

24 *Barr.* 55 C3. Cf. 36.30.4–5.

25 Elatia: *Barr.* 55 D3 (Elateia); Spercheus (Spercheios) C3.

under the sun's orb.[23] Lucius Aemilius Regillus, to whom the fleet had fallen as his province, also set out at the same time as the consul. Lucius Arunculeius was assigned the task of constructing thirty quinqueremes and twenty triremes by the senate because it was reported that Antiochus was, following the naval battle, rebuilding his fleet on a considerably larger scale.

When their ambassadors brought the news back from Rome that there was no hope of peace, the Aetolians seized Mt. Corax[24] to block the Romans' approach. All their coastline facing the Peloponnese had been laid waste by the Achaeans but they were thinking more about their danger than their losses as they had no doubt that at the start of spring the Romans would return to attack Naupactus. Because he knew that this was what they expected Acilius thought it a better idea to try a surprise maneuver and attack Lamia. Its people, he reasoned, had been brought to the verge of destruction by Philip and, besides, they could on that occasion be caught off guard because they had no fear of such a move. Setting off from Elatia, Acilius first pitched camp in enemy territory close to the River Spercheus.[25] From there he advanced at night, and at dawn attacked the city walls with a cordon of troops.

5. There followed the great alarm and uproar that usually attends an unexpected event. Even so the inhabitants that day defended their city with greater resolve than one might have expected of them in the face of such sudden danger; the men were doing the fighting and the women carrying to the walls weapons of all types and rocks, even though scaling ladders had already been set up at many points. Acilius sounded the retreat and led his troops back to camp at about midday. When their bodies were revived

cibo et quiete refectis corporibus, priusquam praetorium
dimitteret, denuntiavit ut ante lucem armati paratique
essent; nisi expugnata urbe se eos in castra non reductu-
3 rum. eodem tempore quo pridie pluribus locis adgressus,
cum oppidanos iam vires iam tela iam ante omnia animus
deficeret, intra paucas horas urbem cepit.

Ibi partim divendita partim divisa praeda, consilium
4 habitum quid deinde faceret. nemini ad Naupactum iri
placuit occupato ad Coracem ab Aetolis saltu. ne tamen
segnia aestiva essent, et Aetoli non impetratam pacem ab
senatu nihilo minus per suam cunctationem haberent,
oppugnare Acilius Amphissam statuit. ab Heraclea per
Oetam exercitus eo deductus.

5 Cum ad moenia castra posuisset, non corona, sicut
Lamiam, sed operibus oppugnare urbem est adortus. pluribus simul locis aries admovebatur, et cum quaterentur
muri, nihil adversus tale machinationis genus parare aut
6 comminisci oppidani conabantur; omnis spes in armis et
audacia erat; eruptionibus crebris et stationes hostium et
eos ipsos qui circa opera et machinationes[6] erant turba-
bant.

6. Multis tamen locis decussus murus erat, cum allatum est successorem Apolloniae exposito exercitu per
2 Epirum ac Thessaliam venire. cum tredecim[7] milibus peditum et quingentis equitibus consul veniebat. iam in

---

[6] machinationes *BψAE*: machinati omnes *P*: machinas *ed.
Rom.*

[7] tredecim *Sig.*: tribus *Bχ*

---

[26] Amphissa, Heraclea, Oeta: *Barr.* 55 C3.

with food and rest, and before he dismissed his council of war, he gave notice that they were to be in arms and ready to move before dawn and that he would not lead them back to camp unless the city were taken. He then attacked at several points at the same hour as he had the previous day, and since the townspeople lacked strength, weapons and, more than anything, the morale to resist, he took the city in a few hours.

There some of the spoils were sold off and some distributed among the troops, and a council was held to consider his next move. No one wanted to go to Naupactus since the pass at Corax was held by the Aetolians. However, not to have the summer frittered away and the Aetolians nevertheless enjoying through his hesitation a peace that they had failed to obtain from the senate, Acilius decided to attack Amphissa. The army was led down there from Heraclea over Oeta.[26]

When he had established camp before the walls, Acilius used siege works—not a cordon of troops, as at Lamia—to attack the city. Battering rams were brought up in several places simultaneously, and as the walls were being pounded the townspeople made no attempt to prepare or devise any countermeasures for this kind of instrument. All their hopes lay in their weapons and courage; and with persistent counterattacks they harried the advance posts of their enemy and even those who were manning the earthworks and siege engines.

6. Nevertheless, the wall had been shattered at several points when Acilius was brought word that his successor had set his army ashore at Apollonia and was now proceeding through Epirus and Thessaly. The consul was coming with 13,000 infantry and 500 cavalry. He had already

sinum Maliacum venerat;[8] et praemissis Hypatam qui tradere urbem iuberent, postquam nihil responsum est nisi
ex communi Aetolorum decreto facturos, ne teneret se
oppugnatio Hypatae nondum Amphissa recepta, prae-
3 misso fratre Africano Amphissam ducit. sub adventum
eorum oppidani, relicta urbe—iam enim magna ex parte
moenibus nudata erat—in arcem, quam inexpugnabilem
habent[9] omnes armati atque inermes concessere.

4 Consul sex milia fere passuum inde posuit castra. eo
legati Athenienses primum ad P. Scipionem praegressum
agmen, sicut ante dictum est, deinde ad consulem vene-
5 runt, deprecantes pro Aetolis. clementius responsum ab
Africano tulerunt, qui causam relinquendi honeste Aetolici belli quaerens Asiam et regem Antiochum spectabat,
iusseratque Athenienses non Romanis solum ut pacem
6 bello praeferrent, sed etiam Aetolis persuadere. celeriter
auctoribus Atheniensibus frequens ab Hypata legatio Aetolorum venit, et spem pacis eis sermo etiam Africani,
quem priorem adierunt, auxit, commemorantis multas
gentes populosque in Hispania prius deinde in Africa in
fidem suam venisse; in omnibus se maiora clementiae

---

8 sinum Maliacum venerat *Asc. (1510)*: sinu Maliaco venerat
Bχ: sinu Maliaco erat *Weiss. (1862)*
9 habent *Bχ*: habebant *Watt*

---

27 The Thessalian city (*Barr.* 55 C3) was a leading member of
the Aetolian League and the venue of the meeting the previous
year to discuss Glabrio's harsh terms (cf. 36.28.8–9).
28 The present tense (the manuscript reading) is probably a
case of Livy taking over (anachronistically) what he found in Polybius, where it was not an anachronism (I owe this observation to
John Briscoe).

reached the Malian Gulf, and from there he sent men ahead to Hypata[27] to order the inhabitants to surrender the city, but their reply was that they would act only on a communal decision by the Aetolians. So that a siege of Hypata not detain him when Amphissa remained uncaptured, Scipio first sent ahead his brother Africanus and then marched on Amphissa. At their approach, the townspeople abandoned the city, which by now had been largely divested of its walls, and everybody, armed and unarmed alike, retreated to the citadel, which they consider impregnable.[28]

The consul encamped about six miles away. Ambassadors from Athens came there to plead on behalf of the Aetolians, addressing themselves first to Publius Scipio who (as noted above) had gone ahead of the column and, after him, to the consul.[29] They received a more sympathetic response from Africanus, who was looking for a pretext to quit the Aetolian war with honor and had his attention focused on Asia and King Antiochus.[30] He had therefore told the Athenians to convince the Aetolians as well as the Romans to accept peace as a better option than war. Prompted by the Athenians, a large delegation of Aetolians came swiftly from Hypata, and the remarks of Africanus, whom they approached first, increased their hopes of peace, as he reminded them of the many nations and peoples who had put themselves in his hands, in Spain first and then in Africa. In every case, he said, he had left

[29] Polybius, whose account survives (21.4–5), has the delegation come to Africanus but does not mention the consul.

[30] That is, Lucius Cornelius needed to deal quickly with the Aetolians, since glory and a triumph depended on his coming to grips with Antiochus in Asia Minor.

benignitatisque quam virtutis bellicae monumenta reli-
7 quisse. perfecta videbatur res, cum aditus consul idem
illud responsum rettulit quo fugati ab senatu erant. eo
tamquam novo cum icti Aetoli essent—nihil enim nec legatione Atheniensium nec placido Africani responso profectum videbant—, referre ad suos dixerunt velle.

7. Reditum inde Hypatam est, nec consilium expedie-
batur; nam neque unde mille talentum daretur erat, et
permisso libero arbitrio ne in corpora sua saeviretur me-
2 tuebant. redire itaque eosdem legatos ad consulem et
Africanum iusserunt, et petere ut si dare vere pacem, non
tantum ostendere, frustrantes spem miserorum, vellent,
aut ex summa pecuniae demerent, aut permissionem extra
3 civium corpora fieri iuberent. nihil impetratum ut mutaret
4 consul; et ea quoque inrita legatio dimissa est. secuti et
Athenienses sunt; et princeps legationis eorum Echedemus fatigatos tot repulsis Aetolos et complorantes inutili
lamentatione fortunam gentis ad spem revocavit, auctor
indutias sex mensium petendi, ut legatos mittere Romam
5 possent: dilationem nihil ad praesentia mala, quippe quae
ultima essent, adiecturam; levari per multos casus tem-
6 pore interposito praesentes clades posse. auctore Eche-

---

31 The Aetolians, of course, had expected that Lucius would
follow the same line as his famous brother.

them with better reasons for remembering his clemency and generosity than his valor in battle. The problem appeared to be resolved, but when the consul was approached he repeated the response with which the Aetolians had been rebuffed by the senate.[31] Receiving this fresh blow, the Aetolians declared that they wished to report back to their people—they could see that nothing had come of the Athenian embassy and Africanus' indulgent response.

7. The delegates returned from there to Hypata, but no strategy could be worked out: there was no way of raising the thousand-talent payment and they feared that if they put themselves unconditionally in the senate's hands they would be subjected to physical violence. They therefore ordered the same envoys to return to the consul and Africanus and to ask them either to reduce the amount of money or else direct that surrender not entail physical maltreatment of citizens—that is, if they truly wanted to grant peace and not just give them a glimpse of it, thereby frustrating the hopes of hapless men. They failed to make the consul effect any change and that embassy was also dismissed with nothing achieved. The Athenians followed the envoys home. The Aetolians were sickened now by all the rejections and were bemoaning the fortunes of their people with futile laments, but Echedemus, head of the Athenian delegation, revived their hopes with the suggestion that they request a six-month truce so they could send representatives to Rome. The delay, he said, would add nothing to their current ills, which were as bad as they could be, and their present tribulations might possibly be relieved by any number of fortuitous events that could occur in the meantime. On Echedemus' recommendation, the same delegates were sent once more. They met Pub-

demo iidem missi; prius P. Scipione convento, per eum
indutias temporis eius quod petebant ab consule impetra-
7 verunt. et soluta obsidione Amphissae M'. Acilius, tradito
consuli exercitu, provincia decessit, et consul ab Amphissa
Thessaliam repetit, ut per Macedoniam Thraciamque duceret in Asiam.

8 Tum Africanus fratri: "iter quod insistis, L. Scipio, ego
quoque adprobo; sed totum id vertitur in voluntate Phi-
9 lippi: qui si imperio nostro fidus est, et iter et commeatus
et omnia quae in longo itinere exercitus alunt iuvantque,
nobis suppeditabit; si is destituat,[10] nihil per Thraciam
10 satis tutum habebis. itaque prius regis animum explorari
placet; optime explorabitur si nihil ex praeparato agentem
opprimet qui mittetur."

11 Ti. Sempronius Gracchus, longe tum acerrimus iuve-
num, ad id delectus per dispositos equos prope incredibili
celeritate ab Amphissa—inde enim est dimissus—die ter-
12 tio Pellam pervenit. in convivio rex erat et in multum uini
processerat; ea ipsa remissio animi suspicionem dempsit
13 novare eum quicquam velle. et tum quidem comiter acceptus hospes, postero die commeatus exercitui paratos
benigne, pontes in fluminibus factos, vias, ubi transitus
14 difficiles erant, munitas vidit. haec referens eadem qua

---

[10] destituat *Bχ*: destituit *a*: destituet *Briscoe*

---

[32] Ti. Sempronius Gracchus (53) later became Africanus' son-
in-law and father of the famous Gracchi brothers, and as tribune
in 187 (or possibly 184) was a staunch defender of both Africanus
and Lucius Scipio (38.52.9–53.6, 60.4–10). He was an ambassador
to Greece and Macedonia in 185, curule aedile in 182, praetor
and proconsul in Spain in 180–178, and holder of two consulships
(177 and 163). Cf. *MRR* 397–98.

lius Scipio first and through him managed to gain from the consul a truce for the period they requested. The siege of Amphissa was raised and Manius Acilius quit the province after transferring command of the army to the consul. The consul also headed back to Thessaly from Amphissa in order to march into Asia by way of Macedonia and Thrace.

Africanus then spoke as follows to his brother: "The route on which you are setting out has my approval, too, Lucius Scipio, but it all depends on Philip's inclinations. If he loyally supports our authority, he will provide us with a safe passage, provisions and everything that sustains and assists an army on a long march. If he lets us down, you will have no security passing through Thrace. So my feeling is that we should first test the king's disposition, and that will be best tested if the man who is sent takes him by surprise when he is not acting from a prepared script."

Selected for this was Tiberius Sempronius Gracchus,[32] by far the most dynamic young man of the day. By using horses stationed in relays, Gracchus achieved almost unbelievable speed, reaching Pella from Amphissa,[33] the point from which he was sent, in two days. The king was at dinner and was well into the wine, and his relaxed frame of mind allayed all suspicion that he intended any mischief. Furthermore, his visitor was then given a warm welcome, and the next day he saw the provisions that had been liberally stockpiled for the army, the bridges that had been built over rivers, and the roads constructed where passage was difficult. Taking back this news with the speed with which he had come, Gracchus met the consul at

[33] Pella, capital of Macedonia: *Barr.* 50 C3; Amphissa: 55 C3.

ierat celeritate Thaumacis occurrit consuli. inde certiore
et maiore spe laetus exercitus ad praeparata omnia in
15 Macedoniam pervenit. venientes regio apparatu et accepit
et prosecutus est rex. multa in eo et dexteritas et humani-
tas visa, quae commendabilia apud Africanum erant, virum sicut ad cetera egregium, ita a comitate, quae sine
16 luxuria esset, non aversum. inde non per Macedoniam
modo sed etiam Thraciam, prosequente et praeparante
omnia Philippo, ad Hellespontum perventum est.

8. Antiochus post navalem ad Corycum pugnam cum
totam hiemem liberam in apparatus terrestres maritimos-
que habuisset, classi maxime reparandae, ne tota maris
2 possessione pelleretur, intentus fuerat. succurrebat su-
peratum se cum classis afuisset Rhodiorum; quodsi ea
quoque—nec commissuros Rhodios ut iterum morraren-
tur—certamini adesset, magno sibi navium numero opus
fore, ut viribus et magnitudine classem hostium aequaret.
3 itaque et Hannibalem in Syriam miserat ad Phoenicum
accersendas naves, et Polyxenidam quo minus prospere
gesta res erat, eo enixius et eas quae erant reficere et alias
4 parare naves iussit. ipse in Phrygia hibernavit, undique
auxilia accersens. etiam in Gallograeciam miserat; bellico-
siores ea tempestate erant, Gallicos adhuc, nondum exo-

---

34 Thaumaci (*Barr.* 55 C2) is the modern Domokos. Earlier
(32.4.5), Livy provides an unconvincing derivation of the name
from the Greek for "marvel" (thauma [θαῦμα]).

35 That is, Galatia in central Asia Minor, settled by migrating
Celtic tribes who had arrived via the Hellespont in 278 BC.

36 Asia Minor was generally regarded as having an enervating
and degenerating effect on its inhabitants. Livy's claim here that
the Gauls had not yet been there long enough for this to happen

Thaumaci.[34] From there the army, buoyed by more sanguine and positive hopes, came to Macedonia to find everything prepared for it. On their arrival the king welcomed and attended to the Scipios with regal liberality. He seemed possessed of great consideration and civility, qualities that won the approval of Africanus who, an outstanding man in all other respects, was not averse to a cordiality that shunned extravagance. From there the Romans reached the Hellespont, passing through Thrace as well as Macedonia, with Philip escorting them and making all necessary arrangements.

8. After the naval battle at Corycus, Antiochus had all winter free for preparations on land and sea and, not to be completely stripped of his hold on the sea, he had paid particular attention to refurbishing his fleet. It did occur to him that he had been defeated at a time when the Rhodian fleet was not present and that if this armament should also take part in the fighting—and the Rhodians would not make the mistake of lagging behind again—he would need a large number of ships to match his enemy's fleet in strength and size. Accordingly, he had dispatched Hannibal to Syria to fetch Phoenician ships and he also ordered Polyxenidas to refit his remaining vessels and build others—and do it all the more energetically in view of his earlier lack of success. Antiochus himself passed the winter in Phrygia, calling for assistance from every quarter. He had even sent to Gallograecia;[35] its people at that time were more pugnacious—they still possessed their Gallic spirit,[36] since the original strain of the people had not yet

contrasts with what he has Manlius Vulso say in a speech in the following book (38.17.9–12).

5   leta stirpe gentis, servantes animos. filium Seleucum in
Aeolide reliquerat cum exercitu ad maritimas continendas
urbes, quas illinc a Pergamo Eumenes hinc a Phocaea
Erythrisque Romani sollicitabant.

6   Classis Romana, sicut ante dictum est, ad Canas hiber-
nabat; eo media ferme hieme rex Eumenes cum duobus[11]

7   milibus peditum equitibus quingentis venit. is cum magnam praedam agi posse dixisset ex agro hostium qui circa
Thyatiram esset, hortando perpulit Livium ut quinque milia militum secum mitteret. missi ingentem praedam intra
paucos dies averterunt.

    9. Inter haec Phocaeae seditio orta, quibusdam ad

2   Antiochum multitudinis animos avocantibus. gravia hiberna navium erant, grave tributum, quod togae quingen-

3   tae imperatae erant cum quingentis tunicis, gravis etiam
inopia frumenti, propter quam naves quoque et praesidium Romanum excessit. tum vero liberata metu factio
erat quae plebem in contionibus ad Antiochum trahebat;

4   senatus et optimates in Romana societate perstandum
censebant; defectionis auctores plus apud multitudinem
valuerunt.

5   Rhodii, quo magis cessatum priore aestate erat, eo
maturius aequinoctio verno eundem Pausistratum classis

6   praefectum cum sex et triginta navibus miserunt. iam

---

11 duobus *ed. Rom.*: viginti *BχMg*

---

37 Later, Seleucus IV Philopater (cf. *OCD* s.v.), who succeeded Antiochus in 187.

38 At 36.45.8. It was a harbor in Pergamene territory.

39 About thirty-seven miles southeast of Pergamum (*Barr.* 56
F4).

died out. He had left his son Seleucus[37] with an army in Aeolis to keep the coastal cities under control; Eumenes was inciting them to rebellion on the one side (from Pergamum), and the Romans were doing so on the other (from Phocaea and Erythrae).

The Roman fleet was wintering at Canae, as noted above,[38] and about midwinter King Eumenes arrived there with 2,000 infantry and 500 cavalry. He claimed that a large amount of plunder could be taken from enemy territory around Thyatira,[39] and by his urging prevailed upon Livius to send 5,000 men with him. The men who were sent removed a massive quantity of booty in a matter of days.

9. Meanwhile civil unrest arose in Phocaea[40] where some people were trying to win over the masses to support Antiochus. Winter quarters for the ships caused hardship for the Phocaeans; their tribute also caused hardship as 500 togas and 500 tunics had been requisitioned from them; even further hardship came from a shortage of grain and because of that the fleet and Roman garrison left them. With that the faction trying win the support of the commons for Antiochus in their meetings was delivered from fear; and while the senate and aristocrats advocated standing by the Roman alliance, the ringleaders of the disaffection had more influence with the masses.

Compensating for their tardiness the previous summer, the Rhodians were this time early in sending out Pausistratus[41] (the same admiral as before) at the spring equinox, with thirty-six ships. By now Livius had left Ca-

---

[40] For Phocaea see 36.43.11 note.
[41] Cf. 36.45.5 and note.

Livius a Canis cum triginta navibus suis[12] et septem quadriremibus, quas secum Eumenes rex adduxerat, Hellespontum petebat, ut ad transitum exercitus, quem terra
venturum opinabatur, praepararet quae opus essent.

7   In portum quem vocant Achaeorum classem primum
advertit; inde Ilium escendit, sacrificioque Mineruae facto
legationes finitimas ab Elaevnte et Dardano et Rhoetio,
8   tradentes in fidem civitates suas, benigne audivit. inde ad
Hellesponti fauces navigat, et decem navibus in statione
contra Abydum relictis, cetera classe in Europam ad Ses-
9   tum oppugnandam traiecit. iam subeuntibus armatis muros fanatici Galli primum cum sollemni habitu ante portam occurrunt; iussu se matris deum famulos deae venire
memorant ad precandum Romanum ut parceret moeni-
10   bus urbique. nemo eorum violatus est. mox universus senatus cum magistratibus ad dedendam urbem processit.
11   Inde Abydum traiecta classis. ubi cum temptatis per
conloquia animis nihil pacati responderetur, ad oppugnationem sese expediebant.

10. Dum haec in Hellesponto geruntur, Polyxenidas
regius praefectus—erat autem exsul Rhodius—cum au-

---

[12] suis *Madvig: om.* Bχ

---

[42] As had both Xerxes and Alexander: cf. 35.43.3 and note.
[43] *Barr.* 51 G4.
[44] Eunuch priests of the Phrygian fertility goddess Cybele
(only two appear in Polybius [21.6.7]). Brought to Rome in 204
(cf. 29.10.5, 34.3.8), the cult was Romanized and its ecstatic features suppressed (it was, in fact, illegal for Romans to practice it
in the Asiatic manner).

nae with thirty ships of his own and seven quadriremes that King Eumenes had brought with him, and he was heading for the Hellespont to make the necessary preparations for the crossing of the army, which he thought would be arriving by land.

He first set a course for what they call "Port of the Achaeans." From there he went up to Ilium, sacrificed to Minerva[42] and then gave a courteous hearing to deputations from neighboring communities—from Elaeus, Dardanus and Rhoeteum[43]—who wished to put their towns under his protection. From there he sailed to the mouth of the Hellespont, left ten ships stationed off Abydos, and crossed with the rest of the fleet into Europe to launch an attack on Sestus. As his soldiers were already approaching the walls some Galli, the frenzied priests,[44] met them before the gate, dressed in the robes of their cult. They declared that they were the servants of the goddess, the mother of the gods, and that it was at her behest that they came to entreat the Romans to spare their walls and their city. None of them was ill-treated. In a little while the entire senate and the magistrates came forth to surrender the city.

From there the fleet crossed to Abydus. Here, in meetings, the Romans sounded out the feelings of the people and when they received no peaceable response they readied themselves for a blockade.

10. While this was happening in the Hellespont, the king's officer Polyxenidas (he was an exile from Rhodes)

2 disset profectam ab domo popularium suorum classem, et
Pausistratum praefectum superbe quaedam et contemp-
tim in se contionantem dixisse, praecipuo certamine animi
adversus eum sumpto, nihil aliud dies noctesque agitabat

3 animo quam ut verba magnifica eius rebus confutaret. mittit ad eum hominem et illi notum, qui diceret et se Pausistrato patriaeque suae magno usui, si liceat, fore, et a

4 Pausistrato se restitui in patriam posse. cum quonam
modo ea fieri possent mirabundus Pausistratus percuncta-
retur, fidem petenti dedit agendae communiter rei aut

5 tegendae silentio. tum internuntius:[13] regiam classem aut
totam aut maiorem eius partem Polyxenidam traditurum
ei; pretium tanti meriti nullum aliud pacisci quam reditum

6 in patriam. magnitudo rei nec ut crederet nec ut asperna-
retur dicta efficit.[14] Panhormum Samiae terrae petit, ibi-

7 que ad explorandam rem quae oblata erat substitit. ultro
citroque nuntii cursare, nec fides ante Pausistrato facta est
quam coram nuntio eius Polyxenidas sua manu scripsit se
ea quae pollicitus esset facturum esse,[15] signoque suo

8 impressas tabellas misit. eo vero pignore velut auctoratum
sibi proditorem ratus est: neque enim eum, qui sub rege
viveret, commissurum fuisse ut adversus semet ipsum
indicia manu sua testata daret.

9 Inde ratio simulatae proditionis composita. omnium se
rerum apparatum omissurum Polyxenidas dicere; non

---

[13] internuntius *Bχ*: internuntius aperit *Mg*
[14] efficit *Bχ*: effecit *Voss.*
[15] facturum esse *Bψ*: facturum *ϕ*

---

[45] The name, indicating a good anchorage in Greek ("pan" =
all, "hormos" = harbor), was applied to several Mediterranean
ports, here to a bay on the north coast of Samos (*Barr.* 61 D2).

had heard that a fleet of his countrymen had left home and
that its commander Pausistratus had made some arrogant
and offensive comments against him at a public meeting.
His feelings toward the man had therefore become particularly hostile and day and night his thoughts were all
focused on ways to make him eat his disdainful words. He
sent to him a man who was also an acquaintance of his to
say that he, Polyxenidas, if given the opportunity, could be
of great use to Pausistratus and his native land—and he
himself could also be restored to his country through Pausistratus' agency. When, taken by surprise, Pausistratus
asked how this could be done, Polyxenidas asked him to
swear that they would see the affair through together or
else keep it shrouded in silence, and Pausistratus did so
swear. Then the go-between explained that Polyxenidas
would deliver up to him either the whole of the king's fleet
or the greater part of it, and the asking price for such a
great service was merely his restoration to his native land.
So momentous was the proposition that it would permit
Pausistratus neither to believe nor to disregard the message. He made for Panhormus[45] in Samian territory and
moored there to examine in detail the offer that had been
made to him. Messengers went to and fro between the
men, but Pausistratus could not be satisfied until Polyxenidas wrote out with his own hand, in the presence of Pausistratus' messenger, that he would make good on his
promise and sent to him the tablets stamped with his seal.
Pausistratus thought that, having given this pledge, the
traitor really was in his pay, as he believed a man living
under a monarch would not have ventured to provide
evidence against himself in his own handwriting.

After this, the scenario for the fake betrayal was put
together. Polyxenidas said he would drop all preparations

317

remigem non socios navales ad classem frequentes habi-
10 turum; subducturum per simulationem reficiendi quasdam naves, alias in propinquos portus dimissurum; paucas
ante portum Ephesi in salo habiturum, quas, si exire res
cogeret, obiecturus certamini foret.

11 Quam neglegentiam Polyxenidam in classe sua habiturum Pausistratus audivit, eam ipse extemplo habuit: partem navium ad commeatus accersendos Halicarnassum,
partem Samum ad urbem misit[16] ‹. . .› ut paratus esset
12 cum signum adgrediendi a proditore accepisset. Polyxenidas augere simulando errorem; subducit quasdam naves,
alias velut subducturus esset navalia reficit; remiges ex
hibernis non Ephesum accersit, sed Magnesiam occulte
cogit.

11. Forte quidam Antiochi miles, cum Samum rei pri-
vatae causa venisset, pro speculatore deprehensus dedu-
2 citur Panhormum ad praefectum. is percunctanti quid
Ephesi ageretur, incertum metu an erga suos haud sincera
3 fide, omnia aperit: classem instructam paratamque in
portu stare; remigium omne Magnesiam missum; perpau-
cas naves subductas esse et navalia tegi;[17] nunquam inten-

---

[16] misit *lac. post ind. Weiss.* ipse cum reliquis substitit *coniciens*: ipse Panhormi substitit *Crév.*: ipse ad Panhormum mansit
M. Müller   [17] tegi *BEPVL*: regi *AN*: detegi *Weiss. (1873)*

---

[46] That is, he would not have his fleet prepared for a sudden
attack.

[47] So reads the Latin, but the meaning is unclear. Walsh
(37.137) suggests that Pausistratus wants the ships to take grain
on board at the two cities, so that on their return he would be
ready to move when given the signal. This is not convincing and,
as has long been suspected, there may be a lacuna in the text; but
all suggested supplements are, as Briscoe notes, also unconvinc-

and would not keep a large number of oarsmen or, indeed, any other crew members attached to the fleet.[46] He would beach some of his ships on the pretext of repairing them and others he would send off to nearby harbors; but he would keep a few on the open sea before the port of Ephesus to bring into battle if circumstances forced him to put to sea.

When Pausistratus heard that Polyxenidas would be remiss in handling his fleet, he immediately became so himself. He sent some of his ships to Halicarnassus to fetch supplies and others to the city of Samos ⟨. . .⟩[47] so that he would be ready when he received the signal to attack from the traitor. Polyxenidas used more deception to delude him further: he beached a number of ships and rebuilt dockyards to make it look as if he would beach others; and instead of bringing his oarsmen to Ephesus from their winter quarters, he secretly assembled them at Magnesia.

11. When one of Antiochus' soldiers had by chance come to Samos on a private matter, he was arrested as a spy and brought to the commander at Panhormus. Pausistratus asked him what was going on in Ephesus and he—whether from fear or from lack of loyalty to his own people is uncertain—told all. The fleet was anchored in the harbor drawn up and ready for action, he said; all the oarsmen had been sent to Magnesia;[48] very few ships had been hauled ashore, and the docks were being covered over;[49]

ing, and he suggests that "mere indication of a lacuna would be the more prudent course."

[48] Magnesia-on-the-Meander: *Barr.* 61 F2.

[49] The reading (*tegi*) here is uncertain. If it is correct, it probably means that the docks are covered over when the ships are away, as protection from the weather.

4 tius rem navalem administratam esse. haec ne pro veris
audirentur, animus errore et spe vana praeoccupatus fecit.

Polyxenidas satis omnibus comparatis, nocte remige a
Magnesia accersito, deductisque raptim quae subductae
erant navibus, cum diem non tam apparatu absumpsisset
5 quam quod conspici proficiscentem classem nolebat, post
solis occasum profectus septuaginta navibus tectis vento
adverso ante lucem Pygela portum tenuit. ibi cum interdiu
ob eandem causam quiesset, nocte in proxima Samiae ter-
6 rae traiecit. hinc Nicandro quodam archipirata quinque
navibus tectis Palinurum iusso petere, atque inde armatos,
qua proximum per agros iter esset, Panhormum ad tergum
hostium ducere, ipse interim classe divisa, ut ex utraque
parte fauces portus teneret, Panhormum petit.

7 Pausistratus primo ut in re necopinata turbatus parum-
per, deinde vetus miles, celeriter conlecto animo, terra
8 melius arceri quam mari hostes posse ratus, armatos duobus agminibus ad promunturia, quae cornibus obiectis ab
alto portum faciunt, ducit, inde facile ex faucibus telis
ancipitibus[18] hostem summoturus. id inceptum eius Nicander a terra visus cum turbasset, repente mutato consi-
9 lio naves conscendere omnes iubet. tum vero ingens pariter militum nautarumque trepidatio orta, et velut fuga in

18 ex faucibus telis ancipitibus *Walsh*: ex ancipitibus *B*χ: telis
ancipitibus *Asc.*: ex loco superiore telis *Weiss*.

---

50 Six miles south of Ephesus.
51 Site unknown according to Briscoe and Walsh ad loc., but
identified as the northeastern promontory of Samos by *Barrington* (61 E2).

and never had so much effort been put into naval activity. Pausistratus' mind being distracted by delusion and groundless hope ensured that this would not be accepted as the truth.

His preparations complete, Polyxenidas summoned his oarsmen from Magnesia by night and hurriedly launched the ships that had been beached. He then passed the day there, not so much in making preparations as because he did not want his fleet spotted as it moved out; and after sunset he set off with seventy decked ships and, despite facing a headwind, reached the port of Pygela[50] before dawn. There he spent the day at rest—for the same reason as before—and at night crossed to the closest parts of Samian territory. From here he instructed a certain Nicander, a pirate chief, to head for Palinurus[51] with five decked ships and then take a body of troops by the shortest route across country to Panhormus, to the rear of the enemy. Polyxenidas himself meanwhile divided his fleet so that he could hold the harbor mouth on both sides; then he made for Panhormus.

At first Pausistratus was momentarily stunned by the unexpected move but then, experienced soldier as he was, he quickly pulled himself together. Thinking that the enemy could be more easily repulsed on land than on sea, he led his troops in two columns to the promontories, which, with their projecting spits of land, shelter the harbor from the sea. From there he assumed that he would easily push back the enemy from the harbor mouth with projectiles hurled from either side. The sight of Nicander arriving overland thwarted his strategy and, suddenly changing his plan, he ordered everybody to board the ships. Sheer pandemonium then broke out among soldiers and sailors

naves fieri, cum se mari terraque simul cernerent circum-
10 ventos. Pausistratus unam viam salutis esse ratus, si vim
facere per fauces portus atque erumpere in mare apertum
posset, postquam conscendisse suos vidit, sequi ceteris
iussis princeps ipse concitata nave remis ad ostium portus
11 tendit. superantem iam fauces navem eius Polyxenidas
tribus quinqueremibus circumsistit. navis rostris icta sup-
primitur; telis obruuntur propugnatores, inter quos et
12 Pausistratus impigre pugnans interficitur. navium reli-
quarum ante portum aliae aliae[19] in portu deprensae,
13 quaedam a Nicandro, dum moliuntur a terra, captae; quinque tantum Rhodiae naves cum duabus Cois effugerunt,
terrore flammae micantis via sibi inter confertas naves
facta; contis enim binis a prora prominentibus trullis
ferreis multum conceptum ignem prae se portabant.
14 Erythraeae triremes cum haud procul a Samo Rhodiis
navibus, quibus ut essent praesidio veniebant, obviae fugientibus fuissent, in Hellespontum ad Romanos cursum
averterunt.

15   Sub idem tempus Seleucus proditam Phocaeam porta
una per custodes aperta recepit; et Cyme aliaeque eiusdem orae urbes ad eum metu defecerunt.

12. Dum haec in Aeolide geruntur, Abydus cum per
aliquot dies obsidionem tolerasset, praesidio regio tutante

---

[19] aliae aliae *ed. Rom.*: aliae *Bχ*

---

[52] The mechanism, invented by Pausistratus, is described in
somewhat greater detail by Polybius (21.7.1–4; cf. Walbank 3.97,
who provides an Alexandrian drawing of the "fire basket").

alike, and there was a virtual flight to the ships when they saw that they were cut off on land and on sea at the same time. Pausistratus thought there was only one route to safety—if he could force a way through the harbor mouth and break out into the open sea. When he saw that his own men had boarded, he ordered the others to follow and, taking the lead himself, headed for the harbor mouth with his ship rowed at maximum speed. As the vessel was just passing the entrance, Polyxenidas surrounded it with three quinqueremes. Struck by their beaks, the ship went down and the defenders were buried under a hail of missiles, among them Pausistratus, who lost his life putting up a spirited fight. Of the other vessels some were caught before the harbor and others within it; and some were captured by Nicander as they tried to get away from shore. Only five Rhodian ships and two Coan vessels made good their escape and they did so by opening up a path for themselves between the crowded enemy ships by terrifying them with shooting flames; for they each carried before themselves great quantities of fire that they had ignited in iron bowls suspended from two poles projecting from the prow.[52] Not far from Samos some Erythraean triremes met the fleeing Rhodian ships (which they were coming to reinforce), and they changed course to join the Romans in the Hellespont.

Close to this time Seleucus regained Phocaea, which was betrayed to him when one of the gates was opened by the sentries. Cyme and other cities on that coastline also defected to him out of fear.

12. While this was going on in Aeolis, Abydus had been facing its siege for a number of days, with a garrison of the king defending the walls. By now they were all exhausted

2   moenia, iam omnibus fessis, Philota quoque praefecto
praesidii permittente, magistratus eorum cum Livio de
condicionibus tradendae urbis agebant. rem distinebat
quod utrum armati an inermes emitterentur regii parum
3   conveniebat. haec agentibus cum intervenisset nuntius
4   Rhodiorum cladis, emissa[20] de manibus res est; metuens
enim Livius ne successu tantae rei inflatus Polyxenidas
classem quae ad Canas erat opprimeret, Abydi obsidione
custodiaque Hellesponti extemplo relicta, naves quae sub-
5   ductae Canis erant deduxit; et Eumenes Elaeam venit.
Livius omni classe, cui adiunxerat duas triremes Mityle-
naeas, Phocaeam petit. quam cum teneri valido regio
6   praesidio audisset, nec procul Seleuci castra esse, depopulatus maritimam oram et praeda maxime hominum raptim in naves imposita, tantum moratus dum Eumenes cum
classe adsequeretur, Samum petere intendit.
7   Rhodiis primo audita clades simul pavorem simul luctum ingentem fecit; nam praeter navium militumque iac-
turam, quod floris quod roboris in iuventute fuerat amise-
8   rant, multis nobilibus secutis inter cetera auctoritatem
Pausistrati, quae inter suos merito maxima erat; deinde,
quod fraude capti quod a cive potissimum suo forent, in
9   iram luctus vertit. decem extemplo naves, et diebus post
paucis decem alias praefecto omnium Eudamo miserunt,
quem aliis virtutibus bellicis haudquaquam Pausistrato
parem, cautiorem, quo minus animi erat, ducem futurum
credebant.

---

[20] emissa *Voss.*: omissa *Bχ*

---

[53] The harbor of Pergamum (cf. 35.13.6).

and their magistrates proceeded to discuss with Livius terms of surrender, with the acquiescence even of Philotas, the garrison commander. A solution was delayed by their failure to agree on whether the king's men were to be released with or without their weapons. They were negotiating this when news of the Rhodian disaster arrived and the matter was taken out of their hands; for Livius feared that Polyxenidas, encouraged by his success in such a major operation, might swoop down on the fleet stationed at Canae. He immediately discontinued the siege of Abydus and his protection of the Hellespont, and launched the ships that had been hauled ashore at Canae; and Eumenes also came to Elaea.[53] Livius now made for Phocaea with his entire fleet, to which he had added two Mytilenean triremes. On hearing that the town was occupied by a powerful royal garrison and that Seleucus' camp was not far away, he raided the coastline, hurriedly loaded the ships with his plunder (mostly human), and waited only for Eumenes to catch up with his fleet before he set sail for Samos.

At first, the news of the disaster brought widespread panic and grief to the Rhodians: apart from the loss of ships and manpower, they had also been deprived of the best and strongest of their youth—many of their nobles had joined Pausistratus, among other reasons because of his prestige, which was deservedly great among his people. Then, aware that they had been taken by trickery and, worst of all, by one of their fellow citizens, their sorrow turned to anger. They immediately dispatched ten ships and a few days later a further ten, all under the command of Eudamus who, in general military skills, was in no way Pausistratus' equal, but as he was less enterprising they believed he would be a more cautious leader.

10   Romani et Eumenes rex in Erythraeam primum classem applicuerunt. ibi noctem unam morati, postero die
11   Corycum Teiorum[21] promunturium tenuerunt. inde cum
in proxima Samiae vellent traicere, non exspectato solis
ortu, ex quo statum caeli notare gubernatores possent,
12   in incertam tempestatem †miserunt†.[22] medio in cursu,
aquilone in septentrionem verso, exasperato fluctibus
mari iactari coeperunt.

13. Polyxenidas Samum petituros ratus hostes, ut se
Rhodiae classi coniungerent, ab Epheso profectus primo
ad Myonnesum stetit; inde ad Macrin, quam vocant, insulam traiecit, ut praetervehentis classis si quas aberrantes
ex agmine naves posset, aut postremum agmen opportune
2   adoriretur. postquam sparsam tempestate classem vidit,
occasionem primo adgredienti ratus, paulo post increbres-
3   cente vento et maiores iam volvente fluctus, quia perve-
nire se ad eos videbat non posse, ad Aethaliam insulam
traiecit, ut inde postero die Samum ex alto petentes naves
4   adgrederetur. Romani, pars exigua, primis tenebris portum desertum Samiae tenuerunt, classis cetera nocte tota
5   in alto iactata in eundem portum decurrit. ibi ex agrestibus

---

[21] Teiorum *ed. Med. 1505*: Pelorum *Bχ*: *del. Weiss. (1862)*
[22] miserunt *Bχ*: ierunt *Madvig*: transmiserunt *Koch*: *alii alia*

---

[54] Exact location unknown, but it was presumably close to Mt.
Korykos, across the bay from Teos (*Barr.* 56 D5), though it must
be noted that "Tean" is an emendation (see textual note).

[55] The intransitive use of the verb *mittere* is unparalleled, so
the text is probably corrupt here (though accepted without question by Sage).

The Romans and King Eumenes landed first at Ery-thrae, and after waiting there overnight they steered a course for the promontory of Tean Corycus[54] the following day. Wishing to cross from there to the nearest parts of the island of Samos, they did not await sunrise so the helms-men could observe the state of the weather but instead †set out†[55] into uncertain conditions. Halfway through the journey the northeasterly wind veered due north, and they began to be buffeted by a sea roughened with waves

13. Thinking that his enemies would head for Samos to join the Rhodian fleet, Polyxenidas set sail from Ephesus and at first anchored off Myonnesus. From there he crossed to the island called Macris,[56] intending to attack any ships he could that strayed from the line of the enemy fleet as it passed by or to fall on the end of the line if given the chance. After he saw that the fleet had been scattered by the bad weather, he at first thought that he had the opportunity to attack, but a little later the wind increased, producing even higher waves, and he saw that he could not reach the enemy. He therefore crossed to the island of Aethalia[57] so that from there he could pounce upon the ships the next day as they headed for Samos from the open sea. As darkness fell a small number of the Romans made it to a deserted haven in Samian territory and, after spend-ing the whole night storm-tossed out at sea, the rest of the fleet also sought shelter in the same harbor. Learning from

[56] Myonnesos and Makris lay on the west side of what is now the Doganbey peninsula (*Barr.* 61 D1).

[57] Probably an islet off the northeast coast of Samos (possibly St. Nicholas).

cognito hostium naves ad Aethaliam stare, consilium habitum utrum extemplo decernerent an Rhodiam exspecta-
rent classem. dilata re—ita enim placuit—Corycum, unde
6 venerant, traiecerunt. Polyxenidas quoque, cum frustra
stetisset, Ephesum rediit.

Tum Romanae naves, vacuo ab hostibus mari, Samum
7 traiecerunt. eodem et Rhodia classis post dies paucos venit. quam ut exspectatam esse appareret, profecti extemplo sunt Ephesum, ut aut decernerent navali certamine,
aut si detractaret hostis pugnam, quod plurimum intererat
ad animos civitatium, timoris confessionem exprimerent.
8 contra fauces portus instructa in frontem navium acie stetere. postquam nemo adversus ibat, classe divisa pars in
salo ad ostium portus in ancoris stetit, pars in terram mi-
9 lites exposuit. in eos ingentem[23] praedam, late depopulato
agro, agentes Andronicus Macedo, qui in praesidio Ephesi
erat, iam moenibus adpropinquantes eruptionem fecit,
exutosque magna parte praedae ad mare ac naves redegit.
10 postero die, insidiis medio ferme viae positis ad elicien-
dum extra moenia Macedonem, Romani ad urbem agmine
iere; inde, cum ea ipsa suspicio ne quis exiret deterruisset,
11 redierunt ad naves; et terra marique fugientibus certamen
hostibus, Samum, unde venerat, classis repetit.

[23] ingentem . . . iam moenibus *Crév.*: iam ingentem . . . moenibus *B*χ

peasants there that enemy ships were anchored at Aethalia, they held a meeting to decide whether to fight it out immediately or await the Rhodian fleet. Deferring the encounter (such was their decision), they crossed to Corycus, the point from which they had come. After a fruitless wait, Polyxenidas also went back to Ephesus.

With the sea unimpeded by the enemy, the Roman ships now crossed to Samos and the Rhodian fleet arrived at the same destination a few days later. To make it look as if this was all that they had been waiting for, the Romans immediately set sail for Ephesus, intending either to decide the contest with a battle at sea or else to wring an admission of fear from the enemy if he refused engagement—something of great importance vis-à-vis the inclinations of the city-states. They positioned themselves opposite the harbor mouth with their vessels facing it in a line. When no one confronted them, they divided the fleet and while one part rode at anchor on the open sea off the harbor entrance the other put ashore its fighting men. After raiding the countryside far and wide, these were bringing back an enormous quantity of booty when Andronicus the Macedonian, a member of the garrison at Ephesus, made a sortie against them as they approached the walls, stripped them of most of their plunder, and drove them back to their vessels on the shore. The next day the Romans set an ambush about half way between the two sides and then marched in a column toward the city in order to lure the Macedonian outside the walls. Then, when suspicion that this very scheme was afoot deterred anyone from coming out, they returned to their ships; and since the enemy was avoiding engagement on both land and sea, the Roman fleet returned to Samos, its point of departure.

Inde duas sociorum ex Italia duas Rhodias triremes cum praefecto Epicrate Rhodio ad fretum Cephallaniae
12 tuendum praetor misit. infestum id latrocinio Lacedaemonius Hybristas cum iuventute Cephallanum faciebat, clausumque iam mare commeatibus Italicis erat.

14. Piraei L. Aemilio Regillo succedenti ad navale im-
2 perium Epicrates occurrit; qui audita clade Rhodiorum, cum ipse duas tantum quinqueremes haberet, Epicratem cum quattuor navibus in Asiam secum reduxit; prosecutae etiam apertae Atheniensium naves sunt.

3 Aegaeo mari Chium[24] traiecit. eodem Timasicrates Rhodius cum duabus quadriremibus ab Samo nocte intempesta venit, deductusque ad Aemilium praesidii causa se missum ait, quod eam oram maris infestam onerariis regiae naves excursionibus crebris ab Hellesponto atque
4 Abydo facerent. traicienti Aemilio a Chio Samum duae Rhodiae quadriremes, missae obviam ab Livio, et rex
5 Eumenes cum duabus quinqueremibus occurrit. Samum postquam ventum est, accepta ab Livio classe et sacrificio, ut adsolet, rite facto Aemilius consilium advocavit. ibi C. Livius—is enim est primus rogatus sententiam—neminem fidelius posse dare consilium dixit quam eum qui id alteri suaderet quod ipse, si in eodem loco esset, facturus
6 fuerit: se in animo habuisse tota classe Ephesum petere et onerarias ducere multa saburra gravatas, atque eas in fau-

---

[24] Chium traiecit *Crév.*: traiecit Bχ: traiecit Chium *Duker*

[58] Greek Ὑβριστής ("Arrogant"); it is perhaps only a nick-name.
[59] The purification of the fleet under its new commander; cf. 36.42.2 and note.

From there the praetor dispatched two triremes of the Italian allies and two Rhodian triremes, under the command of the Rhodian Epicrates, to defend the strait of Cephallenia. The Spartan Hybristas[58] along with a group of young Cephallonians was rendering the strait perilous with his piracy, and the sea was already closed to supplies from Italy.

14. Lucius Aemilius Regillus, who was succeeding to the naval command, was met in Piraeus by Epicrates. He was told of the Rhodian defeat and, since he had only two quinqueremes, he took Epicrates and his four ships back to Asia with him. Some open-decked Athenian vessels also accompanied them.

Aemilius crossed the Aegean Sea to Chios. The Rhodian Timasicrates also reached the same harbor from Samos at dead of night with two quadriremes. Taken to Aemilius, Timasicrates said that his mission was to serve as a convoy because the king's ships, with their repeated forays from the Hellespont and Abydus, were making that coastline hazardous for freighters. Crossing from Chios to Samos, Aemilius was joined by two Rhodian quadriremes (sent to meet him by Livius) and by King Eumenes with two quinquiremes. When they reached Samos, Aemilius assumed command of the fleet from Livius, duly conducted the customary sacrifice,[59] and called a council of war. At the meeting Gaius Livius (he was the first to be asked his opinion) said that no one could provide more trustworthy advice than the man who encourages another to do what he himself would have done in the same situation. His own intention, he explained, had been to sail to Ephesus with the whole fleet, taking along some transport vessels heavily loaded with gravel, and to sink them in the

7 cibus portus supprimere; et eo minoris molimenti ea claustra esse, quod in fluminis modum longum et angustum et vadosum ostium portus sit. ita adempturum se maris usum hostibus fuisse, inutilemque classem facturum.

15. Nulli ea placere sententia. Eumenes rex quaesivit, quid tandem? ubi demersis navibus frenassent claustra maris, utrum libera sua classe abscessuri inde forent ad opem ferendam sociis terroremque hostibus praeben-

2 dum, an nihilo minus tota classe portum obsessuri? sive enim abscedant, cui dubium esse quin hostes extracturi demersas moles sint, et minore molimento aperturi portum quam obstruatur? sin autem manendum ibi nihilo

3 minus sit, quid[25] attinere claudi portum? quin contra illos, tutissimo portu, opulentissima urbe fruentes, omnia Asia praebente, quieta aestiva acturos; Romanos aperto in mari

4 fluctibus tempestatibusque obiectos, omnium inopes, in adsidua statione futuros, ipsos magis adligatos, impeditosque ne quid eorum quae agenda sint possint agere, quam ut hostes clausos habeant.

5 Eudamus, praefectus Rhodiae classis, magis eam sibi displicere sententiam ostendit quam ipse quid censeret

6 faciendum dixit. Epicrates Rhodius omissa in praesentia Epheso mittendam navium partem in Lyciam censuit, et

7 Patara, caput gentis, in societatem adiungenda. in duas

---

25 quid φ: quit ψ

---

60 That is, campaigning season.
61 *Barr.* 65 B5.

harbor mouth. The difficulty of creating an obstruction was lessened by the fact that the harbor mouth was like a river, he said—long and narrow, and with many shallow spots. In this way he would have deprived the enemy of access to the sea and rendered their fleet useless.

15. Nobody liked the proposal, and King Eumenes asked Livius what the point of it was. After the vessels had been sunk and the allies had blocked the gateway to the sea, would they then, with the fleet now set free, leave the harbor to bring help to the allies and instill terror in the enemy; or would they nevertheless continue to blockade the port with the whole fleet? For if they left, who could doubt that the enemy would raise the submerged wrecks and open the port with less effort than it took to block it? And if they had to stay there anyway, what was the advantage of closing the harbor? In fact, he said, the enemy would then have a peaceful summer,[60] enjoying the benefits of an absolutely secure port and a very wealthy city, with Asia providing everything they needed. The Romans would meanwhile be facing waves and storms on the open sea, short of all supplies, constantly on guard, and themselves being more tied down and restricted in everything that they should be doing apart from maintaining the blockade of the enemy.

Eudamus, admiral of the Rhodian fleet, indicated disapproval of the plan without expressing his own view of what should be done. The Rhodian Epicrates' view was that they should forget Ephesus for the moment and send some of their ships to Lycia and bring Patara,[61] capital of the country, into an alliance. That would prove advantageous in two important ways, he said: with the lands facing

333

magnas res id usui fore: et Rhodios, pacatis contra insulam
suam terris, totis viribus incumbere in unius belli quod
8 adversus Antiochum sit curam posse, et eam classem quae
in Cilicia compararetur intercludi, ne Polyxenidae coniun-
9 gatur. haec maxime movit sententia; placuit tamen Regil-
lum classe tota evehi ad portum Ephesi ad inferendum
hostibus terrorem.

16. C. Livius cum duabus quinqueremibus Romanis et
quattuor quadriremibus Rhodiis et duabus apertis Zmyrnaeis in Lyciam est missus, Rhodum prius iussus adire et
2 omnia cum iis communicare consilia. civitates quas praetervectus est, Miletus Myndus Halicarnassus Cnidus
3 Cous, imperata enixe fecerunt. Rhodum ut ventum est,
simul et ad quam rem missus esset iis exposuit, et con-
suluit eos. adprobantibus cunctis et ad eam quam habebat
classem adsumptis tribus quadriremibus, navigat Patara.
4 Primo secundus ventus ad ipsam urbem ferebat eos,
sperabantque subito terrore aliquid moturos; postquam
circumagente se vento fluctibus dubiis volui coeptum est
5 mare, pervicerunt quidem remis ut tenerent terram; sed
neque circa urbem tuta statio erat, nec ante ostium portus
in salo stare poterant, aspero mari et nocte imminente.
6 Praetervecti moenia, portum Phoenicunta, minus
duum milium spatio inde distantem, petiere, navibus a
7 maritima vi tutum; sed altae insuper imminebant rupes,
quas celeriter oppidani, adsumptis regiis militibus, quos

---

62 Smyrna (mod. Izmir: *Barr.* 56 E5) continued to resist Antiochus (cf. 33.38.3–4, 35.42.2).

63 Coastal cities of Asia Minor, all allies of Rhodes.

64 This is probably Phoenike, actually about six miles due east
of Patara (*Barr.* 65 B5), and further by sea.

their island pacified, the Rhodians could bring all their strength to bear on the one war, that against Antiochus; and, secondly, the fleet being put together in Cilicia would be prevented from joining up with Polyxenidas. This was the suggestion that prevailed; but it was nevertheless decided that Regillus should sail out to the harbor of Ephesus with all his fleet to inspire terror in the enemy.

16. Gaius Livius was sent to Lycia with two Roman quinqueremes, four Rhodian quadriremes and two open-decked vessels from Smyrna[62] with orders to go to Rhodes first and formulate all his plans in concert with the Rhodians. The city-states that he passed—Miletus, Myndus, Halicarnassus, Cnidus and Cos[63]—zealously executed his orders, and when he reached Rhodes he explained to the Rhodians the aim of his mission and also sought their opinion. They were all in favor, and Livius sailed on to Patara, with three quadriremes added to the fleet he commanded.

At first, a favorable wind took them toward the city itself and they had hopes of achieving something by suddenly inspiring panic; but the wind changed, and the sea began to churn with waves rolling in different directions. They did manage to hold close to the land with their oars; but there was no safe anchorage near the city and they could not lie off the harbor mouth on the open sea, either, because the waters were rough and night was coming on.

They sailed past the city walls and headed for the port of Phoenicus, which was less than two miles off[64] and which provided ships with shelter from the fury of the sea. There were, however, lofty cliffs overlooking the harbor, and these the townspeople together with the king's troops, whom they had as a garrison, quickly seized. Against them,

335

8 in praesidio habebant, ceperunt. adversus quos Livius,
quamquam erant iniqua ac difficilia ad exitus loca, Issaeos
9 auxiliares et Zmyrnaeorum expeditos iuvenes misit. hi,
dum missilibus primo et adversus paucos levibus excursionibus[26] lacessebatur magis quam conserebatur pugna, sus-
10 tinuerunt certamen; postquam plures ex urbe adfluebant,
et iam omnis multitudo effundebatur, timor incessit Livium, ne et auxiliares circumvenirentur et navibus etiam
11 ab terra periculum esset. ita non milites solum sed etiam
navales socios, remigum turbam, quibus quisque poterat
12 telis, armatos in proelium eduxit. tum quoque anceps
pugna fuit, neque milites solum aliquot, sed L. Apustius
tumultuario proelio cecidit; postremo tamen fusi fugatique sunt Lycii atque in urbem compulsi, et Romani cum
haud incruenta victoria ad naves redierunt.
13 Inde in Telmessicum profecti sinum, qui latere uno
Cariam altero Lyciam contingit, omissa Patara amplius
14 temptandi spe,[27] Rhodii domum dimissi sunt, Livius praetervectus Asiam in Graeciam transmisit, ut conventis Scipionibus, qui tum circa Thessaliam erant, in Italiam traiceret.

17. Aemilius postquam omissas in Lycia res et Livium
profectum in Italiam cognovit, cum ipse, ab Epheso tem-
2 pestate repulsus, inrito incepto Samum revertisset, turpe

[26] levibus excursionibus *Fr. 2*: levibus *Bχ*: levibus et excursionibus *Mg*: levibus proeliis et excursionibus *H.J.M*
[27] omissa . . . temptandi spe *Fr. 2*: omissa (omisso φ) Patara
amplius temptandi χ: Pataram amplius temptandi *B*: omissa spe
Patara amplius temptandi *Drak.*: omisso consilio Patara amplius
temptandi *Weiss.*

although it was unfavorable terrain and getting out of it was difficult, Livius sent his Issaean auxiliaries[65] and his light infantry from Smyrna. While, at the start, it was skirmishing with missiles and small-scale attacks on limited enemy numbers rather than a battle, these men kept up the fight; but when more people came streaming from the city, and eventually the entire population began pouring out, the fear overtook Livius that his auxiliaries might be cut off and his ships also be put at risk even from the land. He therefore led out into battle not only his marines, but the crews as well—a crowd of oarsmen—all of them armed with whatever weapons they could lay their hands on. Even then the battle remained indecisive and not only did some common soldiers fall in the scrappy fighting but so too did Lucius Apustius. Eventually, however, the Lycians were completely routed and driven back into their city, and the Romans returned to the ships with a victory won not without loss of blood.

From there they set off for the gulf of Telmessus,[66] which washes Caria on one side and Lycia on the other, having abandoned hope of a further attempt on Patara. The Rhodians were sent home and, after skirting the coast of Asia, Livius crossed to Greece in order to meet the Scipios (who were at the time in the area of Thessaly) and then cross to Italy.

17. Aemilius had himself been driven from Ephesus by a storm and had returned to Samos with his enterprise aborted. When he learned that the Lycian campaign had been abandoned and that Livius had left for Italy, he felt

[65] From Issa (mod. Vis), a small island off the Croatian coast (*Barr.* 20 D6) famous for the quality of its sailors.
[66] *Barr.* 65 A4.

ratus temptata frustra Patara esse, proficisci eo tota classe
3 et summa vi adgredi urbem statuit. Miletum et ceteram
oram sociorum praetervecti in Bargylietico sinu escen-
sionem ad Iasum fecerunt. urbem regium tenebat praesi-
4 dium; agrum circa Romani hostiliter depopulati sunt. missis deinde qui per conloquia principum et magistratuum
temptarent animos, postquam nihil in potestate sua responderunt esse, ad urbem oppugnandam ducit.

5   Erant Iasensium exsules cum Romanis; ii frequentes
Rhodios orare institerunt ne urbem et vicinam sibi et
cognatam innoxiam perire sinerent; sibi exsilii nullam
6 aliam causam esse quam fidem erga Romanos; eadem vi
regiorum qua ipsi pulsi sint teneri eos qui in urbe ma-
neant; omnium Iasensium unam mentem esse, ut servitu-
7 tem regiam effugerent. Rhodii moti precibus, Eumene
etiam rege adsumpto, simul suas necessitudines commemorando simul obsessae regio praesidio urbis casum mise-
rando, pervicerunt ut oppugnatione abstineretur.[28]

8   Profecti inde, pacatis ceteris, cum oram Asiae legerent,
Loryma—portus adversus Rhodum est—pervenerunt. ibi
in principiis sermo primo inter tribunos militum secretus
9 oritur, deinde ad aures ipsius Aemili pervenit, abduci classem ab Epheso, ab suo bello, ut ab tergo liber relictus

---

[28] abstineretur *Mg*: absisteretur *Bχ*

---

[67] *Barr.* 61 F3.
[68] *Barr.* 61 G4. Its ruins lie near modern Port Aplothiki.

that the failed attempt on Patara was a disgrace and decided to go there with his entire fleet and launch a full scale attack on the city. He sailed past Miletus and the rest of the coastline that was under allied control and landed at Iasus in the bay of Bargylia.[67] The city was held by a garrison of the king, and the Romans subjected the surrounding countryside to ruthless pillaging. Then a deputation was sent to hold discussions with the leading citizens and magistrates to sound out their inclinations, and when they replied that they were powerless to act Aemilius led out his troops to attack the city.

There were with the Romans some exiles from Iasus; and they proceeded to appeal to the Rhodians in large numbers not to countenance the destruction of an innocent city that was both a neighbor and relative of theirs. The reason for their own exile, they said, was simply their loyalty to the Romans; and those remaining in the city were constrained by the same violence from the king's troops by which they themselves had been driven out; all the people of Iasus had but one purpose, to escape their servitude to the king. The Rhodians were touched by their entreaties, and they also found a supporter in King Eumenes; and by both pointing to their racial ties and expressing pity for the misfortunes of a city at the mercy of the king's garrison, they convinced Aemilius to forego the attack.

With everywhere else pacified, the allies left Iasus and, skirting the coastline of Asia, reached Loryma,[68] a port facing Rhodes. Here some furtive conversation arose in the officers' quarters—among the military tribunes at first, but then reaching the ears of Aemilius himself—that the fleet was being removed from Ephesus, its own theater of

hostis in tot propinquas sociorum urbes omnia impune
10 conari posset. movere ea Aemilium; vocatosque Rhodios
cum percontatus esset possetne[29] Pataris universa classis
in portu stare posset, cum respondissent non posse, causam nactus omittendae rei Samum naves reduxit.

18. Per idem tempus Seleucus Antiochi filius, cum per
omne hibernorum tempus exercitum in Aeolide continuisset partim sociis ferendo opem, partim quos in societatem
2 perlicere non poterat depopulandis, transire in fines regni
Eumenis, dum is procul ab domo cum Romanis et Rhodiis
3 Lyciae maritima oppugnaret, statuit. ad Elaeam primo
infestis signis accessit; deinde omissa oppugnatione urbis
agros hostiliter depopulatus, ad caput arcemque regni
4 Pergamum ducit oppugnandam. Attalus primo stationibus
ante urbem positis et excursionibus equitum levisque ar-
5 maturae magis lacessebat quam sustinebat hostem; postremo, cum per levia certamina expertus nulla parte virium
se parem esse intra moenia se recepisset, obsideri urbs
coepta est.
6   Eodem ferme tempore et Antiochus, ab Apamea
profectus, Sardibus primum deinde haud procul Seleuci
castris ad caput Caici amnis stativa habuit cum magno ex-

---

[29] possetne . . . stare *Mg*: utrumnam . . . stare posset *Bχ*: num
. . . stare posset *Weiss.*

---

[69] Cf. 8.5, above.   [70] Brother of Eumenes (cf. 35.23.10);
he would later become Attalus II of Pergamum (158–138).
[71] Apamea: cf. 35.15.1 and note.   [72] There is some dispute
over whether *caput* here means the mouth or, as it more often
does, the source of the river. For the River Caicus, cf. *Barr.* 56
E3, and for Sardis (Antiochus' main base for the war) G5.

operations, which meant that the enemy, left to their rear, would be free to make all manner of attacks with impunity on many allied cities. This caused Aemilius concern, and summoning the Rhodians he asked them whether it was possible for the whole fleet to ride at anchor in the harbor at Patara. When the Rhodians declared it impossible, he used that as a pretext for abandoning the operation and took the fleet back to Samos.

18. In this same period Antiochus' son Seleucus had kept his army in Aeolis throughout the winter,[69] engaged partly in helping his allies, and partly in conducting raids on those whom he could not inveigle into an alliance. At this time he decided to move into territory that was part of Eumenes' kingdom while the king was far from home with the Romans and the Rhodians attacking the coastal areas of Lycia. He first marched on Elaea; but then, foregoing an assault on the city, he exhaustively plundered its farmlands and led his army forward to attack Pergamum, the capital and citadel of the realm. Attalus[70] at first stationed guard emplacements before the city and launched attacks with his cavalry and light infantry, harassing his enemy rather than resisting him. When he discovered through these minor encounters that he was no match for the foe in any branch of his forces, he finally withdrew within the city walls and a siege of the city commenced.

At about the same time, too, Antiochus, who had left Apamea,[71] established a base first at Sardis and then at the mouth of the River Caicus,[72] not far from Seleucus' camp, with a powerful army made up of various races. His most

7 ercitu mixto variis ex gentibus. plurimum terroris in Gallorum mercede conductis quattuor milibus erat. hos paucis Syris admixtis[30] ad pervastandum passim Pergamenum
agrum milites emisit.[31] quae postquam Samum nuntiata

8 sunt, primo Eumenes avocatus domestico bello cum classe
Elaeam petit; inde, cum praesto fuissent equites peditumque expediti, praesidio eorum tutus, priusquam ho-

9 stes sentirent aut moverentur, Pergamum contendit. ibi
rursus[32] levia per excursiones proelia fieri coepta, Eumene
summae rei discrimen haud dubie detractante. paucos
post dies Romana Rhodiaque classis, ut regi opem ferrent,

10 Elaeam ab Samo venerunt. quos ubi exposuisse copias
Elaeae et tot classes in unum convenisse portum Antiocho
allatum est, et sub idem tempus audivit consulem cum
exercitu iam in Macedonia esse, pararique quae ad

11 transitum Hellesponti opus essent, tempus venisse ratus,
priusquam terra marique simul urgeretur, agendi de pace,

12 tumulum quendam adversus Elaeam castris cepit; ibi peditum omnibus copiis relictis, cum equitatu—erant autem
sex milia equitum—in campos sub ipsa Elaeae moenia
descendit, misso caduceatore ad Aemilium velle se de
pace agere.

19. Aemilius, Eumene a Pergamo accito, adhibitisque[33]
Rhodiis, consilium habuit. Rhodii haud aspernari pacem;

---

30 paucis Syris admixtis *Zingerle*: paucis admixtos *Bχ*: paucis
admixtis *ed. Rom.*: Dahis admixtis *Weiss*.

31 milites emisit *Bχ*: milites misit *Harl. 2671*: misit *Gel.*

32 ibi rursus *χ*: ubi *B*

33 adhibitisque *Mg*: adhibitis et *Bχ*: adhibitisque et *M. Müller*:
et adhibitis *H.J.M*

formidable threat lay in his 4,000 Gallic mercenaries. These, with a few Syrians added, he sent out to lay waste the fields of Pergamum at several points. When the news was brought to Samos, Eumenes, called away by the war at home, first sailed to Elaea with his fleet and then, when cavalry and light infantry became available, he hurried on to Pergamum with them as a protective escort before the enemy became aware of it or made any move. There a number of sorties once more precipitated some light skirmishing, Eumenes quite clearly avoiding a decisive encounter. A few days later the Roman and Rhodian fleets reached Elaea from Samos to assist the king. It was reported to Antiochus that the allies had disembarked their troops at Elaea and that many fleets[73] had converged on the one harbor, and when at about the same time he heard that the consul was already in Macedonia with his army and that the necessary preparations for crossing the Hellespont were under way, he thought the time had come to discuss peace terms, before he came under pressure simultaneously on land and sea. He therefore seized a certain hill facing Elaea for his camp; leaving all his infantry there, he went down with his cavalry, which numbered 6,000, into the plains beneath the very walls of Elaea, having first sent a herald to Aemilius to report that he wished to discuss peace.

19. Aemilius summoned Eumenes from Pergamum and held a meeting to which the Rhodians were also in-

---

[73] Latin *classes* (fleets), but as only three fleets are mentioned, Walsh suggests that here it is a poetic usage meaning simply "ships."

Eumenes nec honestum dicere esse eo tempore de pace
2 agi, nec exitum rei imponi posse: "qui enim" inquit "aut
honeste, inclusi moenibus et obsessi, velut leges pacis
accipiemus? aut cui rata ista pax erit, quam sine consule,
non ex auctoritate senatus, non iussu populi Romani pepi-
3 gerimus? quaero enim, pace per te facta rediturusne extemplo in Italiam sis, classem exercitumque deducturus,
an exspectaturus quid de ea re consuli placeat, quid sena-
4 tus censeat aut populus iubeat. restat ergo ut maneas in
Asia, et rursus in hiberna copiae reductae, omisso bello,
5 exhauriant commeatibus praebendis socios, deinde, si ita
visum iis sit penes quos potestas fuerit, instauremus novum de integro bellum, quod possumus, si ex hoc impetu
rerum nihil prolatando remittitur, ante hiemem dis volentibus perfecisse."

6 Haec sententia vicit, responsumque Antiocho est ante
7 consulis adventum de pace agi non posse. Antiochus, pace
nequiquam temptata, evastatis Elaeensium primum deinde Pergamenorum agris, relicto ibi Seleuco filio, Adramytteum hostiliter itinere facto, petit agrum opulentum
quem vocant Thebes campum, carmine Homeri nobilita-
8 tum; neque alio ullo loco Asiae maior regiis militibus parta
est praeda. eodem Adramytteum, ut urbi praesidio essent,
navibus circumvecti Aemilius et Eumenes venerunt.

---

74 Adramytteum and Plain of Thebe: *Barr.* 56 D2, but it is the
town of Thebe, not the plain, that is mentioned in Homer (as the
domain of Eetion, father of Hector's wife, Andromache [*Il.* 1.366,
6.397]).

vited. The Rhodians were not averse to peace but Eumenes declared it was neither honorable to discuss peace terms at this juncture nor possible to bring the matter to a conclusion. "For," he said, "how shall we honorably accept so-called peace terms when we are shut up within our walls facing a siege? Or who will consider such a peace treaty valid when we shall have concluded it without the consul and without senatorial authorization or the bidding of the Roman people? Supposing that peace *is* made on your authority, I have this question: are you going to return to Italy immediately, withdrawing your fleet and your army? Or are you going wait for word of the consul's pleasure in the matter, for the vote of the senate or the order of the Roman people? Your only option in that case is to stay in Asia and have your troops led back to winter quarters, abandoning the campaign and draining your allies by their provisioning of supplies! And then, if those with the authority see fit, we must start the war all over again, a war that we can have finished before winter, god willing, if none of the impetus in the operation is lost through delay."

This view carried the day and Antiochus was given the reply that peace terms could not be discussed before the arrival of the consul. His attempt to gain peace a failure, Antiochus first laid waste the fields of the people of Elaea and after that those of the Pergamenes. Leaving his son Seleucus in place, he then marched on Adramytteum and headed for the rich land they call the Plain of Thebe, made famous by Homer's poetry.[74] In no other place in Asia was greater booty won by the soldiers of the king. Aemilius and Eumenes, sailing around with their ships, also came to Adramytteum in order to give protection to the city.

20. Per eosdem forte dies Elaeam ex Achaia mille pedites cum centum equitibus, Diophane omnibus iis copiis praeposito, accesserunt; quos egressos navibus obviam
2 missi ab Attalo nocte Pergamum deduxerunt. veterani omnes et periti belli erant, et ipse dux Philopoemenis, summi tum omnium Graecorum imperatoris, discipulus. qui biduum simul ad quietem hominum equorumque et ad visendas hostium stationes, quibus locis temporibusque accederent reciperentque sese, sumpserunt.
3 Ad radices fere collis in quo posita urbs est regii succedebant; ita libera ab tergo populatio erat. nullo ab urbe,
4 ne in stationes quidem qui procul iacularetur, excurrente, postquam semel, compulsi metu, se moenibus incluserunt, contemptus eorum et inde neglegentia apud regios oritur. non stratos non infrenatos magna pars habebant
5 equos; paucis ad arma et ordines relictis, dilapsi ceteri sparserant se toto passim campo, pars in iuvenales lusus lasciviamque versi, pars vescentes sub umbra, quidam somno etiam strati.
6 Haec Diophanes ex alta urbe Pergamo contemplatus arma suos capere et ad portam praesto esse iubet; ipse Attalum adit et in animo sibi esse dixit hostium stationem
7 temptare. aegre id permittente Attalo, quippe qui centum equitibus adversus sescentos, mille peditibus cum quattuor milibus pugnaturum cerneret, porta egressus haud procul statione hostium, occasionem opperiens, consi-

---

75 Diophanes, *strategos* of the Achaean League in 192–191, has a higher profile in Polybius, his fellow Megalopolitan, than in Livy (cf. Walbank 3.93 [Polyb. 21.3b. 2]).

76 For further evidence of Livy's high regard for Philopoemen, cf. 39.50.10–11.

20. At about this time 1,000 infantry and 100 cavalry happened to reach Elaea from Achaea, all of these troops commanded by Diophanes.[75] After disembarking they were escorted to Pergamum at night by men sent by Attalus to meet them. They were all veterans with combat experience and their leader was actually a pupil of Philopoemen, the greatest general among all Greeks at that time.[76] They spent two days resting the men and horses as well as observing the enemy outposts to see the points and times at which they came and went.

The king's men would advance close to the foot of the hill on which the city stood, thus leaving the land behind them clear for plundering. Once the townspeople had confined themselves within their walls from fear, there was no sally made from the city, not even to throw spears at the outposts at long range. Contempt for them therefore arose among the king's men, followed by inattention to duties. Most did not have their horses saddled or bridled. A few remained under arms and in their ranks but the rest had slipped away and dispersed throughout the plain, a number engaging in young men's sports and fun, some eating in the shade, and others even lying asleep on the ground.

Observing this from the heights of the city of Pergamum, Diophanes ordered his men to take up arms and hold themselves in readiness at the gate. He himself went to Attalus and explained that he intended to assault an enemy outpost. Attalus allowed this only reluctantly as he could see that Diophanes would be engaging 600 cavalry with 100, and 4,000 infantry with 1,000; and Diophanes, passing through the gate, installed himself not far from an enemy outpost, awaiting his opportunity. The people in

347

8   det.[34] et qui Pergami erant amentiam magis quam auda-
ciam credere esse, et hostes paulisper in eos versi, ut nihil
moveri viderunt, nec ipsi quicquam ex solita neglegentia,
9   insuper etiam eludentes paucitatem, mutarunt. Diophanes quietos aliquamdiu suos, velut ad spectaculum modo
10 eductos, continuit; postquam dilapsos ab ordinibus hostes
vidit, peditibus quantum adcelerare possent sequi iussis,
ipse princeps inter equites cum turma sua, quam potuit
effusissimis habenis, clamore ab omni simul pedite atque
11 equite sublato, stationem hostium improviso invadit. non
homines solum sed equi etiam territi, cum vincula abru-
pissent, trepidationem et tumultum inter suos fecerunt.
12 pauci stabant impavidi equi; eos ipsos non sternere non
infrenare aut escendere facile poterant, multo maiorem
quam pro numero equitum terrorem Achaeis inferenti-
13 bus. pedites vero ordinati et praeparati sparsos per neglegentiam et semisomnos prope adorti sunt. caedes passim
14 fugaque per campos facta est. Diophanes secutus effusos,
quoad tutum fuit, magno decore genti Achaeorum parto—
spectaverant enim e moenibus Pergami non viri modo sed
feminae etiam—, in praesidium urbis redit.

21. Postero die regiae magis compositae et ordinatae
stationes quingentis passibus longius ab urbe posuerunt
castra, et Achaei eodem ferme tempore atque in eundem
2   locum processerunt. per multas horas intenti utrimque

---

[34] considet *Bχ*: consedit *ed. Med. 1478*

---

[77] An epic touch; cf. Homer *Il.* 3.161–244, Verg. *Aen.* 12.131,
Hor. *Carm.* 3.2.6–8, on which see R. G. M. Nisbet and Niall
Rudd, *A Commentary on Horace, Odes, Book III* (Oxford, 2004),
25.

Pergamum believed this was insanity rather than bravado. The enemy, too, turned their attention to them only for a short while and, seeing no movement, made no alteration to their usual carelessness and, in fact, even jeered at their meager numbers. For some time Diophanes kept his men at a standstill, as if they had been brought out simply to watch; but when he saw that the enemy had slipped away from their positions he instructed the infantry to follow with all the speed they could muster. He himself, leading the cavalry with his own squadron, made a sudden charge on the enemy outpost, galloping as rapidly as possible and with the war cry raised simultaneously by every foot soldier and horseman. Even the horses, and not just the men, were terrified; they burst their reins and created panic and havoc among their own side. A few horses did remain unperturbed but even these their riders could not easily saddle, bridle or mount, because the Achaeans struck far greater terror into them than the number of their cavalry warranted. The infantry, in ranks and well prepared, attacked a foe carelessly disordered and virtually half asleep. There was slaughter and flight throughout the plains. Diophanes chased the scattered enemy as far as was safe and then returned to service in the garrison of the city, having won great glory for the Achaean nation; for the combat had been witnessed from the walls of Pergamum by men and women alike.[77]

21. The following day the king's advance guards established a position a half mile further from the city in better order and closer formation; and the Achaeans went forward at roughly the same time and to the same place as before. For several hours both sides waited intently for the

velut iam futurum impetum exspectavere; postquam haud
procul occasu solis redeundi in castra tempus erat, regii
signis conlatis abire agmine ad iter magis quam ad pugnam
3 composito coepere. quievit Diophanes, dum in conspectu
erant; deinde eodem quo pridie impetu in postremum
agmen incurrit, tantumque rursus pavoris ac tumultus
incussit ut cum terga caederentur, nemo pugnandi causa
restiterit; trepidantesque et vix ordinem agminis servantes
4 in castra compulsi sunt. haec Achaeorum audacia Seleucum ex agro Pergameno movere castra coegit.

Antiochus, postquam Romanos ad tuendum Adramytteum venisse audivit, ea quidem urbe abstinuit; depopulatus agros, Peraeam inde, coloniam Mitylenaeorum, ex-
5 pugnavit. Cotton et Corylenus et Aphrodisias et Prinne[35]
primo impetu captae sunt. inde per Thyatiram Sardis re-
6 diit, Seleucus, in ora maritima permanens, aliis terrori erat
aliis praesidio. classis Romana cum Eumene Rhodiisque
Mitylenen primo, inde retro, unde profecta erat, Elaeam
7 redit. inde Phocaeam petentes, ad insulam quam Bacchium vocant—imminet urbi Phocaeensium—adpule-
runt, et quibus ante abstinuerant templis signisque—
egregie autem exornata insula erat—cum hostiliter
8 diripuissent, ad ipsam urbem transmiserunt. eam divisis
inter se partibus cum oppugnarent, et videretur sine ope-

---

35 et Prinne *BPVL*: Prime *AE*: Crene *Gron.*: Princie *N*

---

78 In fact, Peraea (Greek for "the opposite/farther shore," cf.
32.33.6) must refer not to a specific place but to a strip of the
mainland under Mitylenaean control.

79 Probably towns on the Mytilenaean Peraea, but their location is unknown.

80 Cf. 8.7, above.

attack, which they expected to come at any moment. When, not long before sunset, it was time to return to camp, the king's men brought their standards together and proceeded to march off in a column that was organized more for marching than for fighting. Diophanes remained inactive while they were in sight. Then he bore down on the rear of the column with same ferocity as the day before, and once more struck such panic into them and caused such chaos that although their rear was being cut down no one halted to put up a fight. Terror-stricken and barely keeping their marching column together, they were driven back to their camp. This intrepid feat of the Achaeans obliged Seleucus to withdraw his camp from Pergamene territory.

When Antiochus was told that the Romans had arrived to offer protection to Adramytteum, he kept clear of that city and after laying waste the countryside went on to take by storm Peraea, a colony of the Mitylenaeans.[78] Cotton, Corylenus, Aphrodisias and Prinne[79] were taken with the first assault. From there he returned to Sardis by way of Thyatira,[80] and Seleucus remained on the coast, intimidating some communities and assisting others. The Roman fleet along with Eumenes and the Rhodians came to Mitylene first, and then returned to Elaea, their starting point. From there, heading for Phocaea, they put in at the island they call Bacchium[81] (it overlooks the city of Phocaea), and after savagely plundering its temples and statues, which they had previously spared and with which the island was very well endowed, they crossed to the city itself. After dividing up the various responsibilities, they pro-

---

[81] Not in *Barrington*. It may be the Bacchina mentioned by Pliny (*HN* 5.138) in a list of towns close to Smyrna.

ribus armis scalisque capi posse, missum ab Antiocho praesidium trium milium armatorum cum intrasset urbem, extemplo oppugnatione omissa classis ad insulam se recepit, nihil aliud quam depopulato circa urbem hostium agro.

22. Inde placuit Eumenen domum dimitti et praeparare[36] consuli atque exercitui quae ad transitum Hellesponti opus essent, Romanam Rhodiamque classem redire Samum atque ibi in statione esse ne Polyxenidas ab Epheso moveret. rex Elaeam, Romani ac Rhodii Samum redierunt. ibi M. Aemilius frater praetoris decessit.

Rhodii, celebratis exsequiis, adversus classem, quam fama erat ex Syria venire, tredecim suis navibus et una Coa quinqueremi altera Cnidia Rhodum, ut ibi in statione essent, profecti sunt. biduo ante quam Eudamus cum classe ab Samo veniret, tredecim ab Rhodo naves cum Pamphilida praefecto adversus eandem Syriacam classem missae, adsumptis quattuor navibus quae Cariae praesidio erant, oppugnantibus regiis Daedala et quaedam alia Peraeae castella obsidione exemerunt. Eudamum confestim exire placuit. additae huic quoque sunt ad eam classem quam habebat sex apertae naves. profectus cum quantum adcelerare poterat maturasset, ad portum quem Megisten vocant praegressos consequitur. inde uno agmine Phaselidem cum venissent, optimum visum est ibi hostem opperiri.

---

[36] praeparare *Burn. 200*: praeparari *Bχ*

---

[82] Briefly mentioned by Polybius (21.10.5; Walbank 3.101).

[83] A town on the Rhodian Peraea on the border of Lycia: *Barr.* 65 A4. [84] The town lay on a homonymous island off the Lycian coast: *Barr.* 65 C5.

ceeded with the attack and it looked as if the town could be taken by assault and with scaling ladders, without the use of siege works. However, when a garrison of 3,000 soldiers that had been sent by Antiochus entered the city, the attack was immediately abandoned and the fleet withdrew to the island, having only plundered the enemy territory around the city.

22. It was decided that Eumenes should be sent home from here and that he should undertake for the consul and the army the necessary preparations for crossing the Hellespont. The Roman and Rhodian fleets were to return to Samos and there keep watch in case Polyxenidas moved from Ephesus. The king then returned to Elaea and the Romans and Rhodians to Samos. There Marcus Aemilius, brother of the praetor, died.

When the funeral was over the Rhodians set off with thirteen of their own ships, one Coan quinquereme and a second from Cnidus, to sail to Rhodes where they were to remain on guard against a fleet that was reported to be coming from Syria. Thirteen ships had also been sent from Rhodes against the same Syrian fleet, under the command of Pamphilidas;[82] and two days before Eudamus came from Samos with his fleet they picked up four ships that had been guarding Caria and raised the siege of Daedala[83] and certain other fortresses in the Peraea that the king's troops were blockading. It was decided that Eudamus should leave without delay and he was assigned six opendecked vessels to add to the fleet that he commanded. After setting sail he made all the speed he could and overtook the troops that had gone ahead at the port they call Megiste.[84] From there they reached Phaselis as a single column and it seemed best to await the enemy in that location.

23. In confinio Lyciae et Pamphyliae Phaselis est; prominet penitus in altum, conspiciturque prima terrarum
Rhodum a Cilicia petentibus, et procul navium praebet
prospectum. eo maxime, ut in obvio classi hostium essent,
2 electus locus est; ceterum, quod non providerunt, et loco
gravi et tempore anni—medium enim aestatis erat—, ad
hoc insolito odore ingruere morbi volgo, maxime in re-
3 miges, coeperunt. cuius pestilentiae metu profecti cum
praeteruenerentur Pamphylium sinum, ad Eurymedon-
tem amnem adpulsa classe audiunt ab Aspendiis ad Sidam
4 iam[37] hostes esse. tardius navigaverant regii adverso tempore etesiarum, quod velut statum favoniis ventis est.
Rhodiorum duae et triginta quadriremes et quattuor tri-
5 remes fuere; regia classis septem et triginta maioris formae navium erat; in quibus tres hepteres quattuor hexeres
habebat. praeter has decem triremes erant. et hi adesse
hostes ex specula quadam cognoverunt.

6 Utraque classis postero die luce prima, tamquam eo
die pugnatura, e portu movit; et postquam superavere
Rhodii promunturium quod ab Sida prominet in altum,
extemplo et conspecti ab hostibus sunt et ipsi eos vide-
7 runt. ab regiis[38] sinistro cornu, quod ab alto obiectum erat,
Hannibal, dextro Apollonius, purpuratorum unus, prae-
8 erat; et iam in frontem derectas habebant naves. Rhodii
longo agmine veniebant; prima praetoria navis Eudami

23. Phaselis lies on the border of Lycia and Pamphylia.[85] It juts far out into the sea and is the first land sighted by voyagers heading toward Rhodes from Cilicia; and it also affords a view of ships far away. It was chiefly for that reason that it was chosen as the place to encounter the enemy fleet. There was, however, something that they did not anticipate: because of the insalubrious locality and the time of year (it was midsummer), and also because of an unusual stench, diseases began to spread widely among them, affecting oarsmen in particular. They left the place from fear of the epidemic; but when they were sailing along the Gulf of Pamphylia they put in at the River Eurymedon, and were there told by the people of Aspendus that the enemy was now at Side.[86] The king's navy had made quite a slow voyage because it was the unfavorable season of the Etesians,[87] one almost exclusively given over to northwesterly winds. The Rhodians had 32 quadriremes and 4 triremes; the king's fleet comprised 37 ships of larger dimensions, including 3 galleys with seven banks of oars and 4 with six, and 10 triremes in addition to these. From a lookout tower they, too, perceived that their enemy was close at hand.

The following day both fleets moved from port at dawn assuming that they would fight on that day; and after the Rhodians passed the headland projecting into the sea from Side they were suddenly spotted by the enemy and also sighted them. In the king's fleet Hannibal commanded the left wing, which was on the side of the open sea, and Apollonius, one of the king's courtiers, commanded the right; and they now had their vessels drawn up facing forward in line. The Rhodians started to come up in a long column: the flagship of Eudamus was first; Chariclitus[88] brought up

355

erat; cogebat agmen Chariclitus; Pamphilidas mediae classi praeerat.

9   Eudamus postquam hostium aciem instructam et paratam ad concurrendum vidit, et ipse in altum evehitur, et deinceps quae sequebantur servantes ordinem in frontem

10   derigere iubet. ea res primo tumultum praebuit; nam nec sic in altum evectus erat ut ordo omnium navium ad terram explicari posset, et festinans ipse praepropere cum quinque solis navibus Hannibali occurrit; ceteri, quia in

11   frontem derigere iussi erant, non sequebantur. extremo agmini loci nihil ad terram relicti erat; trepidantibusque iis inter se iam in dextro cornu adversus Hannibalem pugnabatur.

24. Sed momento temporis et navium virtus et usus

2   maritimae rei terrorem omnem Rhodiis dempsit. nam et in altum celeriter evectae naves locum post se quaeque venienti ad terram dedere, et si qua concurrerat rostro cum hostium nave, aut proram lacerabat, aut remos detergebat, aut libero inter ordines discursu praetervecta in

3   puppim impetum dabat. maxime exterruit hepteris regia a multo minore Rhodia nave uno ictu demersa; itaque haud dubie dextrum cornu hostium in fugam inclinabat.

4   Eudamum in alto multitudine navium maxime Hannibal, ceteris omnibus longe praestantem, urgebat; et circumvenisset, ni signo sublato ex praetoria nave, quo dispersam classem in unum conligi mos erat, omnes quae in dextro

the rear; and Pamphilidas was in command of the center of the fleet.

When Eudamus saw the enemy line drawn up and ready to join battle, he too moved out into open water and ordered the ships that were following to face forward in a straight line while maintaining their order. At first, this move caused confusion: Eudamus had not sailed out far enough into the open sea to permit all his ships to be deployed in a line toward the land, and being overhasty he met Hannibal with a mere five vessels. The others, because they had been ordered to make a line, were not following him. At the end of the column there was no room left on the landward side and, while confusion reigned among them, the battle with Hannibal was starting on the right wing.

24. But in a moment the quality of their vessels and their accomplished seamanship removed all fear from the Rhodians. As the ships sailed swiftly into open water, each left behind it space on the landward side for one moving up; and if one collided with an enemy vessel with its beak, it would tear open its prow or shear off its oars, or else, finding an open passage between the lines, would sail past the enemy ship and attack its stern. The greatest dismay arose when a king's ship with seven banks of oars was sunk by a much smaller Rhodian craft after a single impact. As a result, the right flank of the enemy was quite clearly preparing for flight. On the open water Hannibal with his superior number of ships had Eudamus, who was clearly superior in all other respects, under severe pressure, and would have surrounded him had not the usual signal for bringing together a scattered fleet been raised on the flagship. At this all the ships that had been victorious on the

cornu vicerant naves ad opem ferendam suis concur-
5 rissent. tum et Hannibal quaeque circa eum naves erant
capessunt fugam; nec insequi Rhodii ex magna parte ae-
gris et ob id celerius fessis remigibus potuerunt.

6   Cum in alto, ubi substiterant, cibo reficerent vires,
contemplatus Eudamus hostes claudas mutilatasque naves
apertis navibus remulco trahentes, viginti paulo amplius
integras abscedentes, e turri praetoriae navis silentio facto
"exsurgite" inquit "et egregium spectaculum capessite
7 oculis." consurrexere omnes, contemplatique trepidationem fugamque hostium, ac[39] prope una voce omnes ut
8 sequerentur exclamaverunt. ipsius Eudami multis ictibus
volnerata navis erat; Pamphilidam et Chariclitum insequi,
9 quoad putarent tutum, iussit. aliquamdiu secuti sunt;
postquam terrae adpropinquabat Hannibal, veriti ne in-
cluderentur vento in hostium ora, ad Eudamum revecti
hepterem captam, quae primo concursu icta erat, aegre
10 Phaselidem pertraxerunt. inde Rhodum non tam victoria
laeti quam alius alium accusantes, quod cum potuisset,
non omnis submersa aut capta classis hostium foret, redierunt.

11   Hannibal, victus[40] uno proelio adverso, ne tum quidem
praeteruehi Lyciam audebat, cum coniungi veteri regiae
12 classi quam primum cuperet; et ne id ei facere liberum
esset, Rhodii Chariclitum cum viginti navibus rostratis ad
13 Patara et Megisten portum miserunt. Eudamum cum sep-

[39] ac *BψMg: om.* φ: alacri ac *Zingerle*
[40] victus *BMg:* ictus χ

---

[89] That is, when the Rhodians had returned to Rhodes.

right wing had swiftly come together to assist their comrades. Then Hannibal and the ships around him also took flight, and the Rhodians were unable to give chase because most of the oarsmen were in poor health and thus all the more quickly fatigued.

While they were rebuilding their strength with food where they had stopped on the open sea, Eudamus watched the enemy hauling their disabled and damaged vessels with tow ropes from open-decked ships, not many more than twenty moving off unharmed. Calling for silence from the tower of the flagship, he said "Get up and take in with your eyes a wonderful sight." They all rose and, observing the terror-stricken flight of their enemy, cried out with almost one voice that they should give chase. Eudamus' own ship had been damaged in numerous collisions but he ordered Pamphilidas and Chariclitus to follow for as long as they thought safe. They did follow for a while, but when Hannibal began to approach the shore they became afraid of being pinned down by the wind on a coast held by the enemy and so returned to Eudamus. Then, with difficulty, they towed to Phaselis the captured ship with seven banks of oars that had been wrecked in the first collision. They returned from there to Rhodes, not so much elated over their victory as blaming each other for failing to sink or capture the entire enemy fleet when they had the chance.

Although he had suffered only one defeat, Hannibal did not even then[89] venture to sail beyond Lycia, despite his eagerness to join up with the king's original fleet at the earliest opportunity; and so that he should not have the liberty to do so, the Rhodians also sent Chariclitus with twenty beaked ships to Patara and the harbor of Megiste.

tem navibus maximis ex ea classe cui praefuerat Samum
redire ad Romanos iusserunt, ut quantum consilio quantum auctoritate valeret, compelleret Romanos ad Patara
expugnanda.

25. Magnam Romanis laetitiam prius victoriae nuntius,
2 deinde adventus attulit Rhodiorum; et apparebat si Rhodiis ea cura dempta fuisset, vacuos eos tuta eius regionis
maria praestaturos. sed profectio Antiochi ab Sardibus, ne
opprimerentur maritimae urbes, abscedere custodia Io-
3 niae atque Aeolidis prohibuit;[41] Pamphilidam cum quattuor navibus tectis ad eam classem quae circa Patara erat
miserunt.
4 Antiochus non civitatium modo quae circa se erant
contrahebat praesidia, sed ad Prusiam Bithyniae regem
legatos miserat litterasque, quibus transitum in Asiam
5 Romanorum increpabat: venire eos ad omnia regna tol-
lenda, ut nullum usquam orbis terrarum[42] nisi Romanum
6 imperium esset; Philippum Nabim expugnatos; se tertium
peti; ut quisque proximus ab oppresso sit, per omnes velut
7 continens incendium pervasurum; ab se gradum in Bithy-
niam fore, quando Eumenes in voluntariam servitutem
concessisset.
8 His motum Prusiam litterae Scipionis consulis, sed ma-

---

41 prohibuit *Holk. 353*: prohibuerunt *B*χ: *post* Sardibus *suppl.*
metusque *Weiss.* 42 orbis terrarum *B*χ: in orbe terrarum
Madvig: terrarum *Weiss.*

---

90 That is, about Patara, an enemy stronghold on the Lycian
coast. 91 Prusias, king of Bithynia since about 230, remained neutral in the war with Antiochus, but it won him no
credit with Rome, as he was later deprived of Mysia, which was

They ordered Eudamus to return to the Romans on Samos with seven of the largest ships from the fleet that he had commanded so that he could, with all his diplomacy and personal influence, push the Romans into storming Patara.

25. News of the victory and then the arrival of the Rhodians brought the Romans great joy; and it was evident that, had the Rhodians been relieved of that particular concern,[90] they would have been free to provide security for all the waterways in the region. But Antiochus' departure from Sardis prevented them from abandoning their protection of Ionia and Aeolis for fear that the coastal cities might fall to him. The Rhodians sent Pamphilidas with four decked ships to join the fleet that lay off Patara.

Antiochus was not only bringing together the garrisons from the city-states that lay around him but had also sent emissaries to King Prusias of Bithynia[91] with a letter in which he bitterly complained about the Romans' crossing into Asia. They were coming to remove all monarchies, he said, so that there should be no empire anywhere in the world but that of Rome. Philip and Nabis had been conquered and he was now the third under attack. This spreading fire, as it were, would sweep through them all, as each lay beside a defeated neighbor. After him, since Eumenes had already acquiesced in voluntary servitude, their next step would be into Bithynia.

Prusias was worried by this but a dispatch from the consul Scipio and, more importantly, one from Scipio's

returned to Eumenes II (38.39.15). He subsequently gave shelter to Hannibal but agreed to surrender him to Flamininus in 183, thus precipitating his suicide (39.51).

gis fratris eius Africani, ab suspicione tali averterunt; qui
praeter consuetudinem perpetuam populi Romani au-
gendi omni honore regum sociorum maiestatem, domesticis ipse exemplis Prusiam ad promerendam amicitiam
9 suam compulit: regulos se acceptos in fidem in Hispania
reges reliquisse; Masinissam non in patrio modo locasse
regno, sed in Syphacis, a quo ante expulsus fuisset, reg-
10 num imposuisse; et esse eum non Africae modo regum
longe opulentissimum, sed toto in orbe terrarum cuivis
11 regum vel maiestate vel viribus parem. Philippum et Nabim, hostes et bello superatos ab T. Quinctio, tamen in
12 regno relictos. Philippo quidem anno priore etiam stipendium remissum et filium obsidem redditum; et quasdam
civitates extra Macedoniam patientibus Romanis imperatoribus recepisse eum. in eadem dignitate et Nabim futurum fuisse, nisi eum suus primum furor, deinde fraus
13 Aetolorum absumpsisset. maxime confirmatus est animus
regis postquam ad eum C. Livius, qui praetor ante classi
14 praefuerat, legatus ab Roma venit, et edocuit quanto et
spes victoriae certior Romanis quam Antiocho et amicitia
sanctior firmiorque apud Romanos futura esset.

26. Antiochus postquam a spe societatis Prusiae deci-
dit, Ephesum ab Sardibus est profectus ad classem quae
per aliquot menses instructa ac parata fuerat visendam,
2 magis quia terrestribus copiis exercitum Romanum et

---

92 King of the Massylii in Numidia and a Roman ally whose
service for Rome in the Hannibalic war led to his territory being
extended in the peace treaty (cf. 30.44.12, 31.11.8).
93 The reference is to Nabis' authorization of the deaths of
leading Roman supporters in the maritime towns of Laconia
(35.13.1).   94 Cf. 35.35.10–19.

brother Africanus, diverted him from such suspicions. Apart from bringing up the ongoing practice of the Roman people of augmenting the prestige of allied kings with all manner of honors, Africanus brought Prusias to prove himself worthy of his friendship by adducing personal examples. He cited petty chieftains in Spain whom he had made his protégés and left as kings, and Masinissa,[92] whom he had not only set on his father's throne but also on that of Syphax, from which he had been earlier deposed—and, as well as being by far the richest of the kings of Africa, Masinissa could match any king in the entire world in regal majesty and power. Philip and Nabis had been enemies conquered in war by Titus Quinctius but they had nevertheless been left on the throne. Indeed, Philip had even seen payment of his tribute remitted the previous year and his hostage son returned to him. He had also recovered a number of city-states outside Macedonia with the acquiescence of the Roman commanders. Nabis, too, would have been held in the same regard had not his own madness first,[93] and then the Aetolians' treachery,[94] destroyed him. The king's mind was truly made up when Gaius Livius, who had earlier commanded the fleet as praetor, came to him as an envoy from Rome and showed him how much more certain were the Romans' hopes of victory than Antiochus' and how much more inviolate and reliable friendship with the Romans would be.

26. After he lost all hope of an alliance with Prusias, Antiochus left Sardis for Ephesus to inspect the fleet, which for some months had been fitted out and prepared for action. He did this more because he could see it was impossible to resist the Roman army and the two Scipios,

duos Scipiones imperatores videbat sustineri non posse
quam quod res navalis ipsa per se aut temptata sibi unquam feliciter aut tunc magnae et certae fiduciae esset.
3   erat tamen momentum in praesentia spei, quod et magnam partem Rhodiae classis circa Patara esse et Eumenen
regem cum omnibus navibus suis consuli obviam in Hel-
4   lespontum profectum audierat; aliquid etiam inflabat animos classis Rhodia ad Samum per occasionem fraude
5   praeparatam absumpta. his fretus, Polyxenida cum classe
ad temptandam omni modo certaminis fortunam misso,
ipse copias ad Notium ducit. id oppidum Colophonium,
mari imminens, abest a vetere Colophone duo ferme milia
6   passuum. et ipsam urbem suae potestatis esse volebat,
adeo propinquam Epheso ut nihil terra marive ageret
quod non subiectum oculis Colophoniorum ac per eos
7   notum extemplo Romanis esset; quos[43] audita obsidione
non dubitabat ad opem sociae urbi ferendam classem ab
Samo moturos; eam occasionem Polyxenidae ad rem ge-
8   rendam fore. igitur operibus oppugnare urbem adgressus,
ad mare[44] partibus duabus pariter munitionibus deductis,
utrimque vineas et aggerem muro iniunxit et testudinibus
arietes admovit.
9   Quibus territi malis, Colophonii oratores Samum ad L.

---

[43] quos *Bχ*: et hos *Madvig*
[44] ad mare *B*: et ad mare *χ*

---

[95] Polyxenidas' successful duping of Pausistratus (11.4–14, above).

[96] Notium/Colophon: *Barr.* 61 E1. Notium was actually about ten miles from old Colophon.

its generals, with his land forces than because he had ever had any success in naval warfare itself or because he felt any great or solid confidence in it at that time. For the moment, however, he had some cause for hope because he had heard that most of the Rhodian fleet was off Patara and also that King Eumenes had left for the Hellespont with all his ships to rendezvous with the consul; and his spirits were further raised by the destruction of the Rhodian fleet at Samos by a piece of treacherous opportunism.[95] Reassured by these considerations, Antiochus sent Polyxenidas with the fleet to put fortune to the test in any kind of engagement, and he himself led the troops to Notium. This is a Colophonian town overlooking the sea, about two miles distant from old Colophon.[96] He wanted to have the town itself under his control; it lay so close to Ephesus that no activity on land or sea could escape the eyes of the Colophonians and by them it would be immediately made known to the Romans. He did not doubt that when they heard about the siege the Romans would move their fleet from Samos to bring succor to an allied city, and that would be Polyxenidas' opportunity to come to grips with them. He therefore proceeded to invest the city with siege works. He ran parallel walls down to the sea on both sides, and on both he brought siege sheds and a mound up to the wall and advanced the battering rams with the "tortoises."[97]

Cowed by the dangers facing them, the Colophonians sent spokesmen to Lucius Aemilius on Samos begging for

[97] The so-called ram tortoise (*testudo arietaria*), a mechanism for carrying the ram and also protecting the soldiers involved in the operation (cf. Vitr. 10.13.2).

Aemilium, fidem praetoris populique Romani imploran-
10 tes, miserunt. Aemilium et Sami segnis diu mora offende-
bat, nihil minus opinantem quam Polyxenidam, bis nequiquam ab se provocatum, potestatem pugnae facturum
11 esse; et turpe existimabat Eumenis classem adiuvare consulem ad traiciendas in Asiam legiones, se Colophonis
12 obsessae auxilio, incertam finem habituro, adligari. Eudamus Rhodius, qui et ante tenuerat eum Sami cupientem
13 proficisci in Hellespontum, cunctique instare et: quanto[45]
satius esse vel socios obsidione eximere vel victam iam
semel classem iterum vincere et totam maris possessionem eripere,[46] quam desertis sociis, tradita Antiocho
Asia terra marique in Hellespontum, ubi satis esset Eumenis classis, ab sua parte belli discedere.

27. Profecti ab Samo ad petendos commeatus, con-
sumptis iam omnibus, Chium parabant traicere; id erat
horreum Romanis, eoque omnes ex Italia missae onera-
2 riae derigebant cursum. circumvecti ab urbe ad aversa
insulae—obiecta aquiloni ad Chium et Erythras sunt—
cum pararent traicere, litteris certior fit praetor frumenti
vim magnam Chium ex Italia venisse, vinum portantes
3 naves tempestatibus retentas esse; simul allatum est Teios

---

[45] instare et quanto *M. Müller*: instare et dicere quanto *Bχ*:
instare ut duceret *Madvig*
[46] eripere *Bχ*: hosti eripere *Fr. 2*

---

[98] Here, as often, Livy omits the verb of saying (cf. Briscoe
2.12).   [99] That is, from the city of Samos.
[100] Chios/Erythrae: *Barr.* 57 E3.
[101] Teos (*Barr.* 57 E3) had been under Antiochus' control
since about 203.

the protection of the praetor and the Roman people. Aemilius was galled by the long period of delay and inactivity
at Samos, for the last thing he expected was that Polyxenidas, whom he had twice challenged in vain, would give
him an opportunity to engage. He also thought it a disgrace that the fleet of Eumenes should be helping the
consul transport the legions to Asia while he himself was
tied up bringing relief to the beleaguered city of Colophon, an operation with no end in sight. The Rhodian
Eudamus, who had also kept him at Samos earlier when
he wanted to leave for the Hellespont, was now, along with
everybody else, pressing him to stay—much better to raise
the blockade of his allies, they said,[98] or inflict another
defeat on a navy they had already beaten once and thereby
seize total control of the sea. Much better that than to
abandon his allies, surrender mastery of Asia on land and
sea to Antiochus, and leave his own sector of the war to go
to the Hellespont, where the fleet of Eumenes provided
sufficient service.

27. Their provisions by now completely exhausted, the
Romans set off from Samos to look for supplies and were
preparing to cross to Chios (this served as a granary for
the Romans and was a place to which all transport vessels
sent from Italy directed their course). They sailed around
from the city[99] to the other side of the island, which faces
north toward Chios and Erythrae,[100] and as they were preparing to make the crossing the praetor was informed by
dispatch that a large quantity of grain had reached Chios
from Italy but that the ships carrying wine had been held
up by bad weather. Along with this came news that the
people of Teos[101] had liberally supplied the king's fleet

regiae classi commeatus benigne praebuisse, quinque milia vasorum vini esse pollicitos. Teum ex medio cursu classem repente avertit, aut volentibus iis usurus commeatu
4 parato hostibus, aut ipsos pro hostibus habiturus. cum
derexissent ad terram proras, quindecim ferme eis naves
circa Myonnesum apparuerunt, quas primo ex classe regia
praetor esse ratus institit sequi; apparuit deinde piraticos
5 celoces et lembos esse. Chiorum maritimam oram depopulati, cum omnis generis praeda revertentes postquam
videre ex alto classem, in fugam verterunt. et celeritate
superabant levioribus et ad id fabrefactis navigiis, et pro-
6 piores terrae erant; itaque priusquam adpropinquaret
classis, Myonnesum perfugerunt, unde se e portu ratus
abstracturum naves, ignarus loci sequebatur praetor.
7   Myonnesus promunturium inter Teum Samumque est.
ipse collis est in modum metae in acutum cacumen a
fundo satis lato fastigatus; a continenti artae semitae aditum habet, a mari exesae fluctibus rupes claudunt, ita ut
quibusdam locis superpendentia saxa plus in altum quam
8 quae in statione sunt naves promineant. circa ea adpropinquare non ausae naves, ne sub ictu superstantium rupibus
9 piratarum essent, diem trivere. tandem sub noctem vano
incepto cum abstitissent, Teum postero die accessere, et
in portu qui ab tergo urbis est—Geraesticum ipsi appellant—navibus constitutis, praetor ad depopulandum circa
urbem agrum emisit milites.

---

[102] *Barr.* 61 D1.

with provisions, and had promised 5,000 jars of wine. In midjourney Aemilius suddenly turned the fleet toward Teos, intending to take over, with the Teans' assent, the supplies prepared for the enemy or else to treat the Teans themselves as enemies. After they turned their prows landward, some fifteen ships appeared before them off Myonnesus[102] and the praetor, initially believing them to be from the king's fleet, proceeded to give chase. But it then became clear that they were the cutters and skiffs of buccaneers. They had been raiding the coastline of Chios and were returning with all manner of plunder; and when they saw the Roman fleet from the open sea they turned to flight. They had the advantage of speed with their lighter vessels (expressly built for that) and they were also closer to land. As a result, they made good their escape to Myonnesus before the fleet could get near them. The praetor, having no knowledge of the area, began to follow them, thinking he would force the ships out of the harbor.

Myonnesus is a promontory lying between Teos and Samos, and is actually a cone-shaped hill rising from a rather broad base to a sharp peak. On the landward side it is accessible by a narrow pathway, and on the seaward side it terminates with cliffs eroded by the waves, so that in places the overhanging rocks jut out to sea beyond vessels at anchor there. The ships did not venture to approach land in that area in case they came within weapon range of the pirates, who were standing on the cliffs above them, and so they frittered away a day. Finally, with approach of night, they abandoned their abortive enterprise and moved on to Teos the following day. They moored their ships in the harbor behind the town—the local people call it Geraesticus—and the praetor sent his men forth to pillage the countryside around the city.

28. Teii, cum in oculis populatio esset, oratores cum
infulis et velamentis ad Romanum miserunt. quibus purgantibus civitatem omnis facti dictique hostilis adversus
2 Romanos, et iuvisse eos omni commeatu[47] classem hostium arguit, et quantum vini Polyxenidae promisissent;
quae si eadem Romanae classi darent, revocaturum se a
populatione milites; si minus, pro hostibus eos habiturum.
3 hoc tam triste responsum cum rettulissent legati, vocatur
in contionem a magistratibus populus, ut quid agerent
consultarent.
4 Eo forte die Polyxenidas cum regia classe a Colophone
profectus, postquam movisse a Samo Romanos audivit et
ad Myonnesum piratas persecutos Teiorum agrum depo-
5 pulari, naves in Geraestico portu stare, ipse adversus
Myonnesum in insula—Macrin nautici vocant—ancoras
6 portu occulto iecit. inde ex propinquo explorans quid hostes agerent, primo in magna spe fuit quemadmodum
Rhodiam classem ad Samum circumsessis ad exitum faucibus portus expugnasset, sic et Romanam expugnaturum.
7 nec est dissimilis natura loci: promunturiis coeuntibus
inter se ita clauditur portus ut vix duae simul inde naves
8 possint exire. nocte[48] occupare fauces Polyxenidas in
animo habebat, et denis navibus ad promunturia stanti-

[47] omni commeatu *Bχ*: commeatu *Holk. Fr 2*
[48] nocte *Fr. 2*: inde nocte *Bχ*: media nocte *Damsté*

---

[103] Fillets (*infulae*) are headbands of wool worn by suppliants,
and the (usually olive) branches, wrapped in wool, are emblems
carried by them. Cf. 35.34.7.
[104] *Barr.* 61 D1.
[105] Cf. 11.7–12, above.

28. As the pillaging went on before their eyes, the people of Teos sent spokesmen to the Roman commander with the fillets and the branches of suppliants.[103] They attempted to exonerate their community of any hostility shown toward the Romans in either word or deed but Aemilius denounced them for the assistance they had given to the enemy fleet with all manner of provisions and for the quantity of wine they had promised Polyxenidas. He added that if they provided the Roman fleet with the same amounts he would recall his men from their marauding but otherwise would treat them as foes. When the envoys reported this harsh response, the people were summoned to a meeting by the magistrates to discuss what they should do.

Polyxenidas happened to have left Colophon with the king's fleet after hearing that the Romans had moved from Samos, had pursued the pirates to Myonnesus and were now pillaging the fields of the Teians while their ships were at anchor in the harbor of Geraesticus. On that day he happened to drop anchor in a sequestered harbor on an island opposite Myonnesus that seamen call Macris.[104] From there he examined from close at hand what his enemy was doing, and at first he had high hopes of defeating the Roman fleet by the same means as he had the Rhodian fleet at Samos when he had blockaded the narrow exit from the harbor.[105] The natural features of the place are not dissimilar: the harbor is so restricted by two promontories coming together that it is barely possible for two ships to exit at the same time. Polyxenidas planned to seize the harbor mouth at night; then, with ten ships stationed off each of the promontories in order to attack the enemy vessels side-on from both flanks as they came out, he

371

bus, quae ab utroque cornu in latera exeuntium navium
pugnarent, ex cetera classe, sicut ad Panhormum fecerat,
armatis in litora expositis, terra marique simul hostes op-
9 primere. quod non vanum ei consilium fuisset, ni cum Teii
facturos se imperata promisissent, ad accipiendos commeatus aptius visum esset Romanis in eum portum qui
10 ante urbem est classem transire. dicitur et Eudamus Rhodius uitium alterius portus ostendisse, cum forte duae
11 naves in arto ostio implicitos remos fregissent; et inter alia
id quoque movit praetorem ut traduceret classem, quod
ab terra periculum erat, haud procul inde Antiocho stativa
habente.

29. Traducta classe ad urbem ignaris omnibus, egressi
milites nautaeque sunt ad commeatus et vinum maxime
2 dividendum in naves, cum medio forte diei agrestis quidam ad praetorem adductus nuntiat alterum iam diem
classem stare ad insulam Macrin, et paulo ante visas quas-
3 dam moveri tamquam ad profectionem naves. re subita
perculsus praetor tubicines canere iubet, ut si qui per
agros palati essent redirent; tribunos in urbem mittit ad
4 cogendos milites nautasque in naves. haud secus quam in
repentino incendio aut capta urbe trepidatur, aliis in urbem currentibus ad suos revocandos aliis ex urbe naves
cursu repetentibus, incertisque clamoribus, quibus ipsis
tubae obstreperent, turbatis imperiis tandem concursum
5 ad naves est. vix suas quisque noscere aut adire prae tu-

would put ashore soldiers from the rest of the fleet, as he had at Panhormus, and crush the enemy with a simultaneous attack by land and sea. His plan would not have failed him but for the Romans' decision, when the Teians promised to meet their demands, that it was more convenient for the fleet to move to the harbor in front of the city in order to take on board the supplies. It is also said that the Rhodian Eudamus pointed out a defect in the other port when two ships happened to break off their oars that became entangled in the restricted harbor entrance. Among other factors that induced the praetor to transfer the fleet was the danger from the landward side, since Antiochus was encamped not far away.

29. The fleet was brought over to the city without anyone knowing and the soldiers and crews disembarked to distribute the supplies (the wine in particular) among the ships. Then it so happened that at about midday a peasant was brought to the praetor and he reported that a fleet had already been riding at anchor off the island of Macris for two days and that a short time ago a number of its ships appeared to be on the move, as if preparing to sail. Stunned by the unexpected news, the praetor ordered bugles sounded for the return of all those dispersed in the fields and sent the tribunes to the city to bring the soldiers and sailors together at the ships. The ensuing panic was like that caused by a sudden fire or the capture of a city, with some running to the city to fetch their comrades, and others swiftly heading back to the ships from town. And orders were muddled by the confused shouts, which were themselves being drowned out by the bugles; but they finally converged on the ships. It was only with difficulty that anyone could recognize or reach his own ship in the

multu poterat; trepidatumque cum periculo et in mari et
in terra foret, ni partibus divisis Aemilius cum praetoria
nave primus e portu in altum evectus, excipiens insequentes, suo quamque ordine in frontem instruxisset,

6 Eudamus Rhodiaque classis substitissent ad terram, ut et
sine trepidatione conscenderent, et ut quaeque parata esset exiret navis.

7   Ita et explicuere ordinem primae in conspectu praetoris, et coactum agmen ab Rhodiis est, instructaque acies,
velut cernerent regios, in altum processit. inter Myonnesum et Corycum promunturium erant, cum hostem con-

8 spexere. et regia classis, binis in ordinem navibus longo
agmine veniens, et ipsa aciem adversam explicuit laevo
tantum evecta cornu, ut amplecti et circuire dextrum

9 cornu Romanorum posset. quod ubi Eudamus, qui cogebat agmen, vidit, non posse aequare ordinem Romanos et
tantum non iam circuiri ab dextro cornu, concitat naves—
et erant Rhodiae longe omnium celerrimae tota classe—,
aequatoque cornu praetoriae navi, in qua Polyxenidas
erat, suam obiecit.

      30. Iam totis simul classibus ab omni parte pugna
conserta erat. ab Romanis octoginta naves pugnabant, ex
2 quibus Rhodiae duae et viginti erant; hostium classis un-
denonaginta navium fuit; maximae formae naves tres
hexeres habebat, duas hepteres. robore navium et virtute
militum Romani longe[49] praestabant, Rhodiae naves agili-

      [49] longe *Madvig*: longe R(h)odios *BχMg*: longe regias *ed.
Med. 1480*: longe regios *Perizonius*

melee; and the panic could have proved dangerous both on land and sea. Aemilius, however, dividing up duties, led the way from the port into open water with his flagship and, taking charge of the other ships that followed in his wake, set each in its place to form a line facing forward. Eudamus and the Rhodian fleet meanwhile stuck close to shore so that the men could board without disorder and every ship could exit when it was ready.

So it was that the foremost vessels formed up in line before the praetor's eyes and the rear was brought up by the Rhodians; and the whole column advanced into open water in battle formation as if they had the king's men in view. They were between Myonnesus and the promontory of Corycus when they sighted the enemy. The king's fleet, which was approaching in a long line two ships abreast, also formed up facing its foe and extended the left wing far enough for it to be able to overlap and surround the Roman right. Eudamus, who was bringing up the allied rear, saw that the Romans were unable to make their line equal in length to the king's and that they were on the verge of being surrounded on the right wing. Urging on his ships—and the Rhodian vessels were by far the swiftest in the entire fleet—he made the flank equal to the enemy's and then set his own ship in the path of the enemy flagship in which Polyxenidas was sailing.

30. By now battle had been joined everywhere at the same time by the entire fleets. On the Roman side eighty ships were engaged, twenty-two of them Rhodian. The enemy fleet comprised eighty-nine vessels and its largest were three with six banks of oars and two with seven. The Romans were far superior in the sturdiness of their vessels and the courage of their men, while the Rhodian ships

3 tate et arte gubernatorum et scientia remigum; maximo
tamen terrori hostibus fuere quae ignes prae se portabant,
et quod unum iis ad Panhormum circumventis saluti fue-
4 rat, id tum maximum momentum ad victoriam fuit. nam
metu ignis adversi regiae naves, ne prorae concurrerent,
cum declinassent, neque ipsae ferire rostro hostem pote-
5 rant, et obliquas se ipsae ad ictus praebebant, et si qua
concurrerat, obruebatur infuso igni, magisque ad incendium quam ad proelium trepidabant.
6   Plurimum tamen, quae solet, militum virtus in bello
valuit: mediam namque aciem hostium Romani cum rupissent, circumvecti ab tergo pugnantibus adversus Rhodios regiis sese obiecere; momentoque temporis et media
acies Antiochi et laevo cornu circumventae naves merge-
7 bantur. dextra pars integra sociorum magis clade quam
suo periculo terrebantur; ceterum postquam alias circum-
ventas praetoriam navem Polyxenidae relictis sociis vela
dantem videre, sublatis raptim dolonibus—et erat secundus petentibus Ephesum ventus—capessunt fugam, qua-
8 draginta duabus navibus in ea pugna amissis, quarum
decem tres captae in potestatem hostium venerunt, ceterae incensae aut demersae. Romanorum duae naves frac-
9 tae sunt, volneratae aliquot; Rhodia una capta memorabili
casu: nam cum rostro percussisset Sidoniam navem, an-
cora, ictu ipso excussa e nave sua, unco dente, velut ferrea

---

[106] Cf. 11.13, above.

were far superior in mobility, their helmsmen's skill and their oarsmen's proficiency. However, the ships that inspired the greatest terror in the enemy were those carrying fire before them, and what had proved their unique source of salvation when they were surrounded at Panhormus[106] was what now contributed most to their victory. Out of fear of the flames confronting them, the king's ships turned aside to prevent the prows colliding and were unable to strike the enemy with their beaks, while at the same time they exposed themselves to broadside ramming; and any ship that did engage was consumed by the fire that poured onto it—and the sailors were more in dread of the flames than they were of combat.

But, as usual, what counted most in the fighting was the soldiers' courage. After breaking the center of the enemy line, the Romans sailed around and attacked from the rear the king's ships that were engaging the Rhodians; and in a trice the center of Antiochus' line and the ships on the left flank were being surrounded and sunk. The right wing remained intact and the sailors were more frightened by the disaster that had overtaken their comrades than by the peril they faced themselves; but after they saw the other vessels surrounded and Polyxenidas' flagship abandoning their comrades and sailing off, they hurriedly raised their topsails—and there was a following wind for the journey to Ephesus—and took flight. They had lost 42 ships in that battle: thirteen had been captured and fallen into their enemy's hands, and the others had been burned or sunk. On the Roman side two ships were complete wrecks and a number disabled; and one Rhodian vessel was captured through an extraordinary mishap. After ramming a Sidonian ship with its beak, its anchor was flung out of the ship by the very force of the collision and

10   manu iniecta, adligavit alterius proram; inde tumultu
iniecto cum divellere se ab hoste cupientes inhiberent
Rhodii, tractum ancorale et implicitum remis latus alterum detersit; debilitatam ea ipsa quae icta cohaeserat
navis cepit. hoc maxime modo ad Myonnesum navali proelio pugnatum est.

      31. Quo territus Antiochus, quia possessione maris pul-
sus longinqua tueri diffidebat se posse, praesidium ab
Lysimachia, ne opprimeretur ibi ab Romanis, deduci
2   pravo, ut res ipsa postea docuit, consilio iussit. non enim
tueri solum Lysimachiam a primo impetu Romanorum
facile erat, sed obsidionem etiam tota hieme tolerare et
obsidentes quoque ad ultimam inopiam adducere extra-
hendo tempus, et interim spem pacis per occasionem
3   temptare. nec Lysimachiam tantum hostibus tradidit post
adversam navalem pugnam, sed etiam Colophonis obsi-
4   dione abscessit et Sardis recepit se; atque inde in Cappa-
dociam ad Ariarathen qui auxilia accerserent, et quocum-
que alio poterat ad copias contrahendas, in unum iam
consilium, ut acie dimicaret, intentus misit.

5   Regillus Aemilius post victoriam navalem profectus
Ephesum, derectis ante portum navibus, cum confessionem ultimam concessi maris hosti expressisset, Chium,

---

107 In Appian (*Syr.* 27) the episode of the anchor cable takes
precedence and contributes most to the allied victory. Briscoe
(2.333) suggests that the expression here (*hoc maxime modo*)
"perhaps indicates Livy's awareness that he may not have under-
stood Polybius properly at this point."   108 Ariarathes IV of
Cappadocia (ca. 220–164) was Antiochus' son-in-law and did send
him reinforcements at the battle of Magnesia (cf. 40.10, below)
and the following year also sent help to the Galatians against the
Romans (38.26.4).

this gripped the prow of the other ship with its fluke, just as if it were a grappling iron thrown at it. Panic ensued and the Rhodians backed water as they tried to break free of the enemy. The anchor cable was dragged along and, becoming entangled in the oars, it sheered them off one side of the ship. The disabled vessel was then captured by the very one with which it had become entangled after ramming it. Such, by and large,[107] was the action in the sea battle off Myonnesus.

31. Antiochus was terrified by this result because, deprived of his mastery of the sea, he had no confidence in his ability to defend his distant territories. He now ordered his garrison to be withdrawn from Lysimachia for fear of its being overrun there by the Romans—a foolish decision, as subsequent events demonstrated. It would have been easy for him not only to defend Lysimachia against the initial Roman offensive but also to sustain a winter-long siege and even reduce the blockading force to utter privation by letting the operation drag on (and meanwhile he could have explored prospects for peace as opportunities arose). After the naval defeat, he not only delivered Lysimachia to his enemies but also abandoned the siege of Colophon and retreated to Sardis. From there he sent men to Ariarathes in Cappadocia to fetch reinforcements,[108] and to any other place he could for the purpose of gathering troops, as he was now wholly committed to one aim: deciding the matter on the field of battle.

After his victory at sea Aemilius Regillus set sail for Ephesus. Here, lining up his ships before the harbor, he wrested from the enemy a final acknowledgment that they had ceded control of the sea, and then he sailed on to

LIVY

quo ante navale proelium cursum ab Samo intenderat,
6 navigat. ibi naves in proelio quassatas cum refecisset, L.
Aemilium Scaurum cum triginta navibus Hellespontum
ad exercitum traiciendum misit, Rhodios parte praedae et
7 spoliis navalibus decoratos domum redire iubet. Rhodii
impigre praevertere ad traiciendas copias consulis; atque
eo quoque functi officio, tum demum Rhodum rediere.
8   Classis Romana ab Chio Phocaeam traiecit. in sinu
maris intimo posita haec urbs est, oblonga forma: duum
milium et quingentorum passuum spatium murus amplec-
titur; coit deinde ex utraque parte in artiorem velut cu-
9 neum; Lamptera ipsi appellant. mille et ducentos passus
ibi latitudo patet; inde lingua in altum mille passuum ex-
currens medium fere sinum velut nota distinguit. ubi co-
haeret faucibus angustis, duos in utramque regionem
10 versos portus tutissimos habet: qui in meridiem vergit,
Naustathmon ab re appellant, quia ingentem vim navium
capit; alter prope ipsum Lamptera est.
     32. Hos portus tutissimos cum occupasset Romana
classis, priusquam aut scalis aut operibus moenia adgrederetur, mittendos censuit praetor qui principum ma-
gistratuumque animos temptarent. postquam obstinatos
2 vidit, duobus simul locis oppugnare est adortus. altera

---

109 Possibly a legate, though he had not held a senior magis-
tracy (see Briscoe 2.334–35).

110 Trophies from the naval engagement, such as the ramming
beaks from captured ships.

111 For Phocaea, cf. 36.43.11 note.

112 Λαμπτήρ, Greek for "beacon" or "lighthouse."

Chios, to which he had been headed when he left Samos before the naval battle. There he repaired the ships damaged in the engagement and sent Lucius Aemilius Scaurus[109] to the Hellespont with thirty ships to ferry the army across. The Rhodians he instructed to return home, honoring them with a portion of the booty and with the naval spoils.[110] Instead, they enthusiastically turned themselves to ferrying over the consul's forces and finally returned to Rhodes only after they had performed this additional task.

The Roman fleet crossed from Chios to Phocaea.[111] This city lies deep in a bay on the coast and is oblong in shape. It is surrounded by a wall two and a half miles long, and it tapers into a wedge shape at both ends; and local people call it Lampter.[112] The bay at this point has a width of 1,200 yards and from it a spit of land runs a mile into the sea, virtually splitting the bay down the middle like a line. At the point where it is joined to the mainland by a narrow isthmus it forms two very safe harbors facing in opposite directions. The one facing south is called Naustathmos[113] from the fact that it has the capacity to hold particularly large numbers of ships, and the other is close to Lampter itself.

32. The Roman fleet occupied these very safe harbors but before assaulting the city walls with scaling ladders or earthworks the praetor felt he should send a delegation to sound out the feelings of the leading citizens and magistrates. When he saw that they were intransigent, he proceeded with an attack at two points simultaneously. One

---

[113] Ναύσταθμος, Greek for "anchorage" or "harbor."

pars infrequens aedificiis erat; templa deum aliquantum tenebant loci; ea prius ariete admoto quatere muros tur-

3 resque coepit; dein cum eo multitudo occurreret ad defendendum, altera quoque parte admotus aries; et iam

4 utrimque sternebantur muri. ad quorum casum cum impetum Romani milites per ipsam stragem ruinarum face-

5 rent, alii scalis etiam ascensum in muros temptarent, adeo obstinate resistere oppidani ut facile appareret plus in armis et virtute quam in moenibus auxilii esse.

6 Coactus ergo periculo militum praetor receptui cani iussit, ne obiceret incautos furentibus desperatione ac

7 rabie. dirempto proelio, ne tum quidem ad quietem versi, sed undique omnes ad munienda et obmolienda quae rui-

8 nis strata erant concurrerunt. huic operi intentis supervenit Q. Antonius a praetore missus, qui castigata pertinacia eorum maiorem curam Romanis quam illis ostenderet

9 esse ne in perniciem urbis pugnaretur; si absistere furore vellent, potestatem iis dari eadem condicione qua prius C. Livi in fidem venissent se tradendi.

10 Haec cum audissent, quinque dierum spatio ad deliberandum sumpto, temptata interim spe auxilii ab Antiocho, postquam legati missi ad regem nihil in eo praesidii esse rettulerant, tum portas aperuerunt, pacti ne quid hostile paterentur.

---

114 Otherwise unknown.

115 Antiochus was at Sardis, some 160 miles away, so it would appear that the townspeople had negotiated a five-day cessation of hostilities to allow for a return journey of envoys.

area was not densely built up—temples of the gods took up much of the space—and it was here that Regillus first moved up the ram and began to batter the walls and turrets. Then, when large numbers rushed there to defend it, a ram was moved up at the other point and the walls were then being demolished in both locations. Where they collapsed, Roman soldiers attacked over the fallen masonry and others also tried to scale the walls with ladders. So stubbornly did the townspeople resist, however, that it was readily apparent that they received more aid from their arms and their courage than from their fortifications.

The praetor was therefore forced by the danger facing his men to have the retreat sounded as he feared to expose his unwary soldiers to men crazed with frenzied despair. Not even when the battle was interrupted did the townspeople stop to rest; instead they rushed off in all directions to strengthen defenses and fill the gaps where they had been demolished. While they were engaged in this operation, Quintus Antonius[114] approached them, sent by the praetor. He scolded them for their obstinacy and pointed out that the Romans were more concerned than they that the battle not end in the city's destruction. If they were willing to abandon their insane conduct, he said, they were offered the chance of surrendering on the same terms on which they had earlier capitulated to Gaius Livius.

Hearing this, the townspeople took a period of five days to deliberate and during that time tried to ascertain if there was any prospect of help from Antiochus.[115] However, when the envoys they had sent to the king brought word that no assistance was forthcoming, they opened their gates on the understanding that they not be treated as enemies.

11   Cum signa in urbem inferrentur et pronuntiasset praetor parci se deditis velle, clamor undique est sublatus indignum facinus esse, Phocaeenses, nunquam fidos socios,

12 semper infestos hostes, impune eludere. ab hac voce, velut
signo a praetore dato, ad diripiendam urbem passim dis-
currunt. Aemilius primo resistere et revocare, dicendo
captas non deditas diripi urbes, et in iis tamen imperatoris

13 non militum arbitrium esse. postquam ira et avaritia imperio potentiora erant, praeconibus per urbem missis liberos
omnes in forum ad se convenire iubet, ne violarentur; et
in omnibus quae ipsius potestatis fuerunt fides constitit

14 praetoris: urbem agrosque et suas leges iis restituit; et quia
hiemps iam appetebat, Phocaeae portus ad hibernandum
classi delegit.

33. Per idem fere tempus consuli, transgresso Aenio-
rum Maronitarumque fines, nuntiatur victam regiam classem ad Myonnesum relictamque a praesidio Lysimachiam

2 esse. id multo quam de navali victoria laetius fuit, utique
postquam eo venerunt, refertaque urbs omnium rerum
commeatibus velut in adventum exercitus praeparatis eos
excepit, ubi inopiam ultimam laboremque in obsidenda

3 urbe proposuerant sibi. paucos dies stativa habuere, impedimenta aegrique ut consequerentur, qui passim per om-

---

[116] Both of these Thracian coastal towns (Ainos: *Barr.* 51 G3;
Maroneia: F3) had Seleucid garrisons (cf. 60.7, below).

When the standards were carried into the city and the praetor had announced that he wanted the people spared since they had surrendered, the cry went up everywhere that it was a disgrace for Phocaeans to get off scot-free when they had always been implacable enemies and never loyal allies. After these words the men, as though on a signal from the praetor, scattered in all directions to plunder the city. Aemilius at first tried to stop them and call them back, saying that it was captured cities that were ransacked, not those that surrendered, and that in any case the decision lay with the general, not his men. But when their rage and greed proved stronger than his authority, he sent heralds throughout the city and ordered all free men to come to him in the forum to avoid maltreatment. And the praetor was true to his word in all that was subject to his control. He restored to them their city, their lands and their self-government; and because winter was now drawing on he chose the harbors of Phocaea as the winter base for his fleet.

33. At about this time the consul, who had passed through the territory of the Aenians and Maronians,[116] was brought the news that the king's fleet had been defeated off Myonnesus and that Lysimachia had been vacated by his garrison. The latter was far more pleasing news than that of the naval victory, especially after they reached there: the city that received them was well stocked with all manner of provisions, as if in preparation for the army's arrival, when they had imagined themselves facing extreme privation and hardship in blockading it. They encamped there a few days to allow the baggage to catch up with them as well as the sick, who, exhausted by their illnesses and the long march, had been left here and there

385

nia Thraciae castella, fessi morbis ac longitudine viae,
4 relicti erant. receptis omnibus, ingressi rursus iter, per
Chersonesum Hellespontum perveniunt. ubi omnibus
cura regis Eumenis ad traiciendum praeparatis, velut in
pacata litora nullo prohibente, aliis alio delatis navibus,
5 sine tumultu traiecere. ea vero res Romanis auxit animos,
concessum sibi transitum cernentibus in Asiam, quam rem
6 magni certaminis futuram crediderant. stativa deinde ad
Hellespontum aliquamdiu habuerunt, quia dies forte qui-
7 bus ancilia moventur religiosi ad iter inciderant. iidem
dies P. Scipionem propiore etiam religione, quia Salius
erat, diiunxerant ab exercitu; causaque et is ipse morae
erat, dum consequeretur.

34. Per eos forte dies legatus ab Antiocho in castra
venerat Byzantius Heraclides, de pace adferens mandata;
2 quam impetrabilem fore magnam ei spem attulit mora et
cunctatio Romanorum, quos, simul Asiam attigissent, ef-
3 fuso agmine ad castra regia ituros crediderat. statuit tamen non prius consulem adire quam P. Scipionem, et ita
mandatum a rege erat. in eo maximam spem habebat,

---

117 The Thracian Chersonese (the Gallipoli peninsula).

118 Livy refers to an ancient ceremony performed on March
1 to inaugurate the festival of Mars, when the Salian priests took
from the Regia twelve bronze shields (returning them on March
24 at the end of the festival). One of them had purportedly fallen
from the sky during Numa's reign, and as Rome's survival depended on its preservation, eleven others were made to conceal
its identity (cf. *OCD* s.v. Salii). Livy, however, apparently misunderstood Polybius (21.13.10–14) here. The interdiction was not
against armies marching but against a Salian priest changing
residence in this period, so only Scipio's functions as a Salian
delayed the army.

in strongholds throughout Thrace. After recovering all of them, they resumed the march and made their way to the Hellespont through the Chersonese.[117] There, thanks to the efforts of King Eumenes, all had been prepared for the passage over, and they made an orderly crossing to what seemed like pacified shores, meeting no opposition and their ships sailing to different parts of the coast. This fact actually raised the confidence of the Romans: they could see that they had been allowed a crossing to Asia, something they had believed would involve heavy fighting. They remained in camp on the Hellespont for some time because the days of the moving of the shields—when there is a religious injunction against traveling—happened to have come round. Those same days had also separated Publius Scipio from the army as the religious obligations touched him more personally because he was a Salian priest; and he too caused delay for the army until he caught up.[118]

34.[119] As it happened, Heraclides of Byzantium had at that time come to the camp as an emissary from Antiochus bearing instructions for peace negotiations. He was led to high hopes of success by the fact that the Romans, whom he had expected to make for the king's encampment at a rapid pace as soon as they reached Asia, were in fact taking their time and delaying matters. Heraclides decided to approach Publius Scipio first rather than the consul, and such had been his orders from the king. It was in Scipio

[119] For chapters 34 to 36, cf. Polyb. 21.13–15 (Walbank 3.105–8).

praeterquam quod et magnitudo animi et satietas gloriae
4 placabilem eum maxime faciebat, notumque erat gentibus
qui victor ille in Hispania qui deinde in Africa fuisset,
etiam quod filius eius captus in potestate regis erat.
5 Is ubi et quando et quo casu captus sit, sicut pleraque
alia, parum inter auctores constat. alii principio belli, a
Chalcide Oreum petentem, circumventum ab regiis navi-
6 bus tradunt; alii postquam transitum in Asiam est, cum
turma Fregellana missum exploratum ad regia castra, effuso obviam equitatu cum reciperet sese, in eo tumultu
delapsum ex equo cum duobus equitibus oppressum, ita
7 ad regem deductum esse. illud satis constat si pax cum
populo Romano maneret hospitiumque privatim regi cum
Scipionibus esset, neque liberalius neque benignius haberi colique adulescentem quam cultus est potuisse.
8 Ob haec cum adventum P. Scipionis legatus exspectasset, ubi is venit, consulem adit petitque ut mandata audi-
ret.
35. Advocato frequenti consilio legati verba sunt au-
2 dita. is, multis ante legationibus ultro citroque nequiquam
de pace missis, eam ipsam fiduciam impetrandi sibi esse
dixit quod priores legati nihil impetrassent: Zmyrnam
enim et Lampsacum et Alexandriam Troadem et Lysima-

that Antiochus placed his greatest hopes. Apart from the fact that the man's magnanimity and having had more than enough glory made him particularly forgiving, and that the world knew the kind of victor he had been in Spain and subsequently in Africa, his son was also a prisoner of war in the king's hands.

There is, as often, little agreement among the authorities on where, when and in what circumstances the son was taken prisoner. Some say that he was intercepted by the king's ships while making for Oreus from Chalcis at the start of the war. Others claim that his capture dates to a time after the crossing to Asia, when he had been sent on a reconnaissance mission toward the king's camp with a Fregellan squadron. Some enemy cavalry rushed out to confront him and while he was beating a retreat he fell from his horse in the melee and was overpowered together with two cavalrymen and taken to the king. On one thing there is general agreement: had a state of peace still existed then between the king and the Roman people and had there been personal ties of hospitality between him and the Scipios the young man could not have received kinder and more considerate treatment than he did.

It was for these reasons that the emissary had awaited the arrival of Publius Scipio and when he came he approached the consul and asked him to hear the instructions he had been given.

35. A full meeting was convened, and the emissary given a hearing. Many delegations had previously gone to and fro in search of peace, he said, but without success; and yet he felt confident of gaining a treaty precisely because those previous embassies had achieved nothing. For, he explained, Smyrna, Lampsacus, Alexandria Troas

chiam in Europa iactatas in illis disceptationibus esse;
3 quarum Lysimachia iam cessisse regem, ne quid habere
eum in Europa dicerent; eas quae in Asia sint civitates
tradere paratum esse, et si quas alias Romani, quod suarum partium fuerint, vindicare ab imperio regio velint;
4 impensae quoque in bellum factae partem dimidiam regem praestaturum populo Romano.
5 Hae condiciones erant pacis; reliqua oratio fuit ut memores rerum humanarum et suae fortunae moderarentur
6 et alienam ne urgerent. finirent Europa imperium, id quoque immensum esse; et parari singula acquirendo facilius
7 potuisse quam universa teneri posse; quod si Asiae quoque partem aliquam abstrahere velint, dummodo non
dubiis regionibus finiant, vinci suam temperantiam Romana cupiditate pacis et concordiae causa regem passurum.
Ea, quae legato magna ad pacem impetrandam vide-
8 bantur, parva Romanis visa: nam et impensam quae in
bellum facta esset omnem praestare regem aequum cen-
9 sebant, cuius culpa bellum excitatum esset, et non Ionia
10 modo atque Aeolide deduci debere regia praesidia, sed
sicut Graecia omnis liberata esset, ita quae in Asia sint
omnes liberari urbes; id aliter fieri non posse quam ut cis
Taurum montem possessione Asiae Antiochus cedat.
36. Legatus postquam nihil aequi in consilio impetrare

---

120 In Polybius (21.14.2) "Lampsacus, Smyrna and Alexandria, and such other cities of Aeolis and Ionia as had made common cause with Rome" (Loeb trans.).

121 There is nothing corresponding to this in Polybius.

122 The comparison of Greece and Asia is also absent from
Polybius.

and, in Europe, Lysimachia had been contested items in those discussions. In the case of those, the king had already withdrawn from Lysimachia so they could not say that he had possessions in Europe; and he was ready to surrender the cities in Asia and any others they might wish to claim from the king's empire[120] on the grounds that they were supporters of the Roman cause. Furthermore, the king would pay the Roman people half the costs of the war.

Such were his peace-terms. The rest of his address was spent urging the Romans to remember the human condition and be circumspect with regard to their own fortunes and not deal harshly with those of others. He asked them to limit their empire to Europe. Even this was immense, and conquering it bit by bit had been an easier matter than holding the whole could be.[121] But if the Romans wished to take away some part of Asia, too, he continued, he would allow his own moderation to be overcome by Roman acquisitiveness just for the sake of peace and concord—provided that they clearly defined the territorial limits.

What seemed to the emissary like important concessions for obtaining peace seemed insignificant to the Romans. Even with regard to the expenses for the war, they thought it only fair that the king should cover them all since it was through his fault that the war had broken out; and it was not only from Ionia and Aeolis that the king's garrisons must be withdrawn—just as all Greece had been liberated, so too all cities lying in Asia should be liberated.[122] And this could be done only by Antiochus ceding possession of Asia west of the Taurus range.

36. When the emissary thought that he was getting no favorable response in the council, he attempted to sound

se censebat, privatim—sic enim imperatum erat—P. Sci-
2 pionis temptare animum est conatus. omnium primum
filium ei sine pretio redditurum regem dixit; deinde ignarus et animi Scipionis et moris Romani, auri pondus ingens pollicitus, et nomine tantum regio excepto societatem omnis regni, si per eum pacem impetrasset.

3 Ad ea Scipio: "quod Romanos omnes, quod me, ad
quem missus es, ignoras, minus miror, cum te fortunam
4 eius a quo venis ignorare cernam. Lysimachia tenenda
erat, ne Chersonesum intraremus, aut ad Hellespontum
obsistendum, ne in Asiam traiceremus, si pacem tamquam
5 ab sollicitis de belli eventu petituri eratis; concesso vero
in Asiam transitu, et non solum frenis sed etiam iugo accepto, quae disceptatio ex aequo, cum imperium patien-
6 dum sit, relicta est? ego ex munificentia regia maximum
donum filium habebo; aliis, deos precor, ne unquam for-
7 tuna egeat mea; animus certe non egebit. pro tanto in me
munere gratum me in se esse sentiet, si privatam gratiam
pro privato beneficio desiderabit; publice nec habebo
8 quicquam ab illo nec dabo. quod in praesentia dare pos-
sim, fidele consilium est. abi, nuntia meis verbis, bello
absistat, pacis condicionem nullam recuset."

9 Nihil ea moverunt regem, tutam fore belli aleam ra-

out Publius Scipio's feelings in private (for such had been his instructions). The very first thing he said to him was that the king would restore his son without ransom. Then, unfamiliar with Scipio's personality and the Roman character, he promised him an enormous amount of gold and partnership in Antiochus' entire kingdom—the royal title alone excepted—if he succeeded in gaining peace through Scipio's intervention.

In reply Scipio said: "Your ignorance of the Romans in general and of me, the man to whom you have been sent, I find the less surprising when I observe your ignorance of the fortunes of the man from whom you come. You should have held on to Lysimachia to prevent us entering the Chersonese or you should have opposed us at the Hellespont to prevent our crossing to Asia—that is, if you intended to seek peace terms from a foe whom you expected to be worried about the outcome of the war. But after allowing us passage into Asia and after accepting not just our reins but our yoke as well, what room is left for negotiations on equal terms when you must submit to our authority? Personally, I shall regard my son as the greatest gift forthcoming from your king's generosity. As for his other presents, I pray to heaven that my fortune may never have need of them—my heart, at least, will not need them. For so great a service to me he shall find me grateful to him—if he wants personal gratitude for a personal gift. In my official capacity I shall accept nothing from him and I shall give nothing. What I can give him at the moment is some honest advice. Go and tell him this from me: he should give up the war and refuse no terms of peace."

These comments did nothing to sway the king, who felt that war would now be a safe bet since terms were already

tum, quando perinde ac victo iam sibi leges dicerentur. omissa igitur in praesentia mentione pacis, totam curam in belli apparatum intendit.

37. Consul, omnibus praeparatis ad proposita exsequenda, cum ex stativis movisset, Dardanum primum, deinde Rhoeteum, utramque civitatem obviam effusam,[50]
2 venit. inde Ilium processit, castrisque in campo qui est
3 subiectus moenibus positis, in urbem arcemque cum escendisset, sacrificavit Mineruae praesidi arcis, et Iliensibus in omni rerum verborumque honore ab se oriundos Romanos praeferentibus, et Romanis laetis origine sua.

Inde profecti sextis castris ad caput Caici amnis pervenerunt. eo et Eumenes rex, primo conatus ab Hellesponto
4 reducere classem in hiberna Elaeam, adversis deinde ventis cum aliquot diebus superare Lecton promunturium non potuisset, in terram egressus, ne deesset principiis rerum, qua proximum fuit in castra Romana cum parva
5 manu contendit. ex castris Pergamum remissus ad commeatus expediendos, tradito frumento quibus iusserat consul, in eadem stativa rediit. inde plurium dierum praeparatis cibariis consilium erat ire ad hostem, priusquam hiemps opprimeret.

---

[50] utramque civitatem . . . effusam (*fort.* effusa B) Bχ: utraque civitate . . . effusa *ed. Rom.*

---

[123] That is, he had nothing to lose by going to war, since in the event of his losing the terms could not be harsher.

[124] *Barr.* 51 G4 (Rhoeteion).

[125] Cf. 9.7, above.

[126] Rome's Trojan ancestry was by now well established in legend.

being dictated to him as if he were defeated.[123] For the moment he set aside talk of peace and focused his attention entirely on preparing for war.

37. When all was ready for carrying through his plans, the consul moved from his base camp and came first to Dardanus, then to Rhoeteum;[124] and the people of both communities poured out to meet him. From there he advanced to Ilium, and encamped in the plain beneath its walls. He went up to the city and its citadel, and sacrificed to Minerva,[125] protectress of the citadel, while the people of Ilium acknowledged the Romans as their descendants by showing them every mark of respect in their words and actions, and the Romans expressed their happiness with their ancestry.[126]

Setting off from there, they reached the source of the River Caecus[127] after five days' march. King Eumenes also came to this area. He had attempted to bring his fleet back from the Hellespont to winter quarters in Elaea but then, facing contrary winds, had been unable to round the promontory of Lecton[128] for several days; and so, not to miss the early stages of the campaign, he disembarked and with a small detachment hurried to the Roman camp by the shortest route. He was sent back to Pergamum from the camp to organize provisions and, after delivering grain to the people specified by the consul, he returned to the same base camp. The plan was to prepare several days' worth of rations and head out against the enemy from there before winter overtook them.

[127] On the source of the Caecus, cf. 18.6 and note, above.
[128] At the southwest tip of the Troad: *Barr.* 56 C3.

6   Regia castra circa Thyatiram erant. ubi cum audisset Antiochus P. Scipionem aegrum Elaeam delatum, legatos
7   qui filium ad eum reducerent misit. non animo solum patrio gratum munus, sed corpori quoque salubre gau-
8   dium fuit; satiatusque tandem complexu filii "renuntiate" inquit "gratias regi me agere, referre aliam gratiam nunc non posse quam ut suadeam ne ante in aciem descendat quam in castra me redisse audierit."

9   Quamquam sexaginta milia peditum, plus duodecim milia equitum animos interdum ad spem certaminis facie-bant, motus tamen Antiochus tanti auctoritate viri, in quo ad incertos belli eventus omnis fortunae posuerat sub-sidia, recepit se et transgressus Phrygium amnem circa
10   Magnesiam, quae ad Sipylum est, posuit castra; et ne, si extrahere tempus vellet, munimenta Romani temptarent, fossam sex cubita altam duodecim latam cum duxisset,
11   extra duplex vallum fossae circumdedit, interiore labro murum cum turribus crebris obiecit, unde facile arceri transitu fossae hostis posset.

    38. Consul circa Thyatiram esse regem ratus, continuis itineribus quinto die ad Hyrcanium[51] campum descendit.
2   inde cum profectum audisset, secutus vestigia citra Phry-
3   gium amnem, quattuor milia ab hoste posuit castra. eo mille ferme equites—maxima pars Gallograeci erant, et

---

[51] Hycanium *Bχ*: Hyrcanum *α*

---

[129] A very odd suggestion, as Scipio cannot be saying that his own presence at the battle would tilt it in Antiochus' favor. How-ever, Scipio's gratitude for his son's return would in fact figure in the accusations made against him in the following years.

[130] River Phrygius: *Barr.* 56 F4; Magnesia ad Sipylum: E4.

The king's camp was in the neighborhood of Thyatira. Here Antiochus heard that Publius Scipio had fallen ill and been taken to Elaea and he sent a delegation to take his son back to him. This was not just a gift pleasing to the father's heart—his joy was also beneficial to his bodily health. When he had eventually embraced the son to his heart's content, he said: "Report to the king that I thank him but cannot reciprocate in any other way than by urging him not to take the field until he hears that I have returned to camp."[129]

Although his 60,000 infantry and a cavalry force of more than 12,000 occasionally gave him confidence for the battle, Antiochus was moved by the great man's authority; and he had pinned all his hopes on him for help, come what may, as he faced the vicissitudes of war. He therefore withdrew and, crossing the River Phrygius, pitched camp in the area of Magnesia-near-Sipylus.[130] To prevent a Roman assault on his fortifications if he decided to delay matters, he dug a ditch six cubits deep and twelve cubits wide and then surrounded the ditch on the outside with a double rampart. On its inner edge of he raised a wall, with turrets at short intervals, by which the enemy could be easily prevented from crossing the ditch.

38. Supposing the king to be in the vicinity of Thyatira, the consul came down to the Hyrcanian plain by forced marches four days later. When he heard that Antiochus had left, he followed in his tracks on the west side of the River Phrygius and encamped four miles from the enemy. Here about a thousand enemy cavalry crossed the river— they were Galatians for the most part, but with a number

Dahae quidam aliarumque gentium sagittarii equites in-
termixti—tumultuose amni traiecto in stationes impetum
4 fecerunt. primo turbaverunt incompositos; dein, cum longius certamen fieret et[52] Romanorum ex propinquis castris
facili subsidio cresceret numerus, regii, fessi iam et plures
non sustinentes recipere se conati, circa ripam amnis,
priusquam flumen ingrederentur, ab instantibus tergo aliquot interfecti sunt.

5   Biduum deinde silentium fuit, neutris transgredienti-
bus amnem; tertio post die Romani simul omnes transgressi sunt, et duo milia fere et quingentos passus ab hoste
6 posuerunt castra. metantibus et muniendo occupatis tria
milia delecta equitum peditumque regiorum magno ter-
7 rore ac tumultu advenere; aliquanto pauciores in statione
erant; hi tamen per se, nullo a munimento castrorum milite avocato, et primo aequum proelium sustinuerunt, et
crescente certamine pepulerunt hostes, centum ex iis oc-
8 cisis centum ferme captis. per quadriduum insequens
instructae utrimque acies pro vallo stetere; quinto die
9 Romani processere in medium campi; Antiochus nihil
promovit signa, ita ut extremi minus mille pedes a vallo
abessent.

    39. Consul postquam detractari certamen vidit, postero
die in consilium advocavit, quid sibi faciendum esset, si
Antiochus pugnandi copiam non faceret: instare hiemem;

---

[52] et Romanorum *Duker*: Romanorum *B*χ: Romanorumque
Holk. 353

of Dahae and mounted archers from other races among them—and made a tumultuous attack on their forward posts. Since they were not in formation, the enemy at first threw them into confusion; but then, as the battle progressed and Roman numbers increased, with reinforcements easily brought up from the camp nearby, the king's men tired and were unable to cope with the greater numbers. They tried to pull back but before they could make it into the river a number were cut down close to the riverbank by the Romans, who were putting pressure on their rear.

There followed two days of inactivity, with neither side crossing the river; but on the third the Romans all crossed together and pitched camp about two and a half miles from the enemy. They were measuring out the camp and preoccupied with fortifying it when 3,000 elite cavalry and infantry of the king appeared, creating great panic and uproar. The men at the Roman forward post were considerably outnumbered but through their own efforts, and without calling any soldiers away from fortifying the camp, they at first managed to keep the battle even; and as the fighting intensified they drove the enemy back, killing 100 and taking about 100 prisoners. In the four days that followed both lines stood drawn up before their ramparts; and on the fifth day the Romans advanced to the center of the plain. Antiochus did not move his standards forward at all, so that his men at the rear were less than one thousand feet from their rampart.

39. When the consul saw the enemy refusing to engage, he called a meeting the following day to discuss what he should do if Antiochus gave them no opportunity to fight. Winter was coming on, he said, and either the troops

2 aut sub pellibus habendos milites fore, aut si concedere in
hiberna vellet, differendum esse in aestatem bellum.

3   Nullum unquam hostem Romani aeque contempse-
runt. conclamatum undique est, duceret extemplo et ute-
4 retur ardore militum, qui tamquam non pugnandum cum
tot milibus hostium, sed par numerus pecorum trucidan-
dus esset, per fossas per vallum castra invadere parati
5 erant, si in proelium hostis non exiret. Cn. Domitius ad
explorandum iter, et qua parte adiri vallum hostium posset, missus, postquam omnia certa rettulit, postero die
propius admoveri castra placuit; tertio signa in medium
6 campi prolata et instrui acies coepta est. nec Antiochus
ultra tergiversandum ratus, ne et suorum animos minueret
detractando certamen et hostium spem augeret, et ipse
copias eduxit, tantum progressus a castris ut dimicaturum
appareret.

7   Romana acies unius prope formae fuit et hominum et
armorum genere. duae legiones Romanae, duae alae[53]
sociorum ac Latini nominis erant; quina milia et quadringe-
8 nos singulae habebant. Romani mediam aciem cornua
Latini tenuerunt; hastatorum prima signa, dein principum
9 erant, triarii postremos[54] claudebant. extra hanc velut ius-

    [53] duae alae *Crév.*: duae *B*χ

    [54] postremos *B*χ: postremo *Huschke*: postremos ordines *Watt*:
postremam aciem *coni. Briscoe*

---

    [131] That is, two days after the meeting (inclusive counting).

    [132] On the expression, cf. 35.7. 5 note.

    [133] The legion usually numbered fewer than 5,000 men.

    [134] On the composition of the legion at this time, cf. Introduc-
tion to vol. IX (LCL 295), lix–lxv.

would have to be billeted in tents or, if he decided to retire to winter quarters, the campaign would have to be deferred till the summer.

No enemy was ever regarded with such disdain by the Romans. The cry went up on all sides that he should lead them out at once and exploit the fervor of his men who, feeling now that what faced them was not fighting with so many thousands of the enemy but slaughtering so many cattle, were ready to cross ditches and a rampart to reach their camp if the enemy did not come out to fight. Gnaeus Domitius was sent to inspect the path and the direction from which the enemy rampart could be approached and after he came back with a full and reliable report it was decided that the camp should be moved closer to the enemy the next day. On the third day[131] the standards were advanced to the center of the plain, and the deployment of the battle line began. Antiochus also felt he should evade the issue no longer in case his refusal to engage weakened the morale of his men and also raised the hopes of the enemy. He, too, led out his forces, advancing so far from his camp as to make it clear that he intended to fight.

The Roman battle line was more or less uniform in terms both of men and weaponry. There were two Roman legions, and two units of allies and men with Latin rights.[132] Each of these bodies comprised 5,400 men.[133] The Romans formed the center, the Latins the wings. The front line was made up of *hastati,* after which came the *principes,* and the *triarii* brought up the rear.[134] Apart from this

tam aciem a parte dextra consul Achaeorum caetratis im-
mixtos auxiliares Eumenis, tria milia ferme peditum, aequata fronte instruxit; ultra eos equitum minus tria milia
opposuit, ex quibus Eumenis octingenti, reliquus omnis
10 Romanus equitatus erat; extremos Trallis et Cretenses—
11 quingentorum utrique numerum explebant—statuit. laevum cornu non videbatur egere obiectis talibus auxiliis,
quia flumen ab ea parte ripaeque deruptae claudebant;
quattuor tamen inde turmae equitum oppositae.

12   Haec summa copiarum erat Romanis, et duo milia mix-
torum Macedonum Thracumque, qui voluntate secuti
13 erant; hi praesidio castris relicti sunt. sedecim elephantos
post triarios in subsidio locaverunt; nam praeterquam
quod multitudinem regiorum elephantorum—erant autem quattuor et quinquaginta—sustinere non videbantur
posse, ne pari quidem numero Indicis Africi resistunt, sive
quia magnitudine—longe enim illi praestant—sive robore
animorum vincuntur.

40. Regia acies varia magis multis gentibus, dissimili-
tudine armorum auxiliorumque erat. decem et sex milia
peditum more Macedonum armati fuere, qui phalangitae
appellabantur. haec media acies fuit, in fronte in decem

---

135 Men armed with the *caetra,* a light leather-covered shield
(at 28.5.11 Livy compares it with the *pelta,* a light shield used
originally by the Thracians; cf. also 31.36.1).

136 An Illyrian tribe (cf. 31.35.1, 33.4.4, 38.21.2), but nothing
is known of them. Strabo (14.1.42) refers to "Thracian Trallians"
as founders of the city of Tralles in Asia Minor.

137 This was the usual view of the ancients. The modern African elephant is larger than the Indian, but the African elephant
used by the Romans may have been the forest elephant, which
was smaller: cf. Walbank 1.614 (Polyb. 5.84.2–7).

"regular" battle formation, the consul also set on the right flank, lined up with the legions, Eumenes' auxiliaries combined with a number of Achaean *caetrati*,[135] some 3,000 infantrymen in all. Beyond these he positioned as protection fewer than 3,000 cavalry, 800 of them Eumenes' soldiers and all the rest Roman horsemen. On the outer flank he placed the Trallians[136] and Cretans, both of them numbering 500 men. The left wing appeared not to require such an auxiliary force deployed against the enemy because, on that side, the river and its steep banks afforded cover, but four cavalry squadrons were stationed there for protection just the same.

Such was the sum of the Roman troops, and there was also a combined force of 2,000 Macedonians and Thracians who had come along with them as volunteers; these were left to guard the camp. The Romans placed sixteen elephants in reserve to the rear of the *triarii*. It was evident that they could not stand up to the superior number of the king's elephants—there were fifty-four of them—and apart from that African elephants are no match for Indian[137] elephants even when numbers are the same, because they are inferior either in terms of size (the Indian animals are much larger) or in fortitude.

40. The king's line of battle was more diverse, composed as it was of many races with different weaponry and different supporting troops. There were 16,000 infantry called *phalangitae* who were armed in Macedonian fashion.[138] They formed the center of the line, and were divided into ten sections in front. The king separated the

[138] Many would have been Greeks or Macedonians, but what distinguished them as *phalangitae* was their armor, especially the *sarissa* (cf. 36.18.2, where they are called *sarisophori*).

2 partes divisa; partes eas interpositis binis elephantis distinguebat; a fronte introrsus in duos et triginta ordines

3 armatorum acies patebat. hoc et roboris in regiis copiis erat, et perinde cum alia specie tum eminentibus tantum inter armatos elephantis magnum terrorem praebebat.

4 ingentes ipsi erant; addebant speciem frontalia et cristae et tergo impositae turres, turribusque superstantes prae-

5 ter rectorem quaterni armati. ad latus dextrum phalangitarum mille et quingentos Gallograecorum pedites opposuit. his tria milia equitum loricatorum—cataphractos ipsi appellant—adiunxit. addita his ala mille ferme equitum;

6 agema eam vocabant; Medi erant, lecti viri, et eiusdem regionis mixti multarum gentium equites. continens his

7 grex sedecim elephantorum est oppositus in subsidiis. ab eadem parte, paulum producto cornu, regia cohors erat;

8 argyraspides a genere armorum appellabantur; Dahae deinde, equites sagittarii, mille et ducenti; tum levis armatura trium milium, pari ferme numero, pars Cretenses pars Tralles; duo milia et quingenti Mysi sagittarii his

9 adiuncti erant; extremum cornu claudebant quattuor milia, mixti Cyrtii funditores et Elymaei sagittarii.

10 Ab laevo cornu phalangitis adiuncti erant Gallograeci pedites mille et quingenti et similiter his armati duo milia

11 Cappadocum—ab Ariarathe missi erant regi—; inde auxi-

---

139 Cf. 35.48.3 and note.

140 This was the name of the elite corps of cavalry in Macedonian armies. The unit's strength (one thousand) may date back to the military reforms of Alexander the Great, who introduced "chiliarchies" (possibly on the Persian model) later in his campaign.   141 "Silver shields."

sections with pairs of elephants set between them. From the front this grouping extended backward thirty-two ranks deep. This was the main strength of the king's forces and it inspired great fear by its general appearance in the first place, but also because of the elephants that towered so high among the soldiers. The beasts were huge themselves and were made the more striking by their ornaments and crests and by towers set on their backs, with four armed men plus the driver standing in each of them. To the right of the *phalangitae* the king stationed 1,500 Galatian infantry. Next to them he placed 3,000 mail-clad cavalry that the Syrians themselves call *cataphracti*.[139] Added to these was a squadron of some 1,000 cavalry (this they called an *agema*[140]). These were Medes, handpicked men, with an admixture of cavalry from many races in the same region. Close to them, and kept in reserve, was placed a herd of sixteen elephants. On the same side, where the wing was extended a little, was the royal company; they were called *argyraspids*[141] from the sort of arms they bore. Next came the Dahae, 1,200, mounted archers; then the light infantry, 3,000 strong, made up of Cretans and Trallians in roughly equal numbers; and attached to these were 2,500 Mysian bowmen. The far end of the flank was composed of a mixture of Cyrtian slingers and Elymaean archers, totaling 4,000 men.

On the left wing the *phalangitae* were flanked by 1,500 Galatian infantry and 2,000 Cappadocians with arms similar to theirs (these had been sent to the king by Ariarathes[142]). After them came a mixture of all kinds of

[142] Cf. 31.4 note, above.

liares mixti omnium generum, duo milia septingenti, et
tria milia cataphractorum equitum et mille alii equites,
regia ala levioribus tegumentis suis equorumque, alio
haud dissimili habitu; Syri plerique erant Phrygibus et
12 Lydis immixti. ante hunc equitatum falcatae quadrigae et
cameli quos appellant dromadas. his insidebant Arabes
sagittarii, gladios tenues habentes, longos quaterna cubita,
13 ut ex tanta altitudine contingere hostem possent. inde alia
multitudo, par ei quae in dextro cornu erat: primi Tarentini, deinde Gallograecorum equitum duo milia et quingenti, inde Neocretes mille, et eodem armatu Cares et
Cilices mille et quingenti, et totidem Tralles, et quattuor
milia caetratorum—Pisidae erant et Pamphylii et Lycii—.
14 tum Cyrtiorum et Elymaeorum paria in dextro cornu loca-
tis auxilia, et sedecim elephanti modico intervallo distan-
tes.

41. Rex ipse in dextro cornu erat; Seleucum filium et
Antipatrum fratris filium in laevo praeposuit; media acies
tribus permissa, Minnioni et Zeuxidi et Philippo, magistro
elephantorum.

---

143 These were taken over from the Persians but often proved
ineffective (as they were for Darius facing Alexander at Gau-
gamela) and, like elephants, were often merely "status symbols,"
more of a danger to their own side than to the enemy (as Livy
notes in the next chapter).

144 A type of cavalry: cf. 35.28.8 and note.

145 Probably from Knossos, but the term is disputed; cf. Walbank 1.540 (on Polyb. 5.3.1).

146 Antipater is referred to by Polybius (e.g., 5.79.12, 21.16–

auxiliary troops, totaling 2,700; then 3,000 mounted *cataphracti,* plus 1,000 other cavalrymen who formed the royal squadron (their own armor and that of their mounts were lighter, but otherwise they were outfitted not unlike the others). These were mostly Syrian, with an admixture of Phrygians and Lydians. Before this cavalry force there were scythed chariots[143] and the camels they call dromedaries. Riding these were Arab archers holding narrow-bladed swords that were four cubits in length so they could reach the enemy from their elevated position. After them came another horde equal in size to the one on the right wing: Tarentines[144] first of all, then 2,500 Galatian horse, followed by 1,000 Neocretans[145] and 15,000 similarly-armed Carians and Cilicians, the same number of Trallians and 4,000 *caetrati* (these were Pisidians, Pamphylians and Lycians). Then there were Cyrtian and Elymaean auxiliary forces in numbers equal to those stationed on the right wing, and 16 elephants a short distance from them.

41. The king himself was on the right wing; on the left he placed in command his son Seleucus and his brother's son Antipater.[146] The center of the line was assigned to three men: Minnio, Zeuxis, and Philip,[147] the master of the elephants.

17), but Antiochus' only brother (Seleucus III) had no son. Antipater was probably Antiochus' cousin rather than his nephew (cf. Briscoe ad loc.).

[147] For Minnio, cf. 35.15.7 and note. For Philip, an elephantarch at the battle of Raphia, cf. Walbank 1.611 (on Polyb. 5.82.8). Zeuxis is the best known of the three, as a leading general and courtier of Antiochus (cf. Walbank 2.503 [on Polyb. 16.1.8]). He had been *strategos* of Lydia since at least 205.

2   Nebula matutina, crescente die levata in nubes, caligi-
3   nem dedit; umor inde velut ab austro[55] perfudit omnia;
quae nihil admodum Romanis, eadem perincommoda
regiis erant: nam et obscuritas lucis in acie modica Romanis non adimebat in omnes partes conspectum, et umor
toto fere gravi armatu nihil gladios aut pila hebatabat;
4   regii tam lata acie ne ex medio quidem cornua sua conspi-
cere poterant, nedum extremi inter se conspicerentur, et
umor arcus fundasque et iaculorum amenta emollierat.
5   falcatae quoque quadrigae, quibus se perturbaturum hostium aciem Antiochus crediderat, in suos terrorem verterunt.
6   Armatae autem in hunc maxime modum erant: cus-
pides circa temonem ab iugo decem cubita exstantes velut
cornua habebant, quibus quidquid obvium daretur trans-
7   figerent, et in extremis iugis binae circa eminebant falces,
altera aequata iugo, altera inferior in terram devexa, illa ut
quidquid ab latere obiceretur abscideret, haec ut prolap-
sos subeuntesque contingeret; item ab axibus rotarum
utrimque binae eodem modo diversae deligabantur falces.
8   sic armatas quadrigas, quia si in extremo aut in medio loca-
tae forent, per suos agendae erant, in prima acie, ut ante
dictum est, locaverat rex.

[55] velut ab austro *Vielhaber*: ab austro velut *B*χ: ab austro
invectus *Weiss*: ab austro vectus *Walsh*

---

[148] Spikes fifteen feet long protruding above the horses heads
is perhaps a "bizarre picture" (so Walsh ad loc.), but in describing
Darius' scythed chariots Curtius says, "From the end of the chariot pole projected iron-tipped spears" (Curt. 4.9.5). It is possible
that Livy, having never seen such chariots, again misunderstood
Polybius (so Briscoe ad loc.).

There was a morning mist that rose to form clouds as the day advanced and produced overcast conditions. Then a drizzle, like that brought by the south wind, dampened everything. While these factors had no adverse affects on the Romans, they were particularly disadvantageous for the king's troops. Their line being relatively short, the faintness of the light did not hamper the Romans' view in any direction and, their troops being almost all heavy-armed, the drizzle did not take the edge off swords or spears. With such a wide line of battle, the king's men were unable to see from the center to their wings, and much less could the flanks keep each other in sight, while the drizzle had taken the tautness out of bows, slings and spear thongs. Furthermore, the four-horse scythed chariots, with which Antiochus had believed he would throw the enemy line into disarray, instead brought terror to the Syrians themselves.

The chariots were fitted out much as follows. They had spikes ten cubits long projecting like horns from the yoke, on both sides of the pole,[148] designed to transfix anything that came in their way; and at either end of the yoke two blades protruded, one on a level with the yoke, the other below it and pointing toward the ground—the former intended slash through whatever met it on the sides, the latter to catch any who fell or got beneath the chariot. There were also two blades attached in similar fashion to the wheel hubs on both sides and likewise pointing in the different directions. As was observed above, the king had positioned the chariots, armed in this manner, in the front line because it would have been necessary to drive them through his own men had they been placed at the extremities of the line or in the center.

9   Quod ubi Eumenes vidit, haud ignarus pugnae et
quam anceps esset[56] auxilii genus,[57] si quis pavorem magis
equis iniceret quam iusta adoriretur pugna, Cretenses
sagittarios funditoresque et iaculatores cum aliquot turmis[58] equitum non confertos, sed quam maxime possent
dispersos excurrere iubet, et ex omnibus simul partibus
10   tela ingerere. haec velut procella, partim volneribus mis-
silium undique coniectorum partim clamoribus dissonis,
ita consternavit equos ut repente velut effrenati passim
11   incerto cursu ferrentur; quorum impetus et levis armatura
et expediti funditores et velox Cretensis momento declinabant; et eques insequendo tumultum ac pavorem equis
camelisque, et ipsis simul consternatis, augebat clamore
12   et ab alia circumstantium turba multiplici adiecto. ita medio inter duas acies campo exiguntur quadrigae, amotoque
inani ludibrio, tum demum ad iustum proelium signo
utrimque dato concursum est.

42. Ceterum vana illa res verae mox cladis causa fuit:
auxilia enim subsidiaria, quae proxima locata erant, pavore
et consternatione quadrigarum territa et ipsa in fugam
2   versa nudarunt omnia usque ad cataphractos equites. ad

---

[56] pugnae et quam anceps esset χ: pugnae quam anceps esset
et B: generis eius pugnae et quam anceps esset *Koch*: quam anceps esset pugnae et *Fügner*   [57] genus χ: gens B

[58] cum aliquot turmis *supp. Crév.*: <. . .> *lac. ind. Weiss.*: cum
parte suorum *supp. M. Müller*

---

[149] Weissenborn correctly observed that there is a lacuna in
the text here. Crévier's supplement "together with a number of
cavalry squadrons" is only one of many suggestions for what Livy
might have written (see textual note).

Eumenes saw this. He was an experienced soldier and knew the danger inherent in that sort of auxiliary force if one were to strike panic in the horses rather than face them in a regular battle. He therefore ordered his Cretan bowmen, his slingers and his spearmen to rush ahead together with a number of cavalry squadrons,[149] not bunched together but spread out as much as possible, and to hurl their weapons at them from all sides at the same time. It was as if a storm hit the horses—wounds dealt by missiles hurled from every quarter on the one hand, and discordant shouts on the other—and it so terrified them that they suddenly bolted in all directions indiscriminately, as though they had no reins. The light infantry, the lightly equipped slingers and the swift-moving Cretans would instantly swerve to avoid them as they charged; and by their pursuit the cavalry were heightening the confusion and panic in the horses and camels, who were also caught up in the same commotion—and added to it all were the redoubled shouts from the crowd of bystanders. So it was that the chariots were driven away from the ground between the two lines and once this ridiculous sideshow was removed from the scene the signal was given on both sides and they finally proceeded to a regular battle.

42. Nevertheless that futile episode soon proved to be the cause of a real calamity. The panic and confusion among the chariots struck dismay into the supporting auxiliary troops that had been stationed next to them, and they, taking to flight, exposed the entire formation right through to the mail-armored cavalry. Their supporting

quos cum dissipatis subsidiis pervenisset equitatus Romanus, ne primum quidem impetum sustinuerunt; pars
eorum fusi sunt, alii propter gravitatem tegumentorum
3 armorumque oppressi. totum deinde laevum cornu inclinavit, et turbatis auxiliaribus, qui inter equitem et quos
appellant phalangitas erant, usque ad mediam aciem ter-
4 ror pervenit. ibi simul perturbati ordines et impeditus
intercursu suorum usus praelongarum hastarum—sarisas
Macedones vocant—, intulere signa Romanae legiones et
5 pila in perturbatos coniecere. ne interpositi quidem elephanti militem Romanum deterrebant, adsuetum iam ab
Africis bellis et uitare impetum beluae et ex transverso aut
pilis incessere aut, si propius subire posset, gladio nervos
incidere.
6   Iam media acies fere omnis a fronte prostrata erat, et
subsidia circumita ab tergo caedebantur, cum in parte alia
fugam suorum et prope iam ad ipsa castra clamorem
7 paventium accepere. namque Antiochus a dextro cornu,
cum ibi fiducia fluminis nulla subsidia cerneret praeter
quattuor turmas equitum, et eas, dum applicant se suis,
ripam nudantes, impetum in eam partem cum auxiliis et
8 cataphracto equitatu fecit; nec a fronte tantum instabat,
sed circumito a flumine cornu iam ab latere urgebat,

forces were in disorder when the Roman cavalry reached them and they failed to resist even the first charge; some were put to flight and others, weighed down by their protective armor and weapons, were overwhelmed. Then the entire left wing gave way and, after the auxiliary forces posted between the cavalry and the troops that they call *phalangitae* were thrown into disorder, the panic reached as far as the center. The ranks in this quarter were now reduced to confusion, and their use of the long spears—the Macedonians call them *sarisae*—was obstructed by their own men running among them, whereupon the Roman legions advanced and hurled their javelins at their disordered foe. Not even the elephants positioned among the enemy could unnerve the Roman soldiers who, after the African wars, were now accustomed to sidestepping the charging animal and either showering javelins upon it from the side or, if they could get closer, hamstringing it with the sword.

By now the center had been almost completely brought down at the front and the auxiliary troops had been encircled and were being cut to pieces from the rear when the Romans discovered that their comrades were in flight on the other side and heard their panicking shouts close to the camp itself. In fact, Antiochus could see that, because the Romans were trusting to the river, there were no auxiliaries on his right flank, apart from four squadrons of cavalry, and that by sticking close to the main body of their comrades these were leaving the bank exposed. He therefore launched an attack in this direction from the right wing with his auxiliary troops and mail-armored cavalry, not merely exerting pressure on the front but also encircling the wing on the side of the river and driving in

donec fugati equites primum dein proximi peditum effuso cursu ad castra compulsi sunt.

43. Praeerat castris M. Aemilius tribunus militum, M. Lepidi filius qui post paucos annos pontifex maximus
2 factus est. is qua fugam cernebat suorum, cum praesidio omni occurrit et stare primo deinde redire in pugnam
3 iubebat, pavorem et turpem fugam increpans; minae exinde erant, in perniciem suam caecos ruere ni dicto parerent; postremo dat suis signum ut primos fugientium caedant, turbam insequentium ferro et volneribus in hos-
4 tem redigant. hic maior timor minorem vicit; ancipiti coacti metu primo constiterunt; deinde et ipsi rediere in pugnam, et Aemilius cum suo praesidio—erant autem duo milia virorum fortium—effuse sequenti regi acriter obsti-
5 tit, et Attalus, Eumenis frater, ab dextro cornu, quo laevum hostium primo impetu fugatum fuerat, ut ab sinistro fugam suorum et tumultum circa castra vidit, in tempore cum ducentis equitibus advenit.

6 Antiochus postquam et eos quorum terga modo viderat repetentes pugnam, et aliam et a castris et ex acie ad-
7 fluentem turbam conspexit, in fugam vertit equum. ita utroque cornu victores Romani per aceruos corporum, quos in media maxime acie cumulaverant, ubi et robur fortissimorum virorum et arma gravitate fugam impedie-

---

[150] M. Aemilius Lepidus (68) (praetor 191, consul 187 and 175, *pontifex maximus* in 180), but the son is otherwise unknown.

from the flank as well until the cavalry were routed and the nearest of the foot soldiers then driven back to the camp in headlong flight.

43. In command of the camp was the military tribune Marcus Aelius, son of Marcus Lepidus,[150] the one who became *pontifex maximus* a few years after this. Aelius hastened with his entire garrison to the point where he saw his comrades in flight and ordered them first to stop and then to return to the fight, and he berated them for their panic and shameful flight. Next came threats—they were rushing blindly to their own destruction if they did not obey his command, he said—and finally he gave his own men the signal to cut down the leading fugitives and with sword thrusts drive back into the enemy the horde that was following them. This greater fear overcame the other. Facing danger on both sides the men halted at first; then they returned to the fray, and Aemilius with his garrison—they were 2,000 stouthearted men—also resolutely opposed the king's headlong pursuit. Furthermore, when Eumenes' brother, Attalus, saw his comrades fleeing on the left and the commotion around the camp, he made a timely appearance on the scene with 200 cavalry from the right wing, where the enemy's left had been driven back with the first assault.

On seeing the men whom he had just witnessed in flight now returning to battle and another horde of men streaming forward both from the camp and the battle line, Antiochus wheeled his horse around to flee. And so the Romans, victorious on both wings, pushed forward to plunder the camp, crossing over mounds of corpses that they had piled up, especially in the center of the line, where both the resolve of the enemy's finest troops and

8 rant, pergunt ad castra diripienda. equites primi omnium
Eumenis, deinde et alius equitatus toto passim campo se-
quuntur hostem, et postremos, ut quosque adepti sunt,
9 caedunt. ceterum fugientibus maior pestis, intermixtis
quadrigis elephantisque et camelis, erat sua ipsorum
turba, cum solutis ordinibus velut caeci super alios alii
10 ruerent et incursu beluarum obtererentur. in castris quoque ingens et maior prope quam in acie caedes est edita:
nam et primorum fuga in castra maxime inclinavit, et
huius fiducia multitudinis qui in praesidio erant pertina-
11 cius pro vallo pugnarunt. retenti in portis valloque, quae
se impetu ipso capturos crediderant, Romani, postquam
tandem perruperunt, ab ira graviorem ediderunt caedem.

44. Ad quinquaginta milia peditum caesa eo die dicun-
tur, equitum tria milia; mille et quadringenti capti et quin-
2 decim cum rectoribus elephanti. Romanorum aliquot
volnerati sunt: ceciderunt non plus trecenti pedites, quattuor et viginti equites, et de Eumenis exercitu quinque et
viginti.
3 Et illo quidem die victores direptis hostium castris cum
magna praeda in sua reverterunt; postero die spoliabant
4 caesorum corpora et captivos contrahebant. legati ab
Thyatira et Magnesia ab Sipylo ad dedendas urbes vene-
5 runt. Antiochus cum paucis fugiens, in ipso itinere pluribus congregantibus se, modica manu armatorum media

---

151 That is, the strongest troops were in the phalanx, and the
weight of their armor also meant that few ran off. "The conjunc-
tion of ideas is rather odd" (Briscoe ad loc.).

152 *Barr.* 56 F4 (Thyatira), E4 (Magnesia ad Sipylum). Magnesia ad Sipylum is the name, but here Livy has changed the

the weight of their arms had impeded flight.[151] With Eumenes' cavalry in front and the rest of the horse following, they pursued the enemy throughout the plain, killing the rearmost as they overtook them. But a greater handicap for the fugitives was their own disorder, caught up as they were among chariots, elephants and camels. When they broke ranks they would crash into each other like blind men and were trodden under by charging animals. In the camp, too, there were casualties on a massive scale, almost greater than in the battle line. The first to flee had mostly headed for the camp and the soldiers in the garrison there, encouraged by this great enlargement of their numbers, put up a more stubborn defense of the rampart. The Romans were held up at the gateways and the rampart, which they had expected to take simply with their assault, and when they eventually broke through they, in their anger, produced a bloodier slaughter.

44. Up to 50,000 infantry and 3,000 cavalry are said to have been killed that day; 1,400 were captured along with 15 elephants and their drivers. A number of Romans were wounded but no more than 300 infantrymen and 24 cavalrymen lost their lives, and 25 from Eumenes' army.

On that day the victors plundered the enemy camp and returned to their own with masses of booty. The following day they proceeded to strip the bodies of the enemy dead and round up the captives. Ambassadors now came from Thyatira and Magnesia-near-Sipylus[152] to surrender their cities. Antiochus was in flight with just a few men, but more gathered around him on the actual journey and he

preposition and case (Magnesia *ab Sipylo*), as the ambassadors are coming *from* the place.

6 ferme nocte Sardis concessit. inde, cum audisset Seleucum filium et quosdam amicorum Apameam praegressos,
et ipse quarta vigilia cum coniuge ac filia petit Apameam,
Xenoni tradita custodia urbis, Timone Lydiae praeposito;
7 quibus spretis, consensu oppidanorum et militum qui in
arce erant, legati ad consulem missi sunt.

45. Sub idem fere tempus et ab Trallibus et a Magnesia,
quae super Maeandrum est, et ab Epheso ad dedendas
2 urbes venerunt. reliquerat Ephesum Polyxenidas audita
pugna, et classi usque ad Patara Lyciae pervectus, metu
stationis Rhodiarum navium, quae ad Megisten erant, in
terram egressus cum paucis itinere pedestri Syriam petit.
3 Asiae civitates in fidem consulis dicionemque populi Romani sese tradebant. Sardibus iam consul erat; eo et P.
Scipio ab Elaea, cum primum pati laborem viae potuit,
venit.
4 Sub idem fere tempus caduceator ab Antiocho per P.
Scipionem a consule petit impetravitque ut oratores mit-
5 tere liceret regi. paucos post dies Zeuxis, qui praefectus
6 Lydiae fuerat, et Antipater fratris filius venerunt. prius
Eumene convento, quem propter vetera certamina aversum maxime a pace credebant esse, et placatiore eo et sua
et regis spe invento, tum P. Scipionem et per eum con-
7 sulem adierunt; praebitoque iis petentibus frequenti con-

---

153 Apamea: cf. 35.15.1 note. The "friends," of course, are
courtiers.   154 Xenon is probably the general of Seleucus
who campaigned against the king's rebellious satrap Molon
(Polyb. 5.42.5, 43.7). Timon is not otherwise known.

155 Towns inland from Ephesus: *Barr.* 61 F2.

156 Cf. 22.5, 24.12, above.

157 Cf. 41.1 above and notes for Zeuxis and Antipater.

reached Sardis about midnight with a small group of armed men. Then, told that his son Seleucus and some of his friends had gone on to Apamea,[153] he himself also made for Apamea, with his wife and daughter, at the fourth watch, leaving the defense of the city of Sardis to Xenon and putting Timon in command of Lydia.[154] These men were ignored and, following an agreement struck between the townspeople and the soldiers in the citadel, a deputation was sent to the consul.

45. At about this same time envoys also arrived from Tralles, Magnesia (the one on the Maeander)[155] and Ephesus to surrender their cities. After hearing about the battle Polyxenidas had left Ephesus and come by sea as far as Patara in Lycia, but fearing the Rhodian ships stationed at Megiste[156] he then disembarked and with a small retinue took the overland route to Syria. The communities of Asia now began to put themselves in the consul's hands and under the authority of the Roman people. The consul was by this time at Sardis; and as soon as Publius Scipio could endure the fatigue of the journey, he too came there from Elaea.

At about the same time a herald from Antiochus, using Publius Scipio as an intermediary, made a request of the consul (which was granted) that the king be allowed to send spokesmen. A few days later a former governor of Lydia, Zeuxis, and Antiochus' brother's son, Antipater,[157] arrived. They met Eumenes first; they thought that because of their long-standing differences he would be the one most averse to a peace treaty with the king. However, finding him more amenable than either they or the king had expected, they next approached Publius Scipio and, through him, the consul. At their request they were

419

silio ad mandata edenda, "non tam quid ipsi dicamus
habemus"[59] inquit Zeuxis "quam a vobis quaerimus,[60]
Romani, quo piaculo expiare errorem regis, pacem ve-
8 niamque impetrare a victoribus possimus. maximo semper
animo victis regibus populisque ignovistis; quanto id maiore et placatiore animo decet vos facere in hac victoria,
9 quae vos dominos orbis terrarum fecit? positis iam adversus omnes mortales certaminibus haud secus quam deos
consulere et parcere vos generi humano oportet."

10 Iam antequam legati venirent decretum erat quid re-
11 sponderetur; respondere Africanum placuit. is in hunc
modum locutus fertur:

"Romani ex iis quae in deum immortalium potestate
12 erant ea habemus quae di dederunt; animos, qui nostrae
mentis sunt, eosdem in omni fortuna gessimus gerimus-
que, neque eos secundae res extulerunt nec adversae
minuerunt. eius rei, ut alios omittam, Hannibalem ves-
13 trum vobis testem darem, nisi vos ipsos dare possem. postquam traiecimus Hellespontum, priusquam castra regia,
priusquam aciem videremus, cum communis Mars et incertus belli eventus esset, de pace vobis agentibus quas
pares paribus ferebamus condiciones, easdem nunc vic-
14 tores victis ferimus. Europa abstinete; Asia omni, quae cis
Taurum montem est, decedite. pro impensis deinde in
bellum factis quindecim milia talentum Euboicorum dabi-

---

[59] habemus *Mg*: *om.* *B*χ   [60] a vobis quaerimus *Madvig*: ut
a vobis quaeramus *B*χ: ut a vobis quaeramus adsumus *M. Müller*

---

[158] The talent varied in weight from state to state, but the
Euboean, which was the same as the Attic (26.196 kg or 59.752
lbs of silver), was regarded as the standard.

granted a full council to lay out their instructions. "It is not so much a matter of our having proposals to make ourselves," said Zeuxis. "Rather, men of Rome, we ask of you by what act of reparation we can make amends for the king's mistake and gain peace and forgiveness from the victors. You have always, with the greatest magnanimity, pardoned the kings and peoples that you have conquered; how much more magnanimous and conciliatory should your conduct be in this victory, which has made you rulers of the world? Your struggles with all mortals now terminated, you should, just like the gods, show consideration and indulgence to the human race."

The response to be made had already been decided before the arrival of the envoys, and it was agreed that Africanus should make it. He is said to have spoken much as follows:

"We Romans possess as a gift of the gods those things whose granting lies in the power of the immortal gods; our disposition, which is controlled by our own minds, we have kept, and still keep, constant, notwithstanding the vagaries of fortune—success has not inflated it nor misfortune diminished it. As witness to this fact, I might, to pass over others, cite for you your comrade Hannibal—could I not cite yourselves! After we crossed the Hellespont and before we saw the camp of the king and his line of battle, at a time when Mars remained impartial and the outcome of the conflict uncertain—at that point you made overtures for peace and we put before you terms as equals to equals. Now as conquerors to conquered we offer the same terms. Stay out of Europe and withdraw from all of Asia lying west of the Taurus range. You must next pay 15,000 Euboean talents[158] to cover the expenses of the war, 500 im-

tis, quingenta praesentia, duo milia et quingenta cum senatus populusque Romanus pacem comprobaverint; mi-
15 lia[61] deinde talentum per duodecim annos. Eumeni
quoque reddi quadringenta talenta et quod frumenti re-
16 liquum ex eo quod patri debitum est placet. haec cum
pepigerimus, facturos vos ut pro certo habeamus, erit quidem aliquod pignus, si obsides viginti nostro arbitratu
dabitis; sed nunquam satis liquebit nobis ibi pacem esse
populo Romano ubi Hannibal erit; eum ante omnia depos-
17 cimus. Thoantem quoque Aetolum concitorem Aetolici
belli, qui et illorum fiducia vos et vestra illos in nos armavit, dedetis, et cum eo Mnasilochum Acarnana et Chalci-
18 denses Philonem et Eubulidam. in deteriore sua fortuna
pacem faciet rex, quia serius facit quam facere potuit. si
nunc moratus fuerit, sciat regum maiestatem difficilius ab
summo fastigio ad medium detrahi quam a mediis ad ima
praecipitari."
19   Cum iis mandatis ab rege missi erant legati ut omnem
pacis condicionem acciperent; itaque Romam mitti legatos placuit. consul in hiberna exercitum Magnesiam ad
20 Maeandrum et Trallis Ephesumque divisit. Ephesum ad
consulem paucos post dies obsides ab rege adducti sunt,

---

[61] milia *suppl. Grut.*: mille *ed. Rom.*: duodecim milia *Wesenberg*

---

[159] He has not been mentioned since the battle of Side (23.7–
24.11, above). He apparently fled to Crete (Nep. *Hann.* 9) and
subsequently received shelter from Prusias of Bithynia, whom he
aided in operations against Eumenes. His suicide there is reported by Livy in Book 39 (51).

[160] For Thoas, the Aetolian *strategos,* cf. 35.12.4 and note.

mediately, 2,500 when the senate and people of Rome
confirm the treaty, and then 1,000 talents annually for
twelve years. It is also our decision that Eumenes be
awarded 400 talents and the remainder of the grain that
was owed to his father. So that we may have confidence
that you will fulfill the conditions once we have settled
them, we shall have some guarantee if you give us twenty
hostages chosen by us. But we shall never be certain of
peace for the Roman people where Hannibal[159] will be
found, and him we demand before all else. You must also
surrender the Aetolian Thoas, instigator of the war with
the Aetolians;[160] it was he who put you in arms against us
by inspiring your confidence in them, and also put them
in arms against us by inspiring their confidence in you.
Along with him you must surrender the Acarnanian
Mnasilochus and the Chalcidians Philo and Eubulidas.[161]
The king will be negotiating peace from a weaker position
because he is negotiating later than he could have done.
If he delays now let him be aware that it is not so easy for
the prestige of kings to be brought down from the highest
level to mediocrity as it is for it to be hurled from mediocrity to the bottom."[162]

The envoys had been sent by the king under orders to
accept any terms of peace and it was therefore decided
that ambassadors should be sent to Rome. The consul
distributed his forces between Magnesia-on-the-Maean-
der, Tralles and Ephesus to spend the winter. A few days
later the hostages from the king were brought to the con-

---

[161] For Mnasilochus cf. 36.11.8–11; Livy has not mentioned
Philo and Eubulidas by name, but they are perhaps among the
anti-Romans in Chalcis at 35.51.6.

[162] Apparently a maxim of Julius Caesar (cf. Suet. *Iul.* 29.1).

21 et legati qui Romam irent venerunt. Eumenes quoque
eodem tempore profectus est Romam quo legati regis.
secutae eos sunt legationes omnium Asiae populorum.

46. Dum haec in Asia geruntur, duo fere sub idem
tempus cum triumphi spe proconsules de provinciis Romam redierunt, Q. Minucius ex Liguribus, M'. Acilius ex
2 Aetolia. auditis utriusque rebus gestis Minucio negatus
triumphus, Acilio magno consensu decretus; isque trium-
phans de rege Antiocho et Aetolis urbem est invectus.
3 praelata in eo triumpho sunt signa militaria ducenta
triginta, et argenti infecti tria milia pondo, signati tetrachmum Atticum centum decem tria milia, cistophori ducenta undequinquaginta, vasa argentea caelata multa
4 magnique ponderis; tulit et supellectilem regiam argen-
team ac vestem magnificam, coronas aureas, dona socia-
rum civitatium, quadraginta quinque, spolia omnis generis. captivos nobiles, Aetolos et regios duces, sex et triginta
5 duxit. Damocritus, Aetolorum dux, paucos ante dies, cum
e carcere noctu effugisset, in ripa Tiberis, consecutis custodibus, priusquam comprehenderetur gladio se transfixit.
6 milites tantum qui sequerentur currum defuerunt; alioqui
magnificus et spectaculo et fama rerum triumphus fuit.

---

163 The *cistophorus,* an Asian silver coin bearing the image of
the basket of Dionysus used in his worship. Here, however, this
is an anachronism, as such a coin did not exist at this date.

164 Corona ($\sigma\tau\acute{\epsilon}\phi\alpha\nu\sigma$) is often not used literally but means a
gifts of precious metal, coined or uncoined (cf. Walbank 3.86;
Oakley 2.359–60). Here it could be either.

165 *Strategos* of the Aetolian League in 192, he had been im-
prisoned in the Lautumiae (3.8, above). After his boast that the

sul in Ephesus and the ambassadors who were to go to Rome arrived as well. Eumenes also set off for Rome at the same time as the king's embassy, and deputations from all the peoples of Asia followed them.

46. While these events were taking place in Asia two proconsuls arrived in Rome from their provinces at about the same time, hoping for a triumph: Quintus Minucius from Liguria and Manius Acilius from Aetolia. After the senate had heard accounts of the exploits of each man, Minucius was refused a triumph while Acilius was voted one by a large majority, and he rode into the city in triumph over King Antiochus and the Aetolians. Borne before him in that triumph were 230 military standards, 3,000 lbs of uncoined silver, 113,000 Attic four-drachma coins, 249,000 coins stamped with the *cista*,[163] and many embossed silver vessels of great weight. Acilius also included in his procession silver furniture belonging to the king and some splendid clothing, 45 golden crowns that had been gifts from allied states,[164] and all manner of booty. He led along 36 important prisoners of war, generals of the Aetolians and of the king. (A few days earlier the Aetolian leader Damocritus,[165] after escaping from prison by night, fatally stabbed himself with a sword on the bank of the Tiber before he could be overtaken by the guards that were chasing him.) All that was missing were soldiers to attend his chariot; apart from that, the triumph was splendid as a spectacle and as a celebration of Acilius' achievements.

Aetolians would discuss peace with the Romans on the banks of the Tiber (35.33.9–11), the location of his suicide is indeed ironical.

7 Huius triumphi minuit laetitiam nuntius ex Hispania tristis, adversa pugna in Bastetanis ductu L. Aemili proconsulis apud oppidum Lyconem cum Lusitanis sex milia

8 de exercitu Romano cecidisse, ceteros paventes intra vallum compulsos aegre castra defendisse, et in modum fugientium magnis itineribus in agrum pacatum reductos.

9 haec ex Hispania nuntiata.

 Ex Gallia legatos Placentinorum et Cremonensium L.

10 Aurunculeius praetor in senatum introduxit. iis querentibus inopiam colonorum, aliis belli casibus aliis morbo absumptis, quosdam taedio accolarum Gallorum reliquisse colonias, decrevit senatus uti C. Laelius consul, si ei videretur, sex milia familiarum conscriberet quae in eas colonias dividerentur, et ut L. Aurunculeius praetor

11 triumviros crearet ad eos colonos deducendos. creati M. Atilius Serranus L. Valerius P. f. Flaccus L. Valerius C. f. Tappo.

 47. Haud ita multo post, cum iam consularium comitiorum appeteret tempus, C. Laelius consul ex Gallia

2 Romam redit. is non solum ex facto absente se senatus consulto in supplementum Cremonae et Placentiae colonos scripsit, sed ut novae coloniae duae in agrum qui Boiorum fuisset deducerentur et rettulit et auctore eo patres censuerunt.

---

166 Bastetania (also at 28.3.3) was in southern Spain, in what is now Andalusia (*Barr.* 27 4C; TIR J-30, 105–6), but the location of Lyco is disputed (TIR J-30, 225). 167 L. Aemilius Paullus (114), governor of Hispania ulterior (cf. 36.2.6).

168 Modern Piacenza. 169 Half of their territory had been taken from the Boii in 191 (36.39.3, 37.2.5, above). One of the colonies was Bononia (Bologna), founded as a Latin colony in 189 (57.7, below, Vell. 1.15.2). The other is not specified.

The euphoria of the triumph was curtailed by bad news from Spain where there had been a defeat in the war against the Lusitanians at the town of Lyco in the territory of the Bastetani.[166] Six thousand men from the Roman army under the command of the proconsul Lucius Aemilius[167] had lost their lives and the rest had been driven in panic within the palisade of their camp. After barely managing to defend this, they were brought back by forced marches into pacified territory like fugitives. Such was the news from Spain.

Envoys from the peoples of Placentia[168] and Cremona in Gaul were ushered into the senate by the praetor Lucius Aurunculeius. They complained about the dearth of colonists, some of whom had been lost as casualties of war, others through disease, while yet others had abandoned their colonies because they were sick of having Gauls as neighbors. The senate decreed that the consul Gaius Laelius should, if he agreed, enroll 6,000 households to be divided between the colonies involved, and that the praetor Lucius Aurunculeius should establish a board of three to escort the colonists. Chosen for this were Marcus Atilius Serranus, Lucius Valerius Flaccus, son of Publius, and Lucius Valerius Tappo, son of Gaius.

47. Not long afterward, as the time for the consular elections drew near, the consul Gaius Laelius returned to Rome from Gaul. He not only enrolled colonists to supplement the populations of Cremona and Placentia in accordance with the senatorial decree passed in his absence, but he also put forward a motion that two new colonies be founded in what had been territory of the Boii[169] and the senate approved his proposal.

3   Eodem tempore litterae L. Aemili praetoris allatae de navali pugna ad Myonnesum facta, et L. Scipionem con-
4 sulem in Asiam exercitum traiecisse. victoriae navalis ergo in diem unum supplicatio decreta est, in alterum diem quod exercitus Romanus tum primum in Asia posuisset
5 castra, ut ea res prospera et laeta eveniret. vicenis maioribus hostiis in singulas supplicationes sacrificare consul est iussus.
6   Inde consularia comitia magna contentione habita. M. Aemilius Lepidus petebat adversa omnium fama, quod provinciam Siciliam petendi causa non consulto senatu ut
7 sibi id facere liceret reliquisset. petebant cum eo M. Fulvius Nobilior, Cn. Manlius Vulso, M. Valerius Messalla. Fulvius consul unus creatur, cum ceteri centurias non explessent, isque postero die Cn. Manlium, Lepido deiecto—
8 nam Messalla iacuit—, collegam dixit. praetores exinde facti duo Q. Fabii, Labeo et Pictor—Pictor flamen Quirinalis eo anno inauguratus fuerat—, M. Sempronius Tuditanus, Sp. Postumius Albinus, L. Plautius Hypsaeus, L. Baebius Dives.

    48. M. Fulvio Nobiliore et Cn. Manlio Vulsone con-sulibus Valerius Antias auctor est rumorem celebrem
2 Romae fuisse et paene pro certo habitum, recipiendi Sci-

---

170 Offered for major successes or in times of major crises; *victimae lactantes* (sucklings) were offered for lesser ones.

171 On the centuriate assembly, see Introduction to vol. IX (LCL 295), xlviii–l.   172 If no candidate gained the support of a majority of the centuries, a second election was necessary. What Livy probably means here is that the newly-elected Fulvius presided over that and declared Manlius the winner (see further Briscoe 2.365).   173 The priest of Quirinus, an ancient, pur-

At this same time a letter arrived from the praetor Lucius Aemilius with news of the naval battle off Myonnesus and the consul Lucius Scipio's transporting of his army to Asia. Supplication lasting one day was decreed for the naval victory, with a second day added for a successful and felicitous outcome for the campaign, as that was the very first time that a Roman army had pitched camp in Asia. The consul was instructed to do sacrifice with twenty full-grown animals[170] for each of the supplications.

After that came the consular elections, which were hard fought. Marcus Aemilius Lepidus' candidacy was generally unpopular because he had left his province of Sicily to run for office without seeking authorization from the senate. Running against him were Marcus Fulvius Nobilior, Gnaeus Manlius Vulso, and Marcus Valerius Messalla. Only Fulvius was elected consul since the others failed to win a majority of the centuries,[171] and on the next day, Lepidus being disqualified, Fulvius declared Gaius Manlius his colleague,[172] since Messalla had no support. After that the following were elected praetors: the two Quinti Fabii, Labeo and Pictor (Pictor had that year been inaugurated as *flamen Quirinalis*[173]), Marcus Sempronius Tuditanus, Spurius Postumius Albinus, Lucius Plautius Hypsaeus and Lucius Baebius Dives.

48. Valerius Antias records under the consulship of Marcus Fulvius Nobilior and Gnaeus Manlius Vulso that there was rumor widely circulating in Rome and accepted almost as fact that the consul Lucius Scipio and, along with

portedly Sabine, deity worshipped on the Quirinal, often identified with Mars and with Romulus. Little else is known about him; cf. *OCD* s.v. Quirinus.

pionis adulescentis causa consulem L. Scipionem et cum
eo P. Africanum in conloquium evocatos regis et ipsos
3 comprehensos esse, et ducibus captis confestim ad castra
Romana exercitum ductum, eaque expugnata et deletas
4 omnes copias Romanorum esse. ob haec Aetolos sustulisse
animos et abnuisse imperata facere, principesque eorum
in Macedoniam et in Dardanos et in Thraciam ad
5 conducenda mercede auxilia profectos. haec qui nuntiarent Romam, A. Terentium Varronem et M. Claudium
Lepidum ab A. Cornelio pro praetore ex Aetolia missos
6 esse. subtexit deinde fabulae huic legatos Aetolos in senatu inter cetera hoc quoque interrogatos esse, unde audissent imperatores Romanos in Asia captos ab Antiocho
7 rege et exercitum deletum esse; Aetolos respondisse ab
suis legatis se, qui cum consule fuerint, certiores factos.
rumoris huius quia neminem alium auctorem habeo, neque adfirmata res mea opinione sit nec pro vana praetermissa.

49. Aetoli legati in senatum introducti, cum et causa
eos sua et fortuna hortaretur ut confitendo seu culpae seu
2 errori veniam supplices peterent, orsi a beneficiis in populum Romanum et prope exprobrantes virtutem suam in
3 Philippi bello, et offenderunt aures insolentia sermonis, et
eo, vetera et oblitterata repetendo, rem adduxerunt ut

---

174 In fact there were no orders, as there was at this time only
a truce with the Aetolians.

175 The envoys mentioned below (49.1).

176 An odd comment, given Livy's usual dismissal of Antias
and his "piece of fiction" comment above. Walsh's explanation (ad
loc.) that "Livy's agnostic stance refers to the existence of the
rumor, not to the content of it" is unconvincing.

him, Publius Africanus had been invited to a discussion
with the king with a view to recovering the young Scipio.
They had been arrested, according to the rumor and, the
generals now being prisoners, a Syrian army had been
immediately led to the Roman camp, which was then
stormed and the Roman troops entirely wiped out. As a
result the Aetolians had gained some confidence and had
refused to carry out the orders they had been given.[174]
Their leaders had left for Macedonia, Dardania and
Thrace to hire mercenary forces, it was said, and Aulus
Terentius Varro and Marcus Claudius Lepidus had been
sent from Aetolia to Rome by the propraetor Aulus Cornelius to make this report. Antias then appends to this
piece of fiction that the Aetolian envoys[175] were, in the
senate, asked among other things where they had heard
about the capture of the Roman generals in Asia by King
Antiochus and the annihilation of the army. The Aetolians
are supposed to have answered that their information had
come from their own ambassadors, who had been with the
consul. Having no other source for this rumor, I feel the
tale is neither to be accepted as true nor rejected out of
hand.[176]

49. When the Aetolian envoys were brought into the
senate, their case and unfortunate situation required that
they admit their guilt and beg for pardon on bended knee
either for their wrongdoing or their mistake. Instead, they
began by listing their services to the Roman people and
adverted to their valor in the war with Philip in almost
reproachful tones. They offended the senators' ears with
the arrogant tenor of their address, and by harking back

haud paulo plurium maleficiorum gentis quam beneficio-
rum memoria subiret animos patrum, et quibus misericor-
4 dia opus erat, iram et odium inritarent. interrogati ab uno
senatore permitterentne arbitrium de se populo Romano,
deinde ab altero habiturine eosdem quos populus Romanus socios et hostes essent, nihil ad ea respondentes egredi
templo iussi sunt.
5 Conclamatum deinde prope ab universo senatu est
totos adhuc Antiochi Aetolos esse et ex unica ea spe pen-
dere animos eorum; itaque bellum cum haud dubiis hosti-
6 bus gerendum, perdomandosque feroces animos esse. illa
etiam res accendit quod eo ipso tempore quo pacem ab
Romanis petebant Dolopiae atque Athamaniae bellum
7 inferebant. senatus consultum in M'. Acili sententiam, qui
Antiochum Aetolosque devicerat, factum est ut Aetoli eo
die iuberentur proficisci ab urbe et intra quintum de-
8 cimum diem Italia excedere. A. Terentius Varro ad cus-
todiendum iter eorum missus, denuntiatumque si qua
deinde legatio ex Aetolis, nisi permissu imperatoris qui
eam provinciam obtineret et cum legato Romano, venisset
Romam, pro hostibus omnes futuros, ita dimissi Aetoli.

50. De provinciis deinde consules rettulerunt; sortiri

---

177 Probably the temple of Bellona, where foreign delegations
were often received (cf. 36.39.5 note).

178 These events are to be dated to December 190/January
189, and news of them cannot have reached Rome when this
embassy is supposed to have taken place.

179 A. Terentius Varro (80) would be praetor in 184 and govern
Hither Spain for two years (cf. 39.38.3, 56.1) with some success
(cf. 39.42.1).

to things in the past long-forgotten they brought it about that the senators began to recall the nation's misdeeds, which were considerably more numerous than its services; and men who stood in need of compassion succeeded only in provoking anger and resentment. They were asked by one senator whether they left the decision on their fate entirely to the Roman people and by a second whether they would have the same allies and enemies as the Roman people, and when they gave no answer to these questions they were ordered out of the temple.[177]

The cry then arose from virtually the entire senate that the Aetolians were still completely committed to Antiochus and that it was from hopes pinned uniquely on him that they derived they confidence. Accordingly, they said, war had to continue against these avowed enemies and their violent spirit had to be curbed. There was also another thing that irritated the senate: at the very same time that they were seeking a peace treaty from the Romans, the Aetolians were making war on Dolopia and Athamania.[178] On a motion made by Marcus Acilius, who had defeated Antiochus and the Aetolians, a senatorial decree was passed ordering the Aetolians to quit the city that day and leave Italy within fifteen days. Aulus Terentius Varro[179] was sent to give them protection on their journey and notice was formally served that, in the case of any future delegation coming to Rome from the Aetolians, all members would be regarded as enemies unless they came with the permission of the general governing the province and accompanied by a Roman legate. With that the Aetolians were sent on their way.

50. The consuls next brought up the matter of their provinces and it was decided that they should proceed to

2 eos Aetoliam et Asiam placuit; qui Asiam sortitus esset,
3 exercitus ei quem L. Scipio haberet est decretus, et in eum
   supplementum quattuor milia peditum Romanorum, ducenti equites, et sociorum ac Latini nominis octo[62] milia
   peditum quadringenti equites; his copiis ut bellum cum
4 Antiocho gereret. alteri consuli exercitus qui erat in Aetolia est decretus, et ut in supplementum scriberet permissum civium sociorumque eundem numerum quem
5 collega. naves quoque idem consul quae priore anno paratae erant ornare iussus ac ducere secum; nec cum Aetolis
   solum bellum gerere, sed etiam in Cephallaniam insulam
6 traicere. mandatum eidem ut si per commodum rei publi-
7 cae facere posset, ut ad comitia Romam veniret; nam praeterquam quod magistratus annui subrogandi essent, censores quoque placere creari; si qua res eum teneret,
   senatum certiorem faceret se ad comitiorum tempus oc-
8 currere non posse. Aetolia M. Fulvio Asia Cn. Manlio
   sorte evenit.

   Praetores deinde sortiti sunt, Sp. Postumius Albinus
   urbanam et inter peregrinos, M. Sempronius Tuditanus
   Siciliam, Q. Fabius Pictor, flamen Quirinalis, Sardiniam,
   Q. Fabius Labeo classem, L. Plautius Hypsaevs Hispaniam citeriorem, L. Baebius Dives Hispaniam ulteriorem.
9 Siciliae legio una et classis quae in ea provincia erat
   decreta, et ut duas decumas frumenti novus praetor impe-

---

[62] octo *Mg*: sex *Bχ*

---

180 On "allies and Latin rights," cf. 35.7.5 note.
181 Then under A. Cornelius Mammula: cf. 2.7–8 above and
note.   182 The thirty quinqueremes and twenty triremes originally intended for service against Antiochus (cf. 4.5, above).

sortition for Aetolia and Asia. The man drawing Asia was
to be allocated the army that Lucius Scipio then commanded and as supplementary forces he was to have 4,000
Roman infantry and 200 cavalry, plus 8,000 infantry and
400 cavalry from the allies and those with Latin rights.[180]
With these troops he was to prosecute the war against
Antiochus. The other consul was to be allocated the army
in Aetolia,[181] and permitted to supplement it by raising the
same number of citizens and allies as his colleague. The
same consul was commanded to equip and take with him
the ships that had been built the year before[182] and not
only make war on the Aetolians but also cross to the island
of Cephallania. He was further instructed to come to
Rome for the elections if he could do so without detriment
to the interests of the state, for apart from the need to
replace annual magistrates it was also the senate's wish
that censors be elected. If anything held him back, he was
to inform the senate that he could not present himself in
time for the elections. In the sortition Aetolia came to
Marcus Fulvius and Asia to Gnaeus Manlius.

The praetors then drew lots with the following results:
Spurius Postumius Albinus received the Citizen and Foreigners Jurisdiction;[183] Marcus Sempronius Tuditanus
received Sicily; Quintus Fabius Pictor, the *flamen Quirinalis,* received Sardinia; Quintus Fabius Labeo received
the fleet; and Lucius Plautius Hypsaeus received Hither
Spain, and Lucius Baebius Dives Farther Spain.

For Sicily a single legion and the fleet that was in the
province was ordained and the new praetor was to requisi-

[183] If the other five praetors had pressing business, the sixth
served as both praetor urbanus and praetor peregrinus.

raret Siculis; earum alteram in Asiam alteram in Aetoliam
10 mitteret. idem ab Sardis exigi atque ad eosdem exercitus
11 id frumentum ad quos Siculum deportari iussum. L. Baebio supplementum in Hispaniam[63] datum mille Romani
pedites equites quinquaginta, et sex milia peditum Latini
12 nominis, ducenti equites; Plautio Hypsaeo in Hispaniam
citeriorem mille Romani dati sunt pedites, duo milia socium Latini nominis et ducenti equites; cum his supple-
13 mentis ut singulas legiones duae Hispaniae haberent.
prioris anni magistratibus C. Laelio cum suo exercitu prorogatum in annum imperium est; prorogatum[64] et P. Iunio
propraetori in Etruria cum eo exercitu qui in provincia
esset, et M. Tuccio propraetori in Bruttiis et Apulia.

51. Priusquam in provincias praetores irent, certamen
inter P. Licinium maximum pontificem fuit et Q. Fabium
Pictorem[65] flaminem Quirinalem, quale patrum memoria
inter L. Metellum et A.[66] Postumium Albinum fuerat:
2 consulem illum cum C. Lutatio collega in Siciliam ad clas-

---

[63] Hispaniam *Bχ*: Hispaniam ulteriorem *Wesenberg*

[64] prioris anni . . . prorogatum . . . prorogatum *Bχ*: *inter obelos Briscoe*, prioris anni magistratibus *delendum coniciens*

[65] Pictorem *Ald.*: praetorem *Bχ*

[66] A. *H.J.M*: *om. Bχ*

---

[184] The non-Latin allies are almost certainly also included here, and Livy's expression (cf. 35.7.5 and note) is perhaps varied here because of its occurrence in the next sentence.

[185] Cf. 47.8 and note, above.

[186] Two distinguished men: L. Caecilius Metellus (72) was twice consul and also *pontifex maximus;* A. Postumius Albinus (30) held the consulship and censorship. In 242 the *pontifex* Me-

tion from the Sicilians two tithes of grain, one of which he
was to dispatch to Asia and the other to Aetolia. Orders
were given for the same quantity to be levied from the
Sardinians, the grain to be shipped to the same armies as
that from Sicily. To supplement his forces for service in
Spain, Lucius Baebius was given 1,000 Roman infantry
and 50 cavalry, together with 6,000 infantry and 200 cavalry of men holding Latin rights.[184] For Hither Spain Plautius Hypsaeus was granted 1,000 Roman infantry, and
2,000 infantry and 200 cavalry of the allies and those with
Latin rights. The two Spains were each to have a legion
plus the aforementioned additional forces. Of the previous year's magistrates, Gaius Laelius saw his *imperium*
prorogued for a year and retained his army; Publius Iunius, propraetor in Etruria, also had his *imperium* prorogued for a year and kept the army that was in the province, as did Marcus Tuccius, propraetor in Bruttium and
Apulia.

51. Before the praetors could leave for their provinces,
a disagreement arose between the *pontifex maximus*, Publius Licinius, and the *flamen Quirinalis*,[185] Quintus Fabius
Pictor, of the kind that arose within the memory of their
fathers between Lucius Metellus and Aulus Postumius
Albinus.[186] Metellus, in his capacity as *pontifex maximus*,
had detained Albinus, who was a consul, to perform religious ceremonies just when he was setting off for Sicily to

tellus had, on religious grounds, forbidden Albinus, then consul
but also *flamen* of Mars, to leave the city for the Sicilian campaign,
thus robbing him of sharing with his colleague C. Lutatius Catu-
lus the glory of bringing the First Punic War to an end (cf. Livy
Per. 19, Val. Max. 1.1.2).

437

sem proficiscentem ad sacra retinuerat Metellus, pontifex
3 maximus; praetorem hunc, ne in Sardiniam proficisceretur, P. Licinius tenuit. et in senatu et ad populum magnis
4 contentionibus certatum, et imperia inhibita ultro citroque, et pignera capta, et multae dictae, et tribuni appellati,
5 et provocatum ad populum est. religio ad postremum vicit;
ut dicto audiens esset flamen pontifici iussus; et multa
6 iussu populi ei remissa. ira provinciae ereptae praetorem
magistratu abdicare se conantem patres auctoritate sua
deterruerunt, et ut ius inter peregrinos diceret decreve-
7 runt. dilectibus deinde intra paucos dies—neque enim
multi milites legendi erant—perfectis, consules praetoresque in provincias proficiscuntur.

8 Fama dein de rebus in Asia gestis temere volgata sine
auctore, et post dies paucos nuntii certi litteraeque im-
9 peratoris Romam allatae, quae non tantum gaudium ab
recenti metu attulerunt—desierant enim victum in Aetolia Antiochum[67] metuere—, quam a vetere fama, quod
ineuntibus id bellum gravis hostis, et suis viribus et quod
10 Hannibalem rectorem militiae haberet, visus fuerat. nihil
tamen aut de consule mittendo in Asiam mutandum aut
minvendas eius copias censuerunt, metu ne cum Gallis
foret bellandum.

[67] Antiochum *suppl. Madvig*

---

[187] As pontifex, Licinius maintained that the Sardinian command meant Fabius would be absent from Rome and was therefore incompatible with his religious obligations.
[188] That is, the Gauls in Asia, the Galatians.

438

join the fleet with his colleague, Gaius Lutatius; and on this occasion the praetor Fabius was held back from his journey to Sardinia by Publius Licinius.[187] Both in the senate and before the people the dispute raged with acrimonious debates: authority was applied on this side and that, bonds taken, fines issued, applications made to tribunes and then appeals made to the people. Eventually religion won the day, with the *flamen* being ordered to obey the pontiff and a fine on him canceled by order of the people. Angry at seeing his province taken from him, Fabius attempted to resign from his office but the senators exercised their authority to prevent him and decreed that he should accept jurisdiction over foreigners. After this the levies were conducted in only a matter of days, as few soldiers needed to be raised; and the consuls and praetors then left for their provinces.

Idle and groundless gossip then circulated about the campaign in Asia; but it was followed a few days later by some reliable news in a dispatch brought to Rome from the commander. The great elation that this occasioned was not so much because of the recent crisis—the Romans had ceased to fear Antiochus after his defeat in Aetolia—as because of the king's reputation of old, for when the Romans entered the war he had seemed a fearsome enemy both on account of his own strength and because he had Hannibal directing his campaign. Even so they did not vote for any change with regard to sending the consul to Asia or for any diminution of his forces, fearing as they did that they would have to fight the Gauls.[188]

52. Haud multo post M. Aurelius Cotta legatus L. Scipionis cum Antiochi regis legatis et Eumenes rex Rho-
2 diique Romam venerunt. Cotta in senatu primum, deinde
in contione iussu patrum, quae acta in Asia essent exposuit. supplicatio inde in triduum decreta est, et quadraginta maiores hostiae immolari iussae.

3 Tum omnium primum Eumeni senatus datus est. is
cum breviter et egisset gratias patribus quod obsidione se
ac fratrem exemissent regnumque ab iniuriis Antiochi
vindicassent, et gratulatus esset quod terra marique res
4 prospere gessissent, quodque regem Antiochum fusum
fugatumque et exutum castris prius Europa, post et Asia
5 quae cis Taurum montem est, expulissent, sua deinde
merita malle eos ex imperatoribus suis legatisque quam se
commemorante cognoscere dixit.

6 Haec adprobantibus cunctis iubentibusque dicere ipsum, omissa in id verecundia, quid sibi ab senatu populoque Romano tribui aequum censeret—propensius
7 cumulatiusque, si quo possit, prout eius merita sint, senatum facturum—, ad ea rex, si ab aliis sibi praemiorum
optio deferretur, libenter, data modo facultate consulendi
senatum Romanum, consilio amplissimi ordinis usurum
fuisse, ne quid aut immoderate cupisse aut petisse parum
8 modeste videri posset; verum enimvero cum ipsi daturi

---

[189] Supplication: cf. 35.8.3 note; full-grown animals: 47.5
above and note.

52. Not much later Lucius Scipio's legate, Marcus Aurelius Cotta, came to Rome with emissaries from King Antiochus, and King Eumenes and the Rhodians arrived as well. Cotta gave an account of events in Asia, first in the senate and afterward, on the order of the senators, in an assembly of the people. A three-day period of supplication was thereupon decreed, and orders given for the sacrifice of forty full-grown animals.[189]

Then Eumenes was first of all given an audience with the senate. He briefly thanked the senators for delivering his brother and him from the siege and rescuing his kingdom from the aggression of Antiochus; and he congratulated them on their military successes on land and sea, on defeating and routing King Antiochus, taking his camp from him, and driving him first from Europe and afterward from Asia west of the Taurus range. He then declared that he wanted the Romans to learn about his services to them from their generals and legates rather than from his own account.

For this there was applause from all the senators who, nevertheless, told him to put aside his modesty in the matter and state what he felt was a fair reward for him from the senate and people of Rome; the senate would then act all the more promptly and generously to meet his requests, as far as it could, in accordance with his desserts. The king replied that, were he being offered a choice of rewards by people other than the Romans and had he simply been given a chance to consult the Roman senate, he would happily have availed himself of that august body's advice in order to avoid the possibility of seeming too extravagant in his ambitions or too lacking in restraint in his requests. But now that it was they themselves who were going to

441

sint, multo magis munificentiam eorum in se fratresque
9 suos ipsorum arbitrii debere esse. nihil hac oratione eius
patres conscripti deterriti sunt quo minus dicere ipsum
iuberent, et cum aliquamdiu hinc indulgentia hinc modestia inter permittentes in vicem non magis mutua quam
inexplicabili facilitate certatum esset, Eumenes ex templo
excessit.

10 Senatus in eadem perstare sententia, ut absurdum esse
diceret ignorare regem quid sperans aut petens venerit;
quae accommodata regno suo sint ipsum optime scire;
Asiam longe melius quam senatum nosse; revocandum
igitur et cogendum quae vellet quaeque sentiret expro-
mere.

53. Reductus a praetore in templum rex et dicere iussus "perseverassem" inquit "tacere, patres conscripti, nisi
Rhodiorum legationem mox vocaturos vos scirem, et illis
2 auditis mihi necessitatem fore dicendi. quae quidem eo
difficilior oratio erit quod ea postulata eorum futura sunt,
ut non solum nihil quod contra me sit, sed ne quod ad
3 ipsos quidem proprie pertineat petere videantur. agent
enim causam civitatium Graecarum, et liberari eas dicent
debere. quo impetrato, cui dubium est quin et a nobis
aversuri sint non eas modo civitates quae liberabuntur, sed
4 etiam veteres stipendiarias nostras, ipsi autem tanto obli-
gatos beneficio verbo socios, re vera subiectos imperio et

---

190 Eumenes' speech and that of the Rhodians following it are
closely modeled on those in Polybius (21.19.1–21.11, 21.22.5–
23.12). See Walsh 37.180 for a comparison (cf. also Walbank
3.112–16). How "historical" they are is a matter of dispute.

bestow the reward, it was all the more incumbent on them
to judge for themselves how generous they should be toward him and his brothers. The senators were not in the
least deterred by such comments from insisting that he
speak for himself; and when the competition had continued for some time, with generosity shown on one side and
modesty on the other, as both parties tried to yield to each
other with a courtesy that was both reciprocal and providing no solution, Eumenes left the temple.

The senate remained firm in its opinion, going so far as
to say that it was inconceivable that the king should be
unaware of the hopes and objectives with which he came.
He himself knew best what was in the interests of his
realm and he knew Asia far better than the senate did; so
he should be recalled and made to reveal his wishes and
thoughts on the matter.

53. The king was brought back into the temple by the
praetor and told to take the floor. "I should have persisted
with my silence, members of the senate," he said,[190] "were
I not aware that you would soon be calling upon the Rhodian delegation and that, after you had heard them, I
would be obliged to speak. In fact, what I have to say will
be made more difficult because their demands will be
such as to make them appear to be not only asking for
nothing that disadvantages me but even for nothing that
serves their own interests. They will plead the cause of the
Greek states and say that they should be freed. If this is
granted, who can doubt that they will deprive us not only
of the states that will be liberated but also of those that
have long been paying tribute to us, while they themselves
will nominally have them as allies beholden to them for
this great favor, but in reality as peoples subject to their

443

5 obnoxios habituri sint? et, si dis placet, cum has tantas
opes adfectabunt, dissimulabunt ulla parte id ad se pertinere; vos modo id decere et conveniens esse ante factis
6 dicent. haec vos ne decipiat oratio providendum vobis erit,
neve non solum inaequaliter alios nimium deprimatis ex
sociis vestris, alios praeter modum extollatis, sed etiam ne
qui adversus vos arma tulerint in meliore statu sint quam
socii et amici vestri.

7 "Quod ad me attinet, in aliis rebus cessisse intra finem
iuris mei cuilibet videri malim quam nimis pertinaciter in
obtinendo eo tetendisse; in certamine autem amicitiae
vestrae, benevolentiae erga vos, honoris qui a vobis habe-
8 bitur, minime aequo animo vinci possum. hanc ego maximam hereditatem a patre accepi, qui primus omnium
Asiam Graeciamque incolentium in amicitiam venit vestram, eamque perpetua et constanti fide ad extremum
9 vitae finem perduxit; nec animum dumtaxat vobis fidelem
ac bonum praestitit, sed omnibus interfuit bellis quae in
Graecia gessistis, terrestribus navalibus, omni genere
commeatuum, ita ut nemo sociorum vestrorum ulla parte
10 aequari possit,[68] vos adiuvit; postremo, cum Boeotos ad
societatem vestram hortaretur, in ipsa contione intermor-
11 tuus haud multo post exspiravit. huius ego vestigia ingressus voluntati quidem et studio in colendis vobis adicere—
12 etenim inexsuperabilia haec erant—nihil potui; rebus ipsis

[68] possit *B*χ: posset *Ald*.

---

[191] Cf. 26.24.4–9, however, where M. Valerius Laevinus, addressing the Aetolians, states that the Aetolians came first but that
an alliance was offered to Attalus at the same date (211).
[192] Cf. 33.2.2 for his collapse (almost certainly from a stroke),
33.21.1–6 for his obituary.

rule and at their command? And, for heaven's sake, when they will be aspiring to power of this magnitude, they will pretend that there is nothing at all in it for them themselves. They will be saying this is simply the proper course for you, one consistent with your past record. You will have to make sure that you are not hoodwinked by such arguments of theirs, and see to it that you not only avoid humbling some of your allies to an unfair and excessive degree while you overvalue others, but also that men who have borne arms against you do not find themselves better off than your allies and friends.

"As far as I am concerned, I should in other situations prefer to be seen as having ceded to anyone what lay within my rights than as having made too determined an attempt to retain it. But in a competition for your friendship, for goodwill toward you, and for the respect in which one will be held by you, I cannot be at all content to be outdone. This is the greatest inheritance I received from my father, who was the very first of the inhabitants of Asia and Greece to enter into an alliance with you,[191] an alliance that he constantly maintained with unwavering loyalty to the very end of his days. Nor was his loyalty and goodwill toward you merely a matter of sentiment—he took part in all the wars that you fought in Greece and helped you out with land and naval forces and with all kinds of supplies, to a degree that none of your allies can possibly match in any respect. Finally, when he was encouraging the Boeotians to accept an alliance with you he collapsed in the middle of his address and breathed his last shortly afterward.[192] In his footsteps I have followed and, while I have in no way been able to go beyond his goodwill

meritisque et impensis officiorum ut superare possem,
fortuna tempora Antiochus et bellum in Asia gestum prae-

13 buerunt materiam. rex Asiae et partis Europae Antiochus
filiam suam in matrimonium mihi dabat; restituebat extemplo civitates quae defecerant a nobis; spem magnam
in posterum amplificandi regni faciebat, si secum bellum
adversus vos gessissem.

14   "Non gloriabor eo quod nihil in vos deliquerim; illa
potius quae vetustissima domus nostrae vobiscum amicitia

15 digna sunt referam. pedestribus navalibusque copiis, ut
nemo sociorum vestrorum me aequiperare posset, imperatores vestros adiuvi; commeatus terra marique suppedi-
tavi; navalibus proeliis, quae multis locis facta sunt, omnibus adfui; nec labori meo nec periculo usquam peperci.

16 quod miserrimum est in bello, obsidionem passus sum,
Pergami inclusus cum discrimine ultimo simul vitae

17 regnique. liberatus deinde obsidione, cum alia parte Antiochus alia Seleucus circa arcem regni mei castra haberent, relictis meis rebus tota classe ad Hellespontum L.
Scipioni consuli vestro occurri, ut eum in traiciendo exer-

18 citu adiuvarem. posteaquam in Asiam exercitus vester est
transgressus, nunquam a consule abscessi; nemo miles
Romanus magis adsiduus in castris fuit vestris quam ego
fratresque mei; nulla expeditio nullum equestre proelium

19 sine me factum est; in acie ibi steti, eam partem sum tuta-
tus in qua me consul esse voluit.

and enthusiasm in developing his friendship with you (in these areas he could not be surpassed), fortune, circumstances, Antiochus and the war that was fought in Asia offered me the opportunity to surpass him in respect of practical assistance and services to you and in the level of expense incurred by our obligations. Antiochus, king of Asia and part of Europe, offered me his daughter in marriage and was ready to restore immediately the city-states that had defected from us. He offered me strong assurances of later increasing my kingdom if I joined him in making war on you.

"I shall not boast that I have in no way been derelict in my duty to you; rather I shall point to the things that are worthy of my house's long-standing friendship with you. I have aided your commanders with land and naval troops on such a scale that none of your allies could equal me; I have supplied you with provisions by land and sea; I have taken part in all your naval battles, fought in many locations; nowhere did I shrink from hardship or danger. I have suffered the worst fate in warfare, a siege—I was blockaded at Pergamum, my life and kingdom both in critical danger. Then, delivered from the siege, at a time when Antiochus was encamped one side of the citadel of my kingdom and Seleucus on the other, I abandoned my own affairs and hurried to meet your consul Lucius Scipio at the Hellespont with my entire fleet in order to help him ferry across his army. I never left the consul's side after your army had crossed to Asia and there was not a Roman soldier in your camp more devoted than my brothers and I. There was no military enterprise, no cavalry engagement undertaken without me. In battle I took my place and defended my position where the consul wanted me to be.

447

"Non sum hoc dicturus, patres conscripti: 'quis hoc
20 bello meritis erga vos mecum comparari potest?' ego nulli
omnium neque populorum neque regum quos in magno
21 honore habetis non ausim me comparare. Masinissa hostis
vobis ante quam socius fuit, nec incolumi regno cum auxiliis suis, sed extorris expulsus, amissis omnibus copiis, cum
22 turma equitum in castra confugit vestra; tamen eum, quia
in Africa adversus Syphacem et Carthaginienses fideliter
atque impigre vobiscum stetit, non in patrium solum regnum restituistis, sed adiecta opulentissima parte Syphacis
23 regni praepotentem inter Africae reges fecistis. quo tandem igitur nos praemio atque honore digni apud vos
24 sumus, qui nunquam hostes semper socii fuimus? pater
ego fratres mei non in Asia tantum, sed etiam procul ab
domo in Peloponneso in Boeotia in Aetolia, Philippi Antiochi Aetolico bello, terra marique pro vobis arma tuli-
mus.
25   "'Quid ergo postulas?' dicat aliquis. ego, patres conscripti, quoniam dicere utique volentibus vobis parendum
est, si vos ea mente ultra Tauri iuga emostis Antiochum ut
ipsi teneretis eas terras, nullos accolas nec finitimos ha-
26 bere quam vos malo, nec ulla re alia tutius stabiliusque
27 regnum meum futurum spero; sed si vobis decedere inde
atque deducere exercitus in animo est, neminem digni-
orem esse ex sociis vestris qui bello a vobis parta possideat
28 quam me dicere ausim. at enim magnificum est liberare

---

193 In Polybius, Eumenes cites two kings as having received
favorable treatment from the Romans, Masinissa and King Pleuratus of Illyria (Polyb.21.21.2—3). Livy omits Pleuratus to concentrate solely on Masinissa, who figures prominently in his history (cf. esp. 31.11.4–18, and Introduction to vol. IX, xliv–v).

"Members of the senate, I am not going to say: 'Who in this war can stand comparison with me in terms of services to you?' Of all those whom you greatly esteem, whether they be peoples or monarchs, there is none with whom I would not venture to compare myself. Masinissa was your enemy before he was your ally,[193] and he did not come over to you with auxiliary forces when his kingdom was intact. No, he was an exile driven from his land, all his troops lost, and he fled to your camp with a squadron of cavalry. And yet, because he stood by you loyally and energetically in Africa to face Syphax and the Carthaginians, you not only restored him to the kingdom of his forefathers but also made him powerful among the monarchs of Africa by further giving him the richest part of Syphax's kingdom. So, I ask, what reward and what honor do we deserve from you when we have never been your enemies and always been your allies? My father, I myself, and my brothers—we have borne arms for you on land and sea, and not just in Asia but far from home, too, in the Peloponnese, in Boeotia, and in Aetolia, in wars with Philip, Antiochus and the Aetolians.

"'What are you asking for, then?' someone may say. Members of the senate, you want me to speak, come what may, and I must obey you. If you pushed Antiochus back beyond the Taurus range because you had it in mind to possess those lands yourselves, there are no people I prefer to have living beside me as neighbors than you, and I do not expect greater security and stability could be given to my realm by anything else. But if you intend leaving the area and withdrawing your armies, I would venture to say that none of your allies deserves to have the territory you have taken in war more than I. Yes, but, it will be said, it

449

civitates servas. ita opinor, si nihil hostile adversus vos fecerunt; sin autem Antiochi partis fuerunt, quanto est vestra prudentia et aequitate dignius sociis bene meritis quam hostibus vos consulere?"

54. Grata oratio regis patribus fuit, et facile apparebat
2 munifice omnia et propenso animo facturos. interposita Zmyrnaeorum brevis legatio est, quia non aderat[69] quidam Rhodiorum. conlaudatis egregie Zmyrnaeis, quod omnia ultima pati quam se regi tradere maluissent, introducti Rhodii sunt.
3 Quorum princeps legationis, expositis initiis amicitiae cum populo Romano meritisque Rhodiorum Philippi
4 prius deinde Antiochi bello, "nihil" inquit "nobis tota nostra actione, patres conscripti, neque difficilius neque molestius est quam quod cum Eumene nobis disceptatio
5 est, cum quo uno maxime regum et privatim singulis et, quod magis nos movet, publicum civitati nostrae hospi-
6 tium est. ceterum non animi nostri, patres conscripti, nos, sed rerum natura, quae potentissima est, disiungit, ut nos liberi etiam aliorum libertatis causam agamus, reges serva
7 omnia et subiecta imperio suo esse velint. utcumque tamen res se habet, magis verecundia nostra adversus regem

---

[69] aderat *Ruperti*: aderant $B\chi$

is a noble gesture to free enslaved communities. That is what I think, too—if the communities have taken no hostile action against you. If, however, they have sided with Antiochus, then how much more does it befit your good sense and fair-mindedness to consult the interests of allies who have served you well rather than those of your enemies?"

54. The senators were pleased with the king's speech and it was easy to see that they were ready to show generosity and favor toward him in every way. Because one of the Rhodians was not present, a brief audience with an embassy from Smyrna was slipped into the proceedings. The Smyrnaeans were heartily thanked for having been being willing to endure all the extremes of suffering rather than yield to the king, and then the Rhodians were ushered in.

The leader of their delegation began with a discussion of the origins of the Rhodian alliance with the Roman people and of the services rendered by the Rhodians first in the war against Philip and then in that against Antiochus. "In all of this case of ours, members of the senate," he went on, "nothing is more difficult and distasteful for us than the fact that our argument is with Eumenes, the only king with whom our community has very close ties of hospitality both on a private level as individuals and, what troubles us more, on a public level as well. But what separates us, members of the senate, is not our personal feelings but the facts of the situation, which are overwhelming: we are free men also advocating the freedom of others, while monarchs want to see everything enslaved and under their power. However, be that as it may, our greatest problem is our respect for the king, not any diffi-

451

nobis obstat quam ipsa disceptatio aut nobis impedita est
aut vobis perplexam deliberationem praebitura videtur.

8 nam si aliter socio atque amico regi et bene merito hoc
ipso in bello, de cuius praemiis agitur, honos haberi nullus

9 posset, nisi liberas civitates in servitutem traderetis ei, esset deliberatio anceps, ne aut regem amicum inhonoratum
dimitteretis, aut decederetis instituto vestro, gloriamque
Philippi bello partam nunc servitute tot civitatium defor-
maretis.

10 "Sed ab hac necessitate aut gratiae in amicum minuen-
dae aut gloriae vestrae egregie vos fortuna vindicat: est
enim deum benignitate non gloriosa magis quam dives
victoria vestra, quae vos facile isto velut aere alieno exso-

11 luat; nam et Lycaonia et Phrygia utraque et Pisidia omnis
12 et Chersonesus, quaeque circumiacent Europae, in vestra
sunt potestate, quarum una quaelibet regi[70] adiecta mul-
tiplicare regnum Eumenis potest, omnes vero datae maxi-

13 mis eum regibus aequare. licet ergo vobis et praemiis belli
ditare socios et non decedere instituto vestro, et meminisse quem titulum praetenderitis prius adversus Philip-

14 pum nunc adversus Antiochum belli, quid feceritis Philippo victo, quid nunc a vobis, non magis quia fecistis
quam quia id vos facere decet, desideretur atque exspec-
tetur. alia enim aliis et honesta et probabilis est causa ar-

15 morum: illi agrum, hi vicos, hi oppida, hi portus oramque
aliquam maris ut possideant; vos nec cupistis haec ante-

[70] regi *Bχ*: regio *Koch*: del. *Novák*

---

[194] That is, Greater Phrygia in central Asia Minor (*Barr.* 62
D4) and Hellespontine Phrygia (the part of Asia Minor closest to
the Hellespont and Propontis [*Barr.* 52 B4]).

culty for us in the dispute itself or the likelihood that it will present you with complex deliberation. For if there were no other way of honoring a friendly and allied king, who had deserved well of you in this very war (the rewards for which are now under discussion), except by delivering free communities into slavery to him, your deliberation would be problematic. You might then either send away a friendly king without appropriate honor or depart from your established practice and sully the glory won in the war with Philip by now subjecting so many communities to slavery.

"However, fortune splendidly releases you from this necessity of diminishing either your gratitude to a friend or your own glory. Thanks to the favor of the gods your victory is as remunerative as it is glorious, so that it can easily deliver you from this debt, as you may call it. For Lycaonia, the two Phrygias,[194] all Pisidia, the Chersonese and the surrounding regions of Europe are in your power. The addition of any one of these can greatly augment Eumenes' kingdom; giving him all of them could put him on a par with the most powerful of kings. You may thus enrich your friends with spoils of war without abandoning your principles. You can call to mind the motive you earlier put forward for your war against Philip and now against Antiochus; and you can remember the measures you took after the defeat of Philip and what measures are wanted and expected of you now, as much because they befit you as because you took them before. Different peoples have different reasons for going to war, both honorable and commendable—some to gain possession of land, others villages, others towns, and others ports and a part

quam haberetis, nec nunc, cum orbis terrarum in dicione
16 vestra sit, cupere potestis. pro dignitate et gloria apud
omne humanum genus, quod vestrum nomen imperium-
que iuxta ac deos immortales iam pridem intuetur,
pugnastis.

"Quae parare et quaerere arduum fuit, nescio an tueri
17 difficilius sit. gentis vetustissimae nobilissimaeque vel
fama rerum gestarum vel omni commendatione humani-
tatis doctrinarumque tuendam ab servitio regio libertatem
suscepistis; hoc patrocinium receptae in fidem et cliente-
lam vestram universae gentis perpetuum vos praestare
18 decet. non quae in solo antiquo[71] sunt Graecae magis
urbes sunt quam coloniae earum, illinc quondam profectae in Asiam; nec terra mutata mutavit genus aut mores.
19 certare pio certamine cuiuslibet bonae artis ac virtutis ausi
sumus cum parentibus quaeque civitas et conditoribus
20 suis. adistis Graeciae adistis Asiae urbes plerique; nisi
21 quod longius a vobis absumus, nulla vincimur alia re. Mas-
silienses, quos, si natura insita velut ingenio terrae vinci
posset, iam pridem efferassent tot indomitae circumfusae
gentes, in eo honore in ea merito dignitate audimus apud
22 vos esse ac si medium umbilicum Graeciae incolerent. non
enim sonum modo linguae vestitumque et habitum, sed
ante omnia mores et leges et ingenium sincerum inte-
grumque a contagione accolarum servarunt.

[71] solo *Crév.*: solo modo *B*χ: solo suo *Harant*: solo illo *Zingerle*

of the coast. You, however, have not harbored ambitions for these things before having them in your control, and now that the world is in your power you *cannot* harbor them. Your fighting has been for respect and prestige in the eyes of all humanity, which has long considered your name and empire as standing next to those of the immortal gods.

"It may be that it is more difficult to protect something that took a great effort to obtain and acquire. You have undertaken to protect from enslavement to a king the independence of an ancient people well-known through the fame of its achievements and through the universal esteem it enjoys for culture and the arts. This defense of an entire race that you have taken under your protection and guardianship you should maintain in perpetuity. The cities on the ancient soil are no more Greek than their colonies that left it for Asia in the past—the change of land did not change their lineage or culture. All our communities have ventured to compete respectfully with their parents and founders in every noble art and sphere of excellence. Most of you have been to the cities of Greece and those of Asia; apart from our greater distance from you, we are in no way inferior to them. If one's innate character could be overcome by what one may term the character of the land, the people of Massilia would long ago have been brutalized by so many uncivilized tribes living around them; but we are told that they are held in as much honor and are deservedly shown as much respect by you as if they were living in the very heart of Greece. They have preserved, pure and untouched by contact with their neighbors, not only the pronunciation of their language, their mode of dress and overall appearance, but above all their culture, laws and character.

23 "Terminus est nunc imperii vestri mons Taurus; quidquid intra eum cardinem est, nihil longinquum vobis debet videri; quo arma vestra pervenerunt, eodem ius hinc
24 profectum perveniat. barbari, quibus pro legibus semper
dominorum imperia fuerunt, quo gaudent reges habeant;
25 Graeci suam fortunam vestros animos gerunt. domesticis
quondam viribus etiam imperium amplectebantur; nunc
imperium ubi est, ibi ut sit perpetuum optant; libertatem
vestris tueri armis satis habent, quoniam suis non possunt.

26 "At enim quaedam civitates cum Antiocho senserunt.
et aliae prius cum Philippo, et cum Pyrrho Tarentini; ne
alios populos enumerem, Carthago libera cum suis legibus
27 est. huic vestro exemplo quantum debeatis videte, patres
conscripti; inducetis in animum negare Eumenis cupidi-
28 tati quod iustissimae irae vestrae negastis. Rhodii et in
hoc[72] et in omnibus bellis quae in illa ora gessistis quam
forti fidelique vos opera adiuverimus vestro iudicio relin-
quimus. nunc in pace consilium id adferimus quod si com-
probaritis, magnificentius vos victoria usos esse quam vi-
cisse omnes existimaturi sint."

Apta magnitudini Romanae oratio visa est.

55. Post Rhodios Antiochi legati vocati sunt. ii volgato
petentium veniam more errorem fassi regis, obtestati sunt
2 patres conscriptos ut suae potius clementiae quam regis

---

[72] et in hoc et *ed. Rom.*: et *B*χ

"The limit of your empire at present is the Taurus range. Nothing within that boundary ought to seem distant to you; your jurisdiction should stretch from here to points as far as your weapons have reached. Let the barbarians, for whom their masters' orders have always served as law, have the monarchies they love. Greeks have their own fortunes but your mentality. They, too, once held an empire by their own strength; now they want the seat of power to remain for ever where it currently resides. They are satisfied to have their liberty protected by your arms since they cannot protect it by their own.

"Yes, you may say that some states sympathized with Antiochus. So did others earlier with Philip, and so did the Tarentines with Pyrrhus; and, not to add other peoples to the list, Carthage is free with her own laws. Members of the senate, just consider the obligation on you set by this precedent of yours and you will resolve to deny to Eumenes' acquisitiveness what you denied to your own justifiable wrath. We Rhodians leave it to you to judge how energetic and loyal we were in assisting you both in this war and in all the wars that you have fought in that region. Now, in peacetime, this is the advice we are offering you, and if you accept it everyone will consider the use to which you put your victory to be more splendid than the victory itself."

The speech seemed in keeping with the greatness of Rome.

55. After the Rhodians the ambassadors of Antiochus were summoned. Following the usual pattern of people asking for pardon, they admitted the king's error and begged the senators to think in their deliberations more about their own clemency than the guilt of the king, who

457

culpae, qui satis superque poenarum dedisset, memores
consulerent; postremo pacem datam a L. Scipione imperatore, quibus legibus dedisset, confirmarent auctoritate
3 sua. et senatus eam pacem servandam censuit, et paucos
post dies populus iussit. foedus in Capitolio cum Antipatro
principe legationis et eodem fratris filio regis Antiochi est
ictum.

4   Auditae deinde et aliae legationes ex Asia sunt. quibus
omnibus datum responsum decem legatos more maiorum
senatum missurum ad res Asiae disceptandas componen-
5 dasque; summam tamen hanc fore, ut cis Taurum montem
quae intra regni Antiochi fines fuissent Eumeni attribue-
rentur, praeter Lyciam Cariamque usque ad Maeandrum
6 amnem; ea ut civitatis Rhodiorum essent; ceterae civitates
Asiae, quae Attali stipendiariae fuissent, eaedem vectigal
Eumeni penderent; quae vectigales Antiochi fuissent, eae
7 liberae atque immunes essent. decem legatos hos decreverunt: Q. Minucium Rufum, L. Furium Purpureonem,
Q. Minucium Thermum, Ap. Claudium Neronem, Cn.
Cornelium Merendam,[73] M. Iunium Brutum, L. Auruncu-
leium, L. Aemilium Paullum, P. Cornelium Lentulum, P.
Aelium Tuberonem.

    56. His quae praesentis disceptationis essent libera
2 mandata; de summa rerum senatus constituit. Lycaoniam
omnem et Phrygiam utramque et Mysiae regias silvas,[74] et

[73] Merendam *Duker*: Merulam *Bχ*

[74] Mysiae regias silvas *McDonald*: My(i)sias regias silvas *Bχ*:
Mysiam regias silvas *Mg*: Mysiam regiam et Milyas *Madvig*

---

[195] Probably Antiochus' cousin rather than his nephew (cf.
41.1 and note, above).   [196] For the terms of the final agreement (the treaty of Apamea), cf. 38.38.2–18.

had more than paid the penalty for his actions. Finally they asked them to ratify by their authority the peace treaty granted by the commander Lucius Scipio on the terms specified by him. The senate did vote to maintain the peace treaty and a few days later the people endorsed it. The treaty was struck on the Capitol with Antipater, the head of the legation, who was also the son of King Antiochus' brother.[195]

Then the other delegations from Asia were also heard. All were given the same answer: that the senate would, following ancestral custom, send ten commissioners to adjudicate and settle affairs in Asia. However, they were also told that the essence of the settlement would be that Eumenes would be awarded those lands west of the Taurus range that had been within the bounds of Antiochus' kingdom, with the exception of Lycia and Caria as far as the River Maeander (these were to belong to the state of Rhodes).[196] The other communities of Asia that had paid tribute to Attalus were also to pay it to Eumenes, and those that had been tributary states of Antiochus would be independent and free of tax. The ten commissioners they selected were the following: Quintus Minucius Rufus, Lucius Furius Purpureo, Quintus Minucius Thermus, Appius Claudius Nero, Gnaeus Cornelius Merenda, Marcus Iunius Brutus, Lucius Aurunculeius, Lucius Aemilius Paullus, Publius Cornelius Lentulus, and Publius Aelius Tubero.[197]

56. These commissioners were given discretionary powers to judge disputes arising on the spot; but the senate established the overall policy. The following were to go to Eumenes: all Lycaonia, the two Phrygias, and the

---

[197] The first three were ex-consuls, the others ex-praetors.

Lydiam Ioniamque[75] extra ea oppida quae libera fuissent
3 quo die cum rege Antiocho pugnatum est, et nominatim
Magnesiam ad Sipylum, et Cariam quae Hydrela appellatur, agrumque Hydrelitanum ad Phrygiam vergentem, et
4 castella vicosque ad Maeandrum amnem et oppida, nisi
quae libera ante bellum fuissent, Telmessum item nominatim et castra Telmessium, praeter agrum qui Ptolomaei
Telmessii fuisset—haec omnia quae supra sunt scripta regi
5 Eumeni iussa dari. Rhodiis Lycia data extra eundem Telmessum et castra Telmessium et agrum qui Ptolomaei
6 Telmessii fuisset; hic et ab Eumene et Rhodiis exceptus. ea
quoque iis pars Cariae data quae propior Rhodum insulam
trans Maeandrum amnem est, oppida vici castella agri qui
ad Pisidiam vergunt, nisi quae eorum oppida in libertate
fuissent pridie quam cum Antiocho rege in Asia pugnatum
est.
7   Pro his cum gratias egissent Rhodii, de Solis urbe, quae
in Cilicia est, egerunt: Argis et illos, sicut sese, oriundos

---

[75] Lydiam Ioniamque *Crév.*: Lydiae Ioniaeque *B*χ

---

[198] The reading is an emendation (A. M. MacDonald, "The
Treaty of Apamea," *JRS* 57 [1967]: n. 8.) If correct it would refer
to a part of Mysia captured by Antiochus in 198.

[199] For its surrender after the battle of Magnesia, cf. 44.4,
above.

[200] Telmessus: *Barr.* 65 B4. Castra Telmessium (not in *Barrington*): probably a "neighboring settlement owing its name to
its origin as a military base" (Walsh ad loc.).

royal forests of Mysia;[198] Lydia and Ionia, apart from those towns that had been independent on the day of the battle with King Antiochus (and Magnesia-near-Sipylus was mentioned by name[199]); the Caria that is called Hydrela, and the territory of Hydrela on the Phrygian side; the strongholds and villages on the River Maeander along with the towns, apart from those that had been free before the war (Telmessus was mentioned by name and Castra Telmessium,[200] apart from the land that had belonged to Ptolemy of Telmessus[201]). Orders were issued for all the aforementioned territories to be awarded to Eumenes. The Rhodians were given Lycia with the exception of Telmessus, just mentioned, of Castra Telmessium and of the territory that had belonged to Ptolemy of Telmessus. (This territory was withheld from both Eumenes and the Rhodians.) They were also given the area of Caria beyond the Maeander and closer to the island of Rhodes, and the towns, villages, strongholds and lands on the side of Pisidia, apart from the towns among them that had been free the day before the battle was fought with King Antiochus in Asia.

After expressing their thanks for these gifts, the Rhodians brought up the question of the city of Soli, which is in Cilicia.[202] The people of Soli were, like themselves, de-

---

[201] The subject of much dispute, he may be the son of Lysimachus and Arsinoe, and grandson of Ptolemy I Soter (cf. Briscoe 2.387–88).

[202] *Barr.* 66 F3 (Soloi).

461

esse; ab ea germanitate fraternam sibi cum iis caritatem
esse; petere hoc extraordinarium munus, ut eam civitatem
8   ex servitute regia eximerent. vocati sunt legati regis Antiochi, actumque cum iis est nec quicquam impetratum
testante foedera Antipatro, adversus quae ab Rhodiis non
9   Solos, sed Ciliciam peti et iuga Tauri transcendi. revocatis
in senatum Rhodiis, cum quanto opere tenderet legatus
regius exposuissent, adiecerunt si utique eam rem ad civitatis suae dignitatem pertinere censerent Rhodii, senatum
10 omni modo expugnaturum pertinaciam legatorum. tum
vero impensius quam ante Rhodii gratias egerunt, cessu-
rosque sese potius adrogantiae Antipatri quam causam
turbandae pacis praebituros dixerunt. ita nihil de Solis
mutatum est.

57. Per eos dies quibus haec gesta sunt legati Massi-
liensium nuntiarunt L. Baebium praetorem in provinciam
Hispaniam proficiscentem ab Liguribus circumventum,
2   magna parte comitum caesa volneratum ipsum cum paucis
sine lictoribus Massiliam perfugisse, et intra triduum ex-
3   spirasse. senatus, ea re audita, decrevit uti P. Iunius Brutus, qui propraetor in Etruria esset, provincia exercituque
traditis uni cui videretur ex legatis, ipse in ulteriorem His-

---

203 L. Baebius Dives (25); for his election cf. 47.8, above.

scended from Argos, said the Rhodians, and there were
feelings of fraternal affection between them because of
this kinship; so they were now asking for a special favor,
that the Romans exempt the community from subjection
to the king. The ambassadors of King Antiochus were
summoned and the issue brought up with them. Nothing
was gained, however, because Antipater pointed to the
terms of the treaty, which, he said, were being contra-
vened by the Rhodians who had designs on Cilicia, not
Soli, and were thus placing themselves across the Taurus
range. The Rhodians were then recalled to the senate,
where the members explained to them the serious objection raised by the king's ambassador but added that if the
Rhodians believed that this was of special concern to the
prestige of their city-state the senate would do all it could
to overcome the intransigence of the king's ambassadors.
At this point the Rhodians became more fulsome in their
thanks than earlier and declared that they would yield to
the arrogance of Antipater rather than afford an excuse for
upsetting the peace treaty. Thus no change was made with
regard to Soli.

57. During the time covered by these events an embassy from Massilia reported that the praetor Lucius Baebius[203] had been ambushed by the Ligurians as he was
setting off for his province, Spain. Most of his retinue had
been killed, they said. Baebius himself had been wounded,
had fled to Massilia with a few comrades and without his
lictors, and had died there within three days. On hearing
this the senate decreed that Publius Iunius Brutus, who
was propraetor in Etruria, should transfer his province
and army to one of his legates whom he thought suitable
and himself set off for Farther Spain, which was now to be

4 paniam proficisceretur, eaque ei provincia esset. hoc senatus consultum litteraeque a Sp. Postumio praetore in
Etruriam missae sunt, profectusque in Hispaniam est P.

5 Iunius propraetor. in qua provincia, prius aliquanto quam
successor veniret, L. Aemilius Paullus, qui postea regem
Persea magna gloria vicit, cum priore anno haud prospere
rem gessisset, tumultuario exercitu conlecto signis conla-

6 tis cum Lusitanis pugnavit. fusi fugatique hostes; caesa
decem octo milia armatorum; duo milia trecenti capti et
castra expugnata. huius victoriae fama tranquilliores in
Hispania res fecit.

7 Eodem anno ante diem tertium kalendas Ianuarias
Bononiam Latinam coloniam ex senatus consulto L. Valerius Flaccus M. Atilius Serranus L. Valerius Tappo trium-

8 viri deduxerunt. tria milia hominum sunt deducta; equitibus septuagena iugera, ceteris colonis quinquagena sunt
data. ager captus de Gallis Boiis fuerat; Galli Tuscos ex-
pulerant.

9 Eodem anno censuram multi et clari viri petierunt.
quae res, tamquam in se parum magni certaminis causam
haberet, aliam contentionem multo maiorem excitavit.

10 petebant T. Quinctius Flamininus, P. Cornelius Cn. f. Scipio, L. Valerius Flaccus, M. Porcius Cato, M. Claudius
Marcellus, M'. Acilius Glabrio, qui Antiochum ad Ther-

11 mopylas Aetolosque devicerat. in hunc maxime, quod

---

204 Cf. Book 44.41–43.   205 Cf. 47.2 and note, above,
where two colonies are authorized. Only Bononia (Bologna) was
founded, perhaps for want of settlers for the second.

206 Unusually large land allotments for a Latin colony, again
possibly because of the difficulty in finding settlers. On the size
of allotments for colonies, cf. Walsh ad loc. and Briscoe 2.158.

his province. This senatorial decree and an accompanying letter were sent to Etruria by the praetor Spurius Postumius, and the propraetor Publius Iunius headed out to Spain. In this province Lucius Aemilius Paullus (who later won great renown for his defeat of Perseus[204]) had the previous year been less than successful in his military enterprises, but some time before his successor arrived he put together a makeshift army and engaged the Lusitanians in pitched battle. The enemy were scattered and put to flight; 18,000 of their troops were killed, 2,300 taken prisoner and the camp taken by storm. Word of this victory brought some tranquility to the situation in Spain.

On December 30th of the same year the triumvirs Lucius Valerius Flaccus, Marcus Atilius Serranus and Lucius Valerius Tappo established a Latin colony at Bononia as authorized by a senatorial decree.[205] Three thousand men were taken there; cavalrymen were granted seventy acres each, the other colonists fifty.[206] The land had been captured from the Gallic Boii and the Boii had driven out the Etruscans.

The same year a large number of distinguished men sought the censorship. As though that were of itself insufficient to raise tensions, it provoked a much more dramatic struggle. Running for the office were: Titus Quinctius Flamininus, Publius Cornelius Scipio son of Gnaeus Scipio, Lucius Valerius Flaccus, Marcus Porcius Cato, Marcus Claudius Marcellus, and Manius Acilius Glabrio (who had defeated Antiochus and the Aetolians at Thermopylae). Popular support was inclining most toward the

multa congiaria dederat[76] quibus magnam partem homi-
12 num obligarat, favor populi se inclinabat. id cum aegre
paterentur tot nobiles, novum sibi hominem tantum prae-
ferri, P. Sempronius Gracchus et C. Sempronius Rutilus,
tribuni plebis,[77] ei diem dixerunt, quod pecuniae regiae
praedaeque aliquantum captae in Antiochi castris neque
13 in triumpho tulisset neque in aerarium rettulisset. varia
testimonia legatorum tribunorumque militum erant. M.
Cato ante alios testes conspiciebatur; cuius auctoritatem
14 perpetuo tenore vitae partam toga candida elevabat. is
testis quae vasa aurea atque argentea castris captis inter
aliam praedam regiam vidisset, ea se in triumpho negabat
15 vidisse. postremo in huius maxime invidiam desistere se
petitione Glabrio dixit, quando quod taciti indignarentur
nobiles homines, id aeque novus competitor intestabili
periurio incesseret.

58. Centum milium multa inrogata erat; bis de ea certatum est; tertio, cum de petitione destitisset reus, nec
populus de multa suffragium ferre voluit, et tribuni eo
2 negotio destiterunt. censores T. Quinctius Flamininus M.
Claudius Marcellus creati.

---

[76] dederat *Zingerle*: habuerat *Bχ*: exhibuerat *Ursinus*: dis-
tribuerat *Wesenberg*: tribuerat *Engel*
[77] tribuni plebis *ed. Rom.*: om. *Bχ*

---

[207] It seems that the abbreviated form (*tr.pl.*) has dropped out
of the manuscript here, as it is unlikely that Livy would have
omitted their office.

[208] That is, because he was seeking office. Aspirants for office
wore the *toga candida,* a special toga fulled with chalk, when they
were "candidates" on campaign (cf. Isid. *Etym.* 19.24.6).

[209] Cato had been Glabrio's legate in the campaign against

last-mentioned because he had distributed considerable largesse by which he had secured the endorsement of a large number of men. Many nobles took it ill that a "new man" was so far ahead of them, and the plebeian tribunes[207] Publius Sempronius Gracchus and Gaius Sempronius Rutilus arraigned him on a charge of not having carried in his triumph or deposited in the treasury a portion of the king's money and the booty that had been taken in Antiochus' camp. The testimony of the legates and military tribunes was conflicting and eyes fell on Marcus Cato more than anybody as a witness, though the authority conferred on him by a career of unswerving morality was diminished by his white toga.[208] Called to give evidence, Cato stated that he had not seen in the triumph the gold and silver vessels that he had seen with the rest of the royal plunder when the camp was taken.[209] Finally, mainly to provoke ill will against Cato, Glabrio declared that he was withdrawing his candidacy since, he said, a candidate as "new" as he was himself was resorting to shameful perjury to attack his popularity, which the nobility accepted with silent resentment.

58. The fine that had been proposed was 100,000 asses. The case had been before the court twice and since by the third occasion the defendant had withdrawn his candidacy, the people were unwilling to vote on the fine and the tribunes abandoned the case.[210] The censors elected were Titus Quinctius Flamininus and Marcus Claudius Marcellus.

Antiochus in 191 and had played a major role in the king's defeat (36.18.8).

[210] There were three separate meetings (*contiones*) before the vote was taken at a fourth and the verdict given.

3 Per eos dies L. Aemilio Regillo, qui classe praefectum
Antiochi regis devicerat, extra urbem in aede Apollinis
cum senatus datus esset, auditis rebus gestis eius, quantis
cum classibus hostium dimicasset, quot inde naves demer-
sisset aut cepisset, magno consensu patrum triumphus

4 navalis est decretus. triumphavit kalendis Februariis. in
eo triumpho undequinquaginta coronae aureae translatae
sunt, pecunia nequaquam tanta pro[78] specie regii triumphi, tetrachma Attica triginta quattuor milia ducenta, cis-

5 tophori centum triginta duo milia trecenti. supplicationes
deinde fuerunt ex senatus consulto, quod L. Aemilius in
Hispania prospere rem publicam gessisset.

6 Haud ita multo post L. Scipio ad urbem venit; qui ne
cognomini fratris cederet, Asiaticum se appellari voluit. et
in senatu et in contione de rebus ab se gestis disseruit.

7 erant qui fama id maius bellum quam difficultate rei fuisse
interpretarentur: uno memorabili proelio debellatum, gloriamque eius victoriae praefloratam ad Thermopylas esse.

8 ceterum vere aestimanti Aetolicum magis ad Thermopylas
bellum quam regium fuit; quota enim parte virium sua-

---

[78] tanta pro *B*χ: pro *Gron.*: tanta nec pro *Seyffert*: quanta pro
Engel

---

[211] At Myonnesus (29.7–30.10, above).

[212] Regillus in fact engaged only one fleet off Myonnesus, so
unless Livy has forgotten this, *classibus* may here mean ships, not
fleets (cf. 18.10 note, above).

[213] How this differed from a normal triumph is uncertain.
Walsh and Engel ad loc. suggest (on the basis of 45.42.2) that the
difference consisted in the absence of captives and spoils in the

In this period Lucius Aemilius Regillus, who had with his fleet defeated King Antiochus' admiral,[211] was given an audience with the senate in the temple of Apollo outside the city. When the senators heard of his achievements, the size of the enemy fleets[212] he had met in battle, and the number of ships he had sunk or captured, he was voted a naval triumph[213] by a large majority. He celebrated the triumph on February 1st. Forty-nine golden crowns were carried in it, but nothing like as much money as a splendid triumph over a king would lead one to expect: 34,200 Attic four-drachma pieces, and 132,300 coins stamped with the *cista*.[214] Following a senatorial decree, there were then supplications in recognition of Lucius Aemilius' success in Spain for the state.

Not long afterward Lucius Scipio came to the city; he wished to be named "Asiaticus"[215] so that he would not be overshadowed by his brother with regard to his *cognomen*. He gave an account of his achievements both in the senate and in a popular assembly. There were some who claimed that the war enjoyed a greater reputation than its difficulty warranted: it had been finished off with a single notable encounter and furthermore the glory of that victory had been forestalled at Thermopylae. But, to look at it fairly, the battle at Thermopylae was more with the Aetolians than the king—for it was with what fraction of his forces

procession, but here (4) Livy mentions golden crowns and comments on the paucity of the money displayed.

[214] Cf. 46.3 note, above.

[215] To commemorate his victory over Antiochus in Asia. In fact, Asiagenes is the correct form (Livy has it right at 39.44.1); "Asiaticus" does not appear until the Augustan period.

rum ibi dimicavit Antiochus? in Asia totius Asiae steterunt vires, ab ultimis orientis terminis[79] omnium gentium contractis auxiliis.

59. Merito ergo et dis immortalibus quantus maximus poterat habitus est honos, quod ingentem victoriam facilem etiam fecissent, et imperatori triumphus est decretus.
2 triumphavit mense intercalario pridie kalendas Martias. qui triumphus spectaculo oculorum maior quam Africani fratris eius fuit, recordatione rerum et aestimatione periculi certaminisque non magis comparandus quam si imperatorem imperatori aut Antiochum ducem Hannibali conferres. tulit in triumpho signa militaria ducenta viginti
3 quattuor, oppidorum simulacra centum triginta quattuor,
4 eburneos dentes mille ducentos triginta unum, aureas coronas ducentas triginta quattuor, argenti pondo centum triginta septem milia quadringenta viginti, tetrachmum Atticorum ducenta quattuordecim milia, cistophoros[80] trecenta viginti unum milia septuaginta, nummos aureos
5 Philippeos centum quadraginta milia, vasorum argenteorum—omnia caelata erant—mille pondo et quadringenta viginti tria, aureorum mille pondo viginti tria. et duces regii, praefecti et[81] purpurati, duo et triginta ante currum
6 ducti. militibus quini viceni denarii dati, duplex centu-

[79] ultimis orientis terminis *Zingerle*: ultimi orientis in *BVLa*: ultimi orientis *φ*: ultimi orientis partibus *ed. Rom.*: ultimis orientis finibus *Weiss.*: in *inter obelos Briscoe* (finibus *errore additum*)
[80] cistophoros *Gron.*: cistophori *Bχ*: cistophorum *Budé*
[81] *et* χ: *om. B*

that Antiochus fought there? In Asia the strength of all Asia stood with him, with auxiliary troops of all its races drawn from the furthest boundaries of the east.

59. There was therefore justification for the greatest possible honor being paid to the immortal gods because they had made the victory easy as well as great, and the commander was awarded a triumph. Scipio triumphed in the intercalary month[216] on the day before the 1st of March. It was a triumph more spectacular than that of his brother Africanus but, if one considers the respective achievements and weighs up the danger and struggle involved for both men, the comparison is as unfair as comparing the one commander with the other or comparing Antiochus as a general with Hannibal. Scipio carried in his triumph 224 military standards, 134 depictions of towns, 1,231 ivory tusks, 234 golden crowns, 137,420 lbs of silver, 214,000 Attic four-drachma pieces, 321,070 coins stamped with the *cista*,[217] 140,000 golden Philippics,[218] 1,423 lbs of silver vases (all with relief carvings), and 1,023 lbs of gold vases. There were also 32 of the king's officers (military captains and courtiers) led before the chariot. The common soldiers were each given twenty-five denarii, a cen-

[216] This, a month of 23/4 days, added between February 23 and 24, was sometimes used to bring the calendar into line with the seasons: cf. Introduction to vol. IX (LCL 295), lxv–lxvii.

[217] Cf 46.3 note, above.

[218] Properly, gold coins minted by Philip II of Macedon in the fourth century, but the name was then applied to coins struck in Macedon and elsewhere by the Successors.

rioni, triplex equiti. et stipendium militare et frumentum
duplex post triumphum datum; proelio in Asia facto duplex dederat. triumphavit anno fere post quam consulatu
abiit.

60. Eodem fere tempore et Cn. Manlius consul in
2   Asiam et Q. Fabius Labeo praetor ad classem venit. ceterum consuli non deerat cum Gallis belli materia; mare
pacatum erat devicto Antiocho, cogitantique Fabio cui rei
potissimum insisteret, ne otiosam provinciam habuisse
videri posset, optimum visum est in Cretam insulam trai-
3   cere. Cydoniatae bellum adversus Gortynios Gnosiosque
gerebant, et captivorum Romanorum atque Italici generis
magnus numerus in servitute esse per totam insulam dice-
batur.
4   Classe ab Epheso profectus cum primum Cretae litus
attigit, nuntios circa civitates misit ut armis absisterent
captivosque in suis quaeque urbibus agrisque conquisitos
redderent,[82] et legatos mitterent ad se, cum quibus de
rebus ad Cretenses pariter Romanosque pertinentibus
5   ageret. nihil magnopere ea Cretenses moverunt: captivos
6   praeter Gortynios nulli reddiderunt. Valerius Antias quattuor milia captivorum, quia belli minas timuerint, ex tota
insula reddita scripsit; eamque causam Fabio, cum rem

---

[82] redderent *Nitsche*: reducerent *Bχ*

---

[219] In fact, Scipio's army had remained in Asia (46.6, above),
so no troops attended the triumph. Livy had presumably forgotten this. The differential between the ranks is the normal one.

[220] It is probably monthly pay that is meant.

turion twice that amount and a cavalryman three times.[219] After the triumph, both the soldier's pay and grain allowance were doubled; and Scipio had already doubled them after the battle in Asia.[220] He celebrated the triumph approximately a year after leaving the consulship.

60. The consul Gnaeus Manlius reached Asia at about the same time as the praetor Quintus Fabius Labeo reached the fleet. The consul was not short of motives for war with the Gauls but since Antiochus' defeat the sea had been peaceful and Fabius, reflecting on the most appropriate course of action to ensure that his provincial administration not appear lethargic, thought it best to cross to the island of Crete. The people of Cydonia had been making war on those of Gortyn and Cnossos,[221] and it was said that a large number of Roman and Italian prisoners were enslaved throughout the island.

Fabius set sail with his fleet from Ephesus and, as soon as he landed on the coast of Crete, sent messengers around the cities ordering the citizens to terminate hostilities, to search out and restore prisoners from their respective towns and country areas, and to send delegates to him so he could discuss with them matters of concern to Cretans and Romans alike. These orders did not provoke much response from the Cretans and none of them restored prisoners, apart from the Gortynians. Valerius Antias has recorded that 4,000 prisoners were restored from the island as a whole through fear when they were threatened with war, and this was the reason for Fabius' successful

---

[221] Cydonia: *Barr.* 60 B1 (Kydonia); Gortyn: C2; Cnossos: D2.

nullam aliam gessisset, triumphi navalis impetrandi ab
7 senatu fuisse. a Creta Ephesum Fabius redit; inde tribus
navibus in Thraciae oram missis ab Aeno et Maronia praesidia Antiochi deduci iussit, ut in libertate eae civitates
essent.

application to the senate for a naval triumph, though he had accomplished nothing else. Fabius returned from Crete to Ephesus and from there dispatched three ships to the coast of Thrace bearing orders for Antiochus' garrisons to be withdrawn from Aenus and Maronea[222] so those states could live in freedom.

[222] *Barr.* 57 E1 (Ainos), D1 (Maronea).

LIBRI XXXVII PERIOCHA

L. Cornelius Scipio cos. legato Scipione Africano fratre (qui se legatum fratris futurum dixerat, si ei Graecia provincia decerneretur, cum C. Laelio, qui multum in senatu poterat, ea provincia dari videretur) profectus ad bellum adversus Antiochum regem gerendum, primus omnium Romanorum ducum in Asiam traiecit. Regillus adversus regiam classem Antiochi feliciter pugnavit ad Myonnesum Rhodiis iuvantibus. filius Africani captus ab Antiocho patri remissus est. victo deinde Antiocho ab L. Cornelio Scipione adiuvante Eumene, rege Pergami, Attali filio, pax data est ea condicione ut omnibus provinciis citra Taurum montem cederet. L. Cornelius Scipio, qui cum Antiocho debellaverat, cognomine fratri exaequatus Asiaticus appellatus.

Colonia deducta est Bononia. Eumenis, quo iuvante Antiochus victus erat, regnum ampliatum. Rhodiis quoque, qui et ipsi iuverant, quaedam civitates concessae. Aemilius Regillus, qui praefectos Antiocho navali proelio devicerat, navalem triumphum deduxit. M'. Acilius Glabrio de Antiocho, quem Graecia expulerat, et de Aetolis triumphavit.

SUMMARY OF BOOK XXXVII

The consul Lucius Cornelius Scipio set off to conduct the war against King Antiochus with his brother Scipio Africanus as his legate, and he was the first of all Roman commanders to cross to Asia (Africanus had declared that he would be his brother's legate if the province was allocated to him, because it looked as if it would be given to Gaius Laelius, who had great influence in the senate). Regillus, with the help of the Rhodians, fought successfully against the royal fleet of Antiochus at Myonnesus. The son of Africanus, who had been captured by Antiochus, was returned to his father. Then Antiochus was defeated by Lucius Cornelius Scipio, assisted by King Eumenes of Pergamum, son of Attalus, and was granted peace on the condition that he withdraw from all the territories this side of the Taurus Mountains. Lucius Cornelius Scipio, who had brought to an end the war with Antiochus, was put on a level with his brother when he was given the cognomen Asiaticus.

A colony was established Bononia. The kingdom of Eumenes, with whose help Antiochus had been defeated, was extended. The Rhodians, who had themselves also given help, were granted a number of cities. Aemilius Regulus, who had crushed the officers of Antiochus in a naval battle, celebrated a naval triumph. Manius Acilius Glabrio triumphed over Antiochus, whom he had expelled from Greece, and over the Aetolians.

INDEX

The Index follows Briscoe's Teubner in citing book and chapter numbers rather than page numbers (as does the former Loeb edition).

INDEX

480